HOLY CONCORD WITHIN SACRED WALLS

HOLY CONCORD WITHIN SACRED WALLS

Nuns and Music in Siena, 1575–1700

Colleen Reardon

UNIVERSITY PRESS

2002

OXFORD
UNIVERSITY PRESS

Oxford   New York
Athens   Auckland   Bangkok   Bogotá   Buenos Aires   Cape Town
Chennai   Dar es Salaam   Delhi   Florence   Hong Kong   Istanbul   Karachi
Kolkata   Kuala Lumpur   Madrid   Melbourne   Mexico City   Mumbai   Nairobi
Paris   São Paulo   Shanghai   Singapore   Taipei   Tokyo   Toronto   Warsaw

and associated companies in
Berlin   Ibadan

Library of Congress Cataloging-in-Publication Data
Reardon, Colleen.
Holy concord within sacred walls : nuns and music in Siena, 1575–1700 /
Colleen Reardon.
p. cm.
Includes bibliographical references (p.) and index.
ISBN 0-19-513295-5
1. Nuns as musicians—Italy—Siena.   2. Church music—Italy—Siena—16th century.
3. Church music—Catholic church—16th century.   4. Church music—Italy—Siena—
17th century.   5. Church music—Catholic church—17th century.   I. Title.
ML290.8.S43 R43 2001
781.71'2'0094558—dc21   2001021586

2 4 6 8 9 7 5 3 1

Printed in the United States of America
on acid-free paper

TO FRANK A. D'ACCONE

ACKNOWLEDGMENTS

On a cold predawn morning in February 1999, our house began to burn down. Flames licked at the window of our study, in which sat my computer, and all my archival notes, musical transcriptions, books, and microfilms; in short, all the material I had collected on Sienese nuns and their music. It is therefore appropriate that I begin these acknowledgments by expressing my most profound gratitude to the men and women of the Binghamton City Fire Department, who arrived within minutes of the 911 call and put out the fire before it consumed six years of research. It is to their credit that everything survived, a bit smoke-damaged perhaps, but intact.

A number of friends, associates, and institutions provided insight, inspiration, and help during the course of this project. Craig Monson and Robert Kendrick were the kindest and most generous colleagues one could hope for: unhesitant about making their work available, and unstinting with advice and encouragement. Elissa Weaver willingly shared her wealth of knowledge on nuns' theater, and Jeffrey Kurtzman helped clarify several issues surrounding seventeenth-century notation. *Un abbraccio forte* for my Sienese friend Stefano Moscadelli, who obtained documents allowing me to enter private archives and accompanied me personally on more than one occasion. He also chased down references in Siena when I was on the other side of the Atlantic. Jonathan and Beth Glixon, Kelley Harness, Robert Holzer, Philippa Jackson, Alyson McLamore, Honey Meconi, Pamela Starr, Lyn Straka, and the late Jean Lionnet all directed me to appropriate bibliography or suggested refinements in ideas or presentation of material. Maribeth Anderson Payne at Oxford University Press was enthusiastic about the project from the beginning and made sure I kept on course. Stan Kauffman in the Graphics Department at Binghamton University produced the map of Siena in chapter 1, and Timothy Rolls computer-processed all the musical examples.

The documents that form the basis of this study were collected in Siena and Rome. I would like to thank Carla Zarrilli, the director of the Archivio di Stato,

Siena, and all the employees there for making me feel so heartily welcome over the years. The staff at the ex-convent of Il Refugio (now a boarding house for young women) allowed me to spend any number of delightful hours wedged (quite literally) in the archive of the Conservatori Riuniti Femminili. Thanks also go to Pietro Elia and to Claudio Pistolozzi at the Opera del Duomo, Siena, and to Franco Daniele Nardi and the administration of the Archivio Arcivescovile, Siena, for admittance to those archives. Daniele Danesi, director of the Biblioteca Comunale, Siena, and the personnel at that venerable institution were cheerful and accommodating. I am grateful to the administration of the Biblioteca Apostolica Vaticana and the Archivio Segreto Vaticano in Rome for allowing me access to documents in their collections. The musical transcriptions in this book are based on microfilms provided by the Biblioteca Apostolica Vaticana, Rome, the Opera del Duomo, Siena, and the University Library, Wroclaw.

This project was supported by a Summer Research Grant from the National Endowment for the Humanities (1994) and by a Summer Support Grant from Binghamton University (1995). An award from the United University Professions helped defray the costs of a research trip to Siena in summer 1999.

I could not have completed this book without the assistance of my husband Nello Barbieri, whose contributions went far beyond the proverbial love and support. He served as an invaluable collaborator for the Italian and Latin transcriptions and translations; he logged many hours on the computer keyboard, designing figures for the book; he was a mine of information on all things Sienese; and throughout it all, he managed to keep both of us sane, not an easy job.

It is with great affection that I dedicate the book to Frank, who knows why.

CONTENTS

x *Contents*

ABBREVIATIONS

AAS	Archivio Arcivescovile, Siena
ACRFS	Archivio dei Conservatorî Riuniti Femminili, Siena
AOMS	Archivio dell'Opera della Metropolitana, Siena
ASF	Archivio di Stato, Firenze
ASS	Archivio di Stato, Siena
ASV, SCVR	Archivio Segreto Vaticano, Sacra Congregazione dei Vescovi e Regolari
BAV	Biblioteca Apostolica Vaticana
BCS	Biblioteca Comunale, Siena
BSSP	*Bullettino Senese di Storia Patria*
DBI	*Dizionario biografico degli Italiani*
DIP	*Dizionario degli Istituti di Perfezione*
JAMS	*Journal of the American Musicological Society*
£.	lire (£.7.13.4 = 7 lire, 13 soldi, 4 denari)
C	canto
A	alto
T	tenor
B	bass
b.c.	basso continuo

A NOTE TO THE READER

All musical transcriptions are the author's. In the musical examples, a whole note equals a semibreve in the original notation. Editorial additions are given above the staff.

All transcriptions and translations of texts are the author's unless otherwise noted. Abbreviations for such commonplace expressions as "Vostra Eminenza" have been resolved without resorting to italics. The original Italian in seventeenth-century documents offers idiosyncratic and often non-standard orthography, which has been reproduced without the addition of "[sic]" except in those cases where clarity of meaning was obscured.

HOLY CONCORD WITHIN SACRED WALLS

INTRODUCTION

In his acclaimed compendium of the lives of famous Sienese, *Le pompe sanesi* (Pistoia, 1649), Isidoro Ugurgieri Azzolini dedicates a chapter to women of distinction from his native city. Near the end of the chapter, after many short biographies devoted to the charms of noblewomen married to prominent aristocrats, he abandons his usual format of separate, numbered entries and instead rushes headlong into paragraphs describing not the rank and status but rather the talents of a number of his Sienese compatriots, most of them unnamed. After citing the accomplishments of these women, who include writers, weavers, dancers, riders, and archers, he turn to musicians:

> Others, by playing all kinds of musical instruments, or by singing the most beautiful little arias or sacred musical compositions, entrance the affections of whoever hears them. The most famous of these women are "la Landa," an Olivetan nun at Ognissanti, "la Giarra," a Gesuate nun at the convent of S. Sebastiano (commonly called "Vallepiatta"), "la Grisona" at S. Niccolò of the Franciscan order, and other almost innumerable women, religious and lay, who not only sing beautifully but are also most learned in counterpoint. Of the women who are marvelous instrumentalists, "la Bargaglia" at Ognissanti is unique. She is mistress of several instruments, but when she plays the theorbo, she makes miracles and produces wonders. (Doc. 1)

Although Ugurgieri Azzolini implies that many Sienese women were musically talented, he names only four, and all are nuns. Clearly, in Siena, as in Milan, Bologna, and Rome, many of the most skilled female musicians lived in convents.[1] And as in those cities, the supposedly impregnable cloister was actually quite permeable, allowing music to flow through the fissures and to connect nuns with their families, friends, patrons, and admirers in the outside world. Now, if the porous nature of the convent wall likens the situation in Siena to that in other Italian urban centers, one feature of musical life in the convents there sets the

Tuscan city apart. Sienese holy women had to cope with far fewer limitations on their musical activities than their sisters elsewhere on the Italian peninsula and were rarely, if ever, forced to resort to elaborate stratagems in order to maintain their musical pursuits. This book thus offers an important counterbalance to the oppositional view of convent music presented in previous research; it demonstrates that musical performance by holy women in early modern Italy was not always characterized by conflict and subject to repression.

Freedom from extensive regulation does not, of course, guarantee a flowering of individual creativity. Despite the favorable circumstances, Siena produced not a single nun who published her music during the Seicento, whereas Bologna can boast one and Milan five. This study does not, therefore, use compositions by Sienese holy women as its central scaffolding; rather, it focuses on cultural products created for nuns (musical, theatrical, and didactic) and on the ritual, devotional, and social contexts in which musical performance took place. A number of Siena's convents provided cloistered girls and women with a lively musical environment, one that extant records allow us to reconstruct with a fair degree of accuracy and in greater detail than is often possible for other cities. Although much of the material is furnished by outside observers of Siena's female monasteries, some of it comes from the nuns themselves, thus adding a personal tone to the narrative. In their not-so-hidden world, the holy women of Siena cultivated their skills as singers and as instrumentalists and regularly displayed them to an admiring public. What emerges is a history of a rich musical practice that was allowed to flourish in order to fulfill vital spiritual, civic, and economic roles in the lives of both early modern nuns and members of the Sienese community at large.

THE STARTING POINT FOR MY investigation is 1575 when, in conformity with the reforms promulgated by the Council of Trent, the apostolic envoy Francesco Bossi made an official visit to all Siena's convents.[2] Bossi's report and his decrees allow for an assessment of the state of the female monastic community during the time that polyphony was establishing itself in the cloister. Records about Sienese nuns, preserved in both Siena and Rome, are plentiful by the last quarter of the sixteenth century, and the confluence of consistent archival accounts thereafter allows for a detailed investigation of the situation during the Seicento, when the public's fascination with convent music and musicians was at its height.

The documentary sources that form the backbone of the following chapters are numerous and varied. Among the most important are those the nuns themselves created, the majority now housed at Siena's Archivio di Stato, in the collection called "Conventi soppressi" ("Con. sopp." in the citations). A few of similar provenance are also found in the city's Archivio dei Conservatori Riuniti Femminili. Such records illustrate the corporate operations of an institution. Financial data is abundant. Account books, with their detailed records of outgoing payments, provide an idea of the monetary resources the monastic community dedicated to support musical activities. *Deliberazioni*—the summaries of discussions nuns held at their periodic meetings—are not so plentiful. Those that do survive furnish insight into convent administration and often provide lists of officers, including women appointed to oversee the music program, if there was one. Rarest of all (and, alas, often the most informative) are chronicles that record the events of importance to the nuns and books of *licenze,* in which the abbess or prioress wrote to the archbishop asking permission to allow men to approach or to enter the cloister. The pointillistic details culled from in-house sources such as these are essential for reconstructing the recurring patterns that characterized life in a convent over long periods of time. When such sources are lost or missing, as is the case with a number of nunneries, what remains are often only records of extraordinary or unusual events written by outsiders.

Among those living outside the walls who remained in very close contact with nuns were Siena's male clergy. From the late sixteenth century onward, all Sienese nuns were subject to the city's archbishop. The course of this relationship is reflected in the various decrees and orders concerning female monasteries promulgated by various archbishops, most preserved in Siena's Archivio Arcivescovile. When the archbishop or the nuns and their relatives wished or needed to defer to a higher authority, they wrote to the Sacred Congregation of Bishops and Regulars (Sacra Congregazione dei Vescovi e Regolari), the standing committee for the control of religious orders set up in Rome after the Council of Trent. The Sacred Congregation had the authority to grant exemptions from established rules or procedures and also served as a court of final appeal in matters of dispute in convents and monasteries the world over. Sienese dispatches to the Sacred Congregation (now in the Archivio Segreto Vaticano) reflect problematic situations and are most plentiful in the waning years of the sixteenth century, when Tridentine reforming zeal was at its peak. The lack of contention over the practice of music in Siena's convents is reflected in the fact that only two of the hundreds of notes that Sienese nuns sent to this body from 1573 to 1670 mention music, and in only one of those is music the central concern. Although the letters are therefore unimportant for tracing musical activities, they are nevertheless useful for understanding several of the economic and administrative issues that confronted Sienese holy women during the Catholic Reformation.

The collection in Siena's Biblioteca Comunale preserves a variety of literature intended for use by nuns, running the gamut from monastic rules to theatrical plays, from devotional exercises to biographies of exemplary holy men and women. Very few sources intended for use at religious rites survive. It is ironic that we have a better idea of what was considered licit for Sienese nuns to read on devotional and recreational occasions than of what they used day in and day out at liturgical services.

Several convents in Siena housed members of the prominent Chigi family, who, it seems, collected every missive, however insignificant, ever written by or sent to a member of the family. The clan's collected correspondence is now at the Vatican Library and includes letters by Chigi nuns and their married female relatives residing in Siena. Passages from these letters offer highly personalized vignettes of life in the convent from both holy women and lay women who retained ties of affection to their cloistered relatives. These candid, intimate letters between family members put a human face on the convent experience in a way that the more numerous formal, official documents meant for general consumption cannot.

From these myriad documentary sources grew five essentially independent but interlocking essays, all modest in scope, each exploring a compelling facet of the musical tradition in early modern Sienese nunneries. As background for the material in the specialized essays, which form the five later chapters of the book, an opening chapter provides a historical overview of the city, with brief sketches of Siena's convents and of their fates during the tempestuous sixteenth century. There follows a perusal of the decrees issued by the apostolic visitor Francesco Bossi and by various Sienese archbishops, especially those regarding musical activities by nuns. These form the basis of my observations on why the experiences of nuns in Siena differed from those of women in nunneries elsewhere on the Italian peninsula. A survey of the many aspects of musical life in Sienese convents is found in chapter 2. Chapter 3 focuses on the "rites of passage" that marked a girl's transition from the secular world to the cloister, with particular attention on the role of music in those ceremonies. Monastic theater, especially plays that include musical interludes of symbolic significance, comes under investigation in chapter 4. Chapter 5 begins with an examination of selected, quite typical biographies of Sienese holy women in order to set into vivid relief what follows: an exceptional spiritual autobiography from a nun-musician in mid-seventeenth-century Siena. In chapter 6, a survey of Chigi operatic patronage in both Siena and Rome serves as an introduction to the examination of the libretto and music from a sacred opera commissioned by the Chigi to celebrate the admission of a member of their family to a Sienese convent. The final chapter of the book is devoted to an analysis of the contents of the single surviving printed volume of sacred works composed specifically for Siena's nuns. Several of the same people, institutions, and monastic customs make appearances in different chapters throughout the book. Given the basically self-contained nature of each chapter, I have decided to err on the side of repetition and provide brief recapitulations of material presented in another context (as well as references to earlier or later discussions).

Although music is clearly the primary focus of the book, my aim throughout has been to include material that would appeal to scholars in a number of fields. With the needs of both nonspecialists and of those unfamiliar with ecclesiastical terminology in mind, I have compiled a brief glossary of musical and conventual terms that appear frequently throughout the text. One often-used word that requires a slightly longer explanation is "noble" (or "aristocratic" or "patrician"). The Sienese nobility was not a closed caste. Candidates for the aristocracy had to reside in the city for a predetermined period, and they had to be upstanding and virtuous men who earned their living in "noble enterprises," including the arts and humanities, large-scale commerce, the manufacture and sale of silk or wool, banking, investment, or the military. Admission to the nobility was a necessary requirement for appointment to certain political offices reserved for this caste. Noble status did not, however, necessarily equate with either political influence or economic affluence, and many aristocratic Sienese fell on very hard times

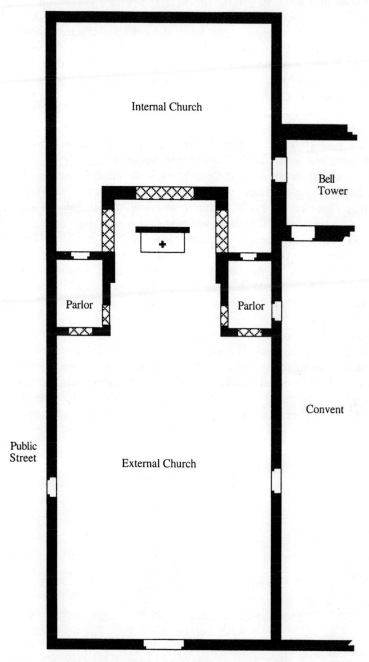

Internal Church

Bell Tower

Parlor

Parlor

Convent

Public Street

External Church

FIGURE 1.   Church at S. Petronilla, 1613

indeed in the seventeenth century. As a result, both power and wealth became concentrated in a mere 16 percent of the city's patrician population. Over the course of the seventeenth and eighteenth centuries, thirty-seven clans held 53 percent of the political appointments reserved for the nobility and accounted for about 64 percent of the income declared by Siena's aristocrats. I refer to these families (and only these families) as the "ruling elite." Among them are found many of the clans who appear as protagonists in the following pages, including the Piccolomini, the Chigi, the Bargagli, the Della Ciaia, the Marsili, the Ugurgieri, and the Gori Pannilini.[3]

It is important that the reader have some understanding of convent architecture in the post-Tridentine period. The only licit communication between cloistered women and those on the outside was supposed to occur through grilles installed at specific locations in the monastery walls. Principal among the places that furnished points of contact was the convent church, which was divided into two separate spheres: the external church, where the public gathered and priests said Mass, and the internal church, where the nuns sang from their own choir and heard the liturgy through the grated openings near the altar. The grated parlors adjoining the convent church were the site of much socializing between the cloistered women and their families and admirers in the outside world. Figure 1, which is based on a 1613 drawing reproducing a portion of the architectural design for the prestigious convent of S. Petronilla, provides a typical example of a convent church.[4]

It was probably in such a church that Ugurgieri Azzolini heard nuns' voices resounding in holy concord. Although his encomium to the cloistered musicians of his native city reflects the apex of their fame, their musical endeavors predate his book by at least a century. Before exploring musical performance in nunneries, however, it will be useful to trace the establishment of the female monastic tradition in Siena and examine how the fate of the convent was tied to the history of the city.

"ILLUSTRIOUS SIENESE WOMEN WORTHY OF REMEMBRANCE"

Nuns and Convent Life in Siena, 1550–1700

The Sienese female monastic tradition is reputed to have begun in 801, when Pepin, son of Charlemagne, ordered the construction of a convent to honor the Roman martyrs Abbondio and Abbondanzio. Angelic intervention determined the very location of the nunnery. It is said that the laborers began to build in a valley near the Tressa river, but on returning to work the next day, they found that the entire foundation had been miraculously transported to a nearby hill. In subsequent centuries, the devout Benedictine nuns of "Santa Bonda" garnered many admirers, among them Blessed Giovanni Colombini (1304–67), the Sienese founder of the Gesuati, and his "companion in poverty," Francesco Vincenti. Both men entrusted their daughters to the care of the nuns and left the convent substantial bequests in their wills. Colombini also specified his wish to be buried in the nuns' cloister. In 1575, the apostolic visitor Francesco Bossi found only fifty-one women at SS. Abbondio e Abbondanzio, but seventy or so nuns are recorded by the turn of the seventeenth century, making it one of the city's most populous convents.[1]

Another group of cloistered Benedictine sisters established themselves at Montecellesi, just north of the city, as early as the eleventh century. The nuns adopted the Cistercian habit and rule early in the thirteenth century and came to live within Siena's walls at a convent dedicated to S. Prospero, located in the area now occupied by the Fortezza. In 1534, after many peregrinations, the women of S. Prospero and those of the convent of S. Agnese joined to form a single community. Shortly afterward, in 1537, the nuns made a public vow to change their name to "Trafisse del Cuor di Maria" ("The Transfixed Ones of Mary's Heart"). Their convent was thereafter known as "Le Trafisse." It held forty women in 1575, a typical number for most medium-sized female religious institutions in Siena.[2] In 1604, Giovanni Battista Piccolomini, the vicar in charge of overseeing the city's nuns, judged Le Trafisse to be the most prosperous convent in the diocese, not only because it had an excellent income from the sisters'

investments and earnings but also because the apostolic visitor had fixed the number of "mouths" the convent could support at a relatively low level, allowing the
women to live "comfortably."[3]

The movement begun by S. Francis found fertile soil in Siena during the
thirteenth century, which saw the founding of the cloistered Clarissan institutions
of S. Petronilla, S. Lorenzo, and S. Chiara, as well as the establishment of S.
Margherita in Castelvecchio, a house for Franciscan tertiaries. S. Niccolò, the
youngest Clarissan institution, was established in the fourteenth century, and the
tertiary house of S. Girolamo in Campansi arose in the fifteenth century. The
origins of yet another convent of tertiaries, the Mantellate di S. Francesco, are
obscure. Of the three institutions that were still uncloistered in 1575, S. Girolamo
and S. Margherita were the largest, the former housing sixty-seven women and
the latter between fifty and sixty. The Mantellate, on the other hand, numbered
only seventeen.[4] All three seem to have attracted members of the aristocracy. S.
Margherita was reputed to house women from Siena's first families.[5] It is difficult,
however, to make generalizations about the financial condition of those families.
A letter from an impoverished nobleman requesting a place for his daughter at
the Mantellate suggests that such convents might have required lower dowries
than cloistered institutions and therefore might have been especially appealing to
the downwardly mobile aristocracy.[6] Certainly, even if dowry was not an issue,
one of the main selling points for tertiary houses was that they were, in fact,
open: young women could be honorably settled in the religious life and still leave
the convent to see their relatives and help out at home if needed.

The premier Clarissan house was S. Petronilla, at which women from rich,
prominent Sienese families professed. The wealth of the convent manifested itself
in its size: sixty-six women lived there in 1575. The nuns owned a miraculous
painting of the Virgin, known as the "Madonna della palla,"[7] and, with the patronage of the Guild of Barbers, they maintained an altar dedicated to S. Apollonia. The institutions of S. Chiara, S. Niccolò, and S. Lorenzo were all well
respected but apparently maintained lower public profiles than S. Petronilla.[8] The
thirty women at S. Lorenzo in 1575 formed one of the smaller convents in Siena.
During the same year, S. Niccolò and S. Chiara housed fifty-one and forty-eight
nuns, respectively.

Of the six Augustinian houses dotting the Sienese urban landscape, all but
one had their origins in the Quattrocento. The exception, SS. Concezione, probably arose later and was never a large institution; in 1575, only twenty-eight nuns
lived there. This may be compared to the forty-nine women at S. Maria degli
Angeli, the sixty-two at S. Maria Maddalena, and the sixty-five at S. Marta, the
three most renowned of the group. S. Maria degli Angeli was an extraurban house
until 1434, when the nuns moved inside Porta Romana and ceded their former
quarters to a local order of monks. In the following centuries, Santuccio (as it
came to be known) grew in size and importance, particularly after coming into
the possession of a much-venerated relic: the head of the Sienese martyr S. Galgano. Although they possessed no such relic, the women of S. Maria Maddalena
made a name for themselves by their skill at copying and illuminating liturgical
and musical manuscripts in their beautiful convent outside Porta Tufi. In the

fifteenth and early sixteenth centuries, the patronage of the Petrucci family helped to enrich the nunnery.[9] The fragmentary state of the surviving documents from this institution offer little insight into the nuns' activities once they were transferred to their new seat inside the city after 1526, but the sheer number of women the convent could support suggests that it continued to prosper. S. Marta began life as a retreat for a small group of aristocratic widows who agreed to live together under the Augustinian rule. Soon after its founding in 1328, however, the institution began to attract professed nuns and then unmarried patrician girls who wished to profess there. The women parlayed their dowries and the gifts bequeathed them into a solid financial base for their nunnery, one of the richest in Siena.[10]

The Augustinian house of S. Paolo did not enjoy the same kind of patronage as her sister institutions in the earliest years. Resources were scarce throughout much of the fourteenth and fifteenth centuries, but by 1575 the convent could easily support forty-three women. A spate of building and remodeling projects in the second half of the seventeenth century suggests that S. Paolo had achieved a position of eminence at that point in time. The nuns at S. Monaca, founded as a home for Augustinian tertiaries, also did not have an auspicious start. After hardscrabble centuries of sustaining themselves by begging, the twenty-eight women there were forced to accept cloistering at the turn of the seventeenth century. Sienese families deserted S. Monaca in droves after a 1619 epidemic in the cloister killed five nuns and two girl boarders; in desperation, the nuns wrote to the Sacred Congregation asking for financial help. Their fortunes then slowly improved. Legend has it that Catherine Medici Gonzaga, who became governor of Siena in 1627, intended to enter the convent after her tenure and was prevented from doing so only by her death in 1629. By midcentury, the women had attracted the patronage of Pope Alexander VII Chigi, who gave them the head of S. Mauro.[11]

Siena had long been home to women who took the Dominican habit and prayed together but resided with their families (S. Catherine being the most famous example). Not until 1479, however, did a group of those women decide to commit themselves to living together in a religious community. In this way, the convent of S. Caterina del Paradiso was born. Fifteen years later, in 1494, a group of women from Paradiso received permission from Cardinal Francesco Piccolomini (later Pope Pius III) to found another Dominican house, S. Giacinto di Vita Eterna. Both were among Siena's open female monasteries and, like some other tertiary institutions, they were much favored by members of Siena's impoverished nobility and by nonaristocrats (such as the daughter of Cathedral maestro Andrea Feliciani).[12] The number of women at Vita Eterna probably never surpassed the thirty-eight prescribed in the document of confirmation. Paradiso, on the other hand, probably housed about fifty women.[13]

Ognissanti was the oldest of the two female monasteries with specifically Sienese roots. It began as a Benedictine convent and was in existence by at least 1288, when the nuns were mentioned as beneficiaries in a will. Although the nuns of S. Giacomo in Bari are given credit for establishing the first female house of the Olivetan order, it seems likely that Ognissanti was in fact the first. The male branch of the congregation took root in Sienese territory at the monastery of Monte Oliveto, founded by Blessed Bernardo Tolomei and other Sienese noblemen in 1319. Pope Clement VI put his official seal of approval on the order in 1344, and it was probably only shortly afterward that the women at Ognissanti took the Olivetan habit. The convent grew in size in the mid-to-late fifteenth century when the sisters of S. Barnaba were forced out of their home and ordered to join ranks with the Olivetan nuns. Ognissanti sheltered fifty-six women in 1575, and it was a stronghold for the rich and powerful Piccolomini clan. The family played a large role in bringing the convent to prominence in the seventeenth century. It was through their agency that the Olivetan nuns could claim that their statue of the Madonna and Child had miraculous powers.[14]

S. Sebastiano in Vallepiatta, the other convent of Sienese origin, was founded by Blessed Giovanni Colombini's cousin, Caterina Colombini. Between 1363 and 1364, she gathered together a group of women who renounced personal property, lived on alms, did manual labor, and freely professed their love of Christ in prayer and through acts of charity. These uncloistered Gesuate called themselves the "Poor sisters of the Visitation of Mary," and like their male counterparts they demonstrated no interest in setting up rigid organizational structures, pursuing theological or doctrinal studies, or promoting special liturgies and rites. Although the male branch of the order was suppressed in 1668, the female branch was allowed to continue. Forty-two nuns made up the community at S. Sebastiano in 1575. After they reluctantly accepted *clausura* at the turn of the seventeenth century, their membership began to include women from important Sienese families such as the Armalei, the Buoninsegni, the Petrucci, and the Venturi.[15]

Two other female institutions with more specialized missions sprang up in Siena at the end of the sixteenth century. The Convertite, reestablished around 1570, provided a refuge for reformed prostitutes who wanted (or were forced) to leave behind the trappings of their former life and take the Dominican habit.[16] The Sienese mystic Caterina Vannini professed there in 1584, and her presence earned the convent fame, respectability, and a certain level of prosperity. The convent grew to become one of the largest in Siena, with over ninety women in 1624.[17] The other institution, Il Refugio, began life in the 1580s as a sanctuary for poor, abandoned girls, perhaps, it was hoped, to spare them the fate of the Convertite.[18] The founder, Domenico Billò, governed the girls until his death in 1593, when they came under the protection of the Chigi family. The new director, Aurelio Chigi, transformed the conservatory into something resembling a female monastery by writing up a rule and insisting that the girls wear a habit. Under Chigi's governance, the institution also began to accept both aristocratic girls whose families had fallen into such poverty that they could not afford a normal convent dowry and rich noblewomen whose dowries helped finance the institution. Aristocrats and commoners were, however, kept strictly separated, and in the 1670s the "Abbandonate" (as the poor, nonaristocratic girls were called) were transferred to a new home at S. Girolamo, the former monastery of the suppressed Gesuati. At that point, those women came under the governance of the hospital of S. Maria della Scala and began to lend their service as nurses there.[19] Il Refugio remained the home of aristocratic girls (rich and impoverished). Il

Refugio was designed to hold forty-eight women. All who desired a place at the house, whether poor or rich, were required to submit to a probationary period of two years before they could take the habit in a ritual ceremony. Afterward, they lived a monastic life of prayer. The Sienese called these women nuns, but in point of fact, they neither took formal vows nor belonged to any established order. Furthermore, they had one privilege denied to every other nun in the city: with appropriate permission from their own chapter, they were free to exit the cloister for a day at a time.[20]

The last female monastic institution founded in Siena before the Napoleonic era was a Capuchin house. In the year 1598, a group of women led by the Sienese mystic Passitea Crogi received permission from Siena's archbishop to build their convent near the old church of S. Egidio. The few extant documents concerning the house show that the Capuchin nuns had a well-earned reputation for their devotion and their dedication to the vow of poverty.[21]

By the turn of the seventeenth century, Siena could therefore boast twenty-one monastic or paramonastic institutions for women.[22] Although a number of them were originally situated outside the city's walls, all but one had moved inside by the mid–sixteenth century. (The exception was SS. Abbondio e Abbondanzio, located beyond Porta San Marco.) The convents were equally distributed among the city's three administrative districts, called *terzi*: the Terzo di Città, which included all the convents near the Duomo and the church of S. Agostino; the Terzo di S. Martino, which incorporated the nunneries near Porta Romana and Porta Pispini, and the Terzo di Camollia, which encompassed the houses lying north of the churches of S. Domenico and S. Francesco (see figure 2).

Table 1.1 shows the distribution of convents by order; bold type identifies the convents at which the nuns cultivated vocal-instrumental ensembles for the performance of polyphonic sacred music during the seventeenth century. Traces of such activity, albeit on a much smaller scale, can be found at S. Margherita in Castelvecchio and S. Monaca, but the loss of archival material makes it difficult to render any judgment about the extent of their enterprises. This is not to deny that nuns at other institutions sang or played musical instruments. S. Niccolò housed one of the four nuns Ugurgieri Azzolini named in his compendium; S. Girolamo in Campansi was the site for the performance of a sacred opera; Il Refugio probably had a nun organist; and a number of the Convertite played plucked string instruments. Existing records suggest, however, that none of these institutions trained and maintained a group of nuns who regularly performed at liturgical rites.

A number of factors characterized those convents that did cultivate their own musical ensembles. One of the most important was the class from which the nunnery drew its members. S. Abbondio, S. Marta, Ognissanti, S. Petronilla, Santuccio, and S. Maria Maddalena were all favored by members of the Sienese nobility and the ruling elite, who were more likely to provide their daughters with musical training and more apt to regard musical performance at the convent as a reflection of family status.[23] The older, cloistered institutions patronized by the aristocracy were also likely to be among the richest, for in addition to the dowries their novices brought, they also found themselves the recipients of tes-

FIGURE 2.　Convents in Siena, c. 1600

tamentary gifts. In addition, the women who professed at such institutions were more apt to receive generous living allowances from their families. Having disposable income to hand helped the nuns purchase and repair instruments, obtain music, and pay for teachers. In this regard, it is notable that S. Paolo, a convent that was not first choice among Siena's prominent families and thus was without great resources in its first centuries of existence, initiated a training program in music once it had attained a solid financial base in the seventeenth century. The formation of the musical ensemble there was, in effect, a sign of the convent's new economic rank and social standing. The Capuchin nuns, on the other hand, with their commitment to poverty, apparently did not learn to perform polyphony. Religious orders that placed an emphasis on ornate ritual were more likely than others to embellish their services with polyphonic music. It is not surprising, for example, that the Benedictines, the Olivetans, and the Cistercians, the only three houses that required women to participate not only in clothing and profession rites but also in elaborate group consecrations, all had musical ensembles. Nuns belonging to orders that fostered the arts were more likely to encourage

TABLE 1.1. Siena's convents: Orders, foundation, population

	Foundation Date	Est. Population 1650*
Augustinian		
S. Maria degli Angeli (Santuccio)	14th cen.?	73
S. Maria Maddalena	1339	62
S. Marta	1328	60
S. Paolo	1330	42
S. Monaca	1338	44
Santissima Concezione	15th cen.?	22
Benedictine		
SS. Abbondio e Abbondanzio	801	70
Capuchin		
Monastero delle Cappuccine	1598	25
Cistercian		
Monastero delle Trafisse	1063	45
Clarissan		
S. Petronilla	1216	55
S. Chiara	13th cen.	44
S. Lorenzo	1257	32
S. Niccolò	Early 14th cen.	42
Dominican		
S. Caterina del Paradiso	1479	50
S. Giacinto di Vita Eterna	1494	36
Franciscan		
S. Girolamo in Campansi	1435	63
S. Margherita in Castelvecchio	Mid–13th cen.?	44
Gesuate		
S. Sebastiano in Vallepiatta	1363–64	45
Olivetan		
Ognissanti	1288	62
Other		
Convertite (reformed prostitutes)	1570	93
Il Refugio (impoverished nobility)	1580	48

Bold: convents with musical ensembles.

musical endeavors. The Olivetans were renowned for promoting the study of art and music. Among the members of the male branch during the seventeenth century was the influential composer and theorist Adriano Banchieri.[24] Thus, the emphasis on music at Ognissanti is not surprising. At the convent of S. Sebastiano, music played an integral role in the expression of the nuns' spirituality. It seems that the women took their cue from the stories surrounding the founder of the Gesuati, Blessed Giovanni Colombini, who was renowed for singing *laude* and who did not hesitate to call on his companions to perform vocal and instrumental music for important visitors.[25] Convents whose nuns considered themselves the custodians of relics that were especially important to the Sienese were also famous for their music. The nuns of S. Petronilla had an altar in their external church dedicated to S. Apollonia, and they also possessed several teeth from this saint so dear to Siena's Guild of Barbers.[26] Every year, guild members came to S. Petronilla with an offering of four pounds of wax and 3 lire. In return, "once the men of the guild had collectively assembled at the church in front of the altar of S. Apollonia, the nuns were obliged to have Mass celebrated according to the long-standing custom, that is, with motets."[27] The sisters of S. Abbondio were entrusted with the care of Blessed Giovanni Colombini's body, and the Augustinian nuns at Santuccio possessed the venerated head of S. Galgano. Both monasteries were renowned for their nun-musicians. It may be that musical ensembles arose at these convents as a way for the nuns to pay manifest homage to the relics entrusted to their care.[28]

Despite some testimony that at least one convent began to cultivate poly-phonic music by the early 1500s, archival records from many nunneries are often spotty until the years immediately following Francesco Bossi's visit to Siena in 1575. The observations of the apostolic visitor provide a wealth of information at a critical juncture in the annals of the city. Not until the 1570s, in fact, were the Sienese, lay and religious, finally beginning to dig their way out of what had been a disastrous century and to rebuild their lives.[29]

The vicissitudes of the Cinquecento had their roots in the political turmoil of the previous century. The long, sometimes glorious, and very well-documented history of republican government in Siena came to an end in 1487 with the coup d'état of Pandolfo Petrucci. When Pandolfo's last heir, his son Fabio, was driven from Siena in 1524, the stage was set for the final debacle. The social and political unrest that characterized Sienese life during the second quarter of the century played out against the backdrop of French and Spanish rivalry for control of the Italian peninsula. Two warring Sienese political factions, the Noveschi (the Nine) and the Libertini (a cross-party group of committed republicans), formed the uneasiest of alliances. The Nine, hoping to renew ties to the Medici, allowed French troops into the city. When the French were defeated at Pavia in February 1525, the Libertini forced those same troops out, killed Alessandro Bichi, leader of the Nine, and took control. This action prompted the pro-French Medici pope, Clement VII, to send his troops to attack Siena. The Sienese defeated the papal forces at the Battle of Camollia in July 1526.

Having rid itself of both French and papal troops, Siena was subject to the garrisoning of imperial soldiers in the city by 1530 and thus to Spanish oversight of internal politics. The Spaniards attempted a reform of political institutions and tried to exercise control of them through the nomination of key government officers. Imperial legates, however, were seen as partial to the Nine, and both the Spanish garrison and the Nine were driven from the city by other political factions in 1545. After two years of unstable self-governance, the Sienese once again saw imperial forces take control and reinstall the Nine. The Spaniards also dispatched the last in a line of incompetent governors to Siena.

The curtain lifted on the final act of the tragedy in 1550 when the Spaniards began to construct a fortress to house their troops. The Sienese lodged protests through diplomatic channels, and several prominent aristocrats left the city and began to plot the overthrow of imperial forces by appealing for help from France.

In July 1552, French and Italian troops led by one of those self-exiled noblemen, Enea Piccolomini, marched on Siena and after a few days of fighting, aided by the people within the city, were able to isolate the Spanish troops inside the still-unfinished fortress. In August, Cosimo I de' Medici, watching the spectacle from a safe distance, was able to negotiate the release of the Spanish soldiers, who marched to Florence. Legend has it that the commander of the imperial garrison issued a warning upon his departure: "You valiant Sienese have struck a most glorious blow. But in the future, be careful, for you have offended too powerful a man."[30]

The warning was prophetic. Less than a year later, Spanish troops entered the Sienese state, arriving at the gates of the city in late January 1554. Cosimo I, furious that the Sienese had put his enemy Piero Strozzi in a position of power, also decided to take action and sent Florentine forces to reinforce the Spaniards. Several skirmishes between French troops and imperial forces followed in 1554, but the major weapon the Spanish and Florentines employed was the siege. It took almost a year to starve the Sienese into submission. Not until April 1555 did they finally capitulate. In 1557, the Spaniards sold Siena to the Medici, and the once independent city was absorbed into the Grand Duchy of Tuscany.

The upheavals of the century were keenly felt by all Siena's nuns. Extraurban female houses were most affected by the nearly constant state of unrest. During the battle of Camollia in 1526, the convent of S. Maria Maddalena, then outside Porta Tufi, was razed by the Sienese to prevent its use by the troops of Clement VII. For the same reason, the nuns of SS. Concezione, located beyond Porta Camollia, were forced to reestablish themselves inside the walls. The battle also witnessed the destruction of S. Prospero and the unwilling transfer of the Cistercian nuns to a new seat. Women at Ognissanti and S. Chiara, outside Porta Romana, and those at S. Petronilla, outside Porta Camollia, saw their monasteries demolished when Spanish and Florentine troops menaced the city at midcentury. Even the nuns of S. Abbondio, beyond Porta San Marco, were constrained to abandon their monastery ahead of the onslaught of armed forces in the 1550s. Six of the twenty Sienese convents existent in 1524 were thus leveled by 1555. Most of the displaced nuns had to seek temporary housing with other religious orders until civic and ecclesiastical authorities could relocate them permanently inside the city walls or until the women could begin construction on a new convent, a process that could take almost half a century, as the sisters of S. Chiara discovered. Even if the nuns did not have to rebuild from the ground up, their new quarters often required extensive architectural modifications and additions so that they might serve as convents. The women of S. Abbondio, the only ones allowed to return to their monastery outside the city, found everything in such a ruined state that ten years of reconstruction (1555–65) were necessary before the place was once again merely habitable.[31]

If the prolonged fighting and political unrest had led to the destruction of many venerable buildings in Siena, the siege had exacted an even more brutal toll on her citizens. The population of Siena in the 1540s is estimated to have reached 22,500. By the end of the siege, about ten thousand Sienese were still alive.[32] The city's holy women suffered along with the rest of the population, their situation doubtless exacerbated by the forced retreat from their abodes in the worst of weather. A chronicle from Santuccio notes that on the raw winter day the nuns of Ognissanti, S. Chiara, and S. Abbondio arrived in Siena, they had to trudge in "mud up to their knees."[33] Sickness and starvation robbed the nuns of many of their congregation during the terrible years that followed. In 1553, fifty-seven choir nuns from S. Abbondio entered the city. By 1565, when they embarked on their return journey, only seventeen of those women were still alive and only six new nuns had joined their ranks.[34]

In the last half of the sixteenth century, therefore, Sienese nuns had to turn a good deal of their energies to the restoration of their convents. Their efforts in that enterprise are recorded in the annals of the Sacred Congregation. From 1576 to 1624, Siena's cloistered nuns most frequently requested permission to do one of two things. First, they sought to clothe women "over the number"; that is, to accept more women than the apostolic visitor deemed their resources could support. Such supernumeraries brought a double dowry, a valuable resource for a financially struggling convent. Second, the nuns appealed for authorization to use *doti anticipate*—the dowries of novices who were expected to take the habit but had not yet taken their final vows—either for construction projects, or to pay off loans, or to buy land. The supplications came both from nuns forced to move during the troubled century (S. Chiara, Le Trafisse, Ognissanti) and from those whose convents survived (Santuccio). It is difficult to know how normal these requests were in the ordinary course of events and whether nuns in other cities entreated similar exemptions at the same rate as Sienese holy women. In any case, the petitions speak to the havoc that both war and neglect wreaked on the convents of Siena and to the determination with which the nuns addressed the problems.

It was during this period of rebuilding that Francesco Bossi came to assure the application of Tridentine directives at the city's holy places; these included such eminent institutions as the Opera of the Cathedral and the hospital of S. Maria della Scala, as well as the female monasteries.[35] Bossi, bishop of Perugia, was a zealous reformer in the mold of Carlo Borromeo.[36] In Borromeo's thumbnail sketch of Bossi we can, however, detect a certain disdain for the Perugian bishop's tastes and lifestyle, which ran to delicate foods, singing birds, dogs with ornate collars, fine glassware, and instrumental music at table. Borromeo also judged Bossi to have a quick temper and too much ambition.[37] Bossi was not a welcome guest. Neither Florentine nor Sienese officials wanted an outsider meddling in their affairs. They were especially loathe to let him examine the accounts from the hospital of S. Maria della Scala and the Cathedral, and they did their best to thwart his efforts. It was through the able diplomacy of then cardinal Ferdinando de' Medici that the Perugian bishop was dispatched to Grosseto and a more sympathetic visitor sent to finish the job in Siena. Before he left, however, Bossi did manage to visit nearly all of Siena's convents and to publish his orders concerning their administration.

Bossi found 926 nuns, novices, and *educande* (girl boarders) inhabiting the convents of Siena in August 1575.[38] The rosiest estimate of Siena's population during Bossi's visit would have found about eighteen thousand inhabitants in the city. Thus, despite, or perhaps because of, the terrible sufferings of war and siege, about 10 percent of Siena's women were religious, a ratio greater than that found in the much larger and less politically tormented urban centers of contemporary Milan and Bologna.[39] Siena's monastic population grew even as the birthrate remained stagnant. By the mid-Seicento, when Siena could still count only eighteen thousand people within her walls, at least 1,057 women—almost 12 percent of the female population—inhabited her cloisters as choir nuns, servants nuns, or novices.[40] Members of one of Siena's civic magistracies, the Balìa, understood the correlation between an impoverished noble class and high marriage dowries on the one hand and an exploding convent population and declining general population on the other. Twice they urged their Florentine overlords to legislate a reduction of secular dowries so as to match those necessary for taking the veil. Nothing came of either effort. For Sienese noble familes, faced with both fewer choices for their daughters in the marriage market and the prospect of disbursing a secular dowry that could amount to over eight times as much as a spiritual dowry, the option of placing daughters in a convent continued to be an extremely viable one in long-term family planning.[41] Although Bossi ordered the archbishop to examine every girl about to take the habit under circumstances where she could "freely state her intentions and state of mind," it is clear that even he could not bring himself to address in a more direct manner the old custom of exploiting the nunnery as a refuge for "superfluous" daughters.[42]

Most of the other decrees Bossi issued were meant to address the typical administrative problems ecclesiastical authorities found in convents during the years immediately following the Council of Trent.[43] Some of his rulings had to do with guidelines for monastic elections and the manner in which officers should discharge their duties. Others outlined procedures for religious rites and devotional customs, among them, how often the nuns should confess and receive communion and when they should sing the Office. Bossi was clearly distressed about the lack of "la vita comune" ("communal living") in many convents. He decreed that all income be shared among the members of the religious community. He also ordered the abbesses to examine each nun's cell and confiscate any personal possessions that could cause scandal.

Bossi's top priority, however, was to restrict nuns' contact with the outside world. The apostolic visitor attacked this issue from all angles. He forbade lay persons from entering the cloister without a license from the archbishop. He took direct aim at convent architecture by providing a detailed account of how the grates in parlors should be constructed. As might have been expected, it was his insistence on absolute clausura for all nuns that created the most controversy. Even at the most well-established, patrician institutions, where the *coriste*, or choir nuns, were indeed cloistered, the *converse*, or servant nuns, who had paid a lower dowry and who were released from participation in the Divine Office so that they could cook, clean, and attend to the most basic chores, were free to exit the convent. Women at some houses—those at S. Abbondio, for example—simply refused to follow Bossi's orders and were able to get away with it for at least a decade.[44] At the open institutions of S. Francesco, S. Girolamo, S. Margherita, S. Monaca, S. Sebastiano, Paradiso, and Vita Eterna, however, there was no hiding behind the

TABLE 1.2.   Siena's archbishops, 1529–1713

Francesco Bandini	1529–88
Ascanio I Piccolomini	1588–97
Francesco Maria Tarugi	1597–1607
Camillo Borghesi	1607–12
Metello Bichi	1612–15
Alessandro Petrucci	1615–28
Ascanio II Piccolomini	1628–71
Celio Piccolomini	1671–81
Leonardo Marsili	1682–1713

excuse that only servants left the convent. Women at all these houses regularly went out to beg for food and money in the streets of the city; their very survival depended on it. Bossi ordered the nuns at several open institutions to pronounce the three solemn vows of poverty, chastity, and obedience and to accept claustration under pain of excommunication, and he gave them two weeks to do so. They refused. Although Bossi was sent packing before the situation reached an explosive point, he had set in motion an unstoppable process that Sienese archbishops would carry out over the next fifty years.

Siena's archbishops maintained, on the whole, an extraordinarily cordial and supportive relationship with the cloistered holy women under their jurisdiction during the sixteenth and seventeenth centuries. (Table 1.2 lists the prelates and their tenures in the position.)[45] That the city's enclosed nuns found episcopal policies acceptable is revealed by the fact that they never protested their treatment to higher authorities. In the years between 1576 and 1624, they wrote not a single letter asking the Sacred Congregation to overturn a decree made by the city's archbishop.

Women at open convents, on the other hand, faced a radically different situation, and their relationship with prelates in both Siena and Rome were much stormier. After Bossi's visit, such women had two options: they could either profess the three solemn vows and allow themselves to be enclosed, or they could keep their doors open but be barred from accepting novices and girl boarders at their institution. Most open convents did not have the economic resources to follow the first path, and choosing the second meant that the convent would eventually cease to exist. Uncloistered women found neither fate acceptable, and the struggle that ensued consumed much of the time and energy of Siena's archbishops.

Although Francesco Bandini was the titular archbishop of Siena from 1529 to 1588, he did not reside in the city, and left the actual day-to-day work to a series of coadjutors. Alessandro Piccolomini, appointed to that post in 1574, was present when Bossi arrived in town but did nothing to enforce the apostolic visitor's directives. In 1578, Ascanio I Piccolomini replaced Alessandro Piccolomini.[46] Probably because he was coadjutor (and not titular archbishop) from 1578–88, Ascanio I at first took a relatively cautious approach to the issue of enclosure.

Families of girls who wished to enter one of the seven open institutions and nuns who wished to bolster their ranks wrote any number of letters to the Sacred Congregation asking for exemptions to the decree forbidding professions, and Ascanio I actually supported their cause on at least one occasion. In May 1583, he requested that the Roman committee allow the female tertiaries at Paradiso to accept twelve novices because then "perhaps they will be disposed to accept perfect clausura, which they have not been able to do until now because they have nothing to live on."[47]

The relationship deteriorated in the late 1580s, when women from open convents did two things not designed to endear them to ecclesiastical authorities. First, they traveled outside the gates of Siena as far as Sinalunga—43 kilometres distant from the city—to beg for alms or, even more shocking, to work in the fields and help with the harvest. Second, they decided to forge ahead and allow young women to profess at their institutions without permission from the Sacred Congregation. The appointment of Ascanio I as titular archbishop in 1588 may have emboldened him to take a stonger stance against such actions, for in August 1591 he placed the offending convents under interdiction. This was lifted in December of the same year but reimposed in 1592 when women from Paradiso and Vita Eterna once again left the city during harvest. In this instance, as on other occasions, the Sienese tertiaries adopted a strategy that nuns in all parts of the peninsula had learned well: they turned to their network of protectors in the ecclesiastic and lay communities.[48] One result of these actions was that members of the Balìa and well-connected male regulars wrote letters on their behalf to Rome. This kind of pressure probably helped the nuns win ground on three issues of utmost importance to their survival. Archbishop Piccolomini either relented (or was compelled to relent) and gave the women permission to leave the city at specific times during the harvest season. He also granted them the right to take in educande. And perhaps most important of all, he was forced to accept the decision by Roman authorities giving all the young women who had taken the habit without official approval to remain among the ranks of the professe at the convents they had surreptitiously entered.[49]

Despite the favorable outcome, the confrontation left women from open convents harboring ill feelings toward their archbishop. An anonymous letter to the Sacred Congregation, dated 1594, accused Ascanio I of "having too high an opinion of himself" and of simultaneously neglecting his pastoral duties and of being too severe with the "poor convents of nuns."[50] With the battle won, most female tertiaries felt no need to make further concessions. The only women to see the handwriting on the wall were the Dominican sisters of Vita Eterna, who voluntarily enclosed themselves in 1595.[51]

The next archbishop, Francesco Maria Tarugi, was far sterner, perhaps because he was not Sienese.[52] In 1599, he stripped all regulars of their authority over the open convents and imposed his own on them. He asked for and apparently received temporary permission from the Sacred Congregation to decide on the admission of girl boarders and supernumerary nuns to the convents of Siena. The prelate clearly wished to have the power to reward convents who submitted to cloistering and, by implication, to make life miserable for those who continued to resist.[53] Between 1600 and 1602, S. Monaca, S. Sebastiano, and S. Margherita all decided to enter into arbitration with the archbishop in order to work out the most favorable conditions possible in return for accepting clausura. Nuns at these institutions bargained for the right to use funds from the dowries of women who had not yet professed to construct their cloisters and walls. They also obtained permission to send out a couple of the oldest members of their congregration to beg for a limited number of years to help increase their income.[54] Tarugi's other victory, if it can be called that, was with the Mantellate of S. Francesco. By 1604, the convent held only five aged tertiaries. Whether they were forced to join with the nuns at S. Margherita (as Ascanio I Piccolomini had desired) or they simply died is not known, but their convent apparently ceased to exist.[55]

Tarugi's successors eventually managed to negotiate the same kinds of arrangements with the remaining holdouts. Metello Bichi saw the enclosure of the Franciscan women of S. Girolamo in Campansi in 1612. It was, in fact, partly through generous donations from the Bichi family that the convent was able to do so. Under Alessandro Petrucci, the tertiaries of Paradiso struck an agreement in 1615, although clausura was not complete until sometime in 1624. The sale of some property and a generous yearly stipend from Maria Maddalena, archduchess of Tuscany, allowed the ninety or so Convertite to enclose themselves in 1624.[56]

Aside from claustration, Sienese archbishops found no issues important enough to warrant setting off a dispute that might provoke the city's nuns into appealing for help from the Sacred Congregation. Sienese families, of course, continued to draft letters to the commission for assistance in resolving issues about dowries, and nuns wrote concerning matters in which the archbishop had to cede authority to Rome, among them, licenses to allow girls to reenter the convent after having left for various reasons, and permission to use dowries paid in advance. But not once in the years between 1576 and 1670 did a nun from a convent in Siena write to the Sacred Congregation in Rome concerning a dispute with the archbishop over musical matters.[57] One could assume that music was not a high priority for women grappling with more pressing concerns, but other records reflect that this was not the case. The inference, in short, is that Sienese archbishops had different attitudes toward the musical activities of the nuns in their city from those of some of their colleagues in Milan, Bologna, and Rome. A brief survey of the few decrees they issued concerning nuns and performance will re-create the musical climate in Siena's convents during the period in question.

Despite his nearly twenty years on the job when Tridentine fervor was at its height, Ascanio I Piccolomini broached the subject of music only once, in a set of rules issued 10 January 1597 that were intended to help the Convertite reform their monastery. Archbishop Piccolomini's words were not ungentle at the beginning of the document: he noted that the women had been deprived of counsel and like lost sheep had been wandering on the wrong path leading to worldly shame and everlasting damnation. In order to show them the straight way to heaven, he thought it best to issue a series of decrees that he hoped they would receive with good will and would think few and sweet rather than many and harsh. His tone then stiffened as he commanded that his rules be obeyed by all of the Convertite under pain of suspension of office, deprivation of the veil, and any other punishments as he saw fit.

Of the twenty-eight decrees outlined in the document, several were similar to those issued by Bossi in 1575. For example, the archbishop ordered the women to keep better records, stipulating that they were to buy two books, one to record professions and the other to keep track of finances. He also commanded that no nun break clausura, that no man be allowed to enter the cloister without a proper license, and that four mature women be elected to monitor all conversations in the parlor. Other decrees, however, seem to be specifically tailored to the Convertite. These "reformed" women were, for instance, forbidden to talk to anyone with whom they had consorted in their former sinful lives. Mandate 13 falls into this category, for it directed the women to remove all lutes and citterns from the convent and never to acquire new ones, for they were both the emblem and the source of "sinful passion."[58]

Piccolomini's successor Tarugi seems to have focused most of his energies on closing down open institutions, and no orders about music have survived from his tenure. In 1608, however, shortly after Tarugi's successor Camillo Borghesi took office, a broadsheet containing several new decrees aimed at all Sienese convents was published. One of Borghesi's mostly highly placed diocesan officials, the vicar-general Fabio Piccolomini, was apparently responsible for circulating the broadsheet, but certainly he must have done so with Borghesi's blessing. In order to avoid confusing these edicts with those promulgated under Ascanio I and Ascanio II Piccolomini, I will therefore give Borghesi credit for them.

In addition to the usual admonitions about the observance of clausura, Borghesi made certain specific recommendations concerning music. Since, as he believed, overly frequent concerts by singers and instrumentalists in the convent's external church could cause a multitude of distractions for women living with "purity of heart," he ordered that nuns limit the number of times lay musicians performed to once or twice a year; that is, on the convent's principal feast days.[59] Clothing ceremonies were another occasion at which Borghesi allowed the presence of professional performers, but he specified that the relatives of the girl taking the habit were to hire the musicians, and not the nuns (the pertinent portions of Borghesi's orders are given in Doc. 2).

If Metello Bichi left little mark during his short reign, Archbishop Alessandro Petrucci showed greater commitment to his pastoral charges.[60] His seventy-two-page compendium of decrees for nuns, issued in 1625 (a year after a visit to all of Siena's convents) is divided into six parts covering nearly all aspects of conventual life: rules and rites; the vows of poverty, chastity, and obedience; and the regulations concerning clausura and the novitiate. Petrucci set the tone for the volume in his preface, where he noted that he had included only the most necessary decrees and had eliminated those that were too harsh. He made several observations concerning the use of music, and it is telling that most were included in the section dedicated to the vow of chastity. Music was evidently considered a force that could lead to sinful corruption if not used wisely. Indeed, Petrucci, like Borghesi, specifically noted the tendency of ill-regulated music to create "distractions." He therefore required the nuns to secure permission from the arch-bishop any time they wished to have music performed in their external churches. He also forbade nuns to perform in their parlors and ordered that they refrain from singing secular tunes at all times. He commanded that convents with a tradition for performing music have a *maestra del canto* and an appropriate rehearsal space situated in such a way that the constant practice of the musicians would not disturb other members of the monastic community. Musical performance was permitted only at divine rites; the music was to be serious and solemn, as it was a sacrilege to sing of divine things with secular music. Apart from services, the nuns were not to sing or play either for lay or ecclesiastical persons in the churches or elsewhere, except when the archbishop came to visit. Petrucci's final obser-vation on music was set out in a section devoted to regulations for novices. He found polyphony of little use to young women at this stage of their careers, and thus he recommended that their musical experiences be restricted to learning plainchant (Doc. 3).

Petrucci's successor was Ascanio II Piccolomini, who served as archbishop for nearly fifty years, from 1628 to 1671. The numerous orders he issued con-cerning nuns dealt with the usual topics: clausura and communal life. He seems to have addressed the issue of music only three times during the course of his long tenure: the first time in a set of decrees stemming from his 1664 visit but not printed until June 1666; again in what appears to be a handwritten addendum to those June decrees, dated August 1666; and for the last time in April 1668.

In the printed volume of 1666, Piccolomini repeated Petrucci's orders that the performance of polyphonic music by singers and instrumentalists be permitted only in the nuns' choir and that performances in the nuns' choir be allowed only for divine rites. He sanctioned the nuns performing or rehearsing anywhere in the convent so long as they could not be heard by lay persons. They could even rehearse in the choir if the doors to the church were locked. He also forbade the use of lay teachers during Advent and Lent (Doc. 4). Piccolomini's handwritten orders of August 1666 modified the first two rules concerning music, issued only two months earlier. He implied that if nuns did not have sufficient light when rehearsing in the choir, they could leave their church doors open. He also declared that nuns who played and sang at the parlor grates should not be seen, tacitly acknowledging that public musical performance was possible outside of divine services and in places other than the choir (Doc. 5). The April 1668 order re-garded teaching practices. Ascanio II forbade both nuns and educande to take music lessons unsupervised.[61]

From the tenor of these decrees, it is evident that performances of sacred music by both nuns and outsiders occurred frequently in Siena's convents and indeed that convent music-making was considered a highly acceptable enterprise from 1575 right through the beginning of the eighteenth century. Neither Ascanio II's successor, Celio Piccolomini, nor the next archbishop, the music-loving Leo-nardo Marsili, saw fit to make any changes that might have disturbed these long-established traditions. The mandates from Siena are striking when compared to those that emanated from ecclesiastical authorities in other urban centers during the same period. A number of Bolognese prelates issued decree after decree from

1580 to 1620 forbidding nuns to study with outside teachers or to hire secular musicians for performances in their churches. In Milan, Carlo Borromeo revoked all licenses for music instructors and forbade the nuns to invite lay musicians to sing and play in their external churches; Borromeo's cousin Federigo barred the presence of male music teachers throughout his long reign (1595–1631). Repeated edicts and bans, stretching well into the mid–seventeenth century, prohibited Roman nuns from inviting male musicians to their churches, either as performers or as instructors.[62] In Siena, by way of contrast, Borghesi simply sought to limit the use of external performers. Petrucci softened the order even further: he desired only that the nuns request permission when they wanted to invite lay musicians to their churches. Whereas the Milanese, Bolognese, and Roman prelates' bans were probably motivated by a fear of the possibility of "illicit" relations between nuns and lay men as well as the "projection of nonepiscopal order" into the city's convents,[63] Petrucci seemed more concerned with scheduling conflicts. As is illustrated in the next chapter, men who performed for nuns were generally on staff at the Cathedral, and though the archbishop could be confident that they were representing his authority, he wanted to be sure that they did so only when they were not needed at their primary place of employment. Lay music teachers were likewise not a concern in Siena so long as they were properly monitored and did not disturb the nuns' duties during the penitential seasons of Advent and Lent.

The issue of performance in the parlors was more problematic for both Petrucci and Ascanio II, as it was for archbishops in other urban centers, because these spaces were the site of much secular music-making. In Milan, decree after decree was aimed at abolishing the custom; Petrucci, too, forbade nuns to sing secular songs and to perform in the parlors.[64] In Siena, as in Milan, it is evident that the decrees were honored more in the breach than in the observance, and so Ascanio II sought to avoid conflict by not mentioning the parlor and simply issuing a regulation that banned public music-making outside the nuns' choir. His addendum demonstrates that when he was forced to confront the matter directly, he capitulated and allowed the practice, so long as the nuns could not be seen by their audience.

More important, however, than the episcopal decrees that placed some loose restrictions on Sienese nuns were those that exhorted the women to take their musical activities seriously. Petrucci's admonitions concerning adequate musical leadership and rehearsal space were clearly designed to encourage high standards of singing and playing and to forestall complaints from nonmusicians about noise. The amended decrees issued by Ascanio II allowed the nuns a great deal of latitude to choose comfortable, well-lighted spaces to rehearse, even if that meant that lay persons could listen in.

This is not to say that the tolerant environment somehow gave Sienese nuns opportunities denied to cloistered women elsewhere on the Italian peninsula. Nuns in Bologna, Milan, and Rome regularly invited secular musicians to sing in their churches. They likewise pursued their studies with male teachers and performed polyphony in their choirs and in their parlors. Indeed, they were far more famous for their musical skills than Sienese holy women, perhaps because they resided in much larger cities, more frequented by travelers. Every so often, they did indeed have to cope with episcopal injuctions seeking to limit or ban music-making, but such decrees were rarely enforced for very long, or the nuns simply decided to ignore them.[65] One wonders, however, why Sienese archbishops never felt the need to impose similar constraints on the women of their city.

Several factors probably came into play. First, Siena's cloistered performers seem to have avoided getting entangled in explosive scandals. Extreme vigilance on the part of ecclesiastical authorities may have played its part in discouraging male musicians allowed within the nuns' precincts from attempting anything that might arouse suspicion. Indeed, Siena was such a small town that men who obtained permission to teach at female monasteries had to be extremely careful about their deportment at all times, even when they were not in contact with the nuns. Giuseppe Piccini, who was hired as a singer and organist at S. Maria in Provenzano in 1658 and supplemented his income there by teaching at the city's nunneries, apparently learned his lesson the hard way. After what was deemed completely unacceptable behavior during the festivities of Carnival in 1664, Archbishop Ascanio II Piccolomini barred him from serving as an instructor at the city's convents. Piccini's behavior apparently lost him his day job as well, for he disappears from the payment registers at Provenzano after 1664.[66]

Siena's cloistered women were by no means saints, and the city's prelates were not bighearted pushovers who simply turned a blind eye on infractions of all the rules. The archbishop did not hesitate to pursue action against nuns who gave or accepted gifts or who spoke too frequently with lay persons. Ognissanti weathered one case involving a nun who received a love letter from a close relative and another regarding a woman who had constructed a secret grate between her house and the adjoining monastic cell in which her granddaughters resided. At S. Paolo, the prioress was punished for allowing outsiders to enter the convent without proper licenses.[67] Whatever the conduct of cloistered nuns, however, they simply could not compete with the scandalous actions associated with women at open convents. A document from papers of the Sacred Congregation, for example, contains a report of a Dominican tertiary in Siena who was impregnated by a friar of the same order—although rumor had it that she had slept with monks from several different orders. She furthermore had managed to hide her condition under her copious habit as she sought alms in the streets of Siena.[68] An incident of this sort quite literally embodied the prelates' worst fears, and it is clear why they concentrated their efforts on forcing the enclosure of open institutions and ignored the relatively minor sins that must have occurred at cloistered houses. It is not possible, alas, to know the precise reasons that prompted Archbishop Ascanio I Piccolomini to ban lutes and citterns at the open monastery of the Convertite—the only mandate of its kind ever issued in Siena, it must be noted—but whatever the precipitating agent, the nuns had two strikes against them: they were former prostitutes and they were resisting control by refusing to cloister themselves.

Sienese convents, whether by luck or by conscious effort on the part of the women enclosed in them, also seem to have escaped the kinds of internal dissension, often exacerbated by family and class tensions, that brought grief to monastic musical organizations elsewhere in Italy. Robert Kendrick has documented cases in Milan where power struggles erupted over which of a convent's two choirs had the prerogative to perform on certain feast days and over singers' rights to transfer their membership from one ensemble to the other. The resulting upheavals in monastic discipline provoked church authorities into barring the nuns from performing polyphonic music altogether.[69] Such strife seems not to have touched Sienese convents, even though the renown of musical ability cut across lines of lineage and social standing. Of course, the reason may be that the monastic population was already in large part segregated by such factors into separate institutions. Of the four nun musicians cited by Ugurgieri Azzolini, Landi was from a noble family and Bargagli, from the ruling elite, and both professed at the patrician house of Ognissanti. The other two were from nonaristocratic clans, and one of them—"la Grisona"—was at S. Niccolò, a Clarissan convent of lesser social and civic standing than Ognissanti. The nonpatrician "la Giarra" was, however, at S. Sebastiano, where she must have collaborated with musical nuns from Siena's thirty-seven elite families (Maria Verginia Accarigi and Passitea Forteguerri, to name but two).[70] In at least some Sienese convents, then, patrician and nonpatrician women joined to make music, and although it cannot be determined that no friction resulted from the mix, it never created a firestorm of great enough proportions to prompt the intervention of outside authorities. If anything, Siena's nuns seem to have cultivated a remarkable esprit de corps in musical matters. In the 1650s, the members of Siena's elite ruling class who had professed at Santuccio (the Borghesi, the Malavolti, the Placidi, and the Ugurgieri, to cite but a few of the prominent surnames among the coriste there) performed sacred music alongside a "poor maiden" of undistinguished family.[71] Another case is recorded at S. Abbondio, where women from noble families were probably taught to play the organ by a commoner residing in their midst. Their loyalty to her and to each other were put to the test in 1593, when they received the disappointing news that the funds in the monastery's treasury were not sufficient to reconstruct the organ as they desired. Such a situation in other monasteries might have offered an excuse for a single nun to seize control by supplying the money herself and cutting out the competition. Not so at S. Abbondio. Together the organists decided to raise the amount needed from their own funds, and each contributed an equal sum to see the job done right—all eleven of them.[72]

But perhaps the reason for the lack of restrictions on music-making in Sienese convents was less the absence of scandal than the presence of a succession of Sienese archbishops who placed great value on musical performances by the city's nuns. This can be partially explained by the fact that only one of the men appointed to the episcopal seat in the sixteenth and seventeenth centuries—Francesco Maria Tarugi—was not a member of the Sienese patriciate. The fate of nuns in small-town Siena was not, as it might have been in larger cites, an abstract issue for the archbishops. Their sisters, aunts, nieces, and an entire network of extended family were, after all, the inhabitants of the city's convents. Because they were members of the aristocracy themselves, the prelates shared the concerns of the Sienese nobility and they strove to make conditions in female monasteries conform to the expectations of their caste. Musical performance was clearly an important component of family honor, and therefore no archbishop made it difficult for nuns at most convents in the city to sing or to play. Ascanio I Piccolomini's order banning plucked string instruments at the Convertite is the exception that proves the rule: these women—and only these women, it might be added—were targeted precisely because they were not members of the Sienese aristocracy. But even the man who issued that decree clearly enjoyed nuns' music-making. On his three-day visit to S. Abbondio in 1593, Ascanio I heard Mass daily in the inner church and requested that the nuns sing polyphony at the Elevation. He also wanted to be present in the inner church for Vespers, when the nuns sang in polyphony with organ accompaniment. An account of Piccolomini's visit notes that the archbishop took "great consolation" in the latter service.[73]

The prelate who had the greatest effect on the musical environment of Siena's convents was, however, Ascanio II Piccolomini, whose indulgent attitude toward nuns' music-making remained unchanged during his remarkably long reign. He stepped into the office in a fortunate period when all the open convents in Siena had accepted cloistering and when the "militant" phase of the Catholic Reformation was ceding to a period that stressed the church triumphant.[74] Ascanio II was well educated, an astute statesman, and a friend of the powerful Barberini family in Rome. He is perhaps best known for his unflagging defense of Galileo Galilei after the latter's denunciation by the Roman Inquisition in 1633. Piccolomini invited Galileo to his palace in Siena, received him warmly, and encouraged him to resume his scientific writing. According to one biographer, Piccolomini's "humanity and understanding literally saved Galileo's life and sanity."[75] Piccolomini also defended his guest so hotly that the Holy Office in Rome received the following anonymous letter from Siena in 1634:

> Galileo has disseminated in this city opinions that are not very Catholic, urged on by this archbishop, his host, who has suggested to many people that Galileo has been unjustly treated by the Holy Office, and that he neither could nor should give up his philosophical opinions that he has sustained with irrefutable and true mathematical arguments; also, that [Galileo] is the first man in the world, and will live forever in his still-prohibited works, and all modern and distinguished men will follow him.[76]

Piccolomini was clearly an independent thinker, and his accomplishments and family connections gave him sufficient power and prestige to do as he saw fit within the walls of his native city. In the 1630s he supported Galileo, and in the 1660s he chose to allow nuns in Siena to have much greater access to lay musicians that his distant relative Pope Alexander VII Chigi thought appropriate for holy women in Rome.[77] Piccolomini deserves much of the credit for allowing the musical traditions that were already well established in Sienese convents to continue to blossom.

For Ascanio II and the other men who served as archbishop, the issue of nuns' music certainly meant more than allowing the urban elite to garner recognition and honor by proxy. Siena was, after all, a subject city. After their absorption by the Grand Duchy of Tuscany, the Sienese were deprived of the republican government that had played such a prominent role in forging and sustaining their political and cultural legacy. At least one historian has noted that, after the fall of the republic, the religious experience itself was one of the few channels through which the Sienese could express and assert their corporate identity and unity.[78] The religious calendar of feasts, tailored over the centuries to civic purposes, put all of Siena's holy places, including its convents, on display one or more times a year and reassured the Sienese of their unique heritage. Musical performances by Siena's holy women thus might have been understood as a demonstration of communal identity in one of the few areas in which the Sienese had autonomy. The benefits of such a policy flowed not only to the nuns but also to the lay community, who clearly appreciated the opportunity to have access to their spiritual daughters: to teach them music, to perform with them, to borrow their relics for ritual processions, to be assured of their spiritual capital in times of need, and, in the words of one admirer, to hear the "sweet and lovely harmony resound[ing] within those sacred walls, as if angelic singers of paradise had descended amongst us."[79]

GL'ANGELI METTANO UNA CORONA ALLA MONACA CHE CANTA

Musical Activities in the Early Modern Sienese Convent

For the nuns of S. Maria degli Angeli, 17 May 1592 was a red-letter day. To be sure, that Sunday marked the feast of Pentecost. The holiday, however, had to share center stage at the convent with another event of great significance to the nuns. It seems that before this date, the convent had often lacked water and the women had decided to build a fountain in their cloister. On 17 May, construction was complete and water began to flow from the aqueduct for the first time. According to the convent scribe, the nuns celebrated the event by going in procession throughout their gardens, weeping tears of joy, and singing the *Te Deum*.[1]

From this short account, preserved not in a chronicle but in a normally dry debit-credit register, we can begin to understand the extent to which music accompanied the obligations, burdensome and joyful, that punctuated each day, each week, and each year within the cloister. Although liturgical rites witnessed the greatest amount of music-making, other occasions, great and small, also called for musical performance, whether well-rehearsed (as was most often the case) or spontaneous, as in the engaging story just related. Official records cannot do justice to the entire range of nuns' musical endeavors, but they can provide a basis for understanding the place of music within the cyclic patterns of convent life. What follows is an introduction to the various musical activities that flourished in the convents of Siena, an overview of the events that warranted performance, and an evaluation of the significance of music-making for the nuns and for the world outside the cloister.

Nuns in many, if not most, Sienese convents regularly sang Gregorian chant under the supervision and direction of the sister or sisters appointed to lead the plainchant choir.[2] Payments made for acquiring books of plainchant or having it copied demonstrate that singing chant continued to be a vital practice for holy women throughout the seventeenth century, especially those in houses with strong musical traditions.[3] The plainchant choir was an important establishment even in nunneries that were not renowned for their vocal-instrumental ensembles. This much is reflected in the subtext of a letter that Francesca Tarari sent to the Sacred Congregation in Rome in 1644. The "gentlewoman from Cagliari" introduced herself as a professed nun at the Dominican convent of S. Caterina del Paradiso and explained that when she took the habit, her relatives provided the usual dowry demanded of a woman who wished to be a corista (and not the lesser dowry required for a conversa). However, because Tarari could neither read nor sing, she had been denied the usual privileges that accompany the rank of corista. Now she was no longer young and could learn neither reading nor singing. Notwithstanding this fact, she asked the Sacred Congregation to command her sister nuns to grant her the privileges that she felt were rightfully hers because of the dowry she paid.[4]

It seems that the nuns at Paradiso, one of the less prominent houses in Siena, had accepted Francesca Tarari and her full dowry on the condition that she learn to read and sing. No evidence suggests that S. Caterina could compete with the richer Augustinian, Benedictine, and Olivetan institutions, whose holy women regularly performed polyphony. We can imagine the Dominican sisters' chagrin, however, when a corista refused to learn the skills that would allow her to contribute her voice to the most basic musical expression in the monastic community: chanting the Divine Office.

Several historical manuscripts preserving plainchant or rules for singing chant are still extant in Siena and pertinent to this study. The most impressive is a choirbook, which contains some fascicles copied in 1543.[5] Although it now forms part of the collection in the Cathedral archives, it is certain that it once belonged to a female monastic community, for a rubric in the manuscript states that "two sisters" should begin the Improperia from the middle of the chorus.[6] The choirbook includes a requiem Mass, a Mass Ordinary, and Mass propers for the most important days in the liturgical calendar (e.g., Nativity, Circumcision, Epiphany, Holy Week, Resurrection, Pentecost, Ascension); that is, feasts that would have been celebrated universally. Despite the fact that there is nothing to identify the specific convent that owned this choirbook, its survival offers testimony to similar treasures that many of Siena's nunneries must have had in their possession.

A much smaller sixteenth-century antiphonary in the Biblioteca Comunale also comes from a Sienese convent, again unidentified. It includes chants for major feasts such as the Purification, Palm Sunday, Ascension, Assumption, Maundy Thursday, and Good Friday, as well as for a burial service.[7] Most striking are the rubrics directing the course of processions that took place on the first four of these feasts. As the nuns moved from their choir to the "old church" to the dormitory to the refectory and finally, to the (new?) church, they embellished their singing with dramatic gestures that turned the procession into a theatrical event. At the last station of the Palm Sunday procession, for instance, as the female cantor began the antiphon *Ave Rex noster*, the entire assembly of nuns sank to the ground on their hands and knees to bow to the cross, and then rose to face it until begining the hymn *Gloria, laus et honor*.[8]

The three remaining historical chant sources can all be connected with Augustinian convents. The first is a seventeenth-century copy of the constitution for the convent of S. Monaca.[9] It is virtually identical to the constitution found in an elegant sixteenth-century source that was the property of the nuns of S. Maria Maddalena, who were once renowned for their skill at copying and illuminating musical manuscripts.[10]

In the constitution that served both convents, the subject of chant is treated at length, and the discussion is sprinkled with a generous number of musical incipits illustrating the most important tones of the Mass and the Office. The constitution also includes a detailed description of the female cantors' duties. Women appointed to this position were responsible for assuring that all the nuns in their half of the choir were assigned antiphons to be sung at services during the Office each week; they also intoned every chant sung during services, sometimes alone, sometimes together, and, on the most solemn feasts, in the company of two additional singers. The cantors were obliged to know the rank of each feast, in order to assure the correct choreography. The rules specify that only on minor feast days did the cantors commence singing from their usual seats in the choir. Double feasts required them to intone chants from in front of the altar, whereas on major doubles, they did so from the pulpit. The source from S. Maria Maddalena suggests that in addition to assigning the chant, the cantors were probably expected to teach, for after the constitution is appended the full text of a treatise entitled "Rules for Singing." The treatise addresses philosophical questions about the definition of music and then tackles the practical matters of how to recognize consonance and dissonance, how to identify the authentic and plagal modes, and how to learn and use solfège. It is a testament to the culture and learning of the nuns at S. Maria Maddalena that the treatise is in Latin and not the vernacular used throughout the rest of the manuscript.[11]

Of more interest here is a manuscript prepared in 1675 "for the most reverend mothers of the venerable convent of S. Maria Maddalena at the request of Sister Caterina Angela Carli, the prioress of the choir." The scribe was a Sienese friar who signed himself Dionysius Amadorius.[12] The source reveals a still-healthy tradition of singing Gregorian chant at the end of the Seicento. It contains antiphons to be sung at First and Second Vespers, and sometimes also at Prime and Terce, for such universal feasts as the Sacred Name of Jesus, S. Gabriel Archangel, and S. Joseph. As might be expected, the manuscript also contains antiphons for holy days of special significance to the Augustinian nuns: S. Monica (mother of S. Augustine), S. Nicholas of Tolentino, "all saints of our [Augustinian] order," and the Feast and the Translation of S. Augustine. Most notable are the antiphons for the feast of S. Thomas of Villanova, the Augustinian archbishop of Valencia and Spanish reformer who was canonized in 1658, and for the Holy Name of Mary, a feast that would not be officially extended to the entire Western church until 1683.[13] Perhaps one of the reasons the nuns commissioned the friar to copy the manuscript was to have on hand chant appropriate for these relatively recent holy days.[14]

If many convents expected all their nuns to sing chant, documentary evidence shows that at least nine Sienese institutions—S. Abbondio, S. Maria degli Angeli, S. Maria Maddalena, S. Marta, Ognissanti, S. Petronilla, S. Paolo, S. Sebastiano and Le Trafisse—supported a group of select musicians who performed polyphony. It is difficult to know just how many women from the convent sang in such elite ensembles. At Le Trafisse, which housed between thirty-two and thirty-seven coriste and novices during the course of the century, women were appointed to fulfill the role of "first singer" (*prima cantora*) and "second singer" (*seconda cantora*). Sometimes "third" and "fourth" singers or "assistant singers" were chosen as well.[15] It seems improbable that these women were the only members of the convent able to sing polyphony. More than likely, the cantore were the strongest vocalists and thus were supposed to act as section leaders in what was probably a small ensemble. Whatever their numbers, the singers who could perform polyphony were held in high regard and were often rewarded for their services in the traditional Sienese manner: with special treats at the dining table. The administration at Santuccio purchased six watermelons to give to the singers after their performance on the feast of the Nativity of the Virgin in September 1663 and in August 1676 regaled them with ravaggioli—a fresh, soft, flattened cheese that was a Tuscan specialty—perhaps in anticipation of the same holiday.[16] The cantore at S. Abbondio were entitled to such delicacies as meatballs, eels, and pigeons.[17]

In addition to singers, the musical establishment at most of the convents renowned for polyphony included instrumentalists. Documentation regarding such players is scarce at S. Abbondio and at Le Trafisse, though some records do show that the former institution was famous for its female organists. When the Sienese priest Filippo Montebuoni Buondelmonti compiled his manuscript of "diverse facts about Siena" during the reign of Urban VIII, he included two entries on women in the section devoted to musicians' biographies. One of those was Suor Orsola Silvestri of S. Abbondio, who was "so graceful at playing the organ that it was truly a miracle of nature."[18] Little is known about Suor Orsola, other than the fact that she was accepted into the convent sometime between 1576 and 1579 and she participated in the consecration ceremony of 1586. A chronicle from S. Abbondio praises her abilities as a teacher and credits her for establishing the legacy of fine organ-playing at the convent. Indeed, in the waning years of the sixteenth century, the convent could boast a total of eleven organists, including Suor Orsola.[19] At Le Trafisse, the woman who served as organist is sometimes named along with the other convent officers appointed every three years.[20]

Among the other nunneries with reputations for polyphony, the organist was supplemented by additional musicians, most of whom probably played plucked or bowed string instruments.[21] Ugurgieri Azzolini praises the theorbist he calls "la Bargaglia" at Ognissanti, and it appears that she had at least one disciple. At S. Marta, nuns learned to play the lute.[22] Debit-credit registers from S. Maria degli Angeli include a reference to a violone repaired in 1651, and books of licenze from S. Paolo indicate that, during the last two decades of the century, one or more nuns there played violin, viola, and theorbo.[23] The total number of instrumentalists at these houses is, once again, difficult to determine. A 1631 inventory from S. Marta, for example, includes an entry for "nine instruments of various sorts," most likely including a lute, but we cannot assume that all nine were used on a regular basis. The instrumental ensemble at S. Petronilla can be partially reconstructed only for the mid-1670s. In those years, documents show payments for cleaning and repairing a spinet (*spinetta*), a violone, and a theorbo. By the 1680s, S. Petronilla's ensemble also included violinists.[24]

Nuns and novices were not the only performers in the cloister. The educande also had the opportunity to learn to sing and play from the convent's musicians. This practice, when carried out too enthusiastically or thoughtlessly, could lead to friction between the teacher-performers and the women for whom music was not a top priority. One such incident is documented in a letter sent by the nuns of S. Petronilla to Archbishop Ascanio II Piccolomini in August 1668. After first asking for the archbishop's help in a separate matter, the nuns bring up the problems connected with teaching activities at their institution:

> Also we present to Your most Illustrious and most Reverend Lordship another, similar problem and cause of unrest. It has been several years since your benevolence found a remedy for this, but it has fallen into disuse with the passing of time. The provision was that, for the tranquility of those who wish to pray and rest, the girl boarders should not come into the dormitories from sunset until after the holy Mass [the next day] and in the summer, not until after the prayer of the communal hour that follows [the Mass]. Truthfully, their being in the dormitories is already considered unacceptable: since they are always there, it deprives us of our cells. We can never have peace because they are being instructed to read aloud all the time, and with the great number of the aforementioned boarders, there is the continuous noise of this activity, not to mention the singing and playing in the dormitories and in the contiguous rooms, which face ours, and create a great disturbance for each of us. . . .
>
> Therefore, we supplicate the incomparable benevolence of Your most Illustrious and most Reverend Lordship to renew the order that the maestre who wish to train the girls to read aloud, to sing, and also to play noisy instruments should seek distant rooms that are not contiguous with the cells, so as not to perturb the communal tranquility. (Doc. 6)

There is every reason to suppose that if the educande were talented enough, they performed with the nuns. In some cases, they were essential members of the convent ensemble. When the nuns of Santuccio wrote to the Sacred Congregation in 1655 asking permission to allow the impoverished nonaristocrat Caterina Alessandri to become an educanda at their convent without paying the usual boarding fees, it was not because they took pity on her poverty but rather because Alessandri was "expert at singing and playing" and they needed someone to sing soprano.[25] A letter from the Sienese noblewoman Olimpia Chigi Gori Pannilini to her brother Cardinal Sigismondo Chigi related how her fifteen-year-old daughter Laura, then a boarder at Il Refugio, was tapped to play the organ for high Mass and for Vespers on a convent feast day when "all Siena" was present.[26]

The task of leading the ensembles of nuns, novices, and boarders in rehearsal and performance was often entrusted to a nun maestra. Only two convents, Le Trafisse and S. Sebastiano, preserve the names of nuns who were regularly elected or appointed to convent offices during most of the seventeenth century, and the woman who directed the polyphonic ensemble has a prominent place on these lists.[27] At Le Trafisse, officers were elected every three years, and those with musical ability often served repeated terms in this capacity. Suor Candida Marzocchi, for instance, was elected to three consecutive terms as maestra di musica in 1626, 1629, and 1632 and took up the mantle again in 1638. The same procedure is evident at S. Sebastiano, though nuns rarely held the same job in consecutive two-year periods. A woman from the ruling elite, Suor Maria Rosalinda Pieri, served as director of the polyphonic ensemble during five terms over a twenty-year period (1677–79; 1683–85; 1687–89; 1691–93; 1695–97).[28] At two other convents, the evidence is neither as plentiful nor as systematic. Only a single allusion to a maestra surfaces in the documents from S. Petronilla and in those from S. Maria Maddalena; the entries are dated 1652 and 1654, respectively, but the women who held the positions are not identified.[29] At S. Maria degli Angeli, references to a maestra di musica appear with some regularity in records from 1673 to the end of the century. Among those holding the post were members of Siena's ruling elite: the Chigi, the Ugurgieri, and the Biringucci. As at Le Trafisse and S. Sebastiano, skilled women were asked to take on the duties of the post more than once. There is even some evidence for a single family dominating musical life at Santuccio during the last two decades of the Seicento. Records show that Suor Nicola Caterina Chigi was maestra in 1683–84 and that in 1686 Suor Maria Geltruda Chigi took over the duties of leading the polyphonic ensemble. The latter then went on to serve at least two more terms as maestra di cappella before the century was over.[30]

If archival records demonstrate that many convents brimmed with various kinds of musical activity, very little remains of the actual repertory the talented monastic singers and instrumentalists performed. Only one printed source of music for Sienese nuns survives: a volume of Lamentations and motets for solo voice and continuo published in 1650 by the aristocrat-composer Alessandro Della Ciaia.[31] Della Ciaia was obviously casting his net wide with these works. They served the needs not only of the first-tier female monasteries that wished to shine a spotlight on one of the singers from their ensembles but also of the second-tier institutions that could not cultivate large-scale polyphony but might have had a talented soloist in their midst (S. Niccolò, for example, which housed one of the four nuns Ugurgieri Azzolini named in his encomium). Solo and duet repertory must have therefore been popular at many convents in the city. This is evident in a 1670 letter that Suor Lutugarda Chigi of S. Margherita wrote to one of her nephews (either Cardinal Flavio or Cardinal Sigismondo). She asked him to maintain his promise to send her motets, adding, "It does not matter to me if the words are missing. It will be sufficient that Your Eminence sends them to me, just as long as they are for soprano and alto."[32] Suor Lutugarda obviously believed that the words could be supplied later, according to the occasion for which the motets were intended; the most important factor was the texture of the setting, which would require only two singers (and an accompanist, one assumes) for performance.

Clearly, however, convents that cultivated and maintained a sizable number of talented women were not content to limit themselves to small-scale works. Descriptions of convent celebrations suggest that devotional and liturgical rites important enough to require polyphony were often graced with larger-scale repertory; double- and triple-choir music was not unheard-of on such occasions. Since no composer published large-scale pieces for Sienese nuns and no evidence has surfaced regarding compositional activity among the nuns themselves, the question arises as to how the holy women obtained such repertory.

One answer would have been for the nuns to acquire printed volumes containing large-scale works with traditional mixed-voice scoring and then to arrange the pieces to suit their requirements, either through upward transposition of vocal lines or by substituting instruments for voices on the lowest parts.[33] But though Sienese nuns apparently did purchase some music,[34] they most often adopted another strategy: they turned to the corps of professional musicians who worked in Siena's various public institutions for help. These musicians not only supplied holy women with appropriate repertory for their feast days but also served the nuns as teachers and as performers. The remarkably tolerant climate in Siena throughout the period under consideration allowed holy women and lay musicians to establish and maintain an unbroken and mutually advantageous partnership.

Professional musicians provided a great deal of the music heard in convents on occasions of particular importance to the nuns during the late sixteenth and early seventeenth centuries. Girolamo Gigli, in his *Diario sanese*, provides a calendar of feast days celebrated at all churches in the city during the early eighteenth century.[35] It appears accurate for the seventeenth century and includes the days celebrated with special pomp at convents (see table 2.1).[36] It was precisely for such feasts that nuns often invited lay choirs to perform. Documents clearly reflect this practice at a number of institutions, including those whose nuns apparently did not maintain ensembles of their own, such as S. Girolamo, S. Lorenzo, and SS. Concezione,[37] as well as those that had a reputation for housing musically talented women: S. Abbondio, S. Petronilla, and S. Marta. At the Benedictine convent of S. Abbondio, for example, men were hired to sing polyphony on 21 March, the feast of S. Benedict, the founder of their order; on 31 July, the day in honor of the local *beato* Giovanni Colombini, whose body was buried in their cloister; and on 16 September, the feast of the saints from whom their house took its name, SS. Abbondio and Abbondanzio. Records of payments extend from 1581 to 1624.[38] At S. Marta, outside musicians are recorded from 1597 to 1610, usually for the feasts of Christmas and S. Martha (29 July), although they were sometimes called in for Holy Saturday, for the feast of S. Augustine, and for the burials of abbesses. Rarely do the documents specify either the number of musicians or their names, although several references in the payment records from S. Marta, three to a "Francesco maestro di cappella" in 1605 and 1606 and one to "maestro di cappella messer Marcantonio" in 1608 can only refer respectively to Francesco Bianciardi and Marcantonio Tornioli, the musical directors at the Duomo.[39] The use of Cathedral musicians is also suggested by a few payment records from S. Abbondio that name Girolamo Gulini, the famous castrato soprano in the cappella.[40] Another document from S. Petronilla clearly identifies the "musicians of the Duomo" as those who came to perform on the feast of S. Thomas Apostle in December 1605.[41] The Cathedral staff seem to have enjoyed a near monopoly on the rights to perform at the city's nunneries, perhaps because

TABLE 2.1. Important convent feasts in Gigli's *Diario sanese*

January	
1/20: S. Sebastian	S. Sebastiano in Vallepiatta
1/21: S. Agnes	Le Trafisse
1/25: Conversion of S. Paul	S. Paolo
Sunday after Octave of Epiphany	Il Refugio
February	
2/4: Exposition: Madonna of the Manger	Ognissanti
2/9: S. Apollonia	S. Petronilla
March	
3/21: S. Benedict	S. Abbondio
April	
4/29: S. Catherine of Siena	S. Caterina del Paradiso
May	
5/1: SS. James and Philip Apostles	S. Chiara
5/4: S. Monica	S. Monaca
5/31: S. Petronilla	S. Petronilla
June	
6/11: S. Barnabas	Ognissanti
6/30: S. Paul Apostle	S. Paolo
First Sunday in June	Convertite
July	
7/2: Visitation	Le Trafisse
7/20: S. Margaret	S. Margherita in Castelvecchio
7/22: S. Mary Magdalen	S. Maria Maddalena
7/29: S. Martha	S. Marta
7/31: Blessed Giovanni Colombini	S. Abbondio / S. Sebastiano
Sunday within Octave of Visitation	S. Sebastiano in Vallepiatta
August	
8/10: S. Lawrence	S. Lorenzo
8/12: S. Clare of Assisi	S. Chiara
8/16: S. Hyacinth	S. Giacinto di Vita Eterna
8/20: S. Bernard	Le Trafisse
September	
9/1: S. Giles	Cappuccine
9/8: Nativity of the Virgin	Santuccio
9/16: SS. Abbondio and Abbondanzio	S. Abbondio
9/30: S. Jerome	S. Girolamo in Campansi

(continued)

TABLE 2.1.   (*continued*)

October	
10/26: S. Rustico	Le Trafisse

November	
11/1: All Saints' Day	Ognissanti
11/25: S. Catherine of Alexandria	S. Maria Maddalena

December	
12/3: S. Galgano	Santuccio / Ognissanti
12/6: S. Nicholas	S. Niccolò
12/8: Immaculate Conception	SS. Concezione
12/13: S. Lucy	S. Petronilla
12/21: S. Thomas Apostle	S. Petronilla

they were the best musicians in the city or perhaps because as employees at the seat of the archbishop they were thought to be above reproach.

The records imply that Siena's nuns depended on lay performers most heavily during the years when they were struggling to rebuild their own groups. War and siege and their long aftermath had apparently taken the same toll on music as on convent buildings and population. It does not mean, however, that the women had absolutely no resources at the time. Although the nuns at S. Abbondio were still inviting professionals from the Cathedral to perform on certain feast days in the early Seicento, in 1584 they were able to celebrate the arrival at their convent of the relics of SS. Abbondio and Abbondanzio with "polyphonic songs and hymns." They were also quite capable of performing polyphony at their own consecration ceremonies by the mid-Cinquecento.[42] Likewise, S. Petronilla hired the choir at S. Maria della Scala to perform at the feast of S. Thomas in 1604, but the nuns themselves had sung the polyphonic Mass on the feast of S. Lucy just a week earlier.[43] All the documentation confirms that by the 1620s, convents where music was important had reestablished self-sufficient ensembles capable of performing polyphony on a regular basis for holidays, devotions, and rites. Because the women so valued their relationship with lay musicians, however, they did not sever their contacts with them. Instead, they found different ways to employ the singers, players, and composers who worked in the world beyond their walls.

From the 1630s onward, Sienese nuns were most likely to encounter male musicians when the latter came to the convent to teach. The custom of hiring secular musicians to serve as instructors for nuns was probably very old. Montebuoni Buondelmonti reports that in 1505, Ser Pietro, *maestro di cappella* at the Cathedral, came to S. Abbondio and

> taught Suor Gismonda d'Agostino the profession of musical song to such perfection that she was raised from the rank of conversa to that of corista because

of her most delicate voice and of the incomparable grace of her singing. It was then that polyphony was introduced in the convent, and it is maintained there today.[44]

Although male teachers may have been common throughout the sixteenth and early seventeenth centuries, the first consistent surviving documentary evidence showing their presence begins around 1620 and grows more abundant after mid-century, especially in the surviving manuscripts of *licenze*, or "licenses."[45] The abbess or prioress used these small, bound volumes to pen notes asking permission for outsiders, including musicians, to come to the convent. She then had the volume delivered to the archbishop's palace, where either the archbishop or (more often) the vicar charged with convent oversight wrote a reply and returned it to the nunnery, generally on the same day, sometimes on the day following. Rarely was a petition of any kind refused.[46] Authorizations for music teachers included formulaic admonitions that the teaching was not to interfere with the nuns' religious duties and that all lessons were to be supervised.[47] They also specified a time limit, barring outsiders during Advent and Lent, as stipulated in the 1666 decree issued by Ascanio II Piccolomini (see Doc. 4). The latter restriction could be relaxed when the circumstances warranted. The nuns of S. Petronilla, for example, were successful at convincing Archbishop Leonardo Marsili that they needed their outside maestro during Advent, as two of the convent's most important feast days (S. Lucy and S. Thomas) fell in mid-to-late December (Doc. 7A).

With the appropriate licenses, lay musicians were able to come to the grates and instruct nuns, novices, and educande, sometimes in groups, sometimes privately. In a few cases, we cannot determine whether private lessons were sponsored by the convent or by the student's family. From 1652 to 1654, for example, Cosimo Fantastichi, one of the most highly regarded members of the Cathedral chapel, went to S. Petronilla to teach a certain "Signora Supplitia Verucci" to sing. From the use of "signora" rather than "suor," it is apparent that Verucci was neither a novice nor a professed nun. Unfortunately, it has not been possible to ascertain whether the nuns were grooming Verucci so that she would make a fine addition to their ensemble when she took the habit or whether her relatives were providing the money to allow the girl to polish her musical skills before marriage.[48]

Most often, however, nuns hired professional musicians—predominantly men associated with the Cathedral—not for the benefit of a single boarder but to improve the standards of performance in the monastic ensemble that furnished music for liturgical rites. Lay teachers taught the nuns to sing both plainchant and polyphony and to play a number of instruments, including lute, guitar, theorbo, viola, organ, and most often, violin. It appears that larger, patrician institutions renowned for their vocal-instrumental ensembles were more likely to call in music teachers from the lay community on a regular basis and to request instruction in skills needed for performing polyphony than those institutions with no such heritage.[49] At S. Petronilla, for example, the fifteen-year period from 1685 to 1700 saw thirty-four requests for men to teach singing, playing, and "concerting" music

TABLE 2.2.   Lay musicians at S. Paolo, 1679–1700

Name/Cathedral post*	Tenure S. Paolo	Duties S. Paolo

Giuseppe Fabbrini
    organist 1672–85
    maestro 1685–1704
	1679–1700	teaching singing and playing

Galgano Rubini
    musico 1670–74
    violinist 1676–1704
	1680	"teaching Fabbrini's disciples so they can concert some new compositions for the upcoming feast day"

Andrea Pontolmi violinist 1680–1704	1682–1700	teaching violin
Giuseppe Cini soprano, violinist 1672–84	1683–95	teaching singing, violin, viola
Giovanni Anso	1685	teaching violin

Domenico Franchini
    singer 1674–85
    organist 1685–1704
	1692	teaching music and organ

Lazzaro Lenzi bass 1675–90	1683–88	teaching plainchant
Francesco Neri	1692–93 1696–97	teaching plainchant
Signor Rampini	1696–1700	teaching theorbo

Giuseppe Cavallini
    musico 1677–80
    musico 1685–1704
	1696–1700	teaching singing and playing

*My records from Siena Cathedral stop at 1704.

and only two requests for a plainchant tutor (Docs. 7B and 7C offer typical examples). A book of licenze from S. Lorenzo, on the other hand, shows that during the forty-year period from 1653 to 1693, the nuns requested music teachers only eight times, and four of those licenze were granted for men to teach plainchant. One exception to this rule occurred at the convent of S. Paolo, where lay teachers appear to have been responsible for creating a musical ensemble where none existed before. Records from the institution reveal no tradition for performance by these Augustinian sisters until the last two decades of the seventeenth century. In April 1679, the abbess obtained a license for Giuseppe Fabbrini, then organist at the Cathedral, to come to the grates and teach music to three nuns. The women were clearly quick studies, for in a request from mid-December of 1679, the abbess asked the vicar to allow Fabbrini to come to the convent to teach during Advent because the upcoming feast day of S. Paolo would be "the first year we perform polyphony inside the cloister" (Doc. 8). The performance must have been a great success, for the music program expanded dramatically in the following decades. Fabbrini remained on staff until 1700 and in those years was joined by a number of other tutors, some long-term and some occasional, who instructed the nuns in everything from plainchant to violin (see table 2.2).

The vicar never denied the nuns access to music teachers, although in 1690, he turned peevish and objected to the number of maestri, insisting that the nuns make do with only two instead of the three requested. The patient nuns simply waited a month and then wrote a separate appeal for the third maestro; the vicar caved in to their demand.[50] By the late 1690s, one plainchant instructor and four other musicians—one for violin, one for theorbo, and two for "singing and playing"—were teaching at S. Paolo on a regular basis (Doc. 9).

The ease with which Sienese nuns could obtain access to music teachers might go a long way toward explaining the utter lack of dowry-reduction requests from Siena received by the Sacred Congregation in Rome during the hundred-year period from 1576 to 1670. Nuns from other urban centers often entreated the Roman committee for permission to admit talented women to their ranks with a lesser dowry or with none at all so that they might have someone in the cloister capable of both performing and teaching.[51] The letter from the women of Santuccio to the Sacred Congregation for authorization to allow an educanda to board with them free of charge so that they could have someone to sing soprano in their choir is the closest any convent in Siena came to asking Rome for a dowry reduction. It is possible, of course, that such requests were handled locally and have still not come to light. The evidence suggests, however, that Sienese nuns might have been reluctant to give up much-needed dowries to gain a teacher in the cloister when talented and readily available lay maestri were so capable of building a program from the ground up (as they did at S. Paolo) for such reasonable fees.[52]

The contributions of the maestri at S. Marta and S. Maria degli Angeli went beyond teaching vocal and instrumental techniques. At S. Marta, for example, payment records of 1618–19 show that the former Cathedral singer Benvenuto Flori, then a chaplain at the convent, was paid for instructing the nuns in plainchant and for "having taught the rules for playing the lute in the organ loft." The personnel rolls from the 1630s demonstrate that the role of the maestro had expanded from teaching to include keeping the instruments in good repair. By 1649, the maestro was also expected to provide the nuns with appropriate "motets" and "music" for their feast days.[53] Among the otherwise mostly anonymous maestri was Cristofano Piochi, music director at the Cathedral. In 1671, 1672, and 1674, the Augustinian nuns at S. Marta reimbursed Piochi for conducting rehearsals and for furnishing them with polyphonic compositions.[54]

The maestri di musica who served at Santuccio beginning in the 1630s and continuing through the end of the century were, again, mostly Duomo employees. The documents specify that they instructed the nuns in the finer points of performing concerted music and that they sometimes accompanied the monastic ensemble.[55] As at S. Marta, they also supplied the women with compositions. Andrea Calderoni, who served as maestro della musica at Santuccio in 1636, received payment for teaching the nuns and "not taking back the music," implying that he allowed the nuns to keep the scores he had provided for them. Giuseppe Fabbrini's name appears in the registers at Santuccio from 1677 to 1700 (years in which he was simultaneously employed at the Cathedral and at the convent of S. Paolo). In addition to teaching music, he gave the nuns "many compositions" and probably arranged works for the vocal-instrumental group to perform.[56]

Documents from Sienese convents therefore offer eloquent testimony to prove that when nuns wished to perform large-scale repertory for voices and instruments on important holidays, they expected their lay maestri to supply compositions tailored precisely to their needs and abilities. Of equal note is the fact that these male professional musicians performed with the nuns on certain occasions. This would explain why both a maestro and a maestra di musica were needed at houses such as Santuccio. A probable scenario unfolded as follows: the male musician composed or arranged works for the nuns to sing on special feast days and gave those works to the nun maestra. She was responsible for having the parts copied, distributing the music, teaching all the musicians their parts, and holding the initial sectional and full rehearsals. The maestro came several times to drill the entire ensemble and to fine-tune the balance so that the group would make the best possible impression in the external church. On the feast day itself, the maestra conducted the monastic ensemble from the internal church, perhaps coordinating it through the grates with a group of lay musicians in the external church. One Bolognese source offers some evidence that, despite strong episcopal prohibitions, male musicians and nuns there occasionally collaborated for performances during liturgical services,[57] but the records from Siena are significant in demonstrating just how extensive and how acceptable this practice was in at least one urban center.

Opportunities for nuns to sing and play were not limited to regularly recurring feast days and monastic rites of passage. Holy women also performed for illustrious guests. Apparently, Sienese archbishops fell into this category, for the chronicle from S. Abbondio takes care to note their visits. In most cases, the women showed their respect with elaborate music, some of which highlighted the warm relations between the convent and the episcopal court. In 1689, when Leonardo Marsili arrived for a visit, the scribe says little about his examination of the nuns. Instead, the focus is on the culminating high Mass at the convent. As the archbishop entered the external church in full episcopal regalia, the nuns greeted him by singing the *Ecce sacerdos magnus* ("Behold a great priest") in polyphony. The archbishop's priests responded with the antiphon *Gaudent in celis* ("They rejoice in heaven") in honor of the monastery's titular saints, Abbondio and Abbondanzio. During the Mass that followed, the nuns put their finest soloists on display in two motets, one for two voices, the other for solo voice.[58] Compare this lovefest to the sojourn of the hard-nosed Francesco Maria Tarugi in January 1599. The chronicle concentrates on certain details of the examination, such as the fact that the first nun called in for questioning was told to pull her black veil down over her eyes and was commanded to tell the rest of the nuns to do the same. According to the scribe, Tarugi left many orders for changes, most of which the women ignored.[59] Although we can assume that Tarugi said Mass on the final day of his visit, the scribe does not mention musical performances by the nuns. There are at least two possible reasons for this: either the nuns pointedly demonstrated their lack of esteem for Tarugi by not singing for him, or the scribe purposefully left out any particulars concerning the musical performance as a way of encoding in the chronicle the nuns' lack of regard for the prelate.

If music-making for archbishops could be interpreted as a sign of admiration, performances for foreign visitors were deemed a duty. Sienese nuns, like those in other Italian cities, considered themselves part of the larger urban network. By performing for their out-of-town guests, they were upholding the honor of their city.[60] A brief chronicle from Santuccio notes two important visits to the monastery that occurred in 1677. At the end of February, Cardinal Antonio Bichi stopped in to visit his cousin Anna Bichi.[61] During the Mass he celebrated in the convent church, which was crowded with people, the monastic ensemble sang "devout motets and played lovely sinfonias with various instruments." In the first days of March, hard on the heels of Bichi's departure, the Polish countess Margarita Kotoska Stolnikova arrived in Siena from Florence. On Friday, 5 March, she attended Mass at Santuccio and heard the nuns sing "a lovely motet for full choir."[62]

A visit that probably inspired a number of extraordinary convent performances took place in 1656. The freshly minted Sienese pope, Alexander VII Chigi, gave permission for his sister-in-law, Berenice Della Ciaia, and five other relatives to enter the cloistered spaces of all Siena's female monasteries. Berenice Della Ciaia hailed from the city's ruling elite and had lived in her native city until the pope called her husband, Mario Chigi, to Rome and made him commander of the papal armies.[63] By obtaining permission to enter all of Siena's convents, Della Ciaia was simultaneously exalting her Sienese origins and flouting her ties to the most powerful prelate in the Western world. For the nuns in Siena, urban pride was certainly at stake but so was the prestige of each individual monastic house. Della Ciaia's request must have set up a competition among the nuns of Siena to see who could do the most to honor the noblewoman and her entourage. Making a good show meant upholding the reputation of Siena, basking in the reflected glory of the Chigi name, and perhaps receiving the more tangible benefits of Chigi patronage. Unfortunately, only one account of Berenice Della Ciaia's pilgrimage has surfaced, but happily it comes from the musical house of S. Maria degli Angeli. According to a chronicle from the nunnery, on 27 July 1656, Berenice Della Ciaia, her daughter Agnese Zondadari, the pope's niece Verginia Chigi Piccolomini, Berenice's sister-in-law Sulpizia Santi (wife of the composer Alessandro Della Ciaia), the pope's niece Contessa Flaminia d'Elci Bulgarini, and Flaminia's daughter Deifile Bulgarini Saracini

> were admitted into the cloister and received with great joy by our superiors and by all of us nuns. Six most elegant chairs of crimson velvet, fringed in gold, were prepared and placed near the cloister door. Once the women were seated, the musical nuns sang the following five-voice madrigal in honor of Her Excellency [Berenice Della Ciaia], composed by me, the writer of these chronicles.[64] The work featured concerted instruments and lovely sinfonias:

> When the regal woman,
> the new star in the sky,
> appears rising from the mountains of the East,

she drives away the shadows in these sacred cloisters
with her splendor.
Look: with purple cloth and with gold,
with scepters and with palms, the Vatican
prepares a joyous display for her offspring.
Her faithful consort
supports the world with a great and profound wisdom
in the company of the sacred Atlas.

Once the performances of the madrigal and the instrumental music were over, the women began their visit of the most interesting places in the convent, and after that, they went to the refectory where an abundant lunch had been prepared with various refreshments and pastries and diverse fruits with all sorts of exquisite chilled wines. While the women were satisfying their appetite and thirst, their ears were grazing on ariette and concerted music of various instruments. (Doc. 10)

The account of Berenice Della Ciaia's visit to S. Maria degli Angeli makes two things clear. First, music served neither as a time-filler nor as background noise. Through the performance of a concerted madrigal with newly composed text and music, the nuns were able to pay lavish compliments to Berenice Della Ciaia (the "regal woman"), her husband Mario (the "faithful consort"), and the pope (the "sacred Atlas"), all the while showing off their own prowess. Second, both nuns and their admirers believed that monastic music was "nourishing:" witness the striking metaphor equating the nuns' polyphonic music with food. Robert Kendrick has noted this tendency in Milanese sources regarding nuns' music and has linked it to Caroline Walker Bynum's argument that it was through control of food resources that "women exercised a degree of individual power and leverage in society."[65] The act of feeding others was, if anything, even more important to cloistered sisters than to lay women, for episcopal orders sharply circumscribed when and how they could prepare and give sustenance to outsiders.[66] Nuns were, however, allowed to feed guests on special occasions, often on the same occasions that required musical performance. In the passage cited here, the scribe explicitly links the two customs, implying that just as the nuns' chilled wines and choice pastries were necessary to satisfy the visitors' empty bellies, their musical delicacies were essential for satiating the listeners' hungry ears.[67]

Nuns' ability to provide devotional, spiritual, and physical nourishment came to the fore most dramatically during those years when they could take a starring role in the annual procession sponsored by the city's lay confraternities. The event always featured a relic of special significance to the Sienese, which the confraternity members came to borrow the day after Easter. They displayed the relic for an entire week in one of the city's churches, and then carried it through the streets of Siena on the Sunday after Easter (Low Sunday, or Domenica in Albis). At the end of the procession, the confraternities returned the venerated object to its owners. At least six times during the seventeenth century, religious companies sought permission to borrow a relic from one of the city's convents for just this purpose. In 1607 and 1684, the confraternities petitioned the nuns at SS. Abbondio e Abbondanzio for the body of Blessed Giovanni Colombini; in 1649, they appealed to the women of S. Maria degli Angeli for the head of S. Galgano; in 1653 and in 1655, they asked the communities at S. Margherita and at S. Petronilla respectively for their paintings of the Virgin (both held to be miraculous); and in 1693, they entreated the nuns of Ognissanti for their miracle-producing sculpture of the "Madonna of the Manger." The nuns who possessed the relic, after a suitable show of reluctance and many assurances (generally backed up by legal documents that specified enormous payments if the item were not returned)[68] always granted the request, for the procession accrued honor to their convent and brought crowds of people and large donations to their church.

Chronicles describing several processions held on Low Sunday show that the nuns exploited these civic and devotional events to strengthen their social ties to the community at large. As on other occasions, music furnished the medium for dialogue between world of the cloister and the world beyond the walls. Nothing, alas, remains of the music, but from reports of the events, its prominent place in the festivities is clear. In 1607, for instance, when the religious companies came to collect the body of Blessed Giovanni Colombini, they entered the convent church of S. Abbondio, and "with lighted torches, with great reverence, and with polyphonic songs, they placed the relic under a canopy."[69] After the procession, the assembled citizenry went to return the relic to its rightful owners. As the convent scribe relates it

> [Colombini's] return was an event of great honor, glory and applause, with so great a multitude of monks, confraternities, lay people, and musicians singing hymns and devotional songs that the honor done him was overwhelming. He returned under a canopy that the confraternity donated to him. When [all these people] had exited the gate of S. Marco, we began to ring the bells and play the organ, and upon the entry of the relic [in our church] we sang many spiritual compositions in polyphony in honor of Holy God and of Blessed Giovanni Colombini. Our father confessor accompanied our singing with a prayer to Blessed Giovanni Colombini. When that was finished, we fed a good lunch to all the confraternities and monks, to all the members of the Colombini family, and to the Gesuati friars. When everything was over and everyone left, greatly consoled, our father confessor placed the relic in the cloister and with the greatest amount of reverence possible, we took the relic in procession, singing litanies in honor of God and of Blessed Giovanni and of all the saints. (Doc. 11)

The interaction among the nuns, religious confraternities, and the lay community was even more elaborate and theatrical in 1684, when the body of Giovanni Colombini was again featured in the Domenica in Albis procession. The company of S. Michele Arcangelo came to take the body of the local saint singing "a beautiful hymn they had composed on the tune *Iste Confessor* and a lovely motet." They took the relic to the Hospital church, where it lay in exposition to the public. The rural municipality of Monistero (where the monastery of S. Abbondio was located) decided to add a special touch to the occasion. They gathered together a group of girls, taught them music, dressed them as angels and sent them into Siena. On the day of the procession, while Colombini's body lay at the hospital of S. Maria della Scala, the girls enchanted the Sienese and moved them to great devotion by pretending to search for Colombini's body, all the while singing songs about how the nuns had lost him. After the body was returned to the monastery, the nuns celebrated by performing a polyphonic Mass and motets for the assembled citizenry.[70]

In terms of sheer spectacle, however, no Low Sunday procession from the seventeenth century could equal that of 1649, when the nuns of S. Maria degli Angeli allowed the confraternities to borrow the head of S. Galgano. The relic was an object of great devotion among the Sienese and a cause of dissension between the Augustinian nuns of Santuccio, who possessed it, and the Olivetan women of Ognissanti, who felt it was rightly theirs. The stage was set for a competitive devotional display through art and music, and the result was superb civic theater, whose participants included most of the citizens of Siena, the music-loving governor, Prince Mattias de' Medici (a devotee of both opera and female monastic music),[71] and the very flora and fauna within the city's walls.

The nuns of Santuccio threw down the gauntlet by adorning their external convent walls with decorative cloth brocades and pictures. The women of Ognis-santi followed suit (as did the women of Il Refugio, right down the street). Before the confraternities arrived to take the relic to the external church, Prince Mattias and his court entered the convent church to hear Mass, at which the nuns per-formed vocal and instrumental music. When the moment came to consign S. Galgano to the representatives of the lay companies, the women of Santuccio made certain that the world knew their grief: they knelt in the courtyard of their convent, their faces covered by black veils, candles in their hands, and tears in their eyes. They recovered quickly enough to sing a solemn Vespers in polyphony to the accompaniment of instruments. Then the confraternities took the relic to the church of Ognissanti, and it was the turn of the Olivetan women. The church instantly filled with people eager to observe the honors the holy women would bestow upon the relic.[72] The nuns did not disappoint.

> At the very moment the [sacred head] entered [the church], the nuns sang the Confessor's hymn from the organ loft in two distinct choirs with most beautiful music concerted with various instruments and after that, a lovely motet in praise of the saint, such that it seemed as if paradise had opened up. (Doc. 12A)

The relic was then returned to the external church of Santuccio to lie in state for a week, during which no day went by without the nuns singing; on five occasions, Prince Mattias was present to hear them. On the Sunday of the public procession, the women performed twice: a polyphonic Mass in the morning and a polyphonic Vespers service in the afternoon, both accompanied by instruments. The Medici prince and his court once again came to the convent church to see the relic returned in the early evening, when the nuns sang motets in honor of their saint. The day was not yet over, however, for the nuns took the relic in procession throughout their own gardens. Because the confraternities could not follow the nuns into the cloister,

> they resolved to go all together to the Porta Santoviene [Pispini], to the place within the walls of the city in the piazza of that gate, which directly faces the convent and cloister of the most reverend mothers of S. Maria degli Angeli, who

were to hold the procession. Because, from that location, they could see every-thing very well and observe with devout curiosity, they stayed there. . . . [A] great number of [other] people came as well, to satisfy their curiosity. When the pro-cession appeared in the cloister, the sacred relic was honored with resounding concords and repeated choruses of trumpets. (Doc. 12B)

The spectators could also observe the women and girls of the four convents close to S. Maria degli Angeli (S. Monaca, Vita Eterna, S. Chiara, Il Refugio) hanging out of their windows and balconies with lighted torches and candles in order to see the procession:

But the venerable and devout convent of S. Monaca, being the closest [to San-tuccio] and adjacent to it, and therefore the one to enjoy the procession the most, wanted to render even greater honor to the relic with an extraordinary demonstration [of devotion]. Indeed, in addition to the other nuns who could be seen in various parts of the convent observing everything, about twenty nuns stood atop a cloister wall bordering the two convents. They were well aligned and had lighted candles in their hands, [a sight] that brought both devotion and delight. And when the procession passed by that wall and arrived under a win-dow of the refectory, one could hear those virtuous women [of S. Monaca] sing, to the accompaniment of the organ, a most beautiful and lovely motet in honor of S. Galgano. . . .

Fifty *professe* [of Santuccio], all with their faces covered by black veils and with lighted candles in their hands, followed singing hymns in praise of S. Gal-gano and made repeated turns around the cloister and courtyard of the monastery. The devout songs of the venerable holy women were accompanied by lovely and graceful little birds, who, from the green boughs of trees and flowering plants of the beautiful cloister, in this smiling season of spring, also competed to sing in harmonious concord the divine praises and honor of our great saint. (Doc. 12C)

If the combination of sets, music, gesture, and choreography seem the work of consummate theatrical professionals, it can be attributed to the nuns' long experience with putting on convent plays, often in the presence of an audience of lay visitors. Several of these theatrical productions included scenes that required the nuns to sing and dance. As the account of the 1649 Low Sunday procession proves beyond a doubt, such experience stood them in good stead even on li-turgical and devotional occasions.[73]

FOR THE NUNS OF Siena, music furnished one of the most effective tools in their arsenal for remaining connected to the outside world. Music was a symbol of a convent's status: it signified wealth and nobility. Houses with musical traditions attracted the daughters of aristocrats and the ruling elite, first as *educande*, then as novices who became nuns, bringing with them their dowries and their talents. Music, like food, was a resource that they could control; by using it to "nourish" their families, friends, and patrons, they created bonds of loyalty that helped to assure their survival. Nunneries had a monopoly on certain saints—the founders of their order or those to whom their churches were dedicated or whose relics they held—and those houses with musical ensembles drew the city's inhabitants to their churches to hear them sing and play on those feasts. Thus, musical prowess guaranteed monastic houses a prominent place on the calendar of religious and devotional festivities that were so important to the civic identity of the Sienese. In this way, nuns played a vital role in the life of their city even from within their enclosed spaces.

A strong musical tradition within Siena's convents also represented an essential economic resource for lay musicians. Most male performers in the city probably could not earn a comfortable living solely on the wages they earned at the Cathedral or Provenzano or the Palazzo Pubblico. Convent jobs—teaching and performing—doubtless provided much-needed extra income and made it possible for a healthy corps of professional singers and instrumentalists to call Siena their home. Female monastic houses furnished lay musicians with artistic opportunities unavailable in their male-dominated world: they were able to teach and to perform with women. In addition, a number of musicians, including those who are known today primarily as performers, were given the chance to arrange or compose works for convent ensembles.

For the Sienese, too, music-making by nuns served more than one function. Musical performances in convents were often seen as a form of entertainment in the small city, as well as a showcase for patrician prestige. "Sunday was a feast day at Il Refugio," wrote Olimpia Chigi Gori to her half-brother Sigismondo, "and all Siena came and stayed right through Vespers because nothing was going on in the Piazza and my Lala played the organ for the high Mass and all Vespers."[74] There is no mistaking the pride of the aristocratic mother in her daughter's talents, displayed for all to hear. This is not to deny the devotional component of the event but merely to stress the prominent role theater, music, and family honor played in attracting the public to religious rites. Siena's nuns clearly knew this and learned how to exploit these factors to their advantage, and not just on rare occasions such as the Low Sunday procession. It is worth noting that in documents describing certain monastic rites, the scribe usually mentions four elements: the superb decorations, the number of choirs needed to perform the music, the great crush of the public, and the universal satisfaction of all.[75] Then, as now, the grandiose and the spectacular were undeniably enticing, and the crowds came not only to hear but sometimes to see the nuns' performances. Tridentine decrees were clearly meant to prevent such occurrences, but in these cases, nuns, archbishops, and citizens were clearly obeying the precepts of Trent to the letter and not a whit further: the nuns did not exit the convent, nor did the public enter the enclosed spaces, but there was no decree concerning city walls that happened to offer a good vantage point for a procession inside a cloister.[76]

The convent was, however, not merely a provider of entertainment. The Sienese, like other urban dwellers in Italy, regarded the female monastery as a "new Jerusalem," a place where the life of the world to come was reproduced on earth.[77] When Archbishop Celio Piccolomini visited Santuccio in early January 1675, he was reported to have said, "If this is the convent of S. Maria degli Angeli, then it must be inhabited by many angels from paradise."[78] Angelic nuns were therefore capable of celestial music, a theme that turns up regularly in descriptions of performances by holy women in other Italian cities during this pe-riod.[79] In Siena, too, nuns were credited with the ability to create divine music. We need only return to the description of the musical performance by the Oliv-etan nuns during the Low Sunday procession of 1649: "it seemed as if paradise had opened up." The Sienese, however, took the trope one step further. The S. Abbondio chronicle relates an incident from the mid–fourteenth century, when the nuns were not cloistered and the lay community could enter the internal church. On Christmas night, when a number of people were at the convent to hear Matins, a little boy in his mother's arms cried aloud, "The angels are crown-ing the nun who is singing."[80] In this account, Sienese nuns are shown to be capable not only of imitating the sounds of angelic choirs but also of calling those angels down to earth to honor their performances. Siena's holy women were triply fortunate: they had the support of their compatriots, the sanction of their archbishops, and the approval of heaven to sing.

VENI, VENI SOROR NOSTRA

Clothing, Profession, and Consecration
Ceremonies in Sienese Convents

In order to flee all tumult, let the young girl who wishes to take on the nun's habit be accompanied in the morning to the convent without pomp by her closest female relatives— no other people should be invited—and let her be admitted alone to the internal church of the convent where, having heard Mass, received communion, and taken part in the other solemn ceremonies, she should be clothed by the bishop or his deputy in the presence of the other nuns. . . . The same should be observed for profession rites.

Thus read the penultimate decree in the series of thirty-six that Francesco Bossi issued in the aftermath of his visit to Sienese convents in 1575. The last rule on the list also concerned the clothing and profession ceremonies: Bossi ordered that the expenses for food were not to exceed 10 scudi.[1] These decrees, so similar in content to those emanating from prelates in Rome, Bologna, Venice, and Piacenza, testify to the customs the ecclesiastical hierarchy wanted observed when a girl entered a nunnery or took her vows.[2] The family invited a large number of friends and relatives to accompany their daughter to the convent and to witness her performance in the solemn ceremonies that marked her admission to and acceptance of life in the cloister. Afterward, family, friends, and nuns were treated to a banquet. Since Bossi was critical of nuns' theater—he issued another decree forbidding that practice—he was doubtless discomfited by the idea that the already dramatic religious rituals could be embellished in such a way that they played out on an even larger stage, with the participation of the public. His words would not be the last on the subject. As late as 1784, Pietro Leopoldo, grand duke of Tuscany, had a set of stern directives printed in Siena prohibiting "refreshments, music, decorations, guests, gifts," and all other festal apparatus when a young woman took the habit or professed her final vows.[3] In Siena, as elsewhere, documentary sources demonstrate that long-standing traditions triumphed over every injunction. During the sixteenth and seventeenth centuries, all the monastic ceremonies that confirmed a woman's status as a nun—clothing, profession and consecration—were open to the public and filled with pageantry. Music played a vital role in enhancing the drama of the rites.

THE CEREMONY OF CLOTHING, or investiture, was performed when a young girl (or her family) decided that she was ready to begin her novitiate, that is, her formal instruction to become a nun. In Siena, rules issued for nuns by Archbishop Alessandro Petrucci in 1625 specified that the girl was to be over twelve years of age to take such a step.[4] Those same rules stated that the professe in the convent had to obtain the archbishop's permission to present the girl's application in a chapter meeting and that they then had to decide her future with a secret vote. If the girl was in the convent for education, her family had to remove her from the premises and she was then to return for the investiture within a period of approximately forty days.[5]

A letter Niccolò Piccolomini wrote in 1580 to his two daughters, Agnesa and Scolastica, both nuns at the convent of SS. Abbondio e Abbondanzio, includes a passage describing a typical clothing rite of the time and its attendant celebrations. Since the letter is a catalogue of the "abuses" Piccolomini found in the convents of his era, his sharply ironical tone is clearly intentional:

> A meal of great expense is laid out for all the nuns and for some of the relatives and the officiating priests, as if it were reasonable that in a wedding with Christ one should spend and eat out of all measure and that the expense should not be less than that for a secular marriage. Rather, because these nuptials are of greater merit, they should be of comparable or greater splendor. The girl, in the presence of everyone, dressed in secular clothes, gives a suitable sermon, speaking of the merits of the vows of chastity, obedience, and voluntary poverty and of how she of her own volition has decided to abandon her father, her mother, her brothers, her sisters, and all that the world prizes. She removes her clothes, made of the most deluxe material she could find, and dresses in the very sumptuous vestments made for nuns and blessed by the priest; the vicar or the bishop cuts her hair. . . . After tonsure, all the nuns celebrate with suitable hymns and instrumental music. At the same time, the new nun, dedicated to religion, sits between two other virgins, who both hold trays, on which every one of the invited guests places an offering. All the money the young girl receives she saves for her own use; and there is much ambitious accounting among the nuns to see who has earned more and who less. (Doc. 13)

In addition to furnishing a vivid (and to his mind, damning) portrait of the festivities that commonly surrounded investiture, Piccolomini's letter shows that, Bossi's orders notwithstanding, family members, friends, and perhaps even lay musicians participated in the rite. A letter that another convent of Sienese sisters wrote in 1585 to the Sacred Congregation in Rome demonstrates how important monastic women considered the public nature of this ceremony to be. In the missive, the nuns freely admit that they have never followed Bossi's orders to hold the rite in the internal church without the presence of relatives, and since they now have been given orders to do so by the archbishop's vicar, they want permission to perform the ceremony in the old way:

> In the city of Siena, Augustinian nuns in a convent called Santa Maria Maddalena have always followed the ancient custom of clothing new nuns in the convent's

external church. The professed nuns stay in the internal church and the woman who is taking the habit gives a speech and says many prayers (as mandated by the holy fathers who founded this order) in the presence of all her relatives. Once the ceremony is finished, while the Te Deum is sung, the relatives give her an offering of about 30 scudi, sometimes more, sometimes less, depending on their financial means.[6]

As Craig Monson has observed, the involvement of the novices' relatives in such rites was important, for it "strengthened [the] informal social ties between convent and community" and thus "extended the convent's circle in new and potentially useful ways."[7] That the participation of a girl's family was, in fact, the determining factor for the choice of the site of the ceremony is apparent from a request that the abbess at S. Marta, Giustina Tolomei, made to the Sacred Congregation in 1616. She informs the Roman committee that her niece is about to embark on her novitiate at the convent. But since the girl's mother is dead and her father out of town and she has no other relatives, "she cannot take the habit in the external church with the ceremonies and gratifications that are usual."[8] The abbess asks (and is given permission) to clothe the girl in the internal church.

As is clear from the letters written by Niccolò Piccolomini and the nuns of S. Maria Maddalena, music was part of the usual "gratifications" at investitures. Although Piccolomini did not specifically attack the custom, he did imply that it was one of the elements that contributed to the lavishness of the rite. The kind and amount of music performed must have depended on both the resources of the girl's family and the traditions of the convent. Apart from the rite itself, it is possible that music accompanied the young woman and her train of family and friends as they went in procession through the streets of the city to the institution.[9] After the ceremony, music might have been heard in convent theatrical productions that were sometimes staged to celebrate the addition of a new member to the monastic community. Several of the sacred comedies printed or copied into manuscripts during the sixteenth and seventeenth centuries in Siena may have served as entertainment on the occasion of a clothing ceremony, and most of those include at least one musical scene.[10] A complete opera was staged at the convent of S. Girolamo in Campansi as part of the celebrations for the 1686 investiture of Olimpia Chigi, daughter of Prince Agostino Chigi and Maria Virginia Borghese. The title page of the "little sacred opera" proclaims that Olimpia's ten-year-old twin sisters (Maria Maddalena and Teresa Maria) and the ten-year-old Geltrude Petrucci, all three of whom were educande at Campansi, took the main roles in the work.[11] The custom of performing plays or operas in conjunction with clothing ceremonies continued right into the eighteenth century. The first production in the theater that the nuns of Il Refugio had constructed for their monastery celebrated the 1717 investiture of Laura Caterina Gori Pannilini.[12] In 1719 the archbishop's vicar gave permission for the musician Domenico Mazzuoli to go to S. Caterina del Paradiso to teach "several ariette" to Girolamo Piccolomini's daughter. She needed to learn the music for a comedy to be presented at the investiture of another young woman at the convent.[13]

If music was optional for the festivities surrounding the ceremony, it was essential at the investiture itself, which took place after Mass.[14] Often, lay musicians were hired to perform. Accounts from the Clarissan convent of S. Lorenzo show that in 1661, the nuns spent 25 lire in "music and Masses" for the investiture of Maria Francesca Zaveria Giusti and in 1669 paid 26 lire for music when two girls from the Cheri family were clothed.[15] Unfortunately, the records specify neither the number of performers nor the repertory. Documents from S. Girolamo in Campansi are only marginally more detailed. The Franciscan women there reimbursed a certain "signor Magini" £. 52.13.4 because he had already paid "the musicians who sang outside [the convent] door" when Angela Chigi entered their church to take the habit as Suor Francesca Serafina in 1680.[16] Magini was probably responsible for assembling and directing the musicians who performed at Angela's investiture. He received a similar payment for music in June 1683, when Angela's sister, Berenice Maria, was clothed at Campansi.[17] Although the nuns at both S. Lorenzo and S. Girolamo in Campansi entered the expenses for music in their debit-credit registers, the payments probably came out of the pockets of the girl's family. A seventeenth-century inventory from S. Marta lists the provisions a young girl needed in order to enter the convent and provides the cost of each. For the investiture, the girl's parents were to be prepared to spend 35 lire "for music [performed] either outside or inside, given the possibilities, and as it pleases the girl."[18] This amount would allow a family to hire a respectable ensemble: approximately three or four singers, an organist, a theorbist or violone player, and a director.[19] Some parents who entrusted their girls to S. Marta were willing to hire an even larger ensemble. In 1629, for example, Giovanbattista Borghesi paid 84 lire to the musicians who sang in the external church during clothing rites for his daughters, Flavia and Faustina. At the 1635 investiture of Dorotea Colomba Conti, however, the expenses included no charge for music, "as it was sung inside," presumably by talented professed nuns.[20] Niccolò Piccolomini's letter of 1580 credits the nuns at his representative convent with performing hymns and instrumental music following a novice's tonsure. Indeed, when lay musicians were hired for an investiture ceremony, they may have served only to augment and accompany the monastic ensemble, especially at nunneries boasting strong musical traditions.

One of the many Sienese convents where music flourished was S. Sebastiano in Vallepiatta. This Gesuate institution never housed large numbers of women. From the 1630s until the end of the century, the number of coriste hovered around thirty-five.[21] The convent's reputation for music was, however, out of all proportion to its size. One of the four nun-musicians whom Ugurgieri Azzolini named in his compendium of famous Sienese men and women was "la Giarra" of S. Sebastiano.[22] The institution maintained two officers (elected biennially) to oversee musical activities: a nun to supervise the singing of plainchant and another to direct polyphonic music.[23] Among the few surviving sources to illuminate the musical tradition at the convent is a seventeenth-century manuscript containing the ritual for investiture.[24] As might be expected, music is an important component of the ceremony.

The Gesuate investiture begins with the officiant praying over the habit, veil, and belt and blessing them with holy water and incense. The prelate then says several prayers for the future novice, whom the rubric directs to be standing just outside the door of the church with several lay women in attendance. After the prayers, the prelate intones the antiphon *Veni sponsa Christi* ("Come, bride of Christ"). While the choir takes up the remainder of the antiphon, the girl walks toward the altar in the church "between two angels"—perhaps two educande dressed for the occasion—and when she arrives there, she says the *Ecce venio ad te* ("Behold, I come to you"). The officiant offers another prayer, after which the girl gives a speech.

As the girl changes out of her secular clothes, the manual specifies that a motet be performed. After further prayers, each item of clothing is blessed and brought to the girl, who remains on her knees as she accepts habit, belt, and scapular. The ornaments on her head are then removed, and as the verse *Tondeo te* is recited, the officiant begins to cut her hair. A series of psalms and antiphons follows: first, the psalm *Conserva me* with its antiphon *Tu es Domine*; next the psalm *Domini est terra* with its antiphon *Haec accipiet*; and finally the psalm *Ecce quam bonum* with its antiphon *Sicut ros Hermon*.[25] At the end of this sequence of psalms, the girl is presented with her veil and more prayers are offered.

The girl, now dressed in the habit of a novice, and still kneeling, is given a lighted candle to hold. The prelate intones the hymn *Veni Creator Spiritus*, and verses and responses follow. The officiant recites a prayer invoking the apostles Peter and Paul as well as the fathers of the order: S. Jerome, S. Augustine, and the Blessed Giovanni Colombini. He then blesses the new novice, recites more verses and responses, and offers individual prayers invoking S. Jerome, S. Augustine, and Blessed Giovanni Colombini and another prayer recalling the Visitation of Elizabeth by Mary. He blesses the new novice once again. Another series of verses and short responses ensues, and then the *Te Deum laudamus* begins.

At this point, the new novice rises and approaches the door of the convent. The professed nuns allow her to enter. She and all the nuns immediately kneel and, after a series of verses and short responses, the prelate offers a prayer to bless the convent itself.

As with rites of passage practiced by other orders, the Gesuate clothing ceremony was filled with symbolism: the girl's pilgrimage from the secular world to the monastic enclosure was physically represented by her passage from the external to the internal church and by the alteration of her personal appearance through tonsure and new clothing.[26] Investiture was the first of the rituals that allied a girl with a company of women whose virginity allowed them to mediate between the human and divine or, to quote a Sienese source, to become "angels of paradise" while still on earth.[27] Music accompanied and abetted the metamorphosis, occurring as it did at the most symbolic and theatrical points in the rite. The manuscript that preserves the Gesuate *ordo* includes complete transcriptions of the chants for the antiphons *Veni sponsa Christi, Tu es Domine, Haec accipiet*, and *Sicut ros Hermon*, as well as incipits for the psalms *Conserva me, Domini est terra*, and *Ecce quam bonum*.[28] The first antiphon was performed as the girl was called into the church, and the subsequent psalms and their antiphons were sung during her tonsure. The manuscript directs that the hymn *Veni Creator Spiritus* be "intoned" after the novice accepts her veil. Certainly the *Te Deum laudamus* that accompanied the novice as she entered the cloister must have also been sung.

The most intriguing rubric in the manuscript is, of course, the one directing that a motet be performed as the girl was shedding her worldly clothes and preparing to accept the vestments of a novice.[29] Since no chant was assigned to this pivotal moment, the Gesuate filled the silence with a composition whose text and music came from outside the rite itself. In this manner, they marked the transformation of a girl into a bride of Christ, able to join the ensemble of celestial voices in the internal church. This symbolic use of polyphony sets the Gesuate ceremony apart from similar clothing rites performed during the same period at the Clarissan monasteries of S. Lorenzo and S. Niccolò.[30] Although both those houses could boast the occasional musical nun, neither seems to have cultivated music-making within the religious community in any consistent fashion. For the Gesuate sisters, on the other hand, the performance of polyphony was as important to their monastic identity as their vows, and the incorporation of a motet in their clothing ceremony announced the fact.

It is possible that the Gesuate also performed polyphonic settings of some or all of the items for which chants were provided in the manuscript. An investiture ceremony that was held in the convent's external church and well attended by a young girl's relatives presented an opportunity for the choir nuns to showcase themselves and their institution. The Gesuate had every incentive to make their music-making as splendid as the ceremony was dramatic. Since they were obliged to remain in the internal church during the rite, musical performance certainly offered them the most practical medium through which to accomplish this goal.

The pomp and circumstance surrounding the entrance of girls into the cloister prompted one Sienese prelate after another to promulgate edicts concerning the clothing rite—apparently to no avail. In 1608, Archbishop Camillo Borghesi's vicar-general, Fabio Piccolomini, attempted to curb the amounts of money spent on the festivities, and in 1625, Alessandro Petrucci ordered that girls should come to the convent quietly, devoutly, and in the company of only their closest relatives.[31] Ascanio II Piccolomini issued no orders regarding the ritual during his long reign, but his successor Celio Piccolomini twice tried to legislate reforms. In 1671, he forbade nuns to give flowers to officiating clergy and families, and in 1676, he sternly condemned the "incongruous and harmful distractions" ("distrationi incongrue e nocive") posed by the retinue of guests. Celio Piccolomini's mandates were obviously ignored, because his successor Leonardo Marsili also endeavored to prohibit ostentatious displays.[32] Whatever their feelings about the extravagant behavior of family and friends at the ceremony, however, not one of these prelates ever took issue with musical performance. It is telling that Archbishop Borghesi, who wanted to restrict the use of polyphonic music in the external churches of the city's convents, made an exception for investiture ceremonies. He decreed only that the lay musicians be summoned by the families and not by the nuns (see Doc. 2).

IF THE CLOTHING RITE FUNCTIONED as a young girl's introduction to the cloister, the profession rite sealed her commitment to it. Profession transformed the novice into a full-fledged member of the monastic community who (in most cases) was able to hold office and to vote in chapter meetings. In contrast to investiture, the rite of profession seems to have provoked little controversy among Sienese church officials. It is true that Bossi's 1575 decree outlawing pompous display at investitures includes a final, tacked-on injunction forbidding the same at professions. The men who filled the archbishop's seat in the following decades, however, appear to have been more concerned with other matters surrounding profession. For instance, Borghesi (1608) and Petrucci (1625) specified that girls were not to profess before the age of sixteen, that they were to have completed not less than a full year as a novice before taking this step, and that they were to know how to read so that they might recite the Divine Office.[33] Although the procedure varied from order to order, profession (like investiture) was meant to be a public ceremony, held in the convent's external church, with music as an important component. The ordo for profession at the convent of S. Sebastiano (preserved in the same manuscript that transmits the clothing rite) provides an example.[34]

The Gesuate profession rite begins with the novice and abbess standing before the grate in the external church as the bishop blesses a cloak and black veil. Subsequently, the prelate intones the antiphon *Veni sponsa Christi*. The psalm *Eructavit* follows, and the antiphon is repeated. The novice can then give a speech, after which she kneels at the bishop's feet, puts her hands in his, and takes the vows of obedience, poverty, and chastity. She also promises to live without personal property, according to the rule of S. Augustine and Giovanni Colombini, and freely commits herself to the care of the abbess. The prelate once again intones the antiphon *Veni sponsa Christi* (which the choir completes). The newly professed nun responds with *Ecce venio ad te*. This is followed by the psalm *Credidi* with its antiphon *Dirupisti Domine*.

Together, the prelate and abbess present first the cloak and then the veil to the newly professed nun. When she accepts, they place the cloak on her back and the veil on her head. The new nun renounces the world for Jesus Christ with the great responsory *Regnum mundi*;[35] short responses, verses, and prayers follow. The antiphon *Veni sponsa Christi* is performed for a fourth time as the professed nun is crowned and a cross put into her right hand. As the hymn *Veni Creator Spiritus* begins, a lighted candle is placed in the nun's left hand. The bishop prays, invoking the names of SS. Peter and Paul and Blessed Giovanni Colombini. This is followed by the Te Deum and individual prayers to S. Augustine, Blessed Giovanni Colombini, and S. Jerome.

A rubric in the manuscript shows that just before the prelate says the final prayer and gives his blessing, a miniature drama is enacted, featuring as protagonists the newly professed nun and the abbess.[36] The scene does not appear in the profession manuals from S. Lorenzo and S. Niccolò, and its presence in the Gesuate rite suggests that convents with strong musical traditions were more likely to exploit theatrical resources as a means of communicating their spirituality to the outside world. By opening with a reworking of verse 9 from *Domini est terra*, a psalm performed during the clothing ritual, the little drama emphasizes how far the young woman has progressed on her journey to profession. The playlet is also clearly intended to reinforce the wedding symbolism that permeates the profession ceremony, with its fourfold repetition of the antiphon *Veni sponsa Christi*. Most of the text for the scene is inspired by colorful and dramatic verses from the Song of Songs, in which the nun can imagine herself in the role of Christ's chaste bride:[37]

[NEW NUN]: Raise up your doors, O virgins! Raise up, O doors of the cloister, and your sister will enter.

[ABBESS]: Who is this sister of ours, well-provided with delights, who rises from the desert, leaning over her beloved?

[NEW NUN]: I am [name inserted here], married to Christ, your beloved.

[ABBESS]: What are you asking for, O daughter? Turn back! Already, the night is falling and the beloved has passed through and hidden himself.

[NEW NUN]: Open to me, O venerable mother. The dew of the night is already wet on my head. Open, open! I will look anxiously for my beloved until I find him. I was holding him and I will not let him go until he blesses my soul.

[ABBESS]: My daughter, you will not enter unless you promise to observe all that is contained in the rule of the order of Blessed Giovanni Colombini.

[NEW NUN]: I promise, and I have confidence that with the favor of the grace and compassion of the beloved Lord Jesus Christ, I can do anything in Him who gives me strength. Bless me, O venerable mother, with the blessing of charity and love, together with the entire choir of these virgins, and deign to receive me in their community to be their companion in the love of my beloved.

[RUBRIC]: The virgin kneels and the abbess gives her blessing. . . . Afterward, the virgin makes a deep bow and returns with the crucifix and candle in her hand in front of the vicar, who says the prayer. Once this is finished, the door is closed and [the nuns] go singing into the choir. (Doc. 14)

Certain aspects of this profession ceremony made it very similar to the clothing rite; for example, the acts of blessing and donning the cloak and veil. These portions were, however, shorter than corresponding portions of the investiture ceremony, because no time had to be set aside for the young woman to change her clothes or have her hair cut. The profession ordo therefore lacks a rubric for a motet (inserted during investiture while the girl changed out of her secular finery) and prescribes only one psalm instead of the three needed for tonsure. The manuscript does include an incipit for the psalm *Credidi* and a complete transcription of its antiphon *Dirupisti Domine*, indicating that both were chanted during the ceremony. Rubrics inform us that the antiphon *Veni sponsa Christi* and the hymns *Veni Creator Spiritus* and *Te Deum* were also sung in plainchant.[38] As if to compensate for the lack of theatrically vivid action at the beginning, the rite's final moments were embellished to create a climax. After the new *professa* and the abbess played out their dialogue, the vicar closed the doors to the convent. In this manner, the nuns' bodies disappeared, but their voices resounded as they went singing into the choir.

In urban centers such as Rome, Milan, and Bologna, the rite of profession appears to have been an occasion for the same revelries as those associated with clothing.[39] In Siena, however, the absence of payments to outside musicians as well as the lack of documents describing theatrical performances and banquets implies that the rite might have been celebrated with fewer members of the lay community present and fewer accompanying festivities than investiture. If this were indeed the case, then the music at the ceremony itself might also have been simpler. In fact, the profession ritual from S. Sebastiano makes no reference to polyphony. We cannot, however, assume that the lack of specific indications equals the absence of complex music. It would make sense, for example, that the nuns who "went singing into the choir" performed a polyphonic composition at the culmination of the rite to confirm their new companion's changed status.

ALL ORDERS OF NUNS practiced ritual investiture and profession. Fewer required the additional ceremony to consecrate a nun's virginity. The rite of consecration (whose history and form have been examined by René Metz)[40] was held for a group of nuns, all of whom were to have reached the age of twenty-five.[41] During the course of the consecration, which closely resembled a marriage rite, each nun, accompanied by a matron escort, was presented to her "bridegroom" (the bishop, acting as Christ's proxy) and received from him a blessed veil, ring, and crown.[42] Although Metz believed the rite was seldom practiced after the fifteenth century, it may have been less rare than he thought.[43] Craig Monson has uncovered a tradition for consecration ceremonies at the Bolognese convent of S. Cristina della Fondazza that lasted until the Napoleonic suppression of 1799.[44] In Siena, the ceremony flourished in three Sienese institutions, all renowned for their musical traditions: the Cistercian house of Le Trafisse, the Benedictine monastery of S. Abbondio, and the Olivetan convent of Ognissanti.[45]

The nuns of Ognissanti held ten consecration ceremonies between 1585 and 1684, each documented in the same manuscript that preserves records of all the women who took the habit, professed, and died at the convent from 1575 to 1738.[46] In most cases, only the barest outline is given: the date, the name of the officiating archbishop, the names and ages of the consacrees, and a few brief notes on the ceremony. The descriptions sometimes include information on the length of the rite (it went on for seven hours in 1633) and its cost to the nuns (153 lire in 1633 and an astonishing £. 693.17.4 in 1684). Always mentioned is the place in which a portal was opened between the external church and the internal church (or the cloister) so that the consacrees could process into the public realm one last time. In 1585, 1598, 1613, and 1619, the scribe alludes to "rehearsals" by the nuns, from which we can infer that musical performance had a place in the ceremony. By 1644, no inference is necessary, for the scribe captures the essence of the rite in a formula that is repeated nearly verbatim in 1656 and 1669: "The function was most beautiful with music for three choirs.[47] The decoration was most superb, attendance was very high, and all was done to universal satisfaction."[48] A passage from a letter Leonardo Marsili addressed to Cardinal Flavio Chigi on 18 September 1669 suggests that the nuns exaggerated neither the magnificence of their decorations nor the attraction the rite held for the populace: "Last Sunday, the archbishop consecrated thirteen nuns at Ognissanti. Those nuns conducted the church ceremony and executed the decoration with all possible sumptuousness, and about half of the city—at least of the nobility—came."[49] The ritual and musical opulence associated with consecrations comes into clearer focus in the more detailed description from 1684. Presiding was Leonardo Marsili, who had become archbishop of Siena in 1682. He brought all the members of his court, three ecclesiastical dignitaries, two canons, and the entire seminary of S. Giorgio to help officiate at the five-hour rite. Marsili's *maestro di casa*, Magini, loaned the nuns an extra organ for the event, which featured double-choir works. An unidentified *maestro di cappella* (perhaps Giuseppe Fabbrini, the Cathedral organist) wrote music for the consacrees, taught them their parts, and directed the performances by the holy women and by the twenty-seven lay musicians hired for the occasion. (Doc. 15)

RECORDS FROM SS. ABBONDIO e Abbondanzio paint a similar picture of the consecration ceremony, although they span a longer time period than the documents preserved from Ognissanti. A chronicle from the Benedictine house registers nearly all consecrations from the early sixteenth century through the beginning of the eighteenth century (although lacunae in the source leave us without information for the years 1617–27 and 1635–65).[50] As at Ognissanti, the notices are brief, generally supplying only the names of the consecrated nuns and the date of the ceremonies (held in 1517, 1523, 1533, 1541, 1564, 1576, 1580, 1586, 1593, 1597, 1608, 1617, 1632, 1666, 1680, 1693, 1702, and 1717). Occasionally, however, some tantalizing details about the rite emerge. The debit-credit registers from the convent also provide descriptions of some consecrations. The scribes, however, often paid more attention to the various kinds and amounts of food prepared and consumed than to the unfolding of the ceremony itself.[51]

One feature that distinguished the consecration rite at S. Abbondio from that at Ognissanti was its location; from 1597 and throughout most of the seventeenth century, it was usually held in the convent's internal church. The nuns explained the reason for this in a letter they sent to the Sacred Congregation in 1680: their internal church was much larger and therefore able to accommodate the "musicians and the other people necessary to the solemnity and decorum of that rite."[52] Sienese archbishops from Ascanio I Piccolomini to Ascanio II Piccolomini apparently allowed relatives, officiating priests, and lay musicians into the convent's internal church on their own authority and permitted other friends and relatives to crowd into the external church. After Ascanio II died, however, his successors Celio Piccolomini and Leonardo Marsili probably asked the nuns to write to the Sacred Congregation for license to continue this practice. In 1680, the Roman committee left the decision up to the archbishop, who granted the nuns permission to hold the consecration in the internal church. In 1693, however, the Sacred Congregation denied the nuns' request. The women must have been very upset by this turn of events, and someone in a position of authority (perhaps Archbishop Marsili) took steps to assure that the families could, as tradition demanded, see their daughters during the ceremony. The solution was similar to that adopted with regularity at Ognissanti, and it demonstrates how resourceful holy women could be when faced with what might appear to be insurmountable obstacles:

> Because it was not possible to obtain a license from the Sacred Congregation to perform the ceremony in the cloister, as is usual, it was necessary to take down the grate, and near the [opening of the grate] was constructed a most beautiful little chapel, with such lovely draperies that it seemed like paradise; it was there that the nuns to be consecrated positioned themselves. When the [nuns] came out for the first time, they were singing the [*Et nunc*] *sequimur*.[53] Where the grate

had been taken down, only about a foot of wall was left near the ground; there sat the archbishop on his throne with all the other priests.[54]

Music became an important part of the ceremony by the second quarter of the sixteenth century, and the convent chronicle traces the gradual increase in the musical splendor associated with the rite over the course of the next two hundred years. The chronicle states that the fourteen nuns consecrated in 1533 were the first to sing the ceremony in plainchant, following the rubrics of the Roman pontifical.[55] By 1564, however, the consacrees

> performed all the usual passages in two-part polyphony and, thanks be to God, received great honor. The archbishop praised the abbess and said that he had never experienced greater consolation than on that day, praise to God, giver of all graces. So many people came to see the ceremony that a guard had to be placed at the door of the church, and notwithstanding, five hundred lay spectators entered.[56]

The nuns consecrated in 1585 sang the same passages in three-part polyphony,[57] and by 1608, figural music had become so commonplace that the scribe merely notes in passing that the nuns performed the rite "in polyphony, with the organ."[58]

As early as 1564, an ensemble from the Cathedral was present at the consecration,[59] and the debit-credit registers from S. Abbondio suggest that Cathedral musicians performed at the rite throughout the seventeenth century. The tenor of the descriptions also makes it clear that the Duomo singers and instrumentalists did not replace the nuns. Rather, as at Ognissanti, they augmented the monastic ensemble and performed with them. It is difficult to determine just how many men the nuns hired at the beginning of the century. The payment record for 1608 mentions only a maestro di cappella and an unspecified number of musicians.[60] An account of the 1617 consecration is more detailed, for it shows that a chapel master and six musicians, including a trombone player, participated in the ceremony. It also records a supplementary payment to the trombone player— who came for two rehearsals before the consecration—and a large sum for the chapel master, who was responsible for teaching the nuns their music, rehearsing them several times, and playing the organ at the rite itself.[61] By 1632, the number of lay musicians increased to twelve and included a theorbist and a violone player, as well as a chapel master, who once again taught the nuns their music, rehearsed them, and played the organ at the ceremony.[62] In 1680, fifteen musicians, including an organist and diverse "sonatori," participated in the ceremony; the ensemble was led by Giuseppe Fabbrini, organist at the Duomo.[63] The easy commerce between the cloister and the community outside the walls, so evident in the preparation for the consecration, continued after the ceremony, when the musicians sat down with the relatives and officiating priests to a feast and then went home not only richer in cash but also laden with food, purses, handkerchiefs, and shirts the nuns had made them.

It is a pity that the descriptions of investitures, professions, and consecrations make no reference to the specific works the nuns performed. As suggested earlier, holy women in Siena probably obtained at least some of their repertory by adapting pieces in publications not specifically aimed at the convent. Elsewhere, I have speculated that Sienese nuns might have exploited for their own purposes a small-scale motet published by the city's most famous early-seventeenth-century composer, Agostino Agazzari.[64] His *Sacrarum cantionum, liber II, opus V*, first published in Milan in 1607 and reprinted in Venice in 1608, 1609, and 1613, includes a setting of *Veni sponsa Christi*, an antiphon that figures prominently in the clothing ceremonies of many orders (including the Gesuate, as I have just shown). Composers in Milan and Naples explicitly or implicitly designated certain settings of this text for monastic use.[65] The nun-composer Caterina Assandra dedicated her own setting of *Veni sponsa Christi* to another woman who had only recently taken the habit.[66] Although Agazzari had a number of relatives in Sienese convents, he probably did not conceive his setting with women in mind, as he set the text for two contraltos in a range that would have proved ungrateful for most female voices.[67] By transposing all voices up a fourth, however, as the composer advocated in his basso continuo treatise (published as a foreword to the reprint editions of this very collection of small-scale sacred concertos), the attractive setting is eminently suitable for performance by two female singers at a clothing, profession, or consecration ceremony.[68]

After the middle of the seventeenth century, Sienese nuns searching for appropriate repertory could also turn to a collection composed specifically for them, Alessandro Della Ciaia's *Lamentationi sagre e motetti ad una voce col basso continuo* (Venice, 1650). The afterword to the volume informs the reader that the Sienese aristocrat wrote the pieces, all scored for solo soprano, "to satisfy both his talents and the pious requests of some friends on behalf of their relatives who are nuns." Among the nine motets in the print are at least two that are appropriate for use at nuns' rites of passage. Della Ciaia and his publication are discussed in greater detail in chapter 7. Here, suffice it to say that these monodic works could serve a wide variety of needs. They could be exploited by families or nuns who wanted music at clothing, profession, or consecration ceremonies but did not wish to spend a great deal of money on the performance. They could also be used by institutions that wished to feature a talented soloist during a ritual dominated by large-scale repertory. In either case, the convent had to have a virtuoso singer on hand. Both works call for a soprano with a wide range, a flexible voice, and an ability to sing dramatically.

As attractive as these small-scale pieces are, however, they offer examples of only one facet of nuns' music-making. What of the larger-scale works that documents suggest were so common at the rites of passage? The most efficient way of obtaining such repertory was to commission it, and the description of the 1684 consecration at Ognissanti makes it clear that the Olivetan nuns did exactly that (see Doc. 15). The unnamed maestro received payment not only for rehearsing and directing the assembled musicians but also for composing the music used at the ceremony. This was doubtless the usual procedure followed for many of the rites at which lay and monastic musicians combined their musical resources. Such music would have had little use outside the convent walls; most of it was probably never published and is now lost.[69] Fortunately, one such work survives. It is contained in the third and last printed collection of works by Alessandro Della

Ciaia, who is, as it turns out, the only composer known to have published music for Sienese nuns. His *Sacri modulatus ad concentum duarum, trium, quatuor, quinque, octo, novemque vocum accomodati* (Bologna: Iacobi Monti, 1666), preserved in the archives of Siena Cathedral and apparently acquired for use by the musicians of that establishment, contains twenty-eight motets. Twelve motets are designated "ad libitum" and the rest are labeled for performance on specific occasions ("for martyrs," "for a confessor," "on Pentecost"). Among the latter is a five-voice work (CCATB), *Veni, veni soror nostra*, identified as appropriate for "the entrance of a virgin in a convent" ("in ingre[s]su virginum in monasterium").

Much of the text of *Veni, veni soror nostra* is inspired by passages from the Song of Songs, including the opening three phrases (a paraphrase of chapter 5, verse 1), and the last two phrases (chapter 5, verse 10, and chapter 2, verse 10). The slight changes rung on the Canticle text transform the original—an intimate supplication from the bridegroom to his beloved—into a corporate invitation from a community of sisters to a new bride as she arrives at the garden of her spouse. The bride's voice is not heard, but the words of her beloved are quoted in the last phrase of the motet:

> Veni, veni soror nostra in domum Domini. Veni, veni dilecta nostra in hortum sponsi tui. Veni, veni ad dilectum tuum et noli tardare. O vere felicissima anima quia facta es sponsa Christi. Exulta et laetare formosa filia Syon quia hodie sponsa Christi facta es. Veni, veni cum festinatione ad dilectum tuum. Dilectus tuus candidus et rubicundus, electus ex millibus. Audi voces sponsi tui dicentis surge propera amica mea et veni.

Robert Kendrick has noted that the constant alternation of literary voice in the canticle links it closely to the traditions of musical dialogues.[70] This legacy surely must have influenced Della Ciaia, for despite the single literary voice present in the text of *Veni, veni soror nostra*, the composer transformed the setting into a dialogue by assigning several passages to female soloists who speak to the bride in confidential tones, thus differentiating them from a larger group of well-wishers who praise the bride and exhort her to come to the wedding:

> SOLO SOPRANO: Come, come, sister of ours into the house of the Lord. Come, come, our beloved into the garden of your spouse and do not be late.
>
> DUET FOR TWO SOPRANOS: O truly happy soul, because you became a bride of Christ.
>
> CHORUS: Exult and rejoice, beautiful daughter of Sion, because today you became a bride of Christ. Come, come quickly to your beloved.
>
> DUET FOR TWO SOPRANOS: Your beloved is white and red, chosen among thousands.
>
> CHORUS: Listen to the voice of your spouse saying, "Rise and make haste, my beloved and come."

Such a motet could have been performed either by an all-male group of secular musicians or, with some transposition of parts or the use of instruments on the bass and tenor lines, by an all-female convent ensemble. Della Ciaia, however, seems to have composed his work with an eye toward the possibility of collaboration between lay and cloistered singers. Such a performance would have been the most satisfying symbolically, as it would have mirrored the social context of the rite, in which a young girl was led to the external monastic church by her family and friends and greeted by her new companions in the cloister, that is, the "garden" of her spouse. By incorporating lengthy solo and duet passages in his motet, Della Ciaia not only created variety in the work and offered the chance to showcase talented soloists, he also solved the most pressing practical problem posed by the performance situation in question: he reduced the amount of music for mixed chorus to a point that posed few problems for the lay and monastic directors who needed to coordinate two ensembles that might never have rehearsed together before the day of the ceremony.

Veni, veni soror nostra (Ex. 3.1) opens with text appropriate for a professed nun, who, on behalf of her entire congregation, invites her "sister" to join her and the others in the "house of the Lord." Della Ciaia exploits melismas to paint the delights of the garden; the florid passages are juxtaposed with intentionally long note values for the text "and do not be late" (mm. 1–20).[71] The subsequent duet is suitable for two professed nuns: the passage invokes the happiness and unity of the new bride and her spouse with lines that either move together in thirds or toss the same motive back and forth (mm. 21–34).

A half-chorus of lay musicians on alto, tenor, and bass parts enters for the triple-time exhortation to "exult and rejoice." They are quickly echoed by a half-chorus of high voices (C1, C2, A), doubtless assigned to the full complement of monastic singers in the internal church (mm. 35–52). The choirs, one representing the lay community and one the monastic community, join to carry forward the homophonic, dance-like entreaty urging the bride to make haste (mm. 53–62).

The sensuous sound of the two solo voices singing in thirds or alternating runs is appropriate for the text describing the physical beauty of the beloved. As with the earlier duet, this one was doubtless intended for two monastic women (mm. 63–75). Della Ciaia saved his most texturally complex choral passage for the end of the work, perhaps mindful that by then, the monastic and lay choirs would be accustomed to the sound of their combined voices in consort. The final exhortation for the bride to rise up at the voice of her beloved is the only passage set in imitative polyphony (mm. 83–103).

IT IS OF MORE than passing interest that the only surviving music for women in convents of Siena was not the work of a professional composer but of a Sienese aristocrat. Alessandro Della Ciaia came from one of the most affluent families in all of Siena, and his publications reflect his pride in his social standing. The nuns for whom Della Ciaia wrote his motets and Lamentations of 1650 were relatives of friends who undoubtedly hailed from families with bloodlines similar to his. The composer's choice of Cardinal Flavio Chigi as the dedicatee of his *Sacri modulatus* might seem an opportunistic stroke on the composer's part, an attempt to link his music to Chigi fortunes, which were running high in 1666. It certainly did not hurt that Cardinal Flavio was nephew to a reigning pope, but Della Ciaia's decision to dedicate the volume to him was probably also based on the fact that

Flavio was his own blood relative, an avid lover of music, and a fellow member of the Sienese ruling elite.[72] For families of such standing in Siena, as in other urban centers, the clothing, profession, and consecration of daughters, sisters, aunts, and nieces held a significance beyond the religious. Robert Kendrick has observed that they became occasions "to show liturgical pomp, family ties, wealth and, not least, musical ability."[73] It could be argued, in fact, that as the seventeenth century wore on in Siena, a city undergoing a decline in population and the gradual extinction of patrician families, musical display by women in convents assumed an ever greater importance as an emblem of the vitality of the remaining Sienese nobility.[74] An aristocrat would be among those most sensitive to the issue; an aristocrat-composer could turn his talents to writing pieces destined for the nuns in his city and publish them without worrying about the costs associated with going to press. Publication was probably an important and necessary step for Della Ciaia, because it carried the music and therefore the reputation of Siena, its aristocracy, and its monastic women beyond the walls of the city. The act of publication probably also ensured the survival of Della Ciaia's music, which is all that remains today of what was a rich body of works associated with rites of passage for young women in the convents of seventeenth-century Siena.

Ex. 3.1. Della Ciaia, *Veni, veni soror nostra* (1666)

Ex. 3.1. (*continued*)

Ex. 3.1. (*continued*)

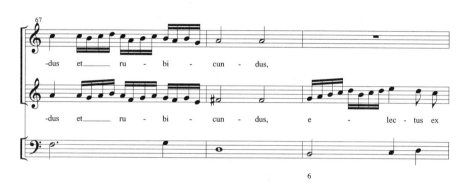

Ex. 3.1.   (*continued*)

Ex. 3.1. (*continued*)

73

FOOLISH VIRGINS

Music in Sienese Convent Theatrical Productions during the Seventeenth Century

One of the liveliest artistic traditions in Sienese convents was the staging of theatrical productions.[1] The plays, most often based on stories from the Bible or the lives of saints, were ostensibly intended as spiritual recreation for the nuns but were often performed as entertainment for members of the lay community. In addition to providing yet another point of contact with the outside world, convent theater allowed nuns to showcase their dramatic prowess and to display their musical skills, for scenes requiring songs, dances, and instrumental music were often incorporated into the spectacle. Documents suggest that these convent productions were frequent; nevertheless, only a handful of the many plays that survive in Siena show signs that they were composed specifically for female monasteries. Musical scenes are incorporated at standard points for traditional reasons in most of those works. Although no scores for those scenes have yet come to light, the plays still have much to tell about the variety of music known and performed in the convents of Siena and about the arguments that must have circulated concerning the musical genres deemed most appropriate for cloistered women.

IN THEIR ENTHUSIASTIC CULTIVATION of sacred theater, Sienese nuns were merely reflecting their own city's long tradition in that arena. Chronicles report, for example, that public performances of sacred plays were staged to commemorate the canonization of S. Bernardino in 1450 and the elevation of Enea Silvio Piccolomini to the papacy in 1458.[2] Such works continued to mark important religious celebrations in the following centuries. At least two *sacre rappresentazioni* about different aspects of Catherine of Siena's life were written and performed publicly for the saint's feast day: the first in the contrada of Fontebranda in 1569 and another in 1601.[3] Plays on religious subjects were sometimes produced with the goal of promoting civic morality. Ercolano Ercolani, a member of the Confraternity of the Sacred Nails (Congregazione dei Sacri Chiodi), recognized the public's need for recreation but was dismayed by the "profane and lascivious" qualities of the plays produced for this purpose. He took it upon himself to write spiritual comedies in order to entice young people away from such dangerous works; his plays were performed in Siena to "universal applause."[4] Sacred theater also had another role in civic life: it served as entertainment for visiting dignitaries. Grand Duke Cosimo II and his entourage took delight in the production of *Santa Dippa*, which young Sienese noblemen staged for them at the Jesuit monastery of S. Vigilio on 9 November 1612. The religious company of S. Croce performed Annibale Lomeri's *Cicilia sacra* at S. Agostino for members of the Medici family on 18 June 1621.[5] The latter play, dedicated to the nuns of S. Cecilia in Rome, includes two scenes that might have been inspired by convent traditions. In both, Cecilia, who is offstage, sings while accompanying herself on the organ.[6] The *mise en scène*—an unseen female singer at the organ—was doubtless intended to be emblematic of nuns' music-making, although holy women were rarely "disembodied voices" when performing convent plays.

Sienese nuns would have had little trouble finding suitable repertory for their theatrical ventures. A great number of *sacre rappresentazioni*, many originally published in Florence during the mid-Cinquecento, were reprinted in Siena during the last decades of the sixteenth century and in the first decades of the seventeenth century by the publisher at the Loggia del Papa.[7] Certainly many of them could have served for public productions, perhaps by lay confraternities or by seminarians, but several seem most appropriate for convent performance. The protagonists in a number of these works are saints who gave their names to female monasteries (S. Caterina, S. Margherita, S. Chiara, S. Maria Maddalena) or whose relics were venerated at a nunnery (S. Apollonia).[8] In other plays, such as the *Rappresentatione di Santa Eufrasia*, the protagonist is a nun and the setting is a convent.[9] To be sure, convent productions were not necessarily limited to plays about female saints. As I will show, it is possible that the women at S. Margherita in Castelvecchio performed a work that featured S. Galgano as protagonist.

Convent drama, however popular among nuns, was one of the artisitic activities of which ecclesiastical authorities were most suspicious.[10] When Francesco Bossi visited the convents of Siena in 1575, musical performance seems to have concerned him not at all. Tales of convent drama, however, apparently perturbed him, for he asked repeatedly if the women staged plays. The nuns at S. Maria degli Angeli were the most cautious: they told Bossi that they had not done plays for quite some time. The abbesses at S. Lorenzo, S. Chiara, S. Paolo and SS. Concezione declared that no plays had been staged since the death of Cosimo I. As he had died less than a year and a half before the visit, this was hardly an admission that they had forsaken the boards forever. At S. Marta, Suor Anna told Bossi that in the past the nuns had occasionally put on plays, but in the present they did so rarely, because they did not want to borrow clothes from lay persons. The theatrical legacy must have been strongest at SS. Abbondio e Abbondanzio and at S. Petronilla. The abbess at the former institution admitted that the nuns staged dramas "once in a while" and had done so the previous year. The spokeswoman for the convent of S. Petronilla defended the use of theatrical works; she gave the subject of the play produced that year (a work based on the life of S.

Agata) and noted that the nuns performed only "among themselves" without allowing outside visitors. Bossi's interrogations obviously led him to believe that many female institutions, even those not among the wealthiest, such as S. Paolo, performed plays on a frequent basis. Despite the nuns' protestations of proper protocol, Bossi decided that this was not a practice he wanted to continue, and so he issued an order barring convent performances of any comedies, even those with a spiritual subject, and forbidding the nuns to possess false beards, wigs, and costumes that might come in handy for such productions.[11]

Bossi's ban on convent theater was never enforced, for records show that nuns continued to present plays through the end of the Cinquecento and into the Seicento and that ecclesiastical authorities in Siena made no attempt to stop them.[12] Archbishop Alessandro Petrucci, it is true, issued a decree against the performance of profane comedies in convents, but he did allow for the presentation of "devout plays" by the nuns. And though he forbade them to remove their religious clothes for such productions, he did permit them to put on "serious" costumes over their habits.[13] Ascanio II Piccolomini requested only that the nuns vet any production plans with his vicar and that they not be seen in costume (leaving open the possibility that they could wear costumes when not performing for the public).[14] Despite relative freedom in matters theatrical, however, two convents found themselves in hot water in 1597. During Carnival season, the nuns at S. Sebastiano in Vallepiatta and those at S. Margherita in Castelvecchio not only performed sacred comedies, they also allowed lay women "of every kind" into the cloister to see the productions, and then hosted several of the visitors overnight. The archbishop promptly put all the women involved under interdict.[15] The nuns of Vallepiatta reacted quickly and penitently, admitting their actions and asking for absolution.[16] The women at Castelvecchio also wrote to ask absolution, but the tone of their letter is much sharper than the one from Vallepiatta, perhaps because the aristocratic women could count on the support of their prominent families. The scribe implies that the archbishop's vicar was responsible for stirring up the trouble and questions both the depth of the vicar's convictions and his authority. The scribe is also careful to cast the nuns in a very favorable light by suggesting that they are making their request on behalf of others:

> The nuns of S. Margherita in Siena, called the "poor ones of Castelvecchio," having performed a play that several unmarried lay women attended and having used a room where (so it's said) anyone can enter because they are uncloistered nuns who can go outside, have been placed under interdict by the archbishop's vicar, even though in the past this practice has always been allowed and one might doubt the validity of this interdiction. The nuns turn to this Sacred Congregation, humbly supplicating them to order the vicar to clear up the entire matter and to absolve not just the nuns but especially the lay women who are under interdict, so that in these holy days of Lent, they may not be deprived of Masses, communion, sermons, and other spiritual food.[17]

Both nuns and lay women were doubtless absolved—the matter may have been rendered even simpler by the death of the archbishop early in May 1597—for no letters were sent about the matter to the Sacred Congregation in the following year or thereafter, the usual procedure when an affair was not settled to the petitioner's satisfaction.[18]

The archbishop's (or vicar's) response to the infractions by the nuns of Vallepiatta and Castelvecchio may have had more to do with ecclesiastical politics—they were two of the open monasteries in Siena that the archbishop was trying to persuade to accept claustration—than with the presence of a lay audience at their dramatic presentations. Documents from the sixteenth and seventeenth centuries indicate that outside visitors, including men, were routinely present at nuns' theater.[19] This much is clear in the foreword to the *Rappresentatione delli santi Giuliano e Basilissa*, in which the author addresses the nuns for whom he wrote the play:

> Even if I was at first most desirous (or under so much obligation, considering your many merits) to please you, nevertheless, I remained so content and satisfied (as did many other honored guests) by the noble recitation of the lovely play on S. Galgano that you performed, that I would have thought it not a small failing (even though the undertaking was far from my profession) if I had not quickly satisfied you by trying with great affection to write another for you to recite this year for your pleasure and the pleasure of the others who will, by chance, have the opportunity to hear it, among whom I hope to be.[20]

The Italian grammatical structure indicates that the author is a man. Despite the convoluted syntax of his dedication, it is evident that he was present when the nuns performed his earlier play and that he hoped to be among the members of the audience (both male and female) who would see the new production.[21] A highly placed devotee of nuns' theater was Catherine Medici Gonzaga, governor of Siena from 1627 to 1629. In a letter of 1 March 1628, she wrote her sister-in-law, Maria Maddalena of Austria, that she was attending performances of sacred comedies, "which the nuns here [in Siena] do very well."[22]

The date of Catherine Medici Gonzaga's letter confirms that Carnival was the preferred period for convent drama, although some plays may have also been performed on special feast days or as part of the festivities surrounding the clothing of new nuns.[23] More difficult to determine is the actual space in which the dramas were staged. Documents offer no evidence that any seventeenth-century Sienese convent had an actual theater room; it is more likely that the parlors served as theatrical venues.[24] Although none of the plays includes detailed descriptions of scenery, an occasional rubric suggests that the nuns must have been quite resourceful at devising a variety of appropriate sets, props, and costumes for their productions. The script for the *Rappresentatione dello sposalitio d'Isac e di Rebecca*, for instance, directs that when Rebecca prepares to leave with Malco to journey to her new home, she be "mounted on a horse, if possible."[25]

The high quality of the productions that Catherine Medici Gonzaga attended in Sienese convents may have had something to do with the fact that it was normal for the coriste to take part in such plays and not just the novices.[26] The performer who recited the prologue to the 1608 comedy *Eufrosina*, for example, described herself as a "baptized Christian and a professed nun."[27] Doubtless, however, the biggest roles fell to the youngest and most energetic women. In a letter of 1671, the thirty-two-year-old Suor Maria Pulcheria Chigi at S. Girolamo in Campansi informed her brother (either Cardinal Sigismondo Chigi or Prince Agostino Chigi) that she took a role in just one of the two comedies that the convent was mounting during Carnival not only because illnesses were creating difficulties for her but also because "now I should leave place for the young ones, as my time is past."[28]

The "young ones" may or may not have included the educande, the girls who were placed in monastic institutions for education before marriage or the declaration of vows. In the convents of S. Maria degli Angeli and S. Petronilla, the educande had their own separate musicotheatrical tradition. They participated in the old Tuscan custom celebrating the return of spring through the *maggio* ("May song"). Although it originally involved just singing and dancing, a dramatic story (based on an epic, chivalric, or religious subject) was later incorporated in the celebration. The poetic construction of the maggio was quite rudimentary, consisting of four-line stanzas with eight-syllable lines rhyming *abba* or *abbx*. The poetry was sung to a simple recitation formula that could be ornamented by more talented singers; the recitation could be interrupted to insert more musically sophisticated arias or choruses.[29] At S. Petronilla, the singing of maggi can be documented from 1623; at Santuccio, from 1634. In both institutions, it apparently continued through the end of the century.[30] Unfortunately, no scripts for these performances survive.[31] We have only the account entries noting that the girls performed the works "for their own recreation," that they were given a small gratuity, and that the nuns reimbursed them for the purchase of prosciutto and cheese, which was probably consumed as a special treat after the performance.[32]

THE SIX WORKS LISTED IN table 4.1, one printed and five in manuscript, can be definitively linked to Sienese convents. The print is dated, as are two of the manuscripts. The remaining plays appear to have been copied in the late Cinquecento or during the course of the Seicento.

Men wrote three of the plays. Although we cannot identify the male author of *Giuliano e Basilissa*, we know that *Santa Marina* was penned by Domenico Tregiani, a member of the Accademia degli Insipidi.[33] Tregiani was a poet and playwright by profession. As he implies in the foreword, he wrote the drama in honor of the clothing of a certain "Camilla" (probably a relative) at the convent.[34] Benvenuto Flori, the author of *L'evangelica parabola*, served Siena Cathedral in various guises—as singer, sacristan, and chaplain—from 1579 until his death in 1642.[35] The authorship of the other works remains a mystery.

The specific convent for which each play was written can be easily determined in three cases. Tregiani named the Convertite on the title folio of *Santa Marina*; the author of *Giuliano e Basilissa* declared that the work was intended for the "Gesuate sisters" (that is, the nuns of S. Sebastiano in Vallepiatta); and Flori dedicated his sacred comedy to the Olivetan nuns of Ognissanti, who had requested that he write it.[36] The author of *Isac e Rebecca* was, alas, less specific. The prologue furnishes the only clue, for the speaker refers to "divine Augustine, who guides us in this convent."[37] We can thus infer that the work was originally penned for one of the six Augustinian houses in Siena. If, as I suspect, musical

TABLE 4.1.　Convent plays with musical scenes in the BCS

Manuscripts	
MS G.XI.53	*La rappresentatione e festa di Santo Galgano in ottava rima*
MS G.XI.56	*La devota rappresantasione di Santa Marina Vergine fatta novamente da il Desioso Insipito senese a riquitione delle molto Reverende Convertite di Siena, il dì 25 di settembre l'anno 1589*
MS G.XI.58	*Rappresentatione delli santi Giuliano e Basilissa composta ad istantia delle venerabili e devote suore Giesuate di Siena per doversi recitare dalloro*
MS G.XI.59	*Eufrosina comedia spirituale nuova 1608*
MS K.X.53	*Rappresentatione dello sposalitio d'Isac e di Rebecca, nuovamente posta in luce*
Printed works	
Flori, Benvenuto	*L'evangelica parabola delle vergini prudenti e delle stolte.* Siena: Ercole Gori, 1642

and theatrical traditions went hand in hand, then Santuccio, S. Maria Maddalena, S. Marta, and S. Paolo are the likeliest candidates. The problem becomes thornier with *Eufrosina*, whose author not only leaves us in the dark concerning his identity but also furnishes no hints about the cloistered women for whom the play was created. *Santo Galgano* provides an excellent example of the difficulty of assigning plays to convents based on theme or topic. In this case, the subject chosen by the anonymous author would seem to make it particularly suitable for performance at S. Maria degli Angeli, whose nuns came into possession of the Sienese saint's head in the mid-sixteenth century. However, a note on the flyleaf of the manuscript informs us that it belonged to Suor Flavia Chigi (sister of Pope Alexander VII), a nun at the Franciscan convent of S. Margherita in Castelvecchio.[38] Of course, this does not necessarily prove that the play was performed there; it may have been copied for devotional reading rather than actual performance.[39]

Of these six plays, two exploit music-making either summarily or not at all and therefore will not be examined in depth here. Tregiani's *Santa Marina* includes no explicit or implicit directions for music. In *Santo Galgano*, the script specifically calls for music-making at only one point. In the final scene, the characters playing the roles of the officiating prelates are directed to "sing something" as they bury the saint; the author, however, neither provides a text nor suggests a tune.[40] Music may have also opened the work, although the rubrics are not as clear. In the introductory scene, "a young boy comes out with a cittern" and is given three eight-line stanzas (*ottave*) to "say."[41] It seems plausible that the nun assigned this character sang the ottave, if only to a simple recitation formula, while accompanying herself on a cittern.

The remaining four plays employ music much more liberally. So important is the role of music in Flori's work that I will consider it separately after first examining *Isac e Rebecca*, *Giuliano e Basilissa*, and *Eufrosina*. Although the musical aspect of the plays is the main focus, the subject matter and themes of each also offer fertile ground for exploring several issues surrounding the claustration of women.

THE TWO-PART *ISAC E REBECCA* is based on the biblical story in Genesis 24. Abraham orders his servant (named Malco in the play) to go to Mesopotamia and seek a wife for his son Isaac. Malco makes the journey and stops at a well outside the far-off village. He already has an understanding with God: if he asks a young woman for a drink, and she happily offers water both to him and to his camels, he will know that she is the one chosen for Isaac. Rebecca appears and offers the water. Malco presents Isaac's proposal of marriage to her family (who are revealed to be Abraham's kin), and Rebecca accompanies Malco back to Canaan to wed Isaac. The play ends with the festivities celebrating the union of Isaac and his "chaste bride."

The spouses remain chaste in *Giuliano e Basilissa*. The three-act play opens with Giuliano and his parents at odds: he wants to retain his purity and to serve God; they want him to marry and produce children. Giuliano agrees to the marriage his parents so fervently desire after being instructed to do so by Christ, who appears to him in a vision. On his wedding night, he finds that his bride Basilissa is only too happy to preserve her virginity (and thus his as well) in order that they may preach their faith. Both sets of parents die conveniently soon after the wedding, leaving the young couple free to follow their calling. Giuliano gathers about him a group of young men and Basilissa a group of young woman, all dedicated to serving God, but they run afoul of the emperor Diocletian. Basilissa and her virginal escort are slaughtered, and Giuliano, too, chooses to suffer a martyr's death rather than sacrifice to pagan deities.

The plot of the five-act spiritual comedy *Eufrosina* is taken from an old legend of the Alexandrian saint, and, just as in Tregiani's *Santa Marina*, the female protagonist spends a good deal of the play pretending to be a man.[42] Destined for marriage to Dardano by her father Pafnutio, Eufrosina asks for a reprieve of six months. Near the end of this period, she manages to slip away from her home, clothed as a man. Thus disguised, she enters a monastery of monks and lives out her life there as Fra Smaraldo. Pafnutio searches far and wide for her, eventually stopping at a monastery where a monk comforts him greatly. That monk sickens and on the point of death reveals that "he" is Eufrosina; thus reunited with her father, Eufrosina dies in his arms. Pafnutio returns home and decides that he still wants Dardano in his family. He sends for his niece Fausta, who has been living in a convent but does not want to become a nun, and, to everyone's great joy, arranges for her to be wed to Dardano.

The authors of these three plays exploit the theme of marriage, a theme central to the lives of all early modern women, including the "brides of Christ." They present various paths to that destination: the nuns are invited to see themselves either as the chaste Rebecca, whose betrothal to Isaac is ordained by God and whose marriage requires that she leave her family and travel to her husband's land; as Basilissa, who is both virgin and spouse and is ready to face martyrdom for her faith; or as Eufrosina, who must defy her family by rejecting earthly vows for celestial ones. It is noteworthy that in the perfect world of the playwright, the convent is only for those with a true vocation. In *Eufrosina*, Pafnutio provides a dowry to a serving girl who wishes to become a nun but is without the needed financial resources. Fausta, on the other hand, does not wish to be a nun, and when she makes her feelings clear, her family heeds her: she is taken out of the convent and suitably married.[43] In the real world, of course, young women often had no choice in the matter and were sometimes placed in nunneries against their wishes.[44] Perhaps this is why the author of *Eufrosina* reminds the nuns for whom the play was intended that their state may be better than that of their married sisters. The prologue, for example, observes that "the married woman, burdened with children and often desperate with anguish, always regrets not having become a nun."[45] In a later scene, two poor women, Marcuccia and Togna, discuss Togna's horrific marriage. Togna informs Marcuccia that her husband frequented taverns, gambled, sought out other women, swore, and shunned work. He spent her dowry without a care and beat her like a snake. Togna "raised her hands to heaven" in thanks when he died.[46]

In addition to a common focus on marriage, the plays stress the theme of obedience, one of the three monastic vows. The marriage-minded mother in *Giuliano e Basilissa* informs her husband that Giuliano would not dare disobey them, as they are his parents; Eufrosina notifies her confessor that she will be joined in matrimony to whomever pleases her father.[47] Divine intervention assures that Giuliano can both submit to the will of his parents and follow his desire to remain a virgin; Eufrosina, on the other hand, must disobey her earthly father in order to fulfill her greater obedience to her divine father.[48] The theme is also clear in the dealings between the "good" servants and their employers. In *Giuliano e Basilissa*, the servant Lisabetta refuses her friend Camilla's invitation to stay and chat because she does not want to show disobedience to her mistress.[49] Perhaps the most pointed monastic reference occurs in *Isac e Rebecca*. After her engagement to Isaac, Rebecca rejects her parents' plea to stay at home for several more days, citing her new allegiance:

> My dear father, now it must please me
> to be obedient to my spouse;
> as I am already under his authority,
> I must do what pleases him.[50]

Various aspects of convent life emerge in the details of certain scenes as well. In *Isac e Rebecca*, Rebecca's mother insists that her daughter would not go to the well "senza licentia."[51] Although this means "without permission," the nuns would have related the word "licentia" to the written license they were required to obtain from the archbishop for a host of actions, from letting doctors in the cloister to receiving music teachers at the grates. A passage from *Giuliano e Basilissa*, in which the young groom asks his bride if she wants to remain a chaste spouse, must have struck the nuns as remarkably like the question posed to them by the officiating cleric in the examination before the clothing ceremony:

> Therefore, if you have been spurred by holy inspiration
> and it pleases you to serve God

in the virginal state in which you now find yourself,
you can declare your intention.[52]

Earlier in the same play, after agreeing to the marriage so fervently desired by his
parents, Giuliano expresses only one desire: that the families forgo the customary
luxury in attiring the bride.[53] When Eufrosina bends to Pafnutio's wish that she
marry, she also asks to dress simply for the ceremony.[54] Such passages were no
doubt veiled references to monastic investitures, in which young women were
often clothed as ornately as secular brides. It is telling that Eufrosina's father is
quite disconcerted by her request:

> I think it most harsh, daughter, that you want neither clothes, nor jewels, nor
> ornaments worthy of our peers, and customary in our day. . . . Comply with me
> in this, my daughter: clothe and adorn yourself according to our rank, as other
> girls who are your peers do, for that would be your duty.[55]

The author of *Eufrosina* here implies that at least one motivating factor behind
the lavish trappings associated with nuns' clothing ceremonies was the desire of
aristocratic families to display their proper social status.[56]

The strong ties between cloistered women and the world beyond the walls
are emphasized in two plays. The nurse in *Eufrosina*, returning from a visit to the
convent, notes: "Nothing goes on in the city without the nuns knowing about
it immediately, and although they do not make an effort to find out, nevertheless
people who visit the convent tell them everything."[57] That the remark about the
nuns "not making an effort to find out" is disingenuous is quickly revealed in a
subsequent passage, as the nurse explains why she is late returning home: "By
now, you know how nuns are . . . one asks about one thing, another asks about
another thing: it's necessary to respond to all of them. . . . I had to tell them
everything from A to Z, in detail."[58] The servant Lisabetta in *Giuliano e Basilissa*
has the same experience: "Those nuns detained me a long time (to my annoyance)
with a great deal of chattering, so that it was difficult for me to get away."[59] And
yet Lisabetta was sent to the convent precisely because her mistress realized that
nuns were probably the best source of information on certain important matters,
such as the good character of Giuliano's bride-to-be Basilissa.

Despite these gentle rebukes, the prevailing idea of holy women in these
plays is, as one might expect, a positive one. Nuns are, for instance, perceived as
having singular access to divine favor. When both sets of parents in *Giuliano e
Basilissa* sicken, Lisabetta goes to the convent to ask the cloistered women for
their prayers because she believes them to be especially efficacious.[60] Eufrosina's
excellent qualities are clear even to a servant whom the others tease for his lack
of devotion; his glowing description is a catalogue of all the behaviors associated
with the model nun:

> Eufrosina is a wise girl; she speaks little and does not let herself be heard. She
> stays secluded; one could say that she never goes out of her room or the oratory.
> One sees in her only spirituality and an extraordinary devotion. She disdains the
> world, mortifies her flesh, and carries only such things as spiritual books, rosaries,
> and the like in her hand. Whoever wants her friendship must speak about God,
> about her special advocate the Virgin Mary, and about the saints.[61]

The convent is depicted as a refuge. Marsilia, a young serving girl in *Eufrosina*, wants to enter the cloister because, as she says, "blessed are the nuns, who are removed from so many of the terrible troubles of this evil world."[62] The author of *Giuliano e Basilissa* uses the stronger image of the nunnery as paradise on earth. When the serving woman Camilla encounters Lisabetta, a former servant who has joined the ranks of Basilissa's virgins, and asks her friend how she can endure all the prayers and fasting, Lisabetta responds, "I feel as if I am living among angels, and I am lost without them."[63]

MUSIC IS FEATURED prominently in all three plays and is put to various uses in each. *Isac e Rebecca* deploys music in the most realistic manner, for aside from its appearance in the prologue,[64] singing, playing, and dancing are presented in the context of the wedding festivities. As the guests sit down to eat, a young man with an instrument in his hand greets Abraham and then sings ("in a beautiful manner") eleven ottave, the first of which justifies his presence at the feast:

> To honor such a worthy gathering,
> I resolved to appear before you,
> because I heard this wedding lauded and highly praised
> in the public voice.
> I heard that all should talk and sing of it
> in every street and in every place,
> and therefore I, too, who desire to bestow honor upon the wedding
> will speak of it briefly.[65]

The youth continues to sing stanzas praising God and his creation, the bride, and the groom; he even incorporates a few lines disparaging his "humble style" of singing while in such "noble company." When the young man finishes his song, he sits down to eat while other guests dance. After the dance, all rise to give thanks to God, chanting a series of prayer verses in Latin. Once the prayers are finished, Abraham tells his guests:

> Now that we have given thanks to God,
> and when we have rested a bit,
> it is my will that we celebrate
> with decent, honest music and songs.[66]

The stage directions order the banquet table removed and instruct the performers to sing, dance, and play, although no specific repertory is mentioned.[67]

This lively scene testifies to the skills of the women at the convent. At least one of the nuns must have been a talented soloist who could accompany herself on the lute, and many of the others must have had either vocal or instrumental training. The last part of the scene, in which chanted Latin prayers are followed by songs and dances, may be read as an apology for the performance of nonliturgical music within the convent walls. As long as the nuns gave thanks to God, what harm was there in performing "decent" secular music?

No attempt is made to incorporate music in such a realistic manner in either *Eufrosina* or *Giuliano e Basilissa*. It can therefore serve more varied roles. Musical scenes, for example, often delineate the beginnings and endings of acts. Act I of *Giuliano e Basilissa* opens with a sung madrigal and closes with a *villanella*; Act III, too, begins with a madrigal. In *Eufrosina*, sung *intermedi* separate Act I from Act II, Act II from Act III, and Act III from Act IV; the plays ends with a madrigal.

These works are not, however, mere structural markers. The madrigal that introduces Act I of *Giuliano e Basilissa* foreshadows the unfolding of the drama and condenses its subject matter into one seven-verse stanza:

> Moved by the chaste zeal
> of the new spouses,
> the heavens become serene
> and send the most sublime heroes
> down here among us,
> and all paradise rejoices happily
> at what the future will bring.[68]

The madrigal at the opening of Act III reinforces the play's moral message:

> Whoever hopes to ascend to heaven
> and there enjoy glory forever
> must disdain wordly things
> and put her hope in God.
> Then in paradise
> joy will succeed torments and death.[69]

The intermedi of *Eufrosina* are even more consistently didactic in tone and more specifically aimed at the monastic audience. At the end of Act I, Divine Love battles Cupid (who represents lust) and emerges victorious. After a speech in which an angel warns that life is a continuous war between carnal and divine love, four angels sing:

> O sacred virgins,
> if God with his love
> has inflamed your hearts,
> then Cupid's sparks are extinguished,
> his arrows and bow are broken.
> These cannot harm her
> who has made a nest for God in her heart.[70]

Similarly, at the end of Act II, angels advise those who love true life to store up their treasures in heaven, where they will enjoy eternal life. At the end of Act III, Faith appears with three angels to perform the following:

> Through Faith and her light
> you have by now discovered
> the path that leads to heaven;
> but you, slaves to your senses, do not follow it.
> . . .
> The path to heaven is steep,
> but zeal renders it easy.

Whoever loves God and trusts in God alone
disdains all [worldly] things.[71]

Although it does not serve as a formal marker, the beggars' song in Act I of
Eufrosina shares the didactic function of such scenes. Having received alms from
Eufrosina and her nurse, the grateful beggars sing to the "courteous and pious
women who help the poor" and tell them that their actions set them on the path
to blessedness.[72] Curiously enough, the piece that closes *Eufrosina* abandons the
prevailing edifying tone that characterizes the musical texts throughout the play,
perhaps because much of its text and all of its music might have been taken
directly from a three-voice "canzone alla napolitana" published by Girolamo
Scotto in 1571.[73] The work is sung as the bride Fausta and her bridegroom
Dardano prepare for the wedding:

Sweet, amorous and lovely nymphs,
who with sweet songs and sweet accents,
make echoes resound and calm the winds,
come to sing with us.
O wedding that we so desired,
today you make us happier than all others.[74]

The singers here are not the usual moralizing angels but rather a group of "young
men." More significant is the tone they adopt in addressing the audience, who
are no longer "sacred virgins" but rather "amorous nymphs"; the latter term is
perhaps a reflection of at least one of the roles into which Siena's singing nuns
were cast.

IN ADDITION TO ITS usefulness for marking structural divisions and for reinforcing the themes of the play, music could also increase dramatic impact by adding
to the spectacle. Both *Giuliano e Basilissa* and *Eufrosina* include scenes in which
music accompanies, and thus represents, the divine. In Act IV of *Eufrosina*, the
protagonist, dressed as a man, leaves her home at night to escape to a male monastery. Satan and his demonic underlings Belfagor and Astarot see her flight and
plot to bring her low by tempting her with worldly pleasures. As they start off
after their prey, the archangel Raphael and two of his angelic assistants appear
singing:

Infernal spirits, why do you plot
against the chaste spouse?
Your talons cannot harm her.
She reposes securely
on the breast of Jesus, son of Mary.
Now, evil ones, go down to hell:
remain there in eternal fire and ice.[75]

After the demons disappear, howling in fear as flames of fire rise up from under
the earth, the angels sing another madrigal, directing the "chaste brides of Christ"
to serve the Lord, as he will keep them safe.

Giuliano e Basilissa includes not one but two scenes in which music serves even more pointedly as a kind of special effect, for both are apparition scenes. In Act I, Christ and a group of angels appear to Giuliano; before Christ awakens Giuliano from his sleep, the angels sing a short madrigal to the "faithful servant of God."[76] More spectacular, both visually and musically, is the apparition scene in Act II, which occurs after the two main characters have agreed to remain chaste spouses and to serve God. Giuliano and Basilissa, nearly blinded by a dazzling celestial light, fall to the ground as Christ and Mary appear with angels and virgins. The choirs of angels on Christ's side sing a stanza in honor of Giuliano, and the choir of virgins then perform a stanza in tribute to Basilissa. The two choirs unite for the final stanza:

> Having overcome the deceptions
> of the ancient serpent, do not fear,
> because you have for a banner, rather a shield,
> the God of hosts
> who will bring your desire to harbor.[77]

As examples from these plays clearly demonstrate, the music heard in Sienese convent theater ranged from chant to double-choir compositions. Solo singers, choristers, and instrumentalists all had opportunities to add to the dramatic situation and to display their talents. The nuns not only sang and played a variety of instruments but also danced in these productions. Music was exploited to help define the play's structure, to add realism to the work, to intensify the spectacle, and to drive home the lessons of the play.[78] It could be associated with the humble (the beggars in *Eufrosina*), and it could just as easily represent the divine (the choirs of angels and virgins in *Giuliano e Basilissa*), but it was never put into the mouths of demons. The one question left unanswered is who composed the music. As I have shown, both the text and the music of published works could have been incorporated into the plays. Perhaps the nuns or the men who came to the convent to teach adapted or arranged well-known secular pieces to accommodate newly composed poetry. It is also possible that the nuns asked their lay maestri to compose music for these scenes. Finally, we cannot dismiss the idea that a talented nun took on the task of creating new works to suit the talents of the women chosen to perform in the play.

THE MUSIC IN BENVENUTO Flori's *L'evangelica parabola*, although serving some of the functions already outlined, is more varied and complex than that in any of the three works thus far examined and is thus worthy of close study (see table 4.2). The play merits special attention on other grounds as well. Flori, the playwright, was a working musician, earning his living for many years as a singer at the Cathedral. He knew the nuns at Ognissanti well, for he was their confessor in 1635.[79] More important, he also had experience with music in a convent setting: during 1618 and 1619, when he was chaplain at S. Marta, he taught the Augustinian nuns "the rules for playing the lute in the organ loft" ("la regola del leuto per sonar nel'organo") and instructed them in plainchant.[80] It is, therefore, not surprising that Flori's play furnishes ample musical scenes. Along with the performance opportunities, however, the libretto also offers both implicit and

TABLE 4.2.   Musical scenes in Flori's *L'evangelica parabola* (1642)

	Style or genre of music	Performers
Prologue	recitative	solo voice
Act II, sc. 4	[madrigal?]	4 pilgrims
Act II, sc. 5	[madrigal?]	4 pilgrims
Act III, sc. 3	canzonetta	solos by Sense, 5 foolish virgins, 5 peasants; ensemble performance of last stanza; instrumental accompaniment
Act IV, sc. 5	madrigals	Pleasure, accompanying himself
Act IV, sc. 11	moresca (2 strains)	4 peasants
Act V, sc. 7	[spiritual] madrigals	solos: 5 wise virgins
Act V, [sc. 8]	lauda	5 wise virgins
Act V, sc. 9	lauda	5 wise virgins

explicit messages about the dangers that certain kinds of music could pose for the talented Olivetan nuns.

Flori based his play on a parable from Matthew 25:1–13 and took further inspiration from verses 34–40 of the same chapter. In the first passage, the kingdom of Heaven is compared to ten virgins awaiting the bridegroom. The five wise virgins fill their lamps with oil; the five foolish do not. When the bridegroom arrives late, the wise virgins are ready with their lighted lamps and accompany him into the banquet. The five foolish virgins must go to buy oil, and when they return, they find the doors to the feast locked. In the second passage, Christ invites into heaven those who fed the hungry, clothed the naked, visited the sick and imprisoned, and took in the homeless. The parable of the wise and foolish virgins served as subject for several liturgical dramas before Flori's time. The oldest is found in a late-eleventh-century or early-twelfth-century manuscript from S. Martial de Limoges; another version was performed at Eisenach in 1322.[81] A Flemish retelling of the story dates from the late fifteenth century, and the Biblioteca Riccardiana preserves a sixteenth-century Italian play for use in a Florentine convent.[82] In both the Flemish and Florentine comedies, musical performance takes on symbolic meaning. In the former, the foolish virgins reveal their true character by squabbling over singing.[83] In the latter, Galantina (one of the foolish virgins) seeks to cultivate the talents expected of a Renaissance courtier: she wants to learn to play the lute and to dance.[84] Her prudent sisters, on the other hand, waste no time on such occupations; they confine themselves to singing Latin psalms, hymns, and liturgical items.[85] Whether or not Flori was acquainted with any of these earlier plays, he too designed his libretto so that both musical references and scenes with music carry symbolic weight.

Many features of the play, in fact, suggest that Flori's use of symbols extends beyond music. The very choice of the subject may have been symbolic. Ognissanti was one of a select number of convents in seventeenth-century Siena that preserved the elaborate rite of consecration, in which a passage from the parable of the wise and foolish virgins figured prominently. At that rite, the celebrant recited a prayer and then called the nuns to process into the church with the following antiphon:[86]

> Prudent virgins
> prepare your lamps.
> Look: the bridegroom is coming;
> go to meet him.[87]

Flori's play begins with a spoken prologue and continues with a sung trope on the "prudent virgins" antiphon:[88]

> After the [actress who gives the] prologue leaves, a voice is heard from behind the scenes singing the following verses in recitative style, inviting the virgins to appear with their oil vases and lighted lamps in order to go meet the bride and bridegroom:

> Wise and beautiful virgins
> shake the lazy sleep from your eyes:
> you are called to the imminent wedding
> of two superlative heroes.
> Go to the great court
> where immense, immortal joy reigns.
> The golden stars are already losing their splendor
> at the appearance of the sun in the east;
> the tuneful birds
> are already singing in concert; their sweetness is heard
> on the hills and the plain,
> as they praise their great and sovereign creator.
> Take action;
> for such an important invitation,
> let your will be ready, your foot, swift.
> Hurry, hurry, quickly take the precious liquid
> of the green olive tree,
> and thus prepared,
> light your lamps and make haste to go
> where the loving, heavenly bridegroom invites you
> and awaits you with his celestial spouse.[89]

Flori's commedia then unfolds over the course of five acts and takes as its central metaphor the idea of pilgrimage. After the ten sleepy virgins are roused out of bed at dawn to await the bridegroom, they split into two groups. In one, we find the five foolish virgins, who leave their lamps behind to pursue Pleasure. On their search, they encounter five young men from the countryside, with whom they sing, dance, and play games. The foolish are abetted by an appropriately named character, Sense. Each of the young women, in fact, represents a particular corporeal sense, as her name indicates: Aquilina, the sense of sight; Aurilla, the sense of hearing; Odorosa, the sense of smell; Gustante, the sense of taste; and Tangifila, the sense of touch. In the second group are the wise virgins, each of whom also represents a particular sense but one attuned to spiritual, rather than physical, stimuli: Deifila (sight), Beatrice (hearing), Diletta (smell), Felice (taste), and Innocenza (touch). While waiting for the bridegroom, they resolve to search for the characters Charity and Prudence, whom they expect to find among the poor, the sick, the imprisoned, the orphaned, and the abandoned.

By having the two sets of women go their separate ways, rarely encountering one another dramatically (and never performing music together), Flori preserves the structural separation between the "sacred" main plot and the "profane" sub-plot so typical of the *commedia spirituale*.[90] Nevertheless, it is easy for him to draw parallels between his two dramatic threads. Both groups encounter persons in distress: a sick man, a family of hungry pilgrims, a robbery victim, and a poor widow. The foolish, enslaved to their physical senses, turn aside their requests for help, whereas the wise, more receptive to their spiritual senses, minister gladly to their needs. Act I, scene 5, for example, shows the meeting between the foolish virgins and the sick man (who is being drawn in a cart by another poor soul). Each one of the foolish virgins reacts by referring to the sense dearest to her:

> AURILLA: I hear someone nearby who is yelling for charity in a loud voice.
>
> POOR MAN: For the love of God, good women, help out this miserable, poor man, and for that, Our Lord will reward you a hundred times over in paradise.
>
> AQUILINA: [*indicating the sick man in the cart*] Look at this lovely sight. . . . Take him some place where no one can see him.
>
> POOR MAN: Please have pity on a poor man.
>
> AURILLA: You have already deafened us; by the sound of it, this one is a scoundrel who probably put himself in the cart to extract money from people with the art of deception . . .
>
> ODOROSA: What a fetid smell! What a stink! Go away, schemers! . . .
>
> POOR MAN: [*indicating the man in the cart*] Look at him, touch him, and you will see that I don't tell lies . . .
>
> TANGIFILA: Wretched one! You want me to touch him? Go away! . . .
>
> GUSTANTE: Let's get away from here, because his smell is making the food I enjoyed just a little while ago churn in my stomach.
>
> AURILLA: Let's leave him, and then he can yell all he wants.[91]

The wise virgins also see, hear, smell, touch, and taste, but with completely different results:

> SICK MAN: Oh, if you harbor pity, dear sisters, help me, a miserable, poor man . . .
>
>   . . .
>
> DEIFILA: What do you say, my sweet and dear sisters, you who are full of charity? I would like to be able to carry [the image of] this unlucky one on the pupils of my eyes. I feel my senses moved to pity.
>
> BEATRICE: Whoever hears of the miseries of this man would have a heart of ice and stone if she were not pierced by pity . . .

DILETTA: This will be the perfume with which we shall anoint the feet of the Redeemer . . .

FELICE: Whoever has pity on the miserable ones will gently taste and savor the sweetness of divine love . . .

INNOCENZA: Who could ever experience more delight than she who toils and strives only to please her Lord God and does that work with her own hands?[92]

In later encounters, the playwright need only refer to a few of the senses to communicate the different approaches each group of virgins adopts. He furthermore implies that because the foolish depend solely on their physical senses, those senses are dull, flat, and unable to penetrate beyond the surface. A charming scene in Act II—one of the few in which music serves as pure spectacle—shows the foolish virgins coming across a group of pilgrims singing for alms in Italian heavily larded with French:

Agiuté le povarete,
madame, de le Orete.
Deme a no pitit de pan
che patime de le fame
che le sciele, e l'empie sorte
scie minascene le morte.

Deh per le amor de Die,
abbaglie le carité.
Vi derem l'Ave Marié
se doné pitit de vin,
blanche o claret come
vè ple, vè ple madame,
che le Vergin delle Orete
e San Giacom de Galicie
Lor ve le remerité.

Ladies, help
the poor pilgrims of Loreto.
Give us a little bread
as we suffer from hunger,
and the heavens and wicked fate
menace us with death.

Oh, for love of God,
have pity.
We will say a Hail Mary for you
if you give us a bit of wine,
either white or red,
as it pleases you, my ladies.
The Virgin of Loreto
and Saint James of Galicia
will reward you for this.

The foolish recognize that the pilgrims are foreigners by their accents and become caught up in determining both their nationality and the lands to which their voyages have taken them. Once the foolish find out that the pilgrims are French, they forsake them—ostensibly for fear of contagion—without bothering to hear their story and without giving them even a morsel of food.[93] The wise meet up with the pilgrims shortly thereafter (they also hear them singing for alms). The wise, too, want to know their nationality and the places to which they have traveled, but Beatrice, unlike her foolish counterpart, insists that their full story be heard. The wise virgins invite the pilgrims to their own home to rest and eat.[94]

Flori's adaptation of the parable used in the ceremony calling the nuns to be consecrated thus becomes a vehicle for him to demonstrate how women should comport themselves if they indeed wish to be nuns. The two female groups of protagonists offer splendid examples of correct and incorrect behavior for those aspiring to life in the convent.

This theme is evident not only in the passages showing the different reactions of the two groups of virgins to the people they encounter but also in more subtle ways. Throughout the play, for example, characters identify other characters by their clothing, which was obviously a banner indicating social status and occupation. Just as the virgins recognize the pilgrims and the peasants by what they wear, the lay person would have been able to identify a nun by her habit. It therefore becomes a matter of grave concern to Prudence and Charity when the foolish virgins, having accepted an invitation by a group of peasants to an evening party (*veglia*) decide to abandon their usual garb and dress up as peasant women.[95] Charity rebukes them for their plan "to procure sad and unhappy omens under false clothes and disguises."[96] Later, when Charity actually sees them dressed alla villanella, she notes that they "have changed clothes and put on hats with feathers, showing that their brains are indeed similar to those of birds, who flutter about everywhere."[97]

Even more obvious is Flori's exploitation of walls as metaphors for the convent wall.[98] In Act IV, for example, the foolish virgins tell the wise that instead of seeking Prudence and Charity, they are going to a party "fuor de le porti"— that is, outside the walls, which are clearly meant to be understood as protection for the residents of the city.[99] The image and its meaning are unmistakable in Act V. There, a wall separates the foolish virgins from their wise sisters at the wedding banquet. When the foolish pound on the locked doors to gain entry, the bride of Christ, representing the Church, opens a window and poses a rhetorical question, "Where are your merits that you should be worthy to enter the blessed cloisters?"[100] The foolish, who have been amusing themselves for four acts, are, needless to say, not admitted.

By this point in the play, the moral is clear. The bodily senses, Flori tells his monastic audience, are hazardous liabilities for the unwary, because they can lead one to an unprofitable search for worldly pleasure. Such behavior was clearly to be avoided by women who wished to devote their lives to God. It is, furthermore, noteworthy that the musician Flori singles out the sense of hearing as an especially strong temptation for the foolish virgins. In this he was not alone. A late-sixteenth-century manuscript that probably belonged to an order of Sienese nuns and was intended as a guide to help a monastic woman examine her conscience before confession cautions that the nun who "delighted in or had a desire to hear or pleasure in hearing secular music and songs that stimulated vanity and love of the world" was in a state of sin.[101] Craig Monson has noted that in confessors' manuals of this time, the sense of hearing replaced the sense of sight as the "second most important provocation of lust" (the first was touch).[102] Flori apparently thought hearing at least on a par with touch, for in his play, he spends ample time demonstrating that of all the activities that could lead a woman astray, music ranked highest on the list. In Act I, for example, the foolish ask Sense where to find pleasure and delight. His response focuses in on one sense: Pleasure is found, he says, where one hears singing and dancing. Aurilla, the virgin guided by her ears, immediately suggests that the virgins accompany Sense to seek Pleasure.[103] Charity, lamenting the choice of the foolish virgins, describes worldly pleasures as "deceiving sirens, who entrap with the tenacious lime of song and with sweetness bestow a bitter death."[104] It is likewise significant that on the first encounter between the peasants and the foolish virgins in Act III, Sense describes all of his charges (not just Aurilla) as quick and agile as deer at singing, dancing, and playing instruments; that is, as lovers of music.[105] Such is the power of music that it can corrupt even those whose weaknesses lie elsewhere. In Act IV, for instance, it is Gustante who calls on the heroes of Greek myth to honor the arrival of Pleasure, saying:

> Let Orfeo come, and Amphion with his lyre
> (for whom the birds and the beasts
> used to come out of the forest);
> let them come sweetly playing and singing
> to honor Delight and Pleasure (so dear to all)
> with their tuneful accents.[106]

Aurilla and her companions are given a chance to defend their sensual appetites in Act II, and they do so aggressively with references to the Creation. Aurilla, for example, poses a rhetorical question: why did God put all the discordant and confused elements in tranquil concord to breathe life into fragile bodies with the capacity for hearing if he did not wish them to hear singing voices and the sound of sweet harmonies? She and her sisters—urged on by the character Sense—contend that their perceptive faculties are God-given and thus should not be neglected.[107] Flori clearly wanted to put forth such insidious arguments so that he could refute them, for in the next scene, Prudence sternly informs the virgins that God gave them their senses for their salvation and not their entertainment. She tells Aurilla that her sense of hearing was bestowed on her that she might listen to the doctrine of the Holy Scriptures and hear of the glorious, heavenly realm of the blessed; she furthermore warns her that by giving too much heed to her corporeal sense of hearing, she will close off the ears of her spirit to divine voices.[108]

In a similar manner, Flori allows his foolish virgins (and their audience) a chance to partake of certain sensual pleasures, such as music, during the course of the play so that he can rebuke them later by demonstrating the terrible consequences of such activities. Act III, scene 3 shows the initial encounter between the foolish virgins and the peasants. The peasants take the stage first, and in the dialect common to the Sienese countryside, they describe in detail the activities that must have been typical of the veglie of the day: eating and drinking, singing and dancing to the sound of instruments, and playing games.[109] The scene concludes with the most complex musical number of the comedy: as Sense sings a stanza of a canzonetta inviting all to the dance, the instrumentalists strike up a tune, and the peasants and virgins link hands and circle around the stage. Subsequent stanzas of the canzonetta, whose text is a paean to joy, delight, pleasure, and love (as experienced by the earthly senses) are performed solo by each virgin and each peasant in turn. All join voices for the concluding stanza, which stresses the sense of hearing:

> SENSE: Now sing, now dance
> with delight, zest, and joy;
> drive away all tedium and care
> and praise kind Pleasure.
> . . .
> AURILLA: Clear voices, make your sweet accents
> resound in our ears,
> for greater joy and contentment
> you could not bestow on us.
> . . .
> EVERYONE: Let us now sing with sweet accents
> about the great joy of Pleasure.
> Let all flee tedium and care;
> long live love and its contentments.[110]

Another important scene occurs in the next act, when Pleasure makes his first and only appearance. He arrives onstage playing his lyre and dancing with the foolish virgins, and then proceeds to sing two madrigals, of which this is the first:

> Whoever wishes to banish tedium, vexation, and care
> and drive away pain
> from her heart
> and fill it up with happiness and joy;
> whoever in this world desires
> to have joyful, lively Pleasure, let her come.
> She will experience such delight
> that all hardship, all pain
> will leave her breast,
> will vanish from her heart and fly away.[111]

Even Gustante must admit that his "sweet melodies are far better than those of the singing sirens who inhabit the woods."[112]

It is a dangerous strategy that Flori adopts and, in fact, it very nearly backfires on him, for the scenes just described are the liveliest and most delightful of the entire production, and the music was doubtless just as enchanting. He does not help his cause with the dull scenes he writes for Prudence, Charity, and the wise virgins. The audience cannot help but sympathize with Aurilla in Act IV when she cuts off a series of stern lectures by the wise sisters with a brusque "now let's finish up these long sermons, since you have dazed us."[113] Prudence and Charity are equally ineffective when they try to dissuade the foolish from disreputable activities. In Act IV, scene 8, for example, they attempt to convince the foolish to abandon worldly pleasures, provoking an impassioned debate. Both Aurilla and Gustante couch their arguments in musical metaphors: a world without pleasure would be like an organ without a windchest, a mistuned lyre, a clavichord with neither keyboard nor strings, a strident trumpet, an out-of-tune drum. Prudence and Charity can only respond defensively, informing the virgins that however lovely the sound of Pleasure is to them now, his departure will lead them to the realization that Pleasure itself is a strident trumpet, a mistuned funereal drum.[114]

It is not until Act V that Flori counters the impact of the musicodramatic scenes in which the foolish virgins participate. He finally unleashes his most powerful tool—music—by allowing his wise virgins to sing for the first time. Before doing so, however, he has each of the prudent young women praise her spiritual sense, thus absolving herself from singing for mere sensual pleasure. This much is apparent in the speech by Beatrice, who represents the spiritual sense of hearing. Addressing the still-absent Christ, she rhapsodizes:

> Concede, o sweet Lord,
> that your handmaiden's ears
> can hearken to and hear only
> sweet songs of praise sung to you,
> and those melodies
> of tuneful voices
> from alternating choirs
> of those winged birds in paradise,
> who stand before your divine presence;
> and concede that with them, I can sing
> that sweet new song of love
> saying "Holy, holy."[115]

When Christ and his bride the Church finally arrive, all the prudent virgins greet them with a series of spiritual madrigals in which music is set in its proper sphere; that is, the sphere Flori envisioned as proper for monastic women. Beatrice, for instance, sings the following:

> O you ardent seraphim, divine spirits,
> let us hear lovely songs and sweet singing
> from you, O blessed angels;
> and let us hear harmonies
> from musical instruments
> as you sing sweet laude in a loving way
> for us to the King of heaven and to his bride.[116]

Shortly afterward, the prudent virgins accompany the bridegroom and his bride into the wedding feast, performing a lauda:

> Glory, glory!
> Let us give laud and honor to the Lord
> who gave us that clear and sacred light

and let us fly quickly up to the heavens
and let us do according to the will
of our sweet love, God,
beloved spouse, who crowns souls
with green olive branches and triumphant palms.[117]

The lauda is heard once again in the penultimate scene of the play; the wise virgins perform it from inside the banquet hall as the foolish virgins wail outside the locked doors.[118]

BY THE END OF THE play, it is apparent that Flori has made deliberate choices about the genres of music performed by each of his characters. The message is clear: lay persons may sing madrigals and canzonettas and may dance the moresca, as the peasants do at the end of Act IV.[119] The monastic woman, however, should confine herself to music with texts praising God: spiritual madrigals such as those the prudent virgins sing to greet Christ, laude such as the one they perform when entering the banquet, and liturgical settings such as are implied in Beatrice's Act V speech, in which she imagines herself singing a Sanctus with choirs of angels. Furthermore, the playwright suggests that monastic women should be heard but not seen. It is significant that both the first and the last compositions to be performed in the play—the recitative inviting the sleepy virgins out of their beds and the lauda *Gloria, gloria!*—are sung from behind the scenes, which serve as the metaphorical walls of the convent. The entire play may, in fact, be read as a pilgrimage to the nunnery: it begins with an unseen voice calling out to those with a true vocation, continues by showing the good deeds in which the vocation becomes manifest, and ends with a wedding banquet symbolizing the ceremony in which a woman takes the veil as the bride of Christ. Indeed, before entering the banquet, the prudent virgins listen to a long speech in which the bride of Christ, that is, the Church, extols the sacraments, dwelling at length on the sacrament of marriage.[120] After the wise virgins follow the bridegroom and bride into the wedding feast, or the "blessed cloisters" as the bride later describes them, the doors are locked behind them and their incorporeal voices resound in song.

The occasion for which Flori's theatrical work was written, his reasons for framing such a pointed moral lesson about music, and the nuns' reactions to the comedy remain unknown. Perhaps the work was intended for presentation as part of the ceremonies associated with the investiture of new nuns at Ognissanti. It would have served as a potent reminder of the kind of behavior expected of the young women who had just taken the veil. Perhaps the play was performed at Carnival. The nuns would have been permitted, within the frame of the play, to engage in inappropriate behaviors, as such behaviors would have been sanctioned by the subversive season of the "world turned upside down."[121] Or perhaps Flori was simply following the tradition of exploiting the comic subplot to teach "through negative example the lessons of the play."[122] The foolish virgins' bad end would have been interpreted as a direct result of their frivolous activities, including their choice of music. Singing such music was thus justified for didactic purposes.

Sienese nuns apparently performed secular music on a regular basis, and not always within the context of a theatrical work, much to the displeasure of Alessandro Petrucci. One of the decrees he issued during his reign as archbishop forbade nuns to sing secular tunes of any kind, even if they had been stripped of their original words and supplied with sacred texts (see Doc. 3). Not surprisingly, the decree had little if any effect, and the practice not only continued but doubtless flourished during the reign of Ascanio II Piccolomini. According to Ugurgieri Azzolini, the nuns of Siena sang not only liturgical compositions but also "the most beautiful little arias" (see Doc. 1). Flori's play appears to offer evidence that despite the indulgent attitudes of prelates such as Ascanio II, some Sienese ecclesiastics remained steadfast in their belief that a woman who chose a monastic profession was to leave behind the secular tunes that could lead her astray. Flori himself hinted at the musical ideal for cloistered women in the dedication to this very commedia, in which he praised the convent for its "*holy*, happy and blessed concord, where such sweet and lovely harmony resounds *within* those sacred walls, as if angelic singers of paradise had descended amongst us"(emphasis mine).[123]

It is also possible, of course, to read Flori's play and dedication as subversive documents. The author, although a priest himself, may have enjoyed and approved of nuns singing secular music and may have understood that one way they could actually obtain permission to do so publically without fear of censure was within the framework of a theatrical piece that demonstrated the deleterious effects of such actions. Flori's ecclesiastical status, his long and distinguished career as a musician and chaplain at the Cathedral, and the seemingly obvious moral message of his theatrical piece probably guaranteed that the archbishop's vicar, who was charged with examining all plays slated for convent performance, would give the work his approval.

The women of Ognissanti have not, alas, left us their thoughts on the play. Some nuns may have read Flori's work literally and taken his admonitions to heart. I suspect, however, that whatever the author's intentions, many of the "angelic singers" secretly blessed him because his play offered them an unimpeachable format for incorporating secular music-making into their spiritual fun.

DIVAS IN THE CONVENT

The Role of Music in the vite
of Sienese Holy Women

Among the biographies given a separate entry in Ugurgieri Azzolini's compendium of the famous men and women of his native city is one devoted to an unnamed woman of uncommon devotion who lived at the turn of the fifteenth century. The author relates that this ardent young nun sought to better herself spiritually in any way possible, and so upon hearing of the holy life led by the friars at the Osservanza, she dressed herself as a man and fled from her convent to the monastery. After living there in an exquisitely pious manner for some time after making her profession, her gender finally came to light, and she was taken back to live in a cloistered community of nuns. This "rare and incredible example" of saintly life, according to Ugurgieri Azzolini, should come as no surprise to one who has read the biograhies of S. Eugenia, S. Eufrasia, S. Marina, and S. Eufrosina, who also lived disguised as men in monastic communities (Doc. 17).

Ugurgieri Azzolini offers convincing proof that accounts of a holy woman's life (called a *vita* in Italy) held great fascination for an early modern audience. The medieval tradition of compiling such vite thrived into the sixteenth and seventeenth centuries; prints and manuscripts preserve hundreds of narratives by women who recounted their experiences, ranging from the mundane (the events of their lives leading up to their entrance in the convent) to the extraordinary (their visionary episodes).[1] Usually a male spiritual advisor, often the woman's confessor, was responsible for asking her to provide such information, and his reasons for making such a request varied. When ecclesiastical authorities were suspicious of a holy woman's mystical visions, they asked to have a written account to assure that she did not perpetuate heresy and that she was not under demonic influence. A nun's life could also serve as an example of virtue to others. Some confessors doubtless offered such accounts to the world in order to savor the reflected glory of a woman in their spiritual care; others were probably inspired by civic pride. Certain narratives were left in manuscript for limited, possibly in-convent, consumption; others were published for a wider audience, perhaps to prepare the path for future beatification or canonization. Many of the stories took the form of biographies, presenting the reader with the dilemma of "disentangling" the woman's voice from that of her spiritual advisor.[2] One can also find nuns' autobiographies, but even in these works, readers must be attuned to the devices women exploited in order to protect themselves from accusations of vainglory.[3] Notwithstanding the problems posed by the genre, these vite are of enormous value in understanding the spiritual practices of cloistered women and the behavior that both they and their admirers perceived to be "saintly." The narratives can also shed light on some of the details of day-to-day activities in the convent and the nuns' relationship with the outside world.

In the course of the seventeenth century, a number of Sienese holy women were the subjects of biographies by male ecclesiastics. Most of these works are typical of the genre, linking the nuns not only to their contemporaries in other European cities and New Spain but also to a long line of sante and beate stretching back to the Middle Ages. Biographies of three nuns whose lives span the years from circa 1560 to circa 1650 will lay the groundwork for approaching the literature on two other Sienese holy women in whose spiritual lives music played an important role. One of the latter vite is of special interest as it appears to be unique in emphasizing the connection between a nun's spiritually favored status and her ability as a performer.

THE BIOGRAPHY OF PASSITEA CROGI may be found in at least nine seventeenth- and eighteenth-century manuscripts preserved in the Biblioteca Comunale, Siena. All were apparently copied from an account written by Padre Ventura Venturi sometime before 1628.[4] A printed version of Crogi's life was published by Lodovico Marracci in 1669; he, too, based his account on Venturi's biography.[5]

Venturi relates that Crogi was conceived on the feast of S. Lucy and that her holiness was apparent in the womb, for she did not allow her mother to drink wine or eat meat. She was born on 13 September 1564, the vigil of the Exaltation of the Holy Cross, and fasted even as a baby, abstaining from drinking milk on certain days of the week. When she was gravely ill as a child, the Virgin Mary, in the guise of an unknown woman, came to the house and cured her.

Crogi received her education in an extraordinary manner: angels taught her the Ave Maria, the Pater Noster, the Credo, the Salve Regina, and other prayers, and S. Catherine, in the company of two angels, instructed her in reading and writing (the angels brought the necessary pens and paper).[6] Having once acquired these skills, Passitea pored over the lives of the saints, and this led her to one overzealous act. After reading about S. Marina, who hid her gender and lived disguised as a man in a community of monks, Passitea decided to cut off her own breasts.[7] She succeeded in severing her right breast before fainting from pain. At that point, the Virgin Mary once again intervened in her life, restoring her breast and teaching Passitea to use prudence and discretion in her spiritual life.

Beginning at an early age, Crogi frequented the Mass and the Divine Office, even at night. She started disciplining herself at age seven in imitation of Christ's

Passion. She rarely slept on her tiny, uncomfortable bed and neither ate meat nor drank wine. In fact, she fasted more often than not, and when she did consent to eat, she consumed only bread and water. But her sanctity was not merely a function of her ascetic life and diet; she also performed good deeds in the community. She gave food away to the poor, was charitable toward prisoners, and visited the sick, sucking pus from infected wounds of the afflicted. Illegitimate children were of special concern to her: divine inspiration would lead her to the houses of desperate women giving birth out of wedlock. After Crogi convinced the mother to give her the newborn, milk would miraculously flow from her restored breast, allowing her to feed the child. When the baby was healthy, she consigned it to Hospital of S. Maria della Scala.

After the death of her parents, Crogi gathered a number of young women together and sought permission from Archbishop Ascanio I Piccolomini for her congregation to take solemn vows and to live as a cloistered community. Although Piccolomini reluctantly rejected the proposal—he thought that too many poor orders without proper financial support already existed in the city—his successor, Francesco Maria Tarugi, finally granted Crogi's wish. Through Tarugi's ministrations, the congregation found a home at the church of S. Egidio in 1598.[8] When the building projects finished in 1603, the nuns vowed perpetual clausura and the strict observance of the rule of S. Clare; the convent was one of the poorest and most austere in all Siena.[9] According to Venturi, the order was so strict that even the animals were devout. He recounts that Passitea had a chicken that she trained to go to the oratory when the bells sounded and to convene in the chapter when public confession of faults was held. The chicken, following the example of those who lay flat on the ground, face down, would also distend herself on the ground, wings spread, and cluck out her sins.[10]

The vita treats other aspects of Crogi's public career, including her 1597 sojourn in Florence, when she became especially close to Marie de' Medici. It was at the insistence of Marie de' Medici that Crogi traveled to France in 1602 and again in 1609, although the author is silent upon her role as counselor to the queen.[11] Details of Crogi's spirituality are, however, rendered in full: she was both tormented at the hands of demons and blessed with ecstatic visions in which she received the stigmata and participated in a mystic marriage with Jesus Christ. By the time of her death on 13 May 1615, Crogi had established a reputation as a woman of great humility, a prophetess, and a miraculous healer.[12]

Crogi's position as founder of a convent made her an apt candidate for a biography. Her life could serve as a source of pride to her sisters in Christ (not to mention the community at large). Her ability to practice her faith in the public arena (at least for a time) was not, however, an option for most women in Counter-Reformation Italy, who were confined to the nunnery.[13] That such cloistered women were nevertheless considered worthy of biographical attention is evident from an account published in 1712, in which Padre Giuseppe Scapecchi narrates the life of Suor Chiara Birelli.[14]

Birelli was born on 22 February 1565 in Assisi, her parents' city of origin. When her father died, however, her mother went to live with her brother in Siena and raised her two infant children there. Birelli's vocation showed itself early in her life: so impatient was she to partake of the Eucharist that her confessor agreed to allow her to receive first communion at a very young age. She also resisted her mother's attempts to prepare her for the secular world; instead of wearing sumptuous dresses, she chose to clothe herself in the black habit of S. Catherine as a devotional practice.

As a girl, Birelli fell ill. One night in a dream the Virgin Mary told her to have patience and to adapt herself to her condition, as she would always be unwell. Indeed, she never recovered her health and needed a wheelchair in order to move about. When her mother died, she found herself a poor orphan, but another heavenly voice told her that she would be granted a place among the "Abbandonate" at Il Refugio, the institution established in the 1580s by Domenico Billò to care for orphaned and abandoned girls. The convent usually did not accept young women with incurable illnesses, but Birelli appealed directly to Aurelio Chigi, who had taken over the directorship of the house in 1593; she so impressed him that he admitted her in 1598. In 1608, Aurelio Chigi, his mother Olimpia Chigi, and his sister-in-law (also named Olimpia) all contributed so that Birelli might have a dowry and a habit, and she was vested.

Despite her many physical ailments, Birelli participated in the Divine Office and spent much time contemplating the Passion. Furthermore, she did not spare herself from severe penitential practices. On the day of her profession, for example, Birelli prayed for an invisible crown of thorns, which tormented her for the rest of her life. She also flagellated herself, wore a chain of iron next to her skin, and fasted regularly. Her devotion to the Eucharist was such that she would go into ecstasy when she received communion. She was blessed with the gift of prophecy, and her prayers were reputed to heal the sick. The high esteem in which she was held extended beyond the city of Siena. Federigo Borromeo, archbishop of Milan, came to visit her in 1621. After her death on 11 July 1622, her internal organs were dried into a powder, which was responsible for cures. Even the sheet in which she slept cured illness, and her wheelchair helped a Sienese noblewoman give birth without pain. In 1670, her body was exhumed in order to be reburied inside the new cloister of the Abbandonate: her body was intact, and her heart, conserved separately in a little reliquary of decorated copper, gave off a sweet fragrance.

Suor Colomba Tofanini, a nun in the convent of S. Girolamo in Campansi, was another woman of humble social origins and cloistered life. No author is named on her vita, preserved in a seventeenth-century manuscript; perhaps it was written at Campansi by one of her sister nuns.[15] Although the work is a paean to the humility and holy life of Suor Colomba, it may have also been intended to serve the needs of an important Sienese family that placed many of its female members at Campansi. Indeed, the author makes the point of naming two of Colomba's companions at the convent—Suor Maria Agnese and Suor Maria Pulcheria—and noting that they were, respectively, the sister and niece of "Cardinal Chigi," that is, Fabio Chigi, who ascended to the papacy in 1655 as Alexander VII.[16] Tofanini's cult was doubtless promoted by the Chigi, who could interpret her prophetic statements as a "sacral legitimization" of the family's power in Siena and Rome.[17]

From the biography, the reader learns that Suor Colomba was born in 1583 and baptized Verginia. Even as a girl she wore a hair shirt and sometimes bound her sides with thorns until she was forbidden to do so by her confessor. She was anxious to receive her first communion and at age nine, when she first tasted the host, she went into ecstasy. The Eucharist was central to her devotional practices for the rest of her life. She did not eat on the days she received communion and reported that she tasted savory meat in the host.[18]

On Passion Sunday in 1608, Verginia entered the convent of Campansi (at that time an open monastery). A little over a year later, on 12 April 1609, she was vested as a conversa and took the name Suor Colomba. Some eight years later, in 1617, after contradicting one of her sister nuns, she asked God to deprive her of speech so that she "would never offend Him in any way with her tongue"; her wish was granted.[19] A doctor called in to examine her confirmed that Suor Colomba's muteness was sent by God and refused to intervene with a cure.[20] In addition to suffering her speech infirmity, she disciplined herself twice a day until blood ran and wore a belt of iron with sharp points next to her skin. She also ate very small portions of food and vomited what little she was ordered to eat when ill. Her special talent, developed as a child, was curing illness. In order to conceal the fact that her ability to heal came from God, she would sometimes rub the afflicted person with oil from the lamp that burned before the Sacred Sacrament in the convent church. At other times, she used to lick the wounds of the sick. She was also endowed with an ability to see into the future: she predicted the papacy of Fabio Chigi a number of times, the last just before her death on 7 March 1655.[21]

IF MANY OF THE WAYS these Sienese nuns comport themselves seem remarkably similar, it is because they follow patterns well established by earlier generations of holy women.[22] Catherine Walker Bynum has offered compelling evidence, for example, of the importance of food in late medieval women's piety.[23] As a preparation for the union with Christ in communion, many medieval holy women engaged in extreme forms of fasting. The renunciation of earthly food was coupled not only with a strong devotion to and desire for the Eucharist but also with such practices as sucking pus from festering wounds (or, as in Suor Colomba's case, licking the injuries of the afflicted). Similarly, because these women perceived the bleeding body of Christ on the cross as food, they often imitated his example by distributing food to the needy. Food symbolism—women as providers of food—figures in the legends of miraculous lactation or in stories of women's bodies exuding oil or sweet substances.[24] The somatic spirituality of many medieval women is also reflected in their desire to imitate Christ's Passion by involuntary or voluntary suffering, including the serene acceptance of sickness on one hand and bloody self-flagellation on the other.[25]

Sienese nuns had to look no further than the life of their own S. Catherine for a model of behavior.[26] Indeed, both Crogi and Tofanini considered Catherine of Siena their special advocate.[27] Echoes of Catherine's life—the practice of sucking pus from the wounds of the sick, the ability to provide food for others in a miraculous manner, the stigmata, the mystic marriage with Christ, and especially the active life of public service—emerge most forcefully in Crogi's biography, but important motifs of medieval female piety are unmistakable, for example, in the emphasis on voluntary bodily torment in Tofanini's biography, on the patient suffering of illness in Birelli's vita, and on both women's ascetic diet, devotion to the Eucharist, and ability to effect miraculous cures.

Like their medieval counterparts, the sixteenth- and seventeenth-century holy women were renowned in their day, and their fame spread far beyond the convent walls. In the 1650s, for instance, when Appollonia Generali, a poor girl from Castelmuzio, told her brutal father that she wanted to become a nun, he mocked her earnest wish by saying, "Do you really think that the era of Suor Colomba of Campansi will return? Do you think that you are some kind of saint and that they will accept you for the love of God, and without a dowry?"[28] Clearly, Suor Colomba's story, though not published, had reached into the Sienese countryside and was well known even to those who had little use for religion. Despite her father's objections, Generali did become a conversa at the convent of S. Caterina del Paradiso, taking the name Suor Rosa Maria. The events of her life, narrated in a vita by one of her sister nuns and published by Padre Ambrogio Spannocchi, leave no doubt that she modeled her actions on those of Suor Colomba and other nuns like her.[29] Although the Counter-Reformation Church was increasingly uneasy about mystic manifestations in holy women—especially their abilitites to prophesy and heal—the Sienese of the period apparently had no misgivings.[30] These biographies usually provide names of those who were cured or who heard the predictions of future events; often these witnesses were from important and powerful families.[31] It is with a respectful tone that Leonardo Marsili of Siena describes the following incident in a 1669 letter to Cardinal Flavio Chigi in Rome:

> At Castelvecchio, we lost that good nun named Suor Maria Caterina Stefanoni, considered to be one of God's great servants. The day her body lay in state in the church, an enormous number of people turned out, and they tell of a miracle (although I'm not sure if it's true or not). Signora Alessandra Gori had someone touch the face of the deceased with one of her rings. She then went to a gravely ill person (I don't know who) and placed this ring on his body, and they say that the sick man derived notable relief from this.[32]

Marsili's reservations about the miracle seem to have less to do with the nun's ability to effect cures than with the third- or fourthhand nature of the story. In his letter, we catch both the spontaneous, fervid devotion these "living saints" inspired and the universal respect accorded them in early modern Siena.

THE TWO SIENESE NUNS who now claim our attention, Caterina Vannini and Maria Francesca Piccolomini, were both musicians and renowned as such. Accounts of their lives, therefore, refer not only to the kinds of behaviors just described but also to their musical skills. This is not as uncommon as it might seem from the foregoing Sienese examples, in which music appears only as an accompaniment to mystic visions.[33] Biographies of nuns from seventeenth-century Bologna, for example, occasionally offer anecdotes about musical activities.[34] A passage from the vita of Suor Angela Gozzadini relates that she hated learning to play an instrument; she told her confessor that the two great faults of her youth consisted of wasting her teacher's time and squandering her parents' money in pursuit of musical competence. Her solution was to run pins through her fingers so that she was unable to play.[35] That Gozzadini lacked both enthusiasm and ability is clear in the passage, and the point is less about music than about her great humility and self-deprecation in readily confessing her youthful transgressions. On the other hand, the author of the book on the virtues of the nuns at S. Maria Nuova does not hesitate to draw conclusions about the possible danger of music in the cloister. Suor Maria Vittoria Della Bordella is offered as an example. She was an excellent musician, and although no great scandal ever arose because of her talent, she did fall into the trap of vanity, "adopting now and then for her amusement the practice of music." Once she saw the error of her ways, she forsook music forever, "humbly applying herself to prayer alone."[36] The benefits that musical training could offer are briefly explored by the author of the biography of Giulia Albergati (later Suor Laura Caterina Maria). As a young girl, Giulia learned to play the harpsichord and sing so well that when a mendicant Observant friar used to come to her house asking for alms, he would go into ecstasy upon hearing her. The author is careful to note, however, that Giulia never sang secular songs and turned to music only as a spur to her faith; the ecstasy the friar experienced was induced not only by the "harmony" but also by the "piety" of the spiritual song Giulia performed.[37]

The ambivalent or negative attitudes toward music in these vite may reflect the tendency of the ecclesiastical hierarchy in Bologna to try to restrict performance by nuns there.[38] Positive references to the role music could play in the lives of nuns are much more widespread in writings from Milan, especially during the tenure of Archbishop Federigo Borromeo (reg. 1595–1631). Robert Kendrick documents Borromeo's fervent support of the musical activities of nuns in his pastoral care and links the flowering of polyphony in Milan (especially at convents) with "the prelate's adherence to one strain of Christian optimism, that which saw creation as a manifestation of divine goodness."[39] The harmony of music thus reflected that of creation, and the special status of nuns (as inhabitants of an "earthly Jerusalem") made them the best candidates to convey the angelic harmonies of paradise and to move the listener to devotion. Borromeo actually insisted on musical literacy for novices and encouraged music-making by the nuns in his diocese, as long as it did not give way to ostentatious displays. He went so far as to send a lute and music to Suor Confaloniera at S. Caterina in Brera and reacted with delight at her descriptions of music-making that were intended to encourage piety among her sisters in the convent.[40] It is to this prelate that we owe the biography of the Sienese nun Caterina Vannini.[41]

Vannini was one of the most interesting women in early modern Siena, and Borromeo maintained a close relationship with her: they exchanged gifts and letters in the last two years of her life.[42] Borromeo published Vannini's biography in 1618, more than a decade after her death, and it is not difficult to understand the fascination that this woman's life held for him. Borromeo's model for nuns was Mary Magdalen, and Vannini, a reformed prostitute, was for all practical purposes that model incarnate.

From Borromeo's account, we learn that Vannini was born in Siena in 1562 to a family that fell on hard times: Vannini's father died when she was young, and her mother had to work to support the family.[43] By age eleven, young Catherine was dressing in sumptuous clothes and accepting gifts given under the pretext of Christian compassion. "Bad counsel" led her into sensual pleasures and sin. Promises of greater delights, pleasures, and honors enticed her to go to Rome. During her sojourn in Rome, however, God began to awaken good thoughts in Vannini's soul. She noticed that an image of the Magdalen she kept in her house seemed to glow with a singular light, and she took the saint for her special advocate. In a moment of desperation, when she tried to commit suicide by throwing herself down a well, an unknown force pushed her back from the edge. Nevertheless, she continued to live a life of sin and created such a sensation that in 1574, Pope Gregory XIII imprisoned her. Offered the choice of marriage or forced entry into a convent, Vannini rebelled, saying that she did not desire marriage and if she were to repent, it would be in her native city. The pope banished her from Rome, and she arrived home in very poor health.

Although she confessed and received communion upon her return to Siena, she lapsed into her sinful ways soon after regaining strength. During Advent of 1575, however, she heard a sermon about the Magdalen, and by Christmas her transformation was complete.[44] At that point, the thirteen-year-old girl gave away all her rich clothes, cut her hair, went barefoot, and dressed in sackcloth. In the years that followed, she ate and drank only small amounts of bread and water, flagellated herself often, prayed for and was granted crippling deformities, refused to sleep lying down, and was favored with visions. Word spread throughout Siena of her sanctity, and she obtained the habit of the Dominican tertiaries. Despite this, Vannini's request to join the Convertite was initially refused. Only in 1584, after three years of waiting, did she gain entrance to the convent. She spent the rest of her life there, and for four years was enclosed in a tiny cell with only a small window opening on the church. She was renowned for her humility, for her ability to see into the minds and souls of others and to effect miraculous cures, and for the extreme asceticism of her life. When she died in July 1606, her body gave off a lovely aroma, and sparks of fire were seen to fly from her heart.

In the third and final portion of the biography, Borromeo lists (and illustrates) Vannini's virtues; as part of this discussion, he recounts the events of a typical day in Vannini's life.[45] Before midnight, she began self-flagellation, which she continued for about an hour, sometimes going into ecstasy. Afterward, she meditated on the Passion of Christ or on his life. At dawn, she examined her conscience. In the morning she heard Mass, recited the Divine Office, and took communion; she often went into ecstasy until about midday. The afternoon hours she devoted to reading her psalter. She ate a little bread at Vespers; from Vespers to Compline, she received visitors. At Compline she returned to her prayers, and at the hour of the Ave Maria, she went into ecstasy.

The somatic quality of Vannini's spirituality—her prayers for bodily deformities, her self-flagellation, her ascetic diet, her refusal to sleep lying down—
conformed to long traditions of female piety. To be sure, the suffering she imposed
on her body was meant, in part, to serve as atonement for her former life of sin,
but it was also a means of union with Christ. Borromeo notes specifically that
Vannini spent part of each day contemplating the Passion of Christ; it is noteworthy that both self-flagellation (partaking of Christ's suffering) and communion
(receiving Christ's body in the form of a host) prompted ecstatic episodes.

Interestingly enough, however, nowhere in this "official" biography does
Borromeo allude to the fact that Vannini was a musician. Neither does Vannini
mention her musical abilities in the letters that survive from her correspondence
with Borromeo, although music figures prominently in some of the descriptions
of her visions.[46] For example, when she was at Mass she seemed to see "the
church in great resplendence and to hear an angelic melody that redoubled when
the priest pronounced the words *Sanctus, Sanctus, Sanctus Dominus Deus Sabaoth*
because the same words were repeated by the angels with such a beautiful melody
that her soul was almost on the point of leaving her body."[47] Another time when
Vannini was sick and her physician ordered her to lie down in her bed, she heard
"the sweetest concerto of musical instruments, accompanied by a most beautiful
harmony of angelic voices that for hours sang the laude of Saint George and of
Saint Francis of Paula, whose feast the Church was celebrating that very day."[48]

It is certain that Vannini's musical talents were well known to Borromeo and
to his Sienese contacts. In a letter written shortly after Vannini's death, her confessor, Padre Capacci, informed Borromeo that the nun played many musical
instruments and that when she played the lute, she went into ecstasy.[49] Borromeo
must have also had more specific information either from Vannini or from those
close to her, for he describes one of her frequent raptures in a sermon delivered
to nuns at an unnamed monastery, probably during the 1620s:[50]

> I will give you two more examples of sainted souls who delighted in praising
> God through singing. . . . [T]he other was Catherine from Siena, who played and
> sang very well and sometimes took up her instrument, which was the lute, and
> played it. She put a straw hat on her head that covered her eyes and did this in
> order not to be seen, because having sung and played awhile, she went into
> ecstasy, and notwithstanding that fact, she persevered in playing. Afterward, she
> found herself in great pain because of the hardship of having to move her hands
> while her body was abandoned by her senses. When she came out of ecstasy, she
> sometimes sang so much better than usual, and all who heard her marveled as
> at something never before heard, and she used to say, "Don't be so astonished,
> for I learned this manner of singing in heaven. There, the saints sing in such a
> manner and continuously praise God. It is in imitation of such saints that our
> songs should be composed, and not out of vanity, from which may God preserve
> you."[51]

In another passage, from his book on female mysticism (*De ecstaticis mulieribus
et illusis*, published in 1616),[52] Borromeo does not name Vannini, but the description is so similar to the one just quoted above that he doubtless was thinking of
her:

An ecstatic woman of holy life, who later died in the aura of great sanctity, was sometimes constrained by the pleas of her companions . . . to offer a sign and an example of what the harmony of paradise might be. Because she was most humble and did not think that she was more favored than her companions, she used to at first put up some resistance, but then she would do as they desired with good will and a happy soul. And thus, in their presence alone, she used to take into her hands a lute, which she had learned to play when she was very young, and touching the strings, she used to play a song that was both most delicate and most far removed from the melody and the form of songs that we hear on earth: it has been certified by the worthiest people of faith that here on earth such a manner of singing and such successions of harmonies had never before been heard. Now, this woman continued to sing and play for only a little while before she was enraptured, and although she ceased to sing, she continued to play, never once erring in her choice of harmonies. When some time had passed, she came out of her ecstasy and blushed because she had lost touch with the world of normal sensations in the presence of her companions; and her right arm and hand, with which she plucked the strings [of the lute] hurt her somewhat.[53]

Several particulars in these essentially similar descriptions invite comment. A striking detail in the first is Vannini's use of a theatrical prop—a hat shielding her eyes—ostensibly to prevent others from seeing her during her musical ecstasies. This is reminiscent of a similar action by Vannini's contemporary, the Florentine nun and mystic Maria Maddalena de' Pazzi, who used to paint and embroider in rapture, her eyes sheathed by a blindfold.[54] In each case, the use of a device to cover the eyes seems designed to call attention to the miraculous nature of the event: the body's loss of normal sensation and, in fact, the utter lack of need for the bodily senses while in ecstasy. Both passages just quoted make a point of stressing that it was difficult for Vannini to play in her altered state. Once she returned to her senses, she complained of pain in the hand and arm she had continued to move while enraptured.

Also of note is the kind of music Vannini played while in ecstasy. Robert Kendrick has speculated that she was improvising, and this seems logical in light of the characterization of the resulting sounds as unusual (successions of never-before-heard harmonies).[55] Despite the singular nature of the harmonies, Vannini's touch on the lute is characterized as "unerring," implying that her listeners perceived the music not as bizarre but rather as unworldly, the product of divine inspiration. Because this celestial music emerged only during ecstatic episodes, Vannini was, in essence, allowing celestial forces to play her like an instrument; she was "heard to give honor musically through the inspiration of the Word."[56] Postrapture, the nun was gifted with enhanced vocal abilities, but she was quick to impute all the glory to angelic choirs, from whom she had learned both the songs and style of singing.

Borromeo does not refer to any other kinds of performances by Vannini, and it is unlikely that she engaged in any public musical enterprise. Playing at liturgical services, for example, might have attracted civic audiences to the convent and thus brought on accusations of vanity. As an ex-prostitute at an open convent, Vannini had to tread carefully and find the most appropriate forum for making music, an activity that was clearly important to her. The skeptic might infer that Vannini's musical ecstasies (or reports of those ecstasies) were carefully crafted to conform to Borromeo's expectations. They were unostentatious—restricted to private situations in front of a circle of close companions—and Vannini was modest, assigning all the credit for the heavenly sounds to God. Her performances served to increase religious ardor among her sister nuns by giving them a foretaste of heaven's celestial harmonies. By choosing the role of ecstatic, Vannini was able to become a "focal point of spectacle, commanding an audience of listeners" for her lute-playing.[57]

It was during Vannini's tenure at the Convertite that Ascanio I Piccolomini ordered the women there to give up their lutes and citterns.[58] I noted earlier that the action was politically motivated—punishment for a convent that refused to accept enclosure—but the stories about Vannini suggest that the prelate might have also objected to an ex-prostitute using a lute, the same instrument with which she had entertained paying male customers in her former life, to garner another kind of patronage as a nun.[59] The archbishop died only a few months after promulgating the decrees, and Borromeo's accounts give us every reason to suspect that the ban on lutes and citterns was never enforced at the Convertite. In fact, by the mid–seventeenth century, the practice of playing plucked string instruments, especially lute and theorbo, was well established at a number of the most eminent houses in Siena, including S. Marta, S. Petronilla, and Ognissanti. And it was Ognissanti that housed the only other musical nun in seventeenth-century Siena for whom a vita survives: the theorbist Suor Maria Francesca Piccolomini.

Although Piccolomini, like Vannini, was celebrated as an instrumentalist, the circumstances of her life set her in sharp contrast to the *convertita*. Piccolomini, was born long after Vannini died; she was the child of financially well-off parents from the ruling elite; and she was a virginal young girl when she entered the prominent Olivetan house of Ognissanti. Perhaps most important, Piccolomini was given the chance to write her story in her own words.[60] Like many of her religious contemporaries, Piccolomini penned her spiritual autobiography at the request of her confessor, a certain Padre Sebastiano Conti. Unlike many of her sisters in Europe and New Spain during the same period, however, Piccolomini did not provide a meticulously detailed chronology of her life and visions; instead she related the miraculous cures granted her by the Virgin Mary so that she could play her theorbo on important occasions. The account, along with the biography by Conti that prefaces it, is one of the three or four extraordinary documents that survive to illuminate the musical tradition at Ognissanti.[61] It is also a monument to Piccolomini, who, I will argue, by displaying the much-praised monastic virtues of humility and obedience, was able to manipulate family, monastic, and civic pride to gain fame for her convent and, not incidentally, for herself as a musician.

PICCOLOMINI WAS THE PENULTIMATE child of Alessandro di Francesco Piccolomini and Laura Golia; she was baptized Porzia on 18 October 1631.[62] The oldest of her three sisters, Caterina (baptized on 14 September 1620), entered the Olivetan convent of Ognissanti in January 1636 as Suor Caterina and died there forty-eight years later.[63] From passages in Conti's biography, we also know that at least one of Porzia's other sisters (either Fulvia, baptized 14 March 1630, or Cinzia, baptized 31 May 1633) survived to adulthood.[64] Porzia also had two brothers, Francesco (baptized 5 February 1624) and Niccolò (baptized 22 November 1628), both of whom survived her.[65]

Porzia followed in her sister Caterina's footsteps and was clothed at Ognissanti on 27 November 1645, taking the name Maria Francesca.[66] Both girls were supernumeraries, and therefore their parents had to obtain special permission from Rome and to supply a double dowry before their daughters could enter the convent as novices. Family ties doubtless prompted the parents to go to the extra trouble and expense to send their girls to Ognissanti. Of the forty-seven coriste who signed a legal contract in August 1642, no fewer than six carried the name Piccolomini. Maria Francesca and Caterina thus added their numbers to the already-strong clan there.[67] The sheer number of Piccolomini women at Ognissanti might have also meant that the convent enjoyed a special status in the city during much of the seventeenth century when Ascanio II Piccolomini reigned as archbishop. Ascanio II probably played a role in promoting the cult that grew around Maria Francesca. The nun gained renown by virtue of her musical skills and her special relationship with the Virgin Mary, who manifested her will through a statue at Ognissanti known as the *Madonna del Presepio*, or the "Madonna of the Manger."

Although the Madonna of the Manger plays the largest role in Maria Francesca Piccolomini's autobiography, the young nun begins her story by relating another miracle (attributed to a different statue) that took place before she entered the convent. Beginning when she was seven years old, she tells us, she was prone to extreme dizzy spells that caused her to fall to the ground and frightened her caregivers (Piccolomini was left at a country estate in Radi di Creta with the man and woman who looked after the land there).[68] When her mother heard of this calamity, she prayed for guidance to a local image of the Madonna (the Virgin of Barontori in Campriano), and her daughter was freed from the debilitating attacks.[69] Piccolomini, grateful for the favor shown her, wore a dress patterned like that of the Madonna for over a year after the miraculous cure (28r–v).

Piccolomini then proceeds to relate the circumstances of the first miracle attributed to Ognissanti's miraculous image of the Madonna. She makes it clear that this incident took place shortly after her admission to the convent at age fourteen:

> I applied myself to the study of the theorbo in order to learn to accompany the devout songs of my most religious mothers and dearest sisters in Christ. But soon, all my nails, which had become as tender and fragile as straw, broke when I touched the strings and separated from the flesh on my fingers, so that I could not continue with my lessons. All sorts of remedies were tried, but none were of any use. Thus, I turned to the most efficacious help of our most sacred image of the Madonna of the Manger. I took a hair from her most sacred head and a bit of cotton that was used to wrap the image, and I put this between my nails and the fleshy part of my finger, and the skin and nails grew back together so that I could and can at my pleasure play my theorbo to praise the most glorious

Virgin Mary, who granted this most vile creature such stupendous miracles (28v, 15r).

Piccolomini's reputation as a nun to whom special favors were apt to be granted was, however, based on an incident that occurred after this first miracle and thus is given the most play in her autobiography. Piccolomini relates that in 1650, five years after entering the convent, she fell ill with an unspecified incurable disease. For three years she languished, ridden with fever, barely able to eat or drink, reduced to a skeleton. The malady also affected her left hand, which developed a large, pus-producing wound. By April 1653, her surgeon, Ser Galeazzo, despaired of her life and suggested that she commend her soul to God and the Virgin Mary. Piccolomini told Galeazzo that she had prayed to the Madonna of Castelvecchio, the relic that had been taken through Siena for the traditional Low Sunday procession. The doctor interrupted her to ask why she was praying to that Madonna when Ognissanti possessed its own miraculous image of the Virgin—the Madonna of the Manger. After Galeazzo left, the nun fell into a deep midday sleep in which the convent's Madonna appeared to her and told her that she would free her from all her ills. Upon awakening from this dream, infused with hope, Piccolomini repeatedly requested and finally received one of the rings from the fingers of the sacred image. That evening, after her servant had dressed the wound, the nun placed the ring on the end of the finger of her swollen hand and fell asleep. The next morning, the bandages were gone, the hand was healed, and the ring had descended to its proper place at the base of her finger. News of the miraculous cure spread quickly through the convent; the nuns sang a Te Deum in thanksgiving after having crowded into Piccolomini's room to see the invalid and to kiss her hand. One of the sisters suggested that Piccolomini place the ring on her still swollen, feverish body. When she did so, she was immediately healed. The convent's regular doctor was stupefied by Piccolomini's recovery, but told the nuns not to speak of it until the surgeon, Ser Galeazzo, had confirmed that the skin covering the wound was indeed healthy. Galeazzo arrived the next day, and upon examining the hand, he declared that the nuns should make the miracle known to the entire city. After his visit, the nuns once again sang the Te Deum as well as litanies, this time in polyphony, while Piccolomini knelt in glory among them without the least discomfort of body, though greatly disturbed by her unworthiness at receiving such a great favor (15r–21r).

The next miracle must have take place sometime after 1653. Piccolomini, who had had problems with her knee since childhood, complained to her biological sister Caterina about her pain; her sister advised her to seek the help of the miraculous Madonna and her holy ring. Piccolomini went to the image and took the ring, but instead of placing it on her knee, she placed it on her chest in order to strengthen her weak voice, so that she might recite the Divine Office better. When her sister asked her how her knee felt, Piccolomini replied, "It's worse than ever," but realizing the error of robbing the Virgin of glory for her miracles, she placed the ring on her aching knee and the pain ceased (21r–v).

Yet another cure was granted immediately after the ceremony in which Piccolomini was consecrated as a nun. She had prayed for a debilitating illness so that she might atone for her sins and was rewarded by a ferocious headache as soon as she stepped into the cloister after the ceremony. Doctors tried several medications, but to no avail. After a few days, when she could stand the pain no longer, she put a bit of cotton from the sacred image in her ear and was healed. At first, she pretended that the medications had proved efficacious, but then seeing the sinfulness of lies, she confessed to her sisters in Christ that it was the agency of the Virgin that had cured her (21v–23r).

The final miracle recounted in her autobiography occurred in October 1658. Piccolomini's right shoulder was so inflamed that her arm trembled, and she became unwilling to touch her theorbo, for fear that her playing was not pleasing to the Virgin. With the convent's titular feast of All Saints' Day approaching, Sister Anna Maria Azzoni begged her to ask the miraculous Virgin to favor her. Although at first Piccolomini was reluctant to appear too presumptuous, she was finally won over by Azzoni's exhortations. As she prepared to ask the Virgin for this favor, she thought to herself, "Now I will see if the Virgin wants me to play or not." Kneeling in front of the image, she rubbed her arm with oil from the lamp burning there, then threaded the holy ring through a string and tied it on her arm. She was immediately healed, and therefore was able to play continuously at Mass and Vespers on the feast of All Saints (23r–v).

PICCOLOMINI'S AUTOBIOGRAPHY IS REMARKABLE for several reasons. First of all, the nun leaves no doubt that the Virgin Mary was a champion of her musical talents. By recording her own thoughts before the last cure ("Now I will see if the Virgin wants me to play or not") she makes sure that the meaning of the miracle will not be lost on her reader. In addition, the two "musical" miracles— the healing of Piccolomini's nails and the healing of her arm—quite literally frame the nun's experiences in the convent; as the alpha and omega of her cloistered life, they offer an unambiguous message as to her role there. This frame gives new meaning to the widely witnessed miraculous cure of 1653, for it was her left hand, the hand that held the theorbo, that the Virgin cured first. In fact, the miraculous cure of 1653 appears to have been the turning point in Piccolomini's life, for all of the circumstances were in her favor: the miracle was witnessed by her sister nuns and, perhaps more important, confirmed by the male surgeon who had been taking care of her. Indeed, it was Ser Galeazzo who told the nuns to inform the citizens of Siena what had happened. Humility would have prevented Piccolomini herself from relating the incident. As news of the miracle filtered through the city, it could not have failed to raise Piccolomini's stock on both sides of the convent wall. This was the cure, in essence, that established her reputation as a "living saint."

Two of the other miracles, although they do not directly involve her hands or musical performance, are also rich with symbolism. Piccolomini was doubtless destined to the convent from birth, but the miracle that relieved her of her vertigo spells could be read as a sign that her family had made the right choice. The statue was not the Madonna of the Manger; it was, nevertheless, still a representation of the Virgin. The cure of her headache took place after a most prominent event in the life of the convent, when the young nun would have been in the public eye: the consecration rite. Maria Francesca and three other Piccolomini women (Suor Eufrasia, Suor Honorata, and Suor Maria Colomba) were part of the group of fifteen nuns who participated in the ceremony held at Ognissanti in June 1656. Archbishop Ascanio II Piccolomini officiated at the rite, which was "most beautiful, with music for three choirs, utterly superb decorations, and an enormous audience."[70] As Piccolomini notes (not without a trace of pride), she was in especially good health at the time of the consecration, and she "resisted the various discomforts of the ceremony with better vigor and constancy than [her] companions" (21v). We can infer that she played her theorbo during the rite, probably collaborating with male musicians hired just for the occasion, and made an impression on the gathered public, who were already aware of the miraculous cure granted her in 1653. The new miracle could only increase the young nun's prestige.

The miracle of the knee and the voice is also especially telling, for here we see Piccolomini seizing the occasion to pray not for relief of pain (at least not at first) but for a special gift. A cloistered woman's plea for a stronger voice resonates on many levels and may be read both literally and metaphorically. Was she a singer as well as a theorbist? Or was she consciously or subconsciously pointing to her invisibility as a nun and her desire to be heard in the outside world?

Piccolomini's autobiography is unusual in that it displays little of the tension that seems to be characteristic of such confessor-ordered narratives. She tells her story in a straightforward and sure manner relatively unencumbered with such devices as a rhetoric of humility, despite a couple of stray references to herself as a "most vile creature" or an "undeserving one" (15r, 23r). It is in the biographical preface to her account, provided by Padre Conti, that the tension bubbles to the surface.

The ties that bound nun and confessor were both delicate and complex, and, as noted earlier, the motives that prompted a confessor to ask a nun to write out her experiences must always be examined. We know little about Conti aside from what he tells us himself. The title of his biography makes it clear that he was a Jesuit from Pistoia. His association with Ognissanti apparently began in 1658, when he served the convent as a substitute confessor (2v). Conti's tenure at Ognissanti must have had a profound impact on him, for he never lost his fascination with nuns and with the extraordinary manifestations of their spirituality. Not only did he assume great importance in Piccolomini's life but he also played a part in the stories of two other highly esteemed Sienese holy women. In 1668, he made a special trip to the convent of Paradiso to ask Suor Rosa Maria Generali to pray for Signora Donna Lucrezia Cellesi ne' Rospigliosi, a relative of Pope Clement IX. As soon as Padre Conti had stated his request, Generali replied, "Ah, she rests in peace," a prediction that was borne out soon afterward.[71] Two years later, in 1670, when the Abbandonate were granted permission by Ascanio II Piccolomini to translate the body of Suor Chiara Birelli, Conti was on hand at the exhumation. He successfully pleaded with authorities on behalf of the nuns, who wanted to keep Birelli's heart separate from her body and to bury it under the grate where they received communion.[72]

It was with Piccolomini, however, that Conti forged his most significant relationship. Although most of the nun's miraculous cures took place before Conti's arrival, he was obviously intrigued by her experiences, which doubtless circulated by word of mouth in the convent and the city. It appears that his motives in ordering her to write out her story stemmed from admiration and not distrust. His reverence for her may be inferred from the fact that he allowed her autobiography to circulate in tandem with his own version of her life. His esteem extended to Piccolomini's sisters in the convent and to her biological sisters as well, for he used their comments and observations as important sources of information for his biography, often quoting them word for word (3v–4r; 12v–13r).

This is not to suggest that Conti's motives in writing Piccolomini's story were entirely selfless. He could not resist a bit of self-aggrandizement; by quoting the letter Piccolomini sent to him in August 1659, he was able to show her distress over the fact that he had been ordered to leave Siena for another assignment. Conti further noted that Piccolomini's prayers not to be abandoned were, in a sense, answered by the fact that she died before his departure (11v). Conti's name and his biography also appear in the book dedicated to the story of the Madonna of the Manger that the nuns of Ognissanti published in 1668.[73] All in all, Piccolomini could not have asked for a more sympathetic collaborator than Padre Sebastiano Conti if she were surreptitiously seeking a conduit for her story to the outside world. Conti not only lets the nun tell her own story but also takes it upon himself to act as apologist and to respond preemptively to those who might be skeptical that the Virgin Mary granted cures so that a nun could play her theorbo.

Accordingly, in his biography, Conti sets out to establish Piccolomini's credibility through the well-accepted modes of behavior for monastic women. He first emphasizes her "holy obedience" and her struggle to perfect that virtue. Conti writes that when Piccolomini heard it said that breaking silence and other such behaviors were really not such great transgressions, she responded, "I would rather die that to commit knowingly an inobservance [of the rule]" (2r). It is a theme to which Conti returns later in the essay, noting that when Piccolomini was forbidden to discipline herself, she blurted out "Oh, this obedience!" He further stresses that it was only out of obedience that she overcame her repugnance at writing about the miracles (4r, 5v).

Next, Conti ascertains her purity and innocence by revealing a conversation that she had with him. She anxiously related that she wanted to avoid even the merest shadow of sin in the observance of the three monastic vows, but that she did not know what constituted a sin against chastity. To drive home the point, Conti notes that upon hearing someone say that among nuns there should be no reason to suspect a lack of virginal integrity, she was horrified, and seized by doubt, she removed her monastic ring, as if the merest suggestion of sin rendered her unworthy of that illustrious symbol as a bride of Christ (2v).

Piccolomini's fondness for self-abnegation is introduced next. Prime among the behaviors to demonstrate this quality was self-flagellation. As Conti puts it, "The chief anguish for Maria Francesca was the inability to sate herself with pain." And because of her tendency to beat herself to the point of harming her health, she was allowed to engage in such practices only with the consent of her confessors (3v). The author cites several instances of the violence of her practices in this area. On one occasion, overtaken by a certain "dangerous" thought (Conti is no more specific than that) she left her work, took up a clothesline and beat herself long and hard with it (2v). She thought it appropriate, once she had obtained permission to engage in a limited amount of discipline, to go over the limit by adding three blows for every one of her confessors (3v–4r). Conti cites other kinds of self-abasing deportment as well. For three years, Piccolomini refused to go near a fire during winter, as she wanted to imitate the pains suffered by the forty martyrs on the frozen pond, a feast day celebrated on 10 March. On the days when the miraculous image of the Virgin of the Manger was displayed, Piccolomini was wont to go about the monastery without shoes, notwithstanding that such displays took place during the coldest days of the year: 25 December and 4 February (4v). Piccolomini's diet was also satisfyingly ascetic: her sister nuns reported that she drank water almost exclusively, mixed absinthe with her food, and left the best portions on her plate (4r–v).

Piccolomini's detachment from the things of this world is also stressed. Conti notes that she asked permission of a confessor to show affection to a biological sister with whom she had been raised (probably Fulvia, who was only a year or so older than she and who was not consigned to the nunnery); she desired her affection to spring from obedience and to be motivated by spiritual ties rather than those of blood and family (3r). She abstained from going to the parlor as much as possible, went only when absolutely necessary, and then never spoke or listened with any enthusiasm except when the subject turned to things of the spirit. When Piccolomini's sister (again, probably Fulvia) visited the convent and was unable to interest Maria Francesca in tales of the travails or prosperity of the family, she decided to change the subject by saying: "I understand that your Madonna of the Manger has worked many miraculous favors." Piccolomini at once responded, "You don't know the half of it! I saw her giving a blessing to the nuns as they entered the choir." Fulvia asked, "You've seen her, then?" As if taken aback by her admission of a visionary experience, Piccolomini at once changed her story, saying that another nun had seen the Madonna. Fulvia, sensitive to her sister's distress, responded, "Oh, of course, you couldn't have seen her; I know you well" (3r–v). Conti also briefly alludes to Piccolomini's demeanor during public performances in order to show her apparent disdain for worldly renown: he tells us that when she was in the choir playing, she never looked at the people in the church (3r).

Having established Piccolomini's credentials in matters of chastity, obedience, and self-abnegation, Conti proceeds to demonstrate her "blessed humility." The confessor notes that Piccolomini prayed to the Virgin every morning for this virtue and abominated any praise of herself. She was affable and happy with her sisters in the convent, except when she heard them refer to her as good and without sin and blessed by the Madonna. Conti continues:

> She innocently thought that she could free herself from this persecution of praise and negate the good opinion that others had of her by going about the convent saying that she was full of mortal sins. She did this until she was prohibited by me and by other confessors, who pointed out to her that it would not be a good

thing to say even if it were true, and it was even worse when it was false, as was the case with her. (5r–v)

To further assure that no glory accrued to her because of the favors shown her by the Virgin Mary, she would studiously hide her left hand when she went to the grates so that no one could see the difference in color that marked the miraculously healed wound (5v).

It is only at this point in the narrative, and in this context, that Conti allows himself to discuss Piccolomini's skills as a musician, and when he does, the passage is worded most carefully:

> Being a marvelous theorbo player, and despising any praise because of this, she used to be overjoyed when some disease, especially one affecting her hands, would prevent her from playing. And she never would have ceased supplicating her superiors to release her from playing in public if the Virgin had not miraculously restored the nails that had fallen off her fingers, and another time made a painful inflammation in her right hand cease immediately, and yet another time taken away the spasms and trembling in her right arm. Finally, she was assured that Our Lady approved of being served by her playing at sacred rites. (6r)

Thus Conti singles out for special consideration the miracles involving music. And in a postscript to Piccolomini's autobiography, he mentions two more that Piccolomini recounted to him on her deathbed, one of which also involved musical performance. The first occurred on Christmas 1658. Suffering from a swollen mouth, Piccolomini applied to it a bit of the cotton that was used to wrap the image of the Madonna of the Manger and was healed. The last took place on the morning of 4 February 1659, the very day the convent honored the holy statue of the Madonna. Piccolomini's right hand was so sore and inflamed that she thought she would be unable to play her theorbo in the choir with the other nuns, but when she prayed to the Virgin and put some oil from the lamp on her hand, her pain disappeared, and she was able to perform in honor of her liberator (24v–25r).

The spiritual autobiography of Maria Francesca Piccolomini points up the problems faced by holy women who were talented performers and desired to be acknowledged as such. A nun who enjoyed performing and craved praise of her playing could be accused of the sin of pride. If, however, the Virgin wanted the nun to play (despite the nun's protestations), then performing became an obligation: a humble acquiescence to the will of divine authority. For Piccolomini, as for the lute-playing convertita Vannini, music was an important component of both identity and spirituality. The two women, however, approached music-making in radically different ways. Vannini, perhaps because of her former trade and social status, had to make it clear to her listeners that what she played and sang had nothing to do with her own gifts, because the music was not of this world. Instead, she cast herself as an instrument on which celestial music could be played. In order for her to reproduce this music, it was necessary for her to go into ecstasy; because normal sensations ceased while she was in ecstasy, she did not perceive the pain that resulted from playing while in this divinely inspired state until after her performance. Piccolomini, as a daughter of the ruling elite, needed no pretense to ecstasy. Hers was earthly music, which, one assumes, simply sounded heavenly. Pain was therefore an obstacle to her, for it prevented her from giving her best performance. It was precisely the high quality of the performance, cultivated through her own skills, that made her playing pleasing to Virgin. And no one could question the Virgin's expertise in these matters, for it was celebrated in lesson 6 of the Matins service on the feast of her Nativity (a passage that Piccolomini and her companions recited every year):

> Mary may now play on her instruments, the Mother [may] strike the cymbals with swift fingers. The joyful choruses may sound out and songs alternate with sweet harmonies. Hear, then, how she sings, she who leads our chorus. For she says, "My soul magnifies the Lord, and my spirit rejoices in God my Savior."[74]

By healing Piccolomini, the Virgin Mary was, in essence, validating the nun's need for her full physical capabilities in order to perform well, putting her seal of approval on Piccolomini's talent, and confirming her status as an excellent musician.

It was precisely that status that Piccolomini desired. She had little to fear in the way of censure of her performances, for Ascanio II Piccolomini had very liberal attitudes toward music-making by the nuns in his pastoral care. As Kendrick has pointed out, however, an archbishop who did not restrict the possibilities of polyphony in the cloister encouraged the public attractiveness of such music. Given the Seicento's emphasis on the individual performer, it was impossible to avoid "vanity, individual fame, and public competition."[75] It was during the tenure of Ascanio II that Ugurgieri Azzolini published his encomiastic biographies of famous Sienese, including the citation naming four nuns renowned for their musical talents, two of whom were from Ognissanti (Doc. 1). "La Landa" was Artemisia Landi, who took the Olivetan habit on 22 April 1635 with the name Suor Maria Benedetta.[76] "La Bargaglia" was either Petra or Artemisia Bargagli, both of whom entered the convent on 18 February 1629 and retained their own names at profession.[77] Neither of these women (nor any others, Piccolomini included) are cited as musicians in the convent's necrology. It is only from the passages in the *Pompe sanesi* that we know of Landi's musical prowess and of Bargagli's exceptional gifts as a theorbist. It is clear from Piccolomini's account that she received her training at the convent, perhaps from "la Bargaglia." Indeed, one wonders if Piccolomini knew of Ugurgieri Azzolini's citation and wished for the same kind of lasting renown herself.

Here I return to Piccolomini's account and to two points that require comment. The first concerns the exquisite timing of the musical miracles, which unfailingly occurred at critical junctures in Piccolomini's life or in the life of the convent: a cure so that she could learn to play the theorbo, another so that she could perform on the titular feast of the convent, and yet another to assure her musical participation on the feast dedicated to the statue itself. The second concerns the care Piccolomini took to name the ubiquitous corroborating witnesses, who either urged her to seek the help of the Virgin or beheld or confirmed the miraculous cures: Ser Galeazzo, the nuns in the convent, her sister Caterina, and

Suor Anna Maria Azzoni. In this context, it is indeed strange that she does not cite a single witness to the first miracle attributed to the Madonna of the Manger, the cure that allowed her nails to grow back so that she could continue her theorbo studies. This miracle seems to fall into the category of "what-might-have-happened-had-I-only-thought-of-it-in-time."[78] It led me to wonder why, in 1653, Piccolomini would need to be reminded of the powers of the miraculous Virgin while in the throes of her severe illness when the sacred image had already shown her such favor. Yet I am not questioning the veracity of Piccolomini's story per se; rather I am suggesting that we must confront the question of the roles memory and will played in her autobiographical process and the degree to which self-fashioning extended beyond her writing and into the actual conduct of her life.

Certainly, in 1653, her hand and body were cured in a most spectacular manner, whether the agents of the cure were human or divine. But is it too much to suppose that young Piccolomini was intelligent enough to understand the special status the cure had given her and eager to maintain this status both by rethinking earlier incidents and by cultivating a series of cures that would exalt her musical ability? All Piccolomini's symptoms, though not readily confirmed by objective observation, might have easily resulted from her musical or devotional activities. Catherine Liddell has informed me that beginning theorbists who use a combination of flesh and nail to pluck the strings can indeed have trouble with nails breaking, and that inflamed joints, trembling arms, and aching shoulders can all be induced by repetitive stress or incorrect posture and lack of support while playing the instrument.[79] Piccolomini's habit of mixing absinthe with her food might have caused damage to her nervous system.[80] The strain of the public consecration ceremony could have provoked a physical collapse afterward. And aching knees are sure to result from too much kneeling. But Piccolomini obviously knew how to make a special place for herself in the convent through dramatic behavior and to call attention to herself in ways that were in keeping with the demeanor expected of her as a nun. We see an example of this in her plan to sully her own reputation by saying that she was full of mortal sin: this forced her confessors to tell her that she was not full of mortal sin and therefore should stop making such statements. The behavior, although ostensibly meant to demonstrate her humility, served rather to confirm the high opinion in which she was held. And unlike Catherine of Siena, Piccolomini did not accuse her confessors of "finding excuses for [her] very sins."[81] Her discomfiture at her supposedly unguarded remark to her sister about seeing the Madonna and her practice of hiding her hand at the grates seem to have been designed to stimulate curiosity and to provoke speculation about her extraordinary powers. By using similar tactics, she was able to confirm that she was one of the best, if not the best, theorbist in the convent. Consciously or subconsciously, she chose the most appropriate times to complain about her ailments or to show physical pain, declaring that such pain would leave her unable to play for services on important feast days. When her sister nuns pleaded with her to ask the Virgin for help, she would comply (after a seemly struggle), be healed, and take her place as the star performer. Both her companions on earth and the Virgin Mary in heaven would thus affirm her special musical talents. If this were indeed Piccolomini's modus operandi, then other questions arise. Did Piccolomini actually believe the Virgin to be the source of the cure? Were her practices of self-flagellation and her ascetic diet signs of true devotion or sacrifices necessary to confirm that her actions were those of a holy woman and thus allow her to develop a more specific reputation as a musician with a divine patroness? Was her apparent disdain of the world (her habit of "not looking at the people in the church" when she was in the choir loft playing) paradoxically necessary in order to gain renown in the world that prized humility in its holy women? We shall never know. But we do a disservice to intelligent women such as Piccolomini if we fail to see her as a complex human being who might have been both dedicated to the cloistered life and at the same time desirous of seeking acknowledgment of her musical gifts both by her cloistered community and by the secular world about which she was supposed to care naught and to which she, like most nuns, seems to have been so closely tied.

Of course, Piccolomini's account might not have met with such success if it had not served the larger needs of her extended family, her convent, and the city itself. Piccolomini was fortunate that her clan was so strong at Ognissanti, for she had a built-in core of blood relations who had every reason to promote her as one favored by the Virgin. Nothing suggests that Piccolomini was, like her younger Sicilian contemporary Suor Maria Crocifissa, a family sainthood project, but once the young nun began to manifest all the appropriate signs, one of her relatives was ready to help construct the "living hagiography."[82] In the published volume dedicated to Ognissanti's statue of the Madonna of the Manger, the reader finds not only Maria Francesca Piccolomini's autobiography but also the story of Maria Vittoria Piccolomini.[83] In 1641, while praying to the Madonna of the Manger, Maria Vittoria heard the statue command her to announce the Virgin's desire to have her statue displayed for public veneration. Maria Vittoria, overwhelmed by the order, told a few of her companions, but they did not seem to believe her, and her modesty made her think that perhaps the embassy of conveying the Virgin's desires would be given to other, more devout nuns. Nevertheless, for twelve years, the Virgin continued to address herself to Maria Vittoria alone and to repeat the same command, going so far as to tell the nun, "If you do not follow my orders, I will leave this convent." Maria Vittoria, finally convinced of the certainty of the revelation and cognizant of the obedience she owed her Sovereign Queen, decided to divulge her secret. Once she had so decided, however, the devil (unwilling to see public devotion to the Virgin grow) began to torment the nun, threatening her with death and choking her whenever she tried to proclaim the Virgin's command. In 1653, the nun asked the Virgin to authenticate her desire to be displayed for public devotion. On the night of 22 April, the Virgin appeared at the head of Maria Vittoria's bed and announced: "The miracle has been performed; do not delay making my will known to the confessor in this convent." Indeed, upon waking, she heard of the miraculous healing of Maria Francesca Piccolomini's hand, and it seemed as if the time was ripe to announce the Virgin's wish. After several days spent fighting off the devil, she asked Padre Andrea Bigetti, the convent's confessor, to come to the convent. Maria Vittoria was suffering such great agonies that she had to be carried to the grates, and once there, although she struggled with all her might to tell the confessor what she knew, she could not. Finally, the confessor ordered her to observe the rule of obedience required of her as a nun, and to speak. At that point the devil gave up his hold on her, and she was able to act as ambassador for Mary and to° make known the Virgin's desire to have her statue displayed for public veneration.[84]

Thus was Maria Francesca's miracle immediately substantiated by one of her relatives, and soon the story spread throughout the city.[85] On 10 September 1653, the nuns applied to the archbishop of Siena—Ascanio II Piccolomini, another member of the extended clan—to convene a tribune and examine the evidence for declaring the statue miraculous.[86] It is not surprising that Maria Vittoria Piccolomini was among those who testified. She claimed that the statue healed a fistula in her left eye. She was not, however, alone. Sister nuns (and one educanda) who were members of other prominent Sienese families also came forward: Petra Bargagli (who was perhaps the convent's other famous theorbist), Arcangela Costanti, Egidia Trecerchi, and Laura Orlandini all prayed to the statue for relief of various inflammations and were restored to health. Lay members of important families with relatives at Ognissanti also gave witness. The Virgin's rings cured both Tullio Ugurgieri and the only male child of Lorenzo Cacciaguerra of high fevers. Margherita Griffoli's right thumb was healed by applying to it a bit of the oil from the Virgin's lamp and some of the cotton used to wrap the image. A mystery witness, who for "just reasons" did not wish to be named, used the same cotton from the statue to heal a tumor that an esteemed surgeon had declared incurable.[87] Such testimony led Archbishop Piccolomini to issue a decree, dated 4 February 1654, authenticating the miracles attributed to the statue and declaring it miraculous and thus worthy of veneration. The date of the decree coincided with the day that the nuns had always set aside to honor the statue.[88]

For the Piccolomini clan, the major protagonists in bringing the powers of the statue to light and in declaring it miraculous, the advantages in this entire matter were obvious: they accrued both spiritual and worldly honor. But why were the other nuns so eager to help promote a story that so glorified only one family in the convent? In the face of the much stiffer rules and restrictions for canonization in the post-Tridentine era, Piccolomini perhaps spoke to the convent's need for creating its own local, order-specific saint, unofficial, of course, but no less venerated because of that.[89] That the impulse arose from competition between convents does not seem in doubt. The Convertite had Caterina Vannini; the Cappuccine, Passitea Crogi; the Franciscans of Campansi, Suor Colomba; and the Abbandonate, Chiara Birelli. The Olivetans of Ognissanti clearly needed their own extraordinary nun. Piccolomini fit the typical profile of the seventeenth-century female martyr by demonstrating heroism in the face of sickness; furthermore, her miraculous cure was certified by her surgeon, who replaced a church official as an authority in this matter.[90] The surgeon's opinion was confirmed in a more traditional ecclesiastical manner some months after Piccolomini's death, when her sepulchre was opened and her body was found to be badly decomposed except for her left hand and arm—the site of the 1653 miracle—which were incorrupt.[91] As Bynum has pointed out, "incorruptibility, either of the whole cadaver or of a part, seems a virtual requirement for female sanctity by the early modern period."[92]

For many of the women at Ognissanti, Piccolomini may have been, however, just a means to a more important end: the transformation of their statue into an object with the status of a relic. This was of enormous consequence to the nuns, for the convent had lost an important relic one hundred years previously. During the rising tension between Spanish troops and the Sienese in the mid–sixteenth century, all nuns in convents outside the walls were ordered to come into the city for their own protection. Thus, in the early 1550s, the nuns of Ognissanti left their convent outside Porta Romana for what all thought would be a brief sojourn inside the walls. When the Sienese government ordered the Olivetan house destroyed so that enemy troops could not exploit it during the siege, the nuns needed a new home. They were eventually granted the convent and church that were once the patrimony of the Cistercian monks of S. Galgano.[93]

This turn of events apparently did not please the monks, as they were loathe to sacrifice the church in which the reliquary containing the head of the Sienese martyr S. Galgano had been in exposition since at least 1477.[94] When the Olivetan nuns moved in, however, the relic was in temporary custody of the female monastery of S. Maria degli Angeli. According to a chronicle from Santuccio, the transfer of the relic to their institution was accomplished by miraculous means. The legend narrates that on 23 March 1549, a young blond man of exceeding beauty knocked at the gates of the convent and announced that he had a reliquary containing the head of S. Galgano, which he wanted to give to the nuns for safekeeping. The abbess took the relic into the cloister, but when she returned to thank the young man, he had disappeared. The monastery's servants searched all over the city but were unable to find any trace of the young man. The nuns of Santuccio concluded that the head of S. Galgano was a gift from the angels and kept it in their possession.[95]

The true story is doubtless more prosaic. Giuliano Catoni suggests that when the abbot of S. Galgano realized that the Olivetan nuns were to be given permanent possession of his convent, he refused to restore the reliquary to its special place near the main altar in the attached church. Instead, he bequeathed it to the nuns of Santuccio, and there it remained, despite insistent petitions from the Olivetan nuns for its return.[96] The passage from Maria Vittoria's story in which the statue of the Virgin threatens "If you do not follow my orders, I will leave this convent," seems to have been designed to touch this raw nerve at Ognissanti and to spur the women to rapid and unified action, regardless of the benefit that might accrue to an individual family.

That the women of Ognissanti seem to have placed most of their hopes for increased prestige and a larger role in the civic consciousness on the Madonna of the Manger rather than on Piccolomini seems clear from their course of action. They focused their efforts on having the statue declared miraculous, and they went to press in 1668 with the story of the statue rather than just the account of Piccolomini's cures. This publication allowed the Olivetan nuns to repeat (or perhaps create) a legend for how Ognissanti came into possession of the statue, a legend that had distinct parallels with the story that the nuns of Santuccio used to explain the mysterious appearance of the head of S. Galgano at their convent. The narrative begins in 1446, when the Olivetan nuns were still in their convent outside Porta Romana. Their sacristan during these years, Margarita Credi, often meditated on the image of the Virgin Mary caressing her child and told her sister nuns of her desire to see a statue made in the manner in which she had envisioned this scene so many times. Not long before Christmas 1446, a young man with a beautiful face and a modest and extraordinarily gentle demeanor presented himself at the monastery and inquired if anyone wanted a statue of the Madonna, as he would gladly do the work with the hope of pleasing whomever desired such an image. Credi immediately accepted his offer, and he agreed to make two statues (one of the Virgin and one of the Child) and to deliver them before the feast of the Nativity. At twilight on 16 December, the young man came to the monastery with two boxes and told the nun who acted as porter that his work was finished. When the porter returned with Credi, however, the young man had disappeared, and only the boxes remained. The boxes were duly opened and inside were two extraordinarily beautiful statues in wood. The nuns were delighted and sang songs in praise of the images. They made inquiries after the young artisan, but no one in the city had every heard of him or seen him. Thus, the nuns were persuaded that the Madonna was a gift from the angels.[97]

The tactics the nuns adopted were sound: after the statue was declared miraculous, donations to the convent increased.[98] The holy women must have been especially pleased when, in 1693, the city's confraternities asked the convent to allow them to use the statue for the solemn Low Sunday procession—an honor conferred only on the most important relics, such as the body of Blessed Giovanni Colombini (in the possession of the nuns of SS. Abbondio e Abbondanzio) and the head of S. Galgano.[99]

The story of Maria Francesca Piccolomini and the miraculous statue of the Madonna of the Manger also had larger repercussions for the city of Siena as well. The Sienese, absorbed into the Medici state and lacking political might, had to find ways to preserve their cultural identity and to assert authority in those areas that the Florentines could neither object to nor interfere in. Certainly, a statue of the Virgin that could effect divine cures spoke well for the spiritual power that resided in Sienese convents. Piccolomini's cures prompted a flurry of interest in the statue, especially in the rings that the Madonna wore on her fingers, in the healing oil of the lamp burning before her sanctuary, and in the cotton in which she was wrapped, all agents used by Piccolomini in her own miraculous cures. To stress that the statue's powers were not merely a local phenomenon, the published account from 1668 includes testimony from several non-Sienese witnesses residing outside the city.[100] The 1743 edition of the volume adds the names of a number of Florentines healed by the oil from the Virgin's lamp.[101]

If the published volume strives to show that the statue's powers transcend its place of origin, Piccolomini's description of her relationship with the Virgin seems designed to appeal with particular force to her compatriots. Whereas holy women like Crogi and Vannini recount their mystic marriages with Christ, Piccolomini relates an event that sounds curiously like a mystic marriage to the Virgin: she receives a ring from her finger and experiences a miraculous cure so that she can sing her praises. Conti reinforces this relationship and draws a distinct parallel between Maria Francesca and S. Catherine of Siena by relating that in the final days of her life, Piccolomini felt such sweet pain in her heart, arising out of her love of the Virgin, that she could not go into the choir where the miraculous statue was kept without being overcome by the painful throbbing of her heart. Conti's imagery is taken directly from Raymond of Capua, who reported that S. Catherine's heart would beat so loudly when she beheld the Eucharist that her sister nuns could hear it.[102] Like Raymond of Capua, Conti quotes Psalm 83 to explain this phenomenon, modifying the verse to refer to Piccolomini's love of the Virgin: "My heart and my flesh exulted in my Lady!" This relationship would resonate with special force for the Sienese, who from earliest times had considered the Virgin Mary patroness of their city and had placed themselves under her protection in times of need.[103] As her own special advocate, as a replacement for S. Galgano, and as a symbol of Siena, Maria Francesca Piccolomini could hardly have done better in choosing the agent of her cures.

PICCOLOMINI'S STRATEGY—AND I BELIEVE it was a strategy—was successful. She was universally respected during her life as both a holy woman and, perhaps more important to her, as a musician. Upon her death, her brothers provided her with a pompous and splendid funeral, and nuns in her convent reported seeing her in visions.[104] Although we can never know if the Virgin Mary granted Piccolomini's desire to recite the Divine Office more forcefully in the cloister, Piccolomini herself assured that her voice would resound loud and clear outside its walls through her spiritual autobiography, a portrait of a diva in the convent.

ALLA CITTÀ RITORNA

The Chigi, the Convent, and Opera in Siena, 1669–1686

The Palazzo Pubblico is one of Siena's most impressive buildings. It dominates the Campo, the lovely fan-shaped piazza that lies at the city's heart. For centuries, Sienese leaders convened inside its walls to deliberate the governance of the city. After the fall of the republic in 1555, when the magistracies that met there had little power, the Public Palace came to be exploited for a new purpose: entertainment. In 1560, on the occasion of Cosimo I de' Medici's first visit to his newly acquired dominion, the Great Counsel Hall ("sala grande del Consiglio") was transformed into a theater by the construction of a stage for performers and of galleries for an audience.[1] Eighty years later, Prince Mattias de' Medici, then governor of Siena and a great fan of the new genre of opera, ordered the theater in the Public Palace renovated, possibly along the lines of SS. Giovanni e Paolo in Venice. In 1647, the refurbished venue served as the site of the first operatic performance in Siena. Among the attendees were the English tourists John Raymond and Robert Bargrave, who were especially taken with the elaborate scenery and the machines.[2] Despite the apparent success of the work, over twenty years would pass before another opera was mounted in Siena.

The attempt to revive opera in the city of Siena in the late 1660s differed from the earlier effort in that it appears to have been spearheaded not by the Medici but rather by the Chigi. (Figure 3 presents an abbreviated genealogical table for the prolific family: it includes only those members mentioned in this chapter.) The fortunes of the ancient and powerful Sienese clan soared when Fabio Chigi ascended the papal throne as Pope Alexander VII in 1655. After an apparent struggle with his conscience over the practice of nepotism, the pope finally called his relatives to Rome and began to heap positions and riches upon them. In 1656, he named his brother Mario commander of the papal armies and his nephew Agostino captain of Castel Sant'Angelo and of the papal guards, as well as governor of Benevento and Civitavecchia. The following year, he con-

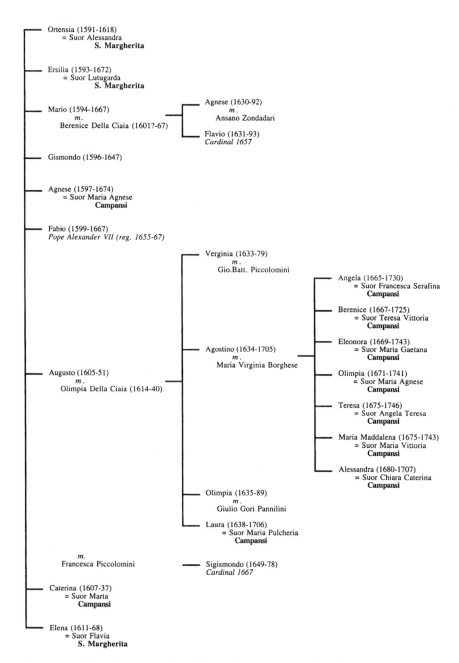

Ortensia (1591-1618)
= Suor Alessandra
S. Margherita

Ersilia (1593-1672)
= Suor Lutugarda
S. Margherita

Mario (1594-1667)
m.
Berenice Della Ciaia (1601?-67)

Agnese (1630-92)
m.
Ansano Zondadari

Flavio (1631-93)
Cardinal 1657

Gismondo (1596-1647)

Agnese (1597-1674)
= Suor Maria Agnese
Campansi

Fabio (1599-1667)
Pope Alexander VII (reg. 1655-67)

Verginia (1633-79)
m.
Gio.Batt. Piccolomini

Agostino (1634-1705)
m.
Maria Virginia Borghese

Angela (1665-1730)
= Suor Francesca Serafina
Campansi

Berenice (1667-1725)
= Suor Teresa Vittoria
Campansi

Eleonora (1669-1743)
= Suor Maria Gaetana
Campansi

Olimpia (1671-1741)
= Suor Maria Agnese
Campansi

Teresa (1675-1746)
= Suor Angela Teresa
Campansi

Maria Maddalena (1675-1743)
= Suor Maria Vittoria
Campansi

Alessandra (1680-1707)
= Suor Chiara Caterina
Campansi

Augusto (1605-51)
m.
Olimpia Della Ciaia (1614-40)

Olimpia (1635-89)
m.
Giulio Gori Pannilini

Laura (1638-1706)
= Suor Maria Pulcheria
Campansi

m.
Francesca Piccolomini

Sigismondo (1649-78)
Cardinal 1667

Caterina (1607-37)
= Suor Marta
Campansi

Elena (1611-68)
= Suor Flavia
S. Margherita

FIGURE 3.   Selected descendants of Flavio Chigi and Laura Marsili

ferred a cardinalate on Mario's son, Flavio. Another Chigi nephew, Sigismondo, was raised to the purple in 1667 (albeit after the death of his uncle).[3]

Fabio Chigi, during his tenure as Pope Alexander VII, is credited with changing the very image of Rome through spectacular building projects. His contributions to the art and architecture of his native city, especially his transformation of the interior spaces of Siena Cathedral, are also well documented.[4] The pope's nephews, cardinals Flavio and Sigismondo Chigi and Prince Agostino Chigi, have not enjoyed the same high reputation for patronage of the plastic arts.[5] As patrons of music, however, none of the Chigi can be easily dismissed. The full extent of their influence on the musical life of mid-seventeenth-century Rome remains to be explored, but the music and documents that have come to light suggest that they had discerning tastes.[6] Despite their residence in the Eternal City, the Chigi nephews also remained strongly attached to Siena and strove to enrich its cultural climate. A brief examination of their involvement with operatic productions in Siena from the late 1660s to 1680 will prepare the ground for the analysis of a "little sacred opera" from 1686 that celebrates both convent life and the Chigi name.

PASSAGES FROM THE CORRESPONDENCE that cardinals Flavio and Sigismondo Chigi received from relatives in Siena offer some of the best information on opera and operatic singing in the city during the second half of the seventeenth century. A letter that Leonardo Marsili wrote to Sigismondo Chigi in September of 1668 shows that the Chigi were deeply involved in the efforts to refurbish (once again) the theater in the Palazzo Pubblico so that it could serve for operatic productions. From the contents of the letter, it appears that the reconstruction was proceeding apace when the committee in charge of choosing an inaugural work hit a snag:

> The deputies of the new theater find themselves disconsolate because *Antigone*, the drama they had chosen to perform there, has lost the singular quality they sought of not having been performed elsewhere. They have asccertained that the work has already been staged in Venice and Bologna and also, they say, in other cities of Lombardy, and now they do not know what opera to choose. If Your Eminence were to ask the Contestabile [Colonna], who is now in Rome, to send us that new comedy he was talking about last summer, which was set to music and never performed, or another that Your Eminence finds appropriate, it would console everyone greatly and be an act of your usual beneficence in a most opportune time of present need.[7]

As the deputies were grappling with this problem, the citizens of Siena were looking forward to another significant musical event: the appearance of an operatic singer in their city. A letter that Suor Maria Pulcheria Chigi wrote in December of 1668 to her half-brother Sigismondo reveals that interest in the musicodramatic genre and its performers was not limited to the secular world but percolated through the convent walls and right into the heart of the cloister: "I hear that Signora Giulia, a famous singer, is going to pass through town. I am told she often comes there [in Rome] to sing. If you were to command her to come here so that I could hear her, please be assured that you would be doing me an immense favor."[8] The "Signora Giulia" in question can be no other than the famous singer Vincenza Giulia Masotti. Masotti, called the "siren of the Tiber" by one of her admirers, was one of the most highly paid singers of her day. She performed in Venetian operatic productions during the 1660s and the early 1670s, while concurrently serving as chamber musician to the duchess of Savoy. After 1673, she moved to Vienna to take up a position at the imperial court.[9] Among Masotti's Roman patrons was Cardinal Sigismondo Chigi, on whose request she probably made the trip to Siena. She arrived in the city on 18 December 1668, and though she did not go to Campansi to perform for Suor Maria Pulcheria, she did indeed sing at a party in the home of her host family, the Della Ciaia.[10] Olimpia Chigi Gori Pannilini, another of Sigismondo's half-sisters, made a report to the cardinal concerning both her appearance and her performance:

> Yesterday, Signora Giulia arrived at the home of the Della Ciaia and yesterday evening, we went to a party there, and truly she sings very well, with great presence and ease, but aside from this, she is a very ugly girl, dressed in a style half like a man. I suppose that when she dresses like a woman, it's much worse. Many ladies and a great number of gentlemen came to hear her.[11]

A report of Masotti's visit also found its way into a letter that Marsili wrote to Cardinal Sigismondo. As it turned out, Masotti played an important role in helping the Sienese choose an opera to replace the rejected *Antigone*:

> After many discussions, the deputies have decided upon another opera. They were newly instigated by me and persuaded by Signora Giulia (who, to the great delight of many ladies and an enormous number of men, sang here the other night on her passage through town) to stage the opera *L'Argia*. Signor Apolloni (who was here) offered to shorten [the work], and we suppose that with the intercession of Your Eminence, we can obtain a copy of the opera from the person who has it so that the parts can be extracted and distributed to the singers.[12]

Antonio Cesti's *L'Argia*, set to a libretto by Giovanni Filippo Apolloni, had enjoyed a number of revivals after its 1655 Innsbruck premiere.[13] The deputies had wisely decided to choose an opera with a proven track record rather than to take a chance on a novelty. Once the opera was selected, the Sienese could focus their energies on the reconstruction of the theatrical venue. In January 1669, Marsili reported to Cardinal Sigismondo that the deputies were trying all methods to make money for the rebuilding project; for example, they printed up two sonnets hoping to prompt the ladies of Siena to contribute money for the ceiling. As Marsili reported, the building was a singular monument in itself, and the astonishing fact that it could be built in such a small city was all thanks to the generous support of the Chigi family.[14]

The opera, planned for mid-May, came in virtually on schedule. The Sienese premiere of *L'Argia* took place on Monday, 27 May, "rich in costumes and scenery and exquisite music, with the continuous assistance of Signor Cesti," and was repeated at least four times over the next weeks.[15] The libretto printed for the occasion does not name the performers; nonetheless, at least two can be securely identified. One is Giacomo Campaluci, a well-known Sienese soprano in the ensembles of both the Cathedral and the Public Palace. His success in *L'Argia* would prompt him to request a leave of absence from his jobs in order to sing in a Grimani production in Venice.[16] He apparently maintained a connection with the Chigi, for in 1673, he appeared in *Adalinda*, an opera produced at Prince Agostino's Ariccia estate.[17] Another role in *L'Argia* was taken by a certain Caterina Angiola Botteghi.[18] It is also possible that Giulia Masotti sang in the opera she had so enthusiastically recommended to the Sienese deputies, for she was fond of it. She had suggested *L'Argia* as a replacement for an opera she did not like during the 1666–67 Venetian season and had taken a role in a Venetian revival of the opera at the Teatro S. Luca in early 1669.[19] In April 1669, Masotti was in Siena and sang on at least four occasions. Although she traveled to Rome at the end of April, she might have easily returned to Siena for the opera premiere, which was still a month off at that point.[20]

From all reports, Cesti's opera delighted audiences. Both Verginia Chigi Piccolomini and her sister Olimpia wrote to Sigismondo in Rome to comment on the performances. Although both women stressed the favorable reaction of "foreigners" to the Sienese production, the emotional temperature of the two letters is different. Verginia provided a succinct evaluation of the performers, focusing on the male lead:

> On Monday, the comedy premiered, after having been delayed from the previous day because Jacomo [Campaluci] caught a cold and on Friday and Saturday, he had a fever. Notwithstanding the circumstances, he did well, and the Florentine gentlemen who were there truly liked him. As for the musicians, none were bad: [most were] good and a few mediocre and the comedy was beautiful. . . . 29 May 1669 . . . Verginia Chigi Piccolomini.[21]

Verginia's sister Olimpia, on the other hand, waxed poetic about the musical experience. Olimpia's missive is of special interest here, for it confirms the porous nature of the Sienese convent walls and suggests that nuns did not necessarily obtain their knowledge of opera secondhand:

> Truly, I think that you would have enjoyed the comedy, which was not staged Sunday because Campaluci caught a cold and Saturday he had a fever, and thus, they staged it yesterday. The opera began at 6:30 in the evening and ended at 12:30 a.m., and truly it was most beautiful, sung and conducted very well. I heard that in Venice the instrumentalists were not as good as those here, and I can tell Your Eminence that both Florentines and other foreigners praised the opera highly. A Frenchman who was passing through here and stopped to see the performance, said that in Paris, they would have charged a doubloon. I assure you that I was entranced, and I do not think that one can hear more refined or elegant music than this . . . for that reason, I am thinking of going to all the performances, and yesterday, *I took all my girls out of the convent and escorted them to the opera.* . . . Olimpia Chigi Gori.[22] (emphasis mine)

So successful was the production and so enthusiastic the Sienese response that a production of Cesti's *La Dori* was planned for the following year. The opera was indeed performed in Florence; among the performers was Campaluci (playing the part of Oronte) and the singer "Il Tiepolo" and his wife. The Sienese production was not to take place, however. All was set for the performance when the grand duke died.[23] Although the extent of Chigi involvment in this opera is unclear, the family probably played some role in two subsequent Sienese Carnival entertainments: the 1677 staging of *Le reciproche gelosie* and the 1682 production of *Ama chi t'ama*. Among the three Sienese noblemen who signed the dedication to the libretto for the first work was Bonaventura Zondadari, nephew to Flavio Chigi (and the cardinal's eventual heir). Bonaventura Zondadari figures as the dedicatee on the libretto of the second work; the dedication came from Sienese with blood ties to the Chigi: the Della Ciaia, the Pannilini, and the Piccolomini. Alesssandro Melani, the composer credited with the music for both operas, had close links to the Roman branch of the Chigi. He dedicated two oratorios—*La morte di Oloferne* (1675) and *Il giudizio di Salomone* (1676)—to Cardinal Sigismondo Chigi. He also composed music performed in 1676 when Laura, the oldest daughter of Agostino Chigi and Maria Virginia Borghese, took the habit at the Roman convent of SS. Domenico e Sisto. A number of Melani's scores, including that for *Le reciproche gelosie*, are preserved in the Chigi archives in Rome.[24]

Chigi family fingerprints are clearly visible in the Sienese performance of Scarlatti's *Gli equivoci nel sembiante*. A libretto of this, Scarlatti's first opera, received with such success in Rome during Carnival of 1679, was printed by a Sienese typographer, from which we can infer that it was staged in the city sometime after the dedication date of 9 May 1680. Frank D'Accone has suggested that Flavio Chigi might have recommended that the work be produced in his native city, though the cardinal did not attend the performance.[25] D'Accone's thesis is strengthened by a payment record from Flavio's account books. On 30 June 1679, Flavio paid for the copying of "several musical works sent to Marchese Salviati in Siena." The justification of this expense reads "opera musicale dei Due Simili" ("the opera of the Two Look-alikes"), certainly shorthand for *Gli equivoci nel sembiante*.[26] Since the dedication to the Sienese libretto makes reference to a "Farnese heroine" and a "most exellent princess," it is probable that the work was staged in honor of Maria Virginia Borghese, princess of Farnese. She and her husband Agostino Chigi were in Siena in May 1680 to celebrate the imminent clothing of their daugher Angela as a nun in the Franciscan convent of S. Girolamo in Campansi. They arrived on 2 May 1680 and did not leave the city until 24 May.[27] Further work with the Chigi correspondence may help fill in the details surrounding this performance.

Although the examples cited make it clear that the Chigi worked to promote public performances of opera, their endeavors in this realm were only one facet of their patronage. The Chigi also cultivated opera in a private sphere during the 1670s, especially at their country estates. Ariccia's own "Academy of the Idlers," whose members included Cardinal Flavio Chigi, Prince Agostino Chigi, the impresario Filippo Acciaiuoli, and the librettist Giovanni Filippo Apolloni, seems to have been created for the express purpose of producing opera. The Acciaiuoli-Apolloni team provided the librettos for *Il Tirinto* and for *L'Adalinda*, which graced the stage at Ariccia in October 1672 and October 1673 respectively.[28] Cardinal

Flavio Chigi enjoyed *L'Adalinda* so much that he probably had it performed at his own Tuscan villa of Cetinale in 1677.[29] These so-called "feudal operas" were meant to exalt the life enjoyed by the aristocracy for whom they were performed. It will soon become clear that they share a close relationship with the *operina sacra* staged privately in 1686 for a select audience at S. Girolamo in Campansi.

S. GIROLAMO IN CAMPANSI was one of two convents still extant in seventeenth-century Siena that had originated as an open house of Franciscan tertiaries. It shared this history and a similar resistance to the imposition of clausura with S. Margherita in Castelvecchio. S. Margherita finally accepted cloistering in 1602, but Campansi held out longer, becoming a cloistered institution only in 1612.[30] Both convents were also favored by members of the Chigi family. Three sisters of Pope Alexander VII—Ortensia, Ersilia, and Elena—all became nuns at S. Margherita in Castelvecchio; another two sisters, Agnese and Caterina, professed at Campansi. The evenhanded distribution of daughters to these institutions ceased with the Pope Alexander's generation. The pope's niece Laura, daughter of his brother Augusto, became a nun at Campansi, and Augusto's son, Agostino, trans-formed Campansi into a Chigi stronghold (see figure 3).

It was Agostino on whom Pope Alexander VII focused his hopes of creating a strong branch of the Chigi in Rome. After conferring several positions on his nephew and watching his success at carrying out his duties, the pope arranged for the twenty-four-year-old young man to marry into one of the most prominent of Roman families, the Borghese. Agostino Chigi and Maria Virginia Borghese wed in 1658, and in order to assure the bridegroom the same social standing as the bride, the Chigi disbursed enormous sums. Although Virginia's splendid dowry was used to purchase the duchy of Ariccia, it was Chigi money (or better yet, money of the papal state) that acquired the feudal property of Farnese (which Pope Alexander VII transformed into a principate) as well as the principate of Campagnano, the Palazzo di Formello, the Villa Versaglia, and a palace in piazza Colonna for Agostino.[31]

Between 1659 and 1681, Agostino and Virginia produced seventeen chil-dren.[32] In 1672, after Virginia had given birth to her tenth child and ninth girl, her sister-in-law, Olimpia, wrote to Cardinal Sigismondo to express her opinion that "now the princess should really be finished with female children, as their number equals that of the choirs of angels and should truly be sufficient."[33] Vir-ginia and Agostino would go on to have seven more children. Of the four boys to whom Virginia gave birth, only Augusto (b. 1662) and the couple's last child, Mario (b. 1681), lived to adulthood. On the other hand, eleven of the thirteen girls survived to become women. The family strategy for dealing with the "choirs of angels" was typical of the time: one was chosen for marriage and the other ten were consigned to the cloister.

Agostino and Maria Virginia could place their daughters in any institution they so desired, and in light of their place of residence, it comes as no surprise that three of the Chigi girls became nuns at the Roman house of SS. Domenico e Sisto.[34] Ties to Siena must have been even stronger, however, for the parents decided to consign seven of their daughters to the Sienese nunnery of S. Girolamo

TABLE 6.1.   Chigi sisters at S. Girolamo in Campansi

Name	Educanda	Investiture	Profession
Angela Francesca Maria	June 1672	June 1680	June 1681
(1665–1730)		Suor Francesca Serafina	
Berenice Maria	June 1676	June 1683	June 1684
(1667–1725)		Suor Teresa Vittoria	
Eleonora Domitilla	June 1676	June 1684	June 1685
(1669–1743)		Suor Maria Gaetana	
Olimpia Maria	June 1679	June 1686	June 1687
(1671–1741)		Suor Maria Agnese	
Teresa Maria	June 1683	June 1691	June 1692
(1675–1746)		Suor Angela Teresa	
Maria Maddalena	June 1683	June 1691	June 1692
(1675–1743)		Suor Maria Vittoria	
Alessandra Caterina	June 1688	June 1697	June 1698
(1680–1707)		Suor Chiara Caterina	

in Campansi, where Agostino's sister, Suor Maria Pulcheria, was waiting to greet them. Angela Francesca came to Campansi as an educanda in 1672; sixteen years later, the youngest and last Chigi daugher, eight-year-old Alessandra Caterina, entered the same convent's gates (see table 6.1). Since the dowries required for nuns in no way equaled those expected in marriage, Agostino and Maria Virginia had ample financial means at their disposal to assure that seven of their daughters could profess at the same convent.[35] They secured their comfort by paying the expenses and dowry for another girl who took vows as a conversa at the same time as the Chigi princess and served as her personal servant. They also guaranteed their daughters' leisure by paying yet another sum to exempt them from having to hold offices in the convent hierarchy. The money the parents disbursed in June 1684 for the clothing of their daughter Princess Eleonora as Suor Maria Gaetana and for the profession of another daughter, Suor Teresa Vittoria, is typical:[36]

For the supernumerary dowry of Signora Donna Eleonora	£. 3200
For the increase in dowry because she is the third sister	£. 1000
For clothes for the same	£. 210
For the meal [served at the clothing ceremony]	£. 420
For tips	£. 133
For room and board during the year of the novitiate	£. 168
For the dowry of Lisabetta Zuccarini, servant	£. 1600
For clothes for the same	£. 105
For the meal [served at the clothing ceremony]	£. 84
For tips	£. 42
For room and board during the year of the novitiate	£. 168
For exemption from holding office for Suor Teresa Vittoria	£. 1400
For the meal at the profession	£. 350
For tips	£. 133

The grand sum of £. 9013—over thirteen times the annual salary of the maestro di cappella at Siena Cathedral in the late seventeenth century—still represents only 37 percent of the amount that would have been required had the family decided to arrange a marriage for either girl with a member of the Sienese ruling elite.[37] The parents could, therefore, afford to be generous when it came to paying for music on the day when each girl took the habit.

Documentary evidence confirms that clothing rites for the first three Chigi princesses did indeed feature musical performance. Leonardo Marsili's majordomo, a certain Magini, was apparently responsible for hiring and directing the musicians who performed at the clothing ceremony for Angela Chigi in June 1680 and at the same rite for her sister Berenice Maria in June 1683.[38] A carpenter was paid to adjust the wooden stands for musicians who sang and played at the investiture of Eleonora Chigi in June 1684.[39] Although the nuns at Campansi listed the cost for music in their own registers, account books from the Chigi household in Rome suggest that the family remunerated the nuns later for those expenditures.[40]

Curiously, no payments for music are recorded in Campansi's registers for the clothing rites of the last four Chigi girls to enter the convent. Nevertheless, the Chigi collection in the Vatican preserves the score of an operina sacra that was performed "when the most excellent Princess Olimpia Chigi was clothed with the Franciscan habit at the venerable convent of San Girolamo, called Campansi, in Siena . . . the year 1686."[41] The title page lists the three characters in the opera and names the singers: Maria Maddalena Chigi, age ten, sang the part of "Divine Love"; Teresa Maria Chigi, age ten, performed the role of "Innocence"; and Geltrude Petrucci, also age ten, took the part of "Delight." Maria Maddalena and Teresa were Olimpia's younger twin sisters, and Geltrude another girl in the convent for education. The only other performers required were a continuo player and two violinists, doubtless drawn from the ranks of the convent's educande, novices, or choir nuns.

No documents have yet come to light providing details about the actual performance of this work; nevertheless, we can speculate as to some of the particulars. Although parlors often doubled as stages for theatrical works in convents, the L-shaped rooms that served this purpose at Campansi seem a cramped and implausible venue for the opera.[42] It is more than likely, considering the status of the family, that the performance took place in one of the convent's interior spaces where the singers, the instrumentalists, and the audience could have been accommodated in comfort. The convent's new church seems a logical site, for Prince Agostino had financed its construction in the early 1680s and Leonardo Marsili had consecrated it in September 1685.[43] The public, social nature of clothing rites and their attendant festivities meant that guests would have included not only Agostino and Maria Virginia, the parents of the Chigi girls, but also relatives such as Olimpia Gori Pannilini and Agnese Zondadari. Members of other important Sienese families to whom the Chigi were related by marriage—the Piccolomini and the Della Ciaia—might have been in attendance. Geltrude Petrucci's kin must have been admitted as well. It is highly probable that Leonardo Marsili, the archbishop of Siena, distant relative to the Chigi, and longtime confidant of the family, was on the guest list. It goes without saying that all the nuns, novices, and boarders inhabiting the convent would have been privy to the entertainment.

The audience for the three-act opera would have recognized, in the anonymous libretto, a sacred allegory appropriate for a young woman about to profess vows as a novice.[44] Delight opens Act I by noting that humankind, depraved and blindfolded, often welcomes false Delight instead of innocent Delight into its heart. He then presents the metaphor of an unsuspecting navigator who takes to the sea when it appears calm, only to find that, once far from port, a sudden shift in wind can whip up a storm. Innocence appears onstage and declares her desire for Delight. Delight responds in kind, but states that he also seeks all other virtues as well. Innocence replies that he is cruel. In the next scene, Innocence encounters Divine Love, and asks him why, if she is so dear to him, she is an object of ridicule and disparged by the world. Divine Love counters by noting that the more she suffers, the greater she will become. Innocence says that she does not want to suffer, and Divine Love begs her not to run away.

Act II finds Innocence regretting her decision to run away from Divine Love. She compares herself to a ship lost at sea, subject to the wrath of the waves, and then wonders who will show her the way. Delight appears and decides to test Innocence; when she asks him how to obtain the palm of martyrdom, he tells her that joy can be found in the pleasures of the world as well as in pain and suffering. Innocence tells him she will not stray from her path and tries to send him away. Because he refuses to go, she flees instead. Delight plunges into despair and wants to kill himself, but Divine Love stops him and Delight agrees to submit to his power. Divine Love sends Delight to seek out Innocence. He finally finds her in a wooded glade, rejoicing in the gentle winds, the song of the nightingale, and the myriad flowers. Delight entreats Innocence to return to the city and to submit to the arrows of Divine Love.

In Act III, Divine Love reveals that the forest to which Innocence had fled was a dangerous place, full of savage beasts. Delight reports to Divine Love that a repentant Innocence has returned to the city and, worried that her heart is too hard, is preparing herself through weeping and sighing for the arrows of Divine Love. Divine Love directs Delight to bring Innocence before him. Innocence finally appears and swears her eternal fidelity to Divine Love, who fires an arrow into her heart. Delight, Innocence, and Divine Love appear on stage together for the first time in the last scene of the opera, when they join to sing a trio expressing their joy.

Certain aspects of the libretto bear a strong resemblance to the emblematic literature so popular throughout Europe in the seventeenth century. Although the first publications of this type concentrated on love emblems, the seventeenth century saw the rise of books that reinterpreted the same pictorial conceits in order to make "ethical and religious truths accessible to all."[45] The adventures of the profane lover and his beloved were replaced by those of Divine Love and Soul. In the former, Love was a sailor, heading for port; in the latter, Soul became the sailor, rowing from the agitated sea to Divine Love on the shore. Another prominent emblem was that of Love (profane or divine, depending on the collection) firing an arrow into the breast of the beloved. As Mario Praz has pointed out, these conceits were not new; they could be traced to the poetry of Petrarch and often back to Ovid. Nevertheless, there are striking similarities between at least two conceits that have a prominent place in the opera—that of a navigator in a stormy sea (expressed at the beginning of the opera by Delight and in the opening of Act II by Innocence) and that of Divine Love as an archer (depicted at the climax of the opera when a rubric in the score directs Divine Love to fire an arrow into the breast of Innocence)—and the two oft-repeated emblems from prints of the time just described. This might suggest that the librettist took inspiration from emblematic literature when constructing the libretto, perhaps in homage to his patrons. The Chigi were not immune to the rage for emblems. For instance, when Fabio Chigi had a carriage constructed for his own use in 1644, he had it decorated with emblems; as Pope Alexander VII, he had another carriage built for Christine of Sweden, and this too, was adorned with emblems.[46] There is still much to be learned about the tastes of the Chigi nephews before any definitive conclusion can be reached concerning this hypothesis, but it is not unreasonable to suggest that many of the sophisticated members of the audience might have understood the opera as an extended musical epigram for well-known emblems of the day.

The musical setting of the anonymous libretto is the product of an unidentified composer.[47] It is probable, however, that the Chigi commissioned the opera from a musician who was familiar with Roman operatic trends of the 1670s and early 1680s, for the musical style of the piece links it closely to the "late Roman school of opera" as exemplified in the works of Bernardo Pasquini and Alessandro Melani.[48] The orchestra is small, consisting of two violins and continuo. The only independent instrumental composition in the score is the opening fifty-two-measure, two-part sinfonia. The vocal parts reign supreme, and there is a sharp distinction between aria and recitative style. In both arias and recitative, one can often find a feature characteristic of the early seventeenth century: the placement of the last syllable of text on the penultimate note of a musical phrase (see Ex. 6.1, mm. 1–3; Ex. 6.8, m. 15; and Ex. 6.9, mm. 6, 10–11). Most of the recitative is fluid, but not extraordinarily rapid. It exploits eighth and sixteenth notes in speechlike patterns and generally moves stepwise melodically over a slow-moving bass line (see Ex. 6.8). The composer lavished the greatest amount of musical attention on the score's twenty-three solo arias, which display attractive but not excessively virtuosic melodic lines. Thirteen arias are in single-stanza ABA form and ten are essentially through-composed. All but four arias begin with a "motto" (see Exs. 6.1, 6.2, 6.9). Eighteen solo arias feature obbligato violin parts. The violins do not provide continuous accompaniment but rather alternate with the vocal line, playing *ritornelli* to introduce the aria and to demarcate important structural points. The remaining five solo arias are accompanied by basso continuo alone, although in four of those five, a violin ritornello punctuates the end of the piece. Eight arias—five in ABA form and three in continuous form, all of them expressing different affections—exploit a modulating ostinato figure in the bass (see Exs. 6.2 and 6.3). Harmonic movement within the arias is generally simple and clear: most modulate briefly to either the dominant, the subdominant, the relative minor, or the relative major, if in a minor key.[49] The modulation occurs at the B section if the aria is in ABA form, or near the midpoint, if the aria is set to continuous music (see Exs. 6.1 and 6.2). An average aria ranges in length from twenty-five to forty-five measures, though the opera also includes two fifteen-measure arias and two monumental arias of 90 and 147 measures, respectively. Rounding out the score are one extended arioso passage, four duets, and one trio.[50]

The Chigi twins and their Petrucci colleague must have received intensive training to prepare them to sing the operina sacra. Since the Chigi princesses were placed at Campansi in June 1683, when both were seven and a half years old, and the Petrucci girl arrived in April 1684, when she was about eight, that training must have taken place inside the convent. No books of licenze survive for Campansi, but lay teachers, probably Cathedral musicians, must have come often to instruct the girls in singing and to help teach them their music. Just how long the girls practiced for their roles is unknown, but considering their tender age, it seems logical to suggest that the opera was composed well in advance of the performance to give them the time necessary to learn their parts.[51]

The youth of the performers did not deter the composer from offering them interpretive challenges. He assigned each of the girls a selection of arias that embody different affections: all three, for example, must be able to express plaintiveness, hope, and ardor in song. Some idea of the variety and contrast inherent in the score is displayed in two arias that follow each other in Act I. In scene 3, Innocence offers a mournful complaint to Divine Love (Ex. 6.1):

> Divine Love, since I save my lilies for you,
> I would prefer that you not be so stern with me.[52]

This tactic apparently disarms Divine Love completely, for in scene 4, after declaring (in recitative) that Innocence is dear to him and beautiful, he launches into an aria of his own (Ex. 6.2):

> Seeing the whiteness of a pure lily,
> I feel a fire inside my heart.
> Seeing the fervor of a spotless lily,
> Sacred Love is won over, and yields.[53]

The aria for Innocence achieves its effect through the repetition of short motives, suggestive of the broken cries of a lament. Because this affection suggests a slow tempo and because the brief motives are often repeated at the same pitch level, the singer must be able not only to shape each carefully with a smooth legato but also to vary the dynamics to achieve some variety without losing sight of the overarching phrase. The aria for Divine Love, on the other hand, requires clear articulation at high speed and the flexibility to move quickly from detached syllabic declamation to flowing melisma, all while maintaining a high level of energy to communicate the character's zeal.

In addition to the interpretive challenges, the singers also faced some technical difficulties. All three girls had to have good breath control in order to perform the melismas that the composer enjoyed using to embellish his vocal lines. Sometimes, these melismas paint the text. In the first aria of the opera, for example,

Ex. 6.1. *Operina sacra* I, 3 (1686), "Divino Amore," mm. 1–10

Ex. 6.2. *Operina sacra* I, 4 (1686), "Al candor di puro giglio," mm. 1–18

Ex 6.2. (continued)

All'— ar - dor d'in-tat-to

gi - glio,   all'— ar - dor d'in-tat-to   gi - glio   vin - to

6 5

ce —   —   —   —   de,   vin-to   ce - de il sa-cro A-mor.

4 3

Delight presents the idea of a calm sea turning stormy on an unsuspecting navigator.[54] Throughout the piece, the waves of the sea are suggested by gently rising and falling melismas, which can stretch to five measures of eighth notes in 3/4 time. More typical, however, are the melismas in the Act III, scene 4 aria for Innocence (Ex. 6.3):

> The voice of heaven is an enchantment for the soul.
> It fights and subdues a heart that resists.
> But in the battle, virtue always has the upper hand,
> and God, the palm of victory.[55]

Here, the running sixteenth notes are, for the most part, decorative. Only the first melisma might have been inspired by the text. It appears on the last two syllables of the word "incanto" ("enchantment"); that is, on the word "canto" ("song"). The composer might have used the melisma as a tongue-in-cheek play on words to depict the "singing" sound of the enchanting "voice from heaven." This particular aria also poses another problem for the singer, for she must project her own line against what amounts to a second melody—the ostinato in the continuo part—and she must be able to control her pitch and effect a chromatic alteration when the continuo pauses momentarily (Ex. 6.3, m. 13).

Another technical demand involves negotiating changes in time signatures. Most of the lyrical solos in the work are in common time. Only one piece, the first in the opera, remains in 3/4 time throughout. In two other arias, both of them for Divine Love, the composer asks the singer to begin in 3/4 and to move to 4/4, mostly to generate musical interest in these through-composed solos. Only in one aria did the composer exploit a rapid shift from 4/4 to 3/4 as a dramatic device to drive home the meaning of the text. In Act II, scene 3, just after Innocence runs away, Delight tells the absent Innocence, "If you want me dead, I will be content."[56] Time signature, tempo, and vocal register all change abruptly not once, but twice, to render the contrast between "death" and "contentment" as striking as possible (Ex. 6.4).

The one concession the composer may have made to the performers regards the range and tessitura of the vocal lines. Most of the arias require a range of approximately an octave, and that octave always lies somewhere between c' and e''. On rare occasions, the singers may be required to touch f' in a melismatic passage, and in two arias, the singer must descend to b. This is still the tessitura considered most appropriate for children with "reasonably trained voices,"[57] and it is more limited than that normally found in arias written for adult sopranos by composers of the time.[58]

The fact that the sacred opera was meant to honor Olimpia Chigi and that two of the performers were Chigi princesses probably induced the librettist to show slight favoritism when it came to assigning arias to his three protagonists. The character of Delight, played by Geltrude Petrucci, has only six arias compared to the eight and nine allocated respectively to Innocence and Divine Love, the roles taken by the Chigi twins. It is true that all three characters are given the opportunity to inaugurate an act: Delight opens Act I; Innocence, Act II; and Divine Love, Act III. Innocence and Divine Love, however, dominate the pro-

Ex. 6.3. *Operina sacra* III, 4 (1686), "La voce del cielo," mm. 1–24

Ex. 6.3.   (*continued*)

-gna ma nel - la pu - gna vir - tù   n'ha sem - pre il van - - - - - to,   Id - di - o,   la pal - ma.

♭6

ceedings in Acts II and III respectively, by singing the greatest number of arias, whereas Delight does not have that advantage in Act I. In this case, however, the composer found a way to compensate the performer for the lack of arias. Delight's initial aria in Act I, at 147 measures, is the longest in the opera, nearly four times the length of the typical solo. To be fair, the librettist also redresses the imbalance in the number of arias allotted to Delight by making her a pivotal dramatic force. She is the catalyst for the action that occurs in the opera, and she has the most sensational theatrical scene in the work: the attempted suicide.

It appears, then, that the librettist knew who would play each character in the little sacred opera and designed the libretto accordingly. The hypothesis seems probable in light of the work's function and its meaning for the performers, the dedicatee, and the audience. As with any sacred allegory, the operina has the didactic goal of driving home explicit morals, concisely summarized by Steven Plank: "suffering is to one's betterment; beauty is in essence a divided quality that must be loved in totality; and pleasure and innocence reach their perfection only with divine love."[59] Plank also makes the logical connection (given the order of nuns at Campansi) between the first of these morals and S. Francis's admonition that the greatest gift the Holy Spirit can bestow is the willingness to endure suffering for the love of Christ.[60] The Franciscan context and the obvious moral message constitute, however, only one layer of meaning in this work. Examinations of the tenor of Catholic faith in the mid–to–late seventeenth century, of the symbolism associated with the post-Tridentine convent, of the devotional and ceremonial practices of Sienese holy women, and of the fortunes of the Chigi family all contribute to a deeper understanding of the operina sacra.

A UNIQUE FEATURE OF the opera in performance was the use of twins in two of the title roles. If, as I suspect, the Chigi twins were identical and not fraternal, that fact does not appear to have escaped the librettist.[61] What little dramatic

Ex. 6.4.   *Operina sacra* II, 3 (1686), "Se morto mi vuoi," mm. 1–7

tension the opera exhibits is created when Innocence, feeling spurned by both Delight and Divine Love, decides to run away. One cause of Innocence's dismay is revealed early in the opera: she is hurt that Delight seeks all virtues (honesty, humility, wisdom, and patience) in addition to her. Delight reproves her with an aria in Act I, scene 2:

> Nature formed beauty
> divided into many aspects.
> Whoever loves only one,
> whoever desires only one
> cannot enjoy it.[62]

Delight is ostensibly referring to all the virtues he listed in his previous aria, but the reference to the Chigi girls would have been clearly represented by the visual spectacle of two identical faces in the roles of Innocence and Divine Love. By extension, of course, the aria could be interpreted as a reference to all six Chigi girls inhabiting the convent by 1686. It is difficult to determine if the librettist was issuing a compliment, a warning, or both. Certainly, the text can be read as a tribute to the "beauty" of all six girls, but a warning is implicit in the fact that the "beauties" are part of a larger clan that acts as a unit to protect family interests above all. In this way, perhaps, the Chigi, through their librettist, were serving notice to members of other families in the nunnery that joyful acceptance of all six (and eventually seven) Chigi princesses was the surest path to the enjoyment of the fruits of Chigi patronage. In the year 1686, in fact, the convent obtained permission from the Sacred Congregation to invest in annuities any money left over from the annual sum that Prince Agostino sent the nuns for his daughters' upkeep. The daughters received the interest generated by those annuities, and could use that money as they saw fit.[63]

If "beauty divided" is indeed a specific reference to the Chigi sisters, other themes in the libretto speak to the kinds of devotional practices those young women would have encountered as a matter of course within the convent. In the libretto, for instance, one of the reasons that Innocence is reluctant to wed herself to Divine Love is her aversion to experiencing pain. As a number of scholars have shown, the practice of self-inflicted suffering in imitation of Christ's Passion was common among holy women in the early modern era. It bears re-peating that this pattern of behavior was an important motif in the biographies of many of the vite examined in chapter 5, including that of Campansi's own "local saint," Suor Colomba Tofanini. This particular holy woman would have had special significance for the Chigi clan, because several times before her death in early March 1655, she predicted to Suor Maria Agnese Chigi and Suor Maria Pulcheria Chigi that Fabio Chigi would ascend to the papacy. Tofanini's special gifts, including that of prophecy, were implicitly attributed to her extraordinary devotion, which manifested itself in various acts of self-torment. She disciplined herself twice a day until blood ran, wore a belt of iron with sharp points next to her skin, and asked God to deprive her of speech so that she would never "offend" with her tongue.[64]

The pampered Chigi girls were certainly not expected to engage in such extreme behavior, but neither were they excused from suffering. The librettist makes this point clear in a duet from Act I, scene 4, in which Divine Love insists on the need for Innocence to experience anguish while Innocence simultaneously spurns the proposal (Ex. 6.5):

> INNOCENCE: No, I do not want to suffer any more; servitude is too tedi-
> ous.
> DIVINE LOVE: Yes, you must still suffer more; servitude is too tedious.[65]

It is, of course, Innocence's lack of willingness to be subject to tribulation that causes her to flee to the forest. Once she returns and accepts the idea that she must suffer, her travails involve nothing more than weeping over her hard heart to soften it in preparation for Divine Love. Indeed, after Divine Love shoots his arrow into her heart, Innocence marvels, "How can it be that a wound brings

Ex. 6.5.   *Operina sacra* I, 4 (1686), "No, che soffrire"

such great delight to the soul?" The choice of the heart as the locus of suffering is particularly apt in light of its prominence in the *vite* of two esteemed Sienese holy women, Catherine Benincasa and Maria Francesca Piccolomini. It links Innocence with these holy women whose love for Christ and for the Virgin manifested itself in the painfully sweet throbbing of their hearts.[66]

In its accent on the idea of pleasurable suffering (perhaps the verb "languishing" is most appropriate in this context) the librettist appears to have been influenced by imagery of the "new mystical optimism" that was manifest in Rome as early as the 1620s. In his study of seventeenth-century Roman oratory, Frederick McGinnis has pointed out that preachers of the early Counter-Reformation relied on martial imagery and calls to battle to inspire devoted Catholics. Later orators, however, chose to exploit joyous images—flowers, light, the mystical marriage of Christ the bridegroom to his bride the Church, the splendors of heaven—in order to move their listeners to delight. Central to religious preaching prevalent in Rome by the mid–seventeenth century was the notion that pleasure both provided an access to virtue and was created as a by-product of virtue.[67]

The difference between these two approaches for motivating the faithful can be best understood by briefly comparing the libretto of the 1686 operina to that of the most famous example of sacred allegory from the beginning of the century, Emilio de' Cavalieri's *Rappresentatione di anima et di corpo*, on a text by Agostino Manni. Manni's libretto begins with a memento mori, "Time flies, life is destroyed," and continues with a cautionary tale involving Body and Soul. After introducing these characters in Act I, Manni gives over the entire second act to their struggles against the temptations of Pleasure, the World, and Worldly Life. The latter are forced to strip and to reveal their essential ugliness by a Guardian Angel. When Body and Soul see the foul nature of Pleasure, the World, and Worldly Life, they are able to resist their attractive lures and to ascend to the realm of heavenly souls.[68] In the 1686 work, however, Delight is not a villain. Though Delight does try to tempt Innocence, it is only to test her virtue. Divine Love does not send Delight away for his mistake but saves him from suicide and gives him the commission to retrieve Innocence. It is Delight, not Divine Love, who convinces Innocence to return to the city. In the end, Delight is an essential partner in the marriage between Innocence and Divine Love.

The idea that Delight is central to the alliance of Innocence and Divine Love is symbolized in the composer's choice to reserve 3/2 meter exclusively for the short but significant duets in the work that document the journey toward the all-important union: the disagreement in Act I between Divine Love and Innocence as to the need for suffering (see Ex. 6.5); the finale of Act II in which Innocence and Delight ask heaven to guide their steps as they return to the city; the reunion of Divine Love and Innocence in Act III; and their subsequent mutual expression of love. The perfect meter receives its perfect setting, however, only in the finale of the work when Innocence, Delight, and Divine Love, on stage together for the first time, sing the concluding trio. The composer stresses the perfection of three by beginning the ensemble in common time, moving into triple only when all three characters join voices (Ex. 6.6):

Ex. 6.6. *Operina sacra* III, 5 (1686), "Il Diletto"

DELIGHT: Delight is perfect,

INNOCENCE: Innocence is beautiful,

DELIGHT, INNOCENCE, DIVINE LOVE: only when Divine Love wounds hearts.[69]

The physical location in which the wedding of Innocence, Delight, and Divine Love takes place is not indicated in the libretto. Indeed, the librettist specifies the physical location of only one scene in the entire opera: the forest ("bosco") of Act II, scene 5.[70] Nonetheless, the setting of the rest of the opera can be inferred from several passages of dialogue between the characters. In Act I, scene 2, after Delight's opening aria, Innocence comes onstage and engages him in conversation, set in recitative. Especially notable is her first question to him:

INNOCENCE: Delight, my friend!

DELIGHT: Amiable Innocence!

INNOCENCE: What desire calls you within these walls?[71]

By using the word *mura*, the librettist restricted its meaning to the thick, defensive walls around a city or a monastery. The librettist, cognizant of the opera's performance site, must have decided to create a passage of dialogue that would have had double meaning for the audience. The question Innocence poses situates not only the imaginary location of much of the opera but also the real performance space of the work "within the walls" of a nunnery. In this regard, it is also noteworthy that Divine Love appears on the scene in response to Innocence's calls and remains "within the walls" for the entire opera. When Innocence flees, Divine Love does not go after her. Rather, he sends Delight to bring her back. This plays into the symbolism of the convent as an "earthly Jerusalem" where divine love (and thus Divine Love) would be most likely to reside.

Innocence's flight, on the other hand, may be read as a dramatization of a normal convent procedure. Before any young girl took vows, her parents withdrew her from the nunnery for a period not to exceed forty days, ostensibly to allow her to reflect on her decision. The Chigi family observed this tradition rigorously, as is clear from a diary recording the details of all their trips to Siena from 1672 to 1704.[72] Each time a Chigi princess was to be clothed, she left the convent for a vacation in the company of her parents and other relatives. This was the reason for the journey that Agostino Chigi and Maria Virginia Borghese made to Siena in May 1680, an event that prompted the Sienese performance of Scarlatti's *Gli equivoci nel sembiante*. The parents were in town to take their daughter Angela out of Campansi for a week-long trip before her investiture. Similarly, in May 1691, when the twins Teresa and Maria Maddalena were of an age to take vows, their parents withdrew them from the convent and took them to S. Quirico d'Orcia, Montalcino, Pienza, and Montepulciano, among other places. In Montepulciano, they visited S. Biagio, the Duomo, the convent of S. Chiara, and the monastery of S. Girolamo, where they saw the body of S. Agnese.[73] After the short vacation, the girls returned to Campansi, where they were clothed within a month.

The official position of the Catholic Church was that the Chigi girls, and others like them, were to have both the vocation and the free will to choose the life of a nun. That this was not always the case has already been established. The maintenance of the facade was, however, absolutely vital in order for the convent-as-repository system to survive. It is notable that in this opera the librettist provides what might be interpreted as a ready-made justification for families such as the Chigi who enclosed most of their female children in convents. In Act III, scene 2, after Delight has reported the return of Innocence to the city, Divine Love commands Delight to bring Innocence before him. Delight obeys, but before leaving the stage, he reflects on the situation. The composer sets his words with the only extended arioso passage of the entire opera, thus endowing them with special significance (Ex. 6.7):

> To serve and obey love, when love is sacred
> Is a gift from heaven, not from destiny.[74]

In other words, it was not the whim of secular Fortune that fated the Chigi girls for the convent but rather the choice of God. The implication is that a heavenly gift cannot be refused. It seems a message meant to reassure the parents and the church hierarchy. Perhaps it was also intended to console the six girls Agostino and Maria Virginia had already consigned to Campansi.

Accepting the "gift from heaven" required a girl to take the habit and to profess, and references to the monastic ceremonies associated with such actions are echoed in the final scenes of the opera. After Innocence returns to the city, she appears before Divine Love in Act III, scene 4. To explain her former behavior, she casts herself in the role prominent in every important rite of passage for early modern nuns: that of the spouse in the Song of Songs.[75] Innocence's statement is followed by a series of questions from Divine Love, to which Innocence responds by declaring her readiness to accept the fate that Divine Love has chosen for her. The questions recall those an archbishop was obliged to pose to a young girl in order to assure that she was committing herself to the cloister out of her own free will and a strong vocation. In answering the queries, Innocence takes vows, as a girl was required to do in a profession ceremony:

> INNOCENCE: I confess that I wandered foolishly, and like a wounded deer, I went in search of the traces of a living fountain; in a secluded wood, in a wild forest, I sought traces of my beloved, just as the enamoured spouse in sacred scripture. . . .
>
> DIVINE LOVE: Therefore, have you truly understood that you must be the target for my arrow?
>
> INNOCENCE: I want it to be so. Thus commands God. . . .
>
> DIVINE LOVE: Tell me, then, do you swear eternal fidelity and love to me?
>
> INNOCENCE: My heart will be yours as long as the sky turns, as long as the sun burns.[76]

As if to emphasize the intimate nature of these last two scenes in the opera, which mark the marriage of Divine Love, Innocence, and Delight, the composer virtually banishes the violins (they play only a five-measure ritornello after the con-

Ex. 6.7.   *Operina sacra* III, 2 (1686), "Il servire"

tinuo aria "La voce del cielo" that Innocence sings in Act III, scene 4) and focuses all musical attention on the voices. The last aria, in Act III, scene 4, and the subsequent final scene of the opera, consisting of recitative, a duet, and the concluding trio, are all accompanied by the continuo part alone.

If one image can be said to dominate the opera, it is that of "the city," mentioned three times in close succession at the end of Act II and the beginning of Act III. In Act II, scene 6, when Innocence tells Delight that she is happy in the forest, he responds to her as follows:

> Believe me, you are wrong.
> Return to the city.
> There, love resides, and wishes to wound your chaste breast.[77]

At the beginning of Act III, Divine Love laments the escape of Innocence to the forest. He commands the rough-living anchorite, accustomed to martyrdom, to stay in the desert—

> But let a gentle lady, on whose beautiful face nature pours,
> with charming liveliness, her rare treasures,
> love the city and flee horror.[78]

In the following scene, Delight informs Divine Love that he has good news as to the whereabouts of Innocence:

> She returns to the city
> repentant of her flight.[79]

Plank interprets the phrase "return to the city" as a call to "come among people and engage in apostolic work."[80] Participation in the kind of active, public religious life suggested by this interpretation was not, however, an option for the Chigi princess to whom the opera was dedicated. Instead, it seems that the city has a much more specific, physical meaning in this opera: it represents the urban convent. To understand this meaning, we must remember that the "city" is set in contrast to the forest to which Innocence flees when she feels rejected by both Delight and Divine Love. In the monologue that opens Act III, Divine Love characterizes the forest as a place replete with wild beasts and unseen dangers. The composer sets the passage in recitative style (Ex. 6.8) and conveys the horrors of the forest through a brief use of biting, dissonant seconds (see mm. 10–11):

> Ill-advised Innocence,
> you wanted to escape and wander about,
> to turn your steps away from me?
> And you think that Divine Love,
> who stops the flow of the rivers,
> and the rotation of the sky and the stars,
> cannot prevent you from walking into disaster?
> You roam through the forests,
> you expose yourself to the voracious fangs of wild beasts,
> and, held fast by hostile claws,
> you neither understand nor see your danger.[81]

This is not at all the impression of the forest that Innocence imparts in Act II, scene 5. She speaks of a place filled with mild breezes, the song of a nightingale, and a multitude of flowers. The listener is more apt to believe Innocence's account because the composer clothes her words in a charming melody characterized by lilting triplets (Ex. 6.9):

> Beautiful hyacinths, lovely violets,
> dear roses, charming amaranths,
> pure lilies, fragrant daffodils,
> you open a sweet wound in my breast.[82]

The enchanting sylvan abode, far from the madding crowd, is reminiscent of the settings featured in operas performed at the Chigi estate of Ariccia in the early

Ex. 6.8. *Operina sacra* III, 1 (1686), "Mal accorta Innocenza," mm. 1–15

Ex. 6.9.   *Operina sacra* II, 5 (1686), "Bei giacinti," mm. 1–16

Ex. 6.9.   *(continued)*

1670s. *Il Tirinto* of 1672 features an "idealized version of Ariccia," including a forest with a view of Jove's temple. In the opera *Adalinda*, performed in 1673, the libretto specifies that the action takes place at Anzio, near Nettuno, the favorite country retreat of Cardinal Flavio Chigi.[83] Lorenzo Bianconi and Thomas Walker have noted that the Ariccia operas celebrate the "virtues of rustic life"; they have also speculated that the performance of the works constituted, for the Chigi, a "public declaration of possession" of their newly acquired feudal properties.[84] Such a life of pastoral bliss was not, however, one that could be enjoyed by the Chigi girls, destined for enclosure. They had to "love the city," a symbol for the female monastery. The walls of the city in the *operina sacra*, just as those that appear in Benvenuto Flori's 1642 theatrical play for the nuns of Ognissanti, were meant to represent the safety and protection offered by the cloister.

The phrases "return to the city" and "love the city" may also have significance in the context of the Chigi family and its fortunes in the 1680s. Pope Alexander VII's goal of establishing a strong branch of the Chigi in Rome had been realized through the amazingly fertile marriage between Agostino Chigi and Maria Virginia Borghese. In Rome, the Chigi had status, land, and heirs. In their native city, however, this branch of the Chigi was dying out.[85] It thus fell to Cardinal Flavio and to Prince Agostino to buttress the position of the Sienese Chigi. To such an end, Flavio Chigi set up his will so that his sister Agnese's son, Bonaventura Zondadari, inherited the feud of San Quirico d'Orcia and the title of marquis (which Grand Duke Cosimo III had conceded to Cardinal Flavio in 1677) as well as Flavio's beautifully constructed and sumptuously decorated villa at Cetinale, 10 kilometres outside Siena in the Montagnola.[86] The only requirement placed on Bonaventura Zondadari was the obligation of taking the Chigi surname and using the Chigi emblems in the family coat-of-arms. In this way, Cardinal Flavio guaranteed the continuation of the family name and assured that his Sienese heirs would have the necessary accoutrements of nobility—a title and a country estate. Prince Agostino Chigi and his wife Maria Virginia, on the other hand, shored up the spiritual capital of the family in Siena by placing seven of their daughters in a single Sienese convent. Never before had a Sienese family consigned so many daughters to a single nunnery, and never again would a Sienese family place such a stake in a similar institution. S. Girolamo in Campansi thus became a monument to Chigi patronage and Chigi piety, and its history was thereafter connected with the family who so richly provided for it. Ultimately, then, the little sacred opera performed for the investiture of Olimpia Chigi in 1686 can be interpreted, much like the operas performed in the early 1670s at Ariccia, as a "public declaration of possession," commemorating, in this case, the addition of a Sienese convent to the Chigi family feudal holdings.

WEEPING AND REJOICING

Lamentations and Motets for Nuns in Seventeenth-Century Siena

In 1650, the Sienese composer Alessandro Della Ciaia allowed his second volume of music to be published under the title *Sacred Lamentations and Motets for one voice with basso continuo.*[1] The use of the verb "allowed" is intentional here, for Della Ciaia appears to have left the painstaking work of seeing the compositions through the press to a certain Bastiano Arditi. It was Arditi who inscribed the volume to Giacomo Carissimi and signed the dedication. Arditi's most important contribution, however, was to provide an afterword in which he informed readers of the genesis and function of the works in the publication:

> O reader, you might perhaps wonder why the present Lamentations and motets that I have gathered are all composed in the soprano clef. The author wrote these works not for professional reasons or out of ambition to have them published but to satisfy both his talents and the pious requests of some friends on behalf of their relatives who are nuns. He therefore composed the works to conform to the range in which the nuns would have to sing them. (Doc. 18)

Della Ciaia's 1650 print takes on particular significance as the sole known source of sacred music composed specifically for Sienese nuns. It also appears to be only the second publication to contain monodic settings of the Lamentations of Jeremiah, which are recited as Lessons 1, 2, and 3 of the first Nocturn from Matins on Maundy Thursday, Good Friday, and Holy Saturday. Della Ciaia's compositions reveal that he perceived Sienese nuns to be not only the custodians of feast days associated with certain saints and martyrs but also the "guardians of Holy Week rites."[2] This chapter sets the composer's motets and Lamentations in the context of mid-Seicento Siena and demonstrates how the works reflect Sienese traditions as well as devotional, liturgical, and musical practices in the city's nunneries. It also explores the symbolism linking the Lamentations of Jeremiah both to the specific setting of the convent and to the general sphere of women's duties.

OFFICIAL SIENESE RECORDS PRESERVE only the barest facts about the activities of the composer Alessandro Della Ciaia. He was born in May 1600 to parents from two Sienese families of the ruling elite: Tiberio Della Ciaia and Ginevra Tolomei. In early 1636, Alessandro married Sulpizia Santi, a young woman from another aristocratic Sienese family, and between 1638 and 1653, at least six children were born to them. We know that by January 1678 he had died, for a financial document names Filippo Della Ciaia as one of his "sons and heirs."[3] Throughout his life, Della Ciaia seems to have insisted on maintaining his identity as a nobleman; he was especially careful not to sully his reputation by leaving any suggestion that he was a professional musician. In the dedication to the 1650 print, Arditi scrupulously noted that Della Ciaia "composed the present volume not for professional reasons, but for sheer pleasure when the gravest affairs of his family permitted him to do so (which was rarely)."[4] He reiterated the same point in the afterword to the print, cited earlier. A similar tone is present in the more informative account Ugurgieri Azzolini provided in his *Pompe sanesi* of 1649:

> Alessandro Della Ciaia, a Sienese nobleman, was a student of doctor Desiderio Pecci in counterpoint or the art of music, and being a fervent emulator of such a teacher, it is not surprising that connoisseurs should recognize in his works that most concise manner of composing. Some of these compositions are in print and are sweet to sing and delightful to hear. He is also in possession of an infinite number of [unpublished] works that virtuosos desire to perform, but he will not allow it out of modesty, for although he is very talented, he does not think highly of himself. In addition to being an intelligent composer and a lovely singer, he also plays the harpsichord, lute, and theorbo most beautifully. Because, as a true nobleman, he does not make a profession of music for money, he gladly composes and plays for his friends, and even more often in service of God, on the occasion of solemn feasts that occur day after day and are celebrated in the churches of Siena. (Doc. 19)

Like his better-known relative Azzolino Della Ciaia, Alessandro may not have made a living as a musician, but he took his compositional studies seriously.[5] Frits Noske characterized the *Lamentatio Virginis in depositione Filii de cruce*, a large-scale dialogue motet from the composer's *Sacri modulatus* of 1666, as "a truly stupendous piece" and noted with wonder that it seemed "incredible that a totally unknown composer was able to write music of such surprisingly high quality."[6] Della Ciaia's teacher was another amateur musician of the ruling elite: the jurist Desiderio Pecci. Pecci was renowned as a singer, instrumentalist, and composer; his works include madrigals, arias, and motets. According to Ugurgieri Azzolini, a number of young gentlemen flocked to Pecci's home to learn the "science of music" and to perform in concerts there.[7] Della Ciaia clearly trusted and revered Pecci for his expertise in the fields of both law and music. He turned to Pecci when he needed a marriage contract written up, and he dedicated his first printed volume, a collection of five-voice madrigals, to his former teacher.[8] Della Ciaia's only other publications—the *Lamentationi sagre e motetti* of 1650 and the *Sacri modulatus* of 1666—both contain sacred music, supporting Ugurgieri Azzolini's assertion that he was especially motivated to compose "in service of God."

Della Ciaia apparently moved in the most rarefied aristocratic circles, and the fact that his 1650 publication is dedicated exclusively to music for nuns who were "relatives of friends" reinforces two points already established by the documentary evidence, but worth repeating here. First, since all the works from this volume call for a soprano with virtuoso capabilities, we can presume that many women of the Sienese nobility received extensive musical training. Second, the families of such young women expected that their daughters would be able to display that training even if destined for the convent.

Arditi cites no specific nunnery as the source of inspiration for Della Ciaia's monodies, and it is most likely that the composer's friends had sisters, daughters, and aunts at more than one of the various institutions whose names are by now familiar from previous chapters.[9] Della Ciaia's connections with the Chigi have already been noted in chapter 6. Prominent members of that family were nuns at the Franciscan institutions of S. Girolamo in Campansi and S. Margherita in Castelvecchio. One document also suggests that Della Ciaia may have forged a strong tie with the convent of Ognissanti. In 1655, the composer signed a financial contract that provided a yearly annuity to two nuns there, Caterina Piccolomini and her sister Maria Francesca, the renowned theorbist who received miraculous cures so that she could perform on important feast days.[10] In the absence of other documents with earlier dates, however, it is not possible to prove that Della Ciaia composed his works with the musically talented Olivetan women in mind. What is clear is that several prominent Sienese female monasteries might have exploited the print for use on many different feast days, including three of the most solemn services belonging to the Proper of the Time.

Lamentations

Holy Week, the week during which Christians commemorate Christ's Passion and death on the cross, had particular meaning for women in convents. Caroline Walker Bynum has asserted that holy women often expressed their spiritual devotion through a body-centered, dramatic *imitatio Christi* in "an effort to plumb the depths of Christ's humanity at the moment of his most insistent and terrifying humanness—the moment of his dying."[11] This thread runs throughout the biographies of Siena's most famous holy women, beginning with S. Catherine of Siena (1347–80), the model for future generations. Catherine told her biographer that it was Christ himself who urged her to embrace the cross and suffering. Her mystical experiences included sharing the Passion of the Lord for several days and receiving invisible stigmata. Suor Caterina Vannini (1562–1606) at the Convertite meditated on the Passion daily. For her, this was far better than thinking about the joys of eternal life. Suor Chiara Birelli (1565–1622) at Il Refugio also included the Passion in her meditations, an appropriate activity for a woman who had requested and received an invisible crown of thorns on the day she took the habit. Suor Colomba (1583–1655) at Campansi and Suor Rosa Maria Generali (1648–80) at Paradiso were similarly devoted to Christ's Passion.[12] Most of these women also engaged in severe self-torture and food asceticism, and some patiently endured debilitating illness, all in an effort to draw nearer to Christ by partaking of his suffering.

Although most nuns in Sienese convents of the seventeenth century did not punish their bodies with the same ferocity as these holy women, all were taught to understand the centrality of the Passion of Christ to their devotional practices. Women about to become "brides of Christ" at the Dominican institution of S. Caterina del Paradiso, for instance, were to contemplate the head, hands, ribs, knees, and feet of the Savior on the cross, and then reflect on the entire Passion in order to prepare themselves for the event. Augustinians at S. Maria degli Angeli who needed inspiration for their Lenten prayers could turn for help to a manuscript containing Suor Domitilla's intensely personal meditations on the Passion.[13] As a preface to the days immediately preceding the feast of the Resurrection, the women at S. Abbondio and S. Monaca both cultivated the tradition of the *lavanda*, in which the abbess washed the feet of all the nuns, reproducing Christ's action of washing his disciples' feet before the Last Supper.[14] All these devotions culminated in the Holy Week liturgy itself, with full participation by the nuns at many convents. In 1626, for example, the nuns of S. Petronilla listed the obligations of greatest importance to their religious community, among them "to give out palms to the public on Palm Sunday and have the Passion recited, and to hold the Matins, Passions, and the other customary services during Holy Week."[15]

From Archbishop Ascanio II Piccolomini's 1666 admonition that nuns should lock the doors of their churches after the end of the Office on the last three days of Holy Week, we can infer that a large number of lay persons came to convent churches on those occasions and then loitered in the parlors afterward, distracting the nuns from their penitential duties.[16] Given the apparent crush of the public, female houses with ensembles of singers and instrumentalists had good reason to incorporate music into the Holy Week Matins services (the so-called Tenebrae).

At least one publication from the first quarter of the seventeenth century offered Sienese monastic singers some works based on texts from the Tenebrae in ranges suitable for their voices. The *Cantiones ac sacrae lamentationes, opus V* (Siena, 1620), by the Sienese composer Annibale Gregori, is the first known print to contain monodic settings of the Lamentations of Jeremiah.[17] Gregori scored his Lamentations (as well as the motets included in the volume) for all voice types ranging from soprano to bass; thus the publication as a whole was not directed exclusively at nuns. That is not to say that Gregori wrote his soprano settings solely for the use of male falsettists or castrati. The high-voice pieces may have been composed in emulation of practices at the nearby Florentine court. Holy Week services for the Medici in Pisa, where the court took up residence for the season, often featured talented female vocalists. The 1599 version of Emilio de' Cavalieri's settings of the Lamentations, for example, included solo passages intended for Vittoria Archilei. Later in the seventeenth century, the renowned Caccini sisters, Francesca and Settimia, performed in Pisa during Holy Week.[18] Even if Gregori's works for soprano were not inspired by the musical prowess of women performers, nothing prevented Sienese nuns from exploiting the three cantus settings of Lamentations in Gregori's print for their own performances.[19]

Against this background, Della Ciaia's 1650 collection of single-voice motets and Lamentations seems a logical successor to Gregori's 1620 print. The critical difference between the two publications is that the pieces in the later print are all specifically intended for performance by holy women. Perhaps the composer was responding to nuns who had availed themselves of Gregori's settings and who wanted (in addition to a new group of motets, all in soprano range) a complete set of Lamentations for high voice in a newer style. Although the 1650 print fits comfortably in the Sienese and larger Tuscan traditions for Holy Week music, it is also an important piece of evidence for Kendrick's thesis concerning the "feminization" of settings of the Holy Week liturgy over the course of the seventeenth century.[20] Why did the Lamentations of Jeremiah so appeal to nuns or why were they considered to be so appropriate for performance by nuns?

A partial answer may be found in the symbolism attached to the female monastery in the seventeenth century. Gabriella Zarri has vividly described the post-Tridentine trend to

> transform female monasteries into protected places, isolated from the external world with keys and grates, but made ever more pleasant on the interior by the enlargement of buildings, courtyards and gardens which, to compensate for the cautious cloistering, would be able to furnish to the minds of both lay citizens and nuns the reproduction on earth of the garden of Eden and a celestial Jerusalem.[21]

As I have shown, the perception of the convent as a "new Jerusalem" was as pervasive in Siena as it was in Bologna and Milan; Kendrick notes that it was probably a "universal mental category" for all early modern convents on the Italian peninsula.[22] The image of the convent as a liminal space in which fortunate souls had a foretaste of heaven finds its most eloquent Sienese expression in the dedication to *L'evangelica parabola*, the 1642 play the Sienese cleric and musician Benvenuto Flori wrote for and addressed to the Olivetan nuns of Ognissanti:

> Neither to adulate you nor to speak ill of others, I dare to say that your religious community is a paradise on earth, where many suns of glorious virtues shine, where laziness is banned; a paradise forever rich and full of spiritual exercises, a divine temple of peace, obedience, and love. The [women] have come from the most noble citizenry of Siena to make themselves citizens of the celestial city of heaven, where among so many souls, one can see only one soul; among so many hearts, one heart; among so many desires, one sole desire: a holy, happy and blessed concord, where such sweet and lovely harmony resounds within those sacred walls, as if angelic singers of paradise had descended amongst us. (Doc. 16)

Who better than the inhabitants of an earthly Jerusalem, the celestial singers of the convents, to embody the city herself as she mourns her fate?

> Aleph. How lonely she is now, the once crowded city! Widowed is she who was mistress over nations; the princess among provinces has been made a toiling slave. . . . Daleth. The roads to Zion mourn for lack of pilgrims going to her feasts; all her gateways are deserted, her priests groan, her virgins sigh; she is in bitter grief.[23]

How appropriate that women enclosed in walls and dedicated to suffering reflect on the tragedy from a first-person perspective, occasionally transforming the voice of the ostensibly masculine speaker into their own as they lament conditions that could reflect the realities of monastic life:

> Aleph. I am a man who knows affliction from the rod of his anger. Aleph. One whom he has led and forced to walk in darkness, not in the light. . . . Beth. He has beset me round about with poverty and weariness. Beth. He has left me to dwell in the dark like those long dead. Ghimel. He has hemmed me in with no escape and weighed me down with chains. . . . Ghimel. He has blocked my ways with fitted stones and turned my paths aside.[24]

Beyond the status of the convent as an "earthly Jerusalem," however, might have been another more powerful stimulus for composers to set the Lamentations for nuns. Deeply ingrained social customs in Italy (as in many cultures the world over) associated women with the task of singing laments over the dead.[25] In medieval and renaissance Florence, for example, women were responsible for the first death rituals, which took place in the home: they washed the deceased in herb-scented water and then gathered around the bier to sing the dirges required by tradition. If a married man died, his widow was expected to lead the lamentations; most often she was joined by other female members of her family and sometimes by close female friends and neighbors.[26] Such behavior was customary by women at all social levels. In 1461, the Mantuan ambassador at the court of Milan reported that as part of the obsequies surrounding the death of Duke Franceso Sforza's mother, Duchess Bianca Maria Visconti and numerous female relatives and friends "performed ritual laments over the body."[27] Although confined to the privacy of the domestic sphere, lamentations by women were clearly considered an important and necessary part of the mourning ritual on the Italian peninsula from the Middle Ages through the Renaissance. Less scholarly attention has been focused on funeral customs in early modern Italy, but evidence suggests that the ancient tradition of women singing laments over the dead survived well into the Seicento and, in fact, did not die out among the upper classes until the eighteenth century.[28] In her study of the behavior of Florentines during the years 1630–31, Giulia Calvi observes that families of plague victims often experienced great distress because the bans on all social interaction meant that the rituals linked to an honorable burial (including lamentations by women) were prohibited.[29]

Cloistered nuns would have had no opportunity to participate in the laments for members of their family who died outside the walls, and it is most difficult to determine what went on inside the walls. Early Christian writers inveighed against the "pagan" practice of singing vernacular dirges at funerals, taking their their cue from biblical passages in which Jesus or his disciples reproached or chased away female mourners before raising the dead.[30] Although ecclesiastical authorities could not interfere in domestic rituals associated with death in secular homes, no documentary evidence suggests that they permitted vernacular laments over the dead in monastic communities, where nuns were often assisted on their deathbeds by priests and confessors called in to administer communion and the last rites.[31]

To all appearances, holy women were mourned and buried strictly following the liturgical rituals established by the Catholic Church.

Customs of such enduring social significance do not, however, simply disappear in convents. Generally, nuns and their families found ways to absorb and transfigure those traditions held to be of greatest importance. It must be remembered that nuns considered themselves "brides of Christ" and that their devotion to their celestial spouse often manifested itself in a body-centered spirituality. The death of Christ would leave the nun a widow, obligated to honor her husband with appropriate mourning rituals. The Lamentations of Jeremiah, sung during Holy Week on the days leading up to, comprising, and immediately following the Crucifixion, offered a compelling vehicle for such mourning within the context of the Church liturgy. The texts treat the downfall of Jerusalem as if it were a death of a family member, and several scholars have noted the use of motifs characteristic of the dirges performed by women at burial ceremonies, especially the stark descriptions of misery and the comparison of the joyous past to the sorrowful present.[32] By setting the nine lessons of the Tenebrae for soprano, Della Ciaia furnished a vehicle for a single nun to give voice to the grief of the entire religious community over the death of Christ in a most expressive manner.

DELLA CIAIA'S 1650 LAMENTATIONS certainly owe a debt to the monodic settings of the same texts by his countryman Gregori.[33] Both men's settings are sectional and through-composed in a largely declamatory style leavened with frequent melismatic passages. They display almost no large-scale repetition of text, with the exception of the final exhortation "Jerusalem, Jerusalem, return to the Lord your God" (a phrase not found in Jeremiah but rather in Osee).[34] Gregori and Della Ciaia repeat either the entire section or some portion of the passage after "Jerusalem, Jerusalem," both for rhetorical emphasis and to lend weight to the end of every setting. Each man's works can be performed only by singers with a wide range, accuracy of pitch, and the flexibility to negotiate winding melismas, sometimes while varying the dynamic level from loud to soft (Gregori) or performing trills (Della Ciaia). Della Ciaia did not, however, resort to passages in triple time or in falsobordone as Gregori was wont to do. Perhaps he considered the employment of triple time too representative of joy and the use of falsobordone too old-fashioned.[35] The thirty years that separated Gregori from Della Ciaia also prompted the latter to require an ever higher level of technical virtuosity than did the former: singers now needed a range of nearly two octaves rather than the octave and a half necessary to perform Gregori's works, and they had to be able to sing longer melismas that incorporated *fuselle* (transcribed in modern notation as thirty-second notes), found in only one of Gregori's settings but in six of those by Della Ciaia. Perhaps most significant, Della Ciaia exploited a much more far-ranging chromaticism than Gregori, making for settings displaying greater contrast and intensity than those fashioned by the earlier composer.

Seven of the nine Lamentations set by Della Ciaia feature a G-final mode with one flat in the signature (*cantus mollis*). The third Lamentation for Maundy Thursday exploits a G-final mode with no flat in the signature (*cantus durus*), and the first Lamentation for Holy Saturday an F-final mode with one flat in the signature. The prominent G-final modes offer the best range for trained female singers. The choice of F-final, cantus mollis mode also lies in a comfortable range for women but may have further significance: it may be Della Ciaia's way of paying homage to the Gregorian formula used to chant the Lamentations, the so-called *tonus lamentationum*, which traverses in a stepwise fashion the distance between F and B♭.[36]

Della Ciaia creates harmonic variety in his Lamentations by alterations in the signature (from mollis to durus or vice versa). These occur in all settings, except the first Lamentation for Good Friday and the first Lamentation for Holy Saturday, and are associated with textual passages that deal with ideas of transformation and reversal, both literal and metaphorical. For example, the text for the second Lamentation on Holy Saturday begins: "How tarnished is the gold, how changed the noble metal."[37] At the word *mutatus* ("changed") the signature "mutates" from mollis to durus (Ex 7.1). Sometimes the signature alters for text that contains extremely poignant or powerful images. One such phrase occurs in the third Lamentation for Good Friday, immediately following the Hebrew letter. The signature converts from mollis to durus at the passage "He has left me to dwell in the dark like those long dead" (Ex. 7.2).[38] Occasionally, both powerful images and ideas of reversal are combined, as in the first Lamentation for Maundy Thursday:

> Plorans ploravit in nocte, et lacrimae eius in maxillis eius; non est qui consoletur eam ex omnibus caris eius; omnes amici eius spreverunt eam, et facti sunt ei inimici.

> Bitterly she weeps at night, tears upon her cheeks, with not one to console her of all her dear ones; her friends have all betrayed her and become her enemies.

Here, the vivid picture of desolation and suffering and the reversal of fortune implied in the idea of betrayal all combined to motivate the composer to change the signature from mollis to durus at the beginning of this passage and then to change back to mollis at the word "enemies" (Ex. 7.3).

Chromaticism is one of Della Ciaia's most effective tools, and it always makes an appearance when the signature mutates, as is demonstrated in examples 7.1–7.3. The composer's application of chromatic alteration, sometimes in very liberal doses, serves an expressive function, helping to illuminate key textual passages dealing with pain, suffering, tears, sin, and darkness.[39] Chromatic passages often call forth unexpected sonorities and frequently lead to a temporary change in modal center, injecting even more harmonic interest into the long settings. One of the most striking and colorful passages occurs in the third Lamentation for Maundy Thursday, at the oft-set text *O vos omnes*:

> O vos omnes, qui transitis per viam,
> attendite, et videte si est dolor sicut dolor meus.

> O, all you who pass by the way,
> come and see if there is any suffering like my suffering.

In eighteen measures, the composer traverses the distance between a C-major chord and a C♯-major chord. The chromatic twists of the melody and the suc-

Ex. 7.1.   Della Ciaia, Holy Saturday, Lamentation 2 (1650), mm. 8–17

cession of surprising harmonies are meant to call attention to the idea of terrible suffering implicit in the text (Ex. 7.4).

Dissonance often goes hand in hand with chromaticism and appears when Della Ciaia wishes to underline selected words. In the musical example just given, for example, the word *dolor* ("suffering") is nearly always set as a dissonant seventh over the bass (Ex. 7.4, mm. 63, 65, 66–67). A portion of the first Lamentation for Maundy Thursday tells of Jerusalem's enemies coming upon her where she is "narrowly confined" (*angustias*), and the composer renders the "anguish" of the situation by writing three successive parallel sevenths (Ex. 7.5).

Della Ciaia also exploits range and virtuoso display in his search for dramatic effect in response to text. In the excerpt given earlier from the third Lamentation on Good Friday (Ex. 7.2), the allusion to death induced the composer to change the signature and to come to a cadence on a chord distantly related to the central mode. The idea of darkness in the same passage is, however, created by the strikingly low range required of the singer. Melismas, too, are often textually motivated: words embodying concepts such as instability, dissipation, or the act of turning or turning away are often set with florid lines. Della Ciaia's melismas sometimes tend to meander unpredictably, but when the composer exploits se-

Ex. 7.2.   Della Ciaia, Good Friday, Lamentation 3 (1650), mm. 65–80

quence, he can write passagework that is both dazzling and graceful. A notable example occurs in the second Lamentation for Holy Saturday: "The babes cry for bread, but there is no one to break it for them."[40] The composer seizes on the concept of "breaking" and interrupts his declamatory line with a melisma (Ex 7.6).

One distinctive feature of all the Lamentations except the last is the division of the text into discrete sections separated by Hebrew letters, which originally functioned as an alphabetical acrostic. Even in homorhythmic settings from the Renaissance, the letters are often "melodically and rhythmically ornate, rather like illuminated initials."[41] Della Ciaia sets the Hebrew letters as separate and self-

Ex. 7.3.   Della Ciaia, Maundy Thursday, Lamentation 1 (1650), mm. 38–58

Ex. 7.4.   Della Ciaia, Maundy Thursday, Lamentation 3 (1650), mm. 53–70

Ex. 7.5.   Della Ciaia, Maundy Thursday, Lamentation 1 (1650), mm. 82–87

sufficient sections in his Lamentations; he precedes each with a strong cadence and separates the end of the letter from the following text with another strong cadence (see Ex. 7.2, mm. 65–72). Since the Hebrew letters consist of one, or at most, two syllables of text, these passages are highly melismatic and always offer the singer a chance to show off her vocal agility, sometimes over slow-moving chords, sometimes in duet with an active continuo line that functions more as a second voice than as a harmony-generating bass. In those passages where the continuo line simply holds chords and the singer is the sole focus of attention, Della Ciaia manages to achieve, through the very unpredictability of his passage-work, the effect of keening, the wailing of the bereaved in a grief that goes beyond words (Ex. 7.7, from the third Lamentation on Good Friday).

The final "Jerusalem, Jerusalem" exhortation also allows the singer to show off her technical skills through liberal application of melisma. The use of repeated musical motives on different pitch levels serves to reinforce the repetition of text always present in this section. The setting of the "Jerusalem" section from the first Lamentation from Holy Saturday is notable for combining high range, chromaticism (to underline the idea of conversion), and rapidly unfolding melisma. From this passage, we can infer the extraordinary virtuosity attained by monastic singers in seventeenth-century Siena (Ex. 7.8).

From the preceding discussion, it might seem that the overall effect of Della Ciaia's Lamentations rests on extreme chromatic alteration or on extraordinary virtuoso display. Certainly, these devices play an important role in the works, and their usefulness for dramatic impact cannot be denied. Not to be overlooked, however, is the composer's gift for producing effective music without obvious fireworks. At one point in the second Lamentation for Good Friday is a passage containing neither striking images nor single colorful words:

Ex. 7.6. Della Ciaia, Holy Saturday, Lamentation 2 (1650), mm. 77–85

Cui comparabo te? vel cui assimilabo te, filia Ierusalem? Cui exequabo te, et consolabor te, virgo filia Sion?

To whom can I liken you? To whom can I compare you, O daughter of Jerusalem? What example can I show you for your comfort, virgin daughter of Zion?

Della Ciaia mirrors the rhetorical repetition in the text through variation of a simple, largely syllabically set melodic motive, which he first places in the commanding higher tessitura of the singer's voice and then treats sequentially in a lower range. The judicious combination of lucid melodic motives, well-directed harmonies, carefully placed chromatic alterations, and piquant 7–6 suspensions creates one of the most moving and memorable passages in all Della Ciaia's Tenebrae settings. In excerpts such as this, we perhaps can discern not only the composer's interpretation of a typical dirge motif—the heartfelt eulogy of the dead—but also his homage to the musical talents of the Sienese "daughters of Jerusalem," whom he found beyond compare (Ex. 7.9).

Ex. 7.7.   Della Ciaia, Good Friday, Lamentation 3 (1650), mm. 52–56

Motets

Della Ciaia's motets inhabit a different world from his works for Holy Week. Despite certain structural and technical similarities—through-composition, sectionalism, a declamatory vocal style, and melismatic passagework—many of the motets display additional features not found in the Lamentations. Although it is true that six of the nine motets exploit G-final modes, three in cantus mollis (*Ecce venio ad te, Domine*; *Ad celestem Ierusalem*; *O dulcissime Domine*) and three in cantus durus (*Cognoscam te, Domine*; *Gaudens gaudebo in Domino*; *Quam dilecta tabernacula tua*), the other three pieces make use of modes not used in the Tenebrae settings. *Gaude, gaude mater Ecclesia* is in a B♭-final mode, *Quemadmodum desiderat cervus* is in an A-final mode, and *Diem faustam* is in C, cantus mollis. Furthermore, no changes in signature (from durus to mollis or vice versa) occur in the course of any of the motets. Since Della Ciaia chooses not to enliven the harmonies by signature changes, he has to create interest in another way. He does so by frequent alternation between common time and triple-time passages within each work. The composer devotes approximately 50 percent or more of the transcribed measures in all motets except *Ecce venio ad te, Domine* to triple meter; the percentage reaches nearly 80 percent in *Gaudens gaudebo in Domino*.

The abundant use of triple meter was doubtless inspired by the texts. As if to counterbalance the nine sorrowful Lamentations, Della Ciaia chose nine joyous motet texts cobbled together from a variety of sources: snippets of liturgical items, quotations or glosses from the Old and New Testaments (with a special emphasis on psalm verses), citations of or variations on hymn stanzas, and what appears to be newly composed devotional prose. Both the length of the motets and certain musical features—the preponderance of small note values, the constant alternation of common time and triple meter, and the increased tendency to repeat short

Ex. 7.8. Della Ciaia, Holy Saturday, Lamentation 1 (1650), mm. 155–72

Ex. 7.9.   Della Ciaia, Good Friday, Lamentation 2 (1650), mm. 25–35

motives in sequence—distinguish Della Ciaia's works in this genre from those by Gregori in his 1620 collection. The most important difference between the two collections is, of course, that Della Ciaia intended his specifically for monastic use. As I will show, both his choice of texts and his musical settings reflect his knowledge of important celebrations in the convent and reveal his sensitivity to spiritual themes of great significance to nuns.

SINCE THE PERFORMANCE OF motets often took place during the Elevation of the host or during communion at Mass, Della Ciaia's *O dulcissime Domine* takes its place in a long line of works associated with the Eucharist. It must be stressed, however, that communion was a particularly momentous event in the lives of many cloistered nuns, who experienced the sacrament in a different way from the laity. Legion are the stories of holy women who so valued the host that they survived on nothing else and often went into ecstasy in the act of receiving it.[42] Even for those nuns who were not mystics, partaking of communion meant encountering the physical body of Christ, the bridegroom.

The text for *O dulcissime Domine* appears to be newly composed except for the last line, an adaptation of Luke 14:17. The singer begins the work by describing communion as if it were a pleasurable banquet and by extolling God. She then proves her worthiness to receive the blessed sacrament by berating herself for failing to appreciate its value (a "rhetoric of humility" common in the *vite* of many holy women).[43] Near the end of the piece, the singer addresses a larger group, most likely her sisters in the convent, and encourages them to accompany her to the feast:

> O most sweet Lord Jesus,
> truly great is the sweetness of a devout soul
> who feasts with you at your banquet
> where no other food is offered but you, sole delight,
> more desirable than all the desires of the heart.
>
> O what a sweet and pleasant banquet since you gave yourself as food!
> O, how wonderful are your deeds, Lord!
> O, how powerful your virtue!
> O, how ineffable your truth!
>
> O heart harder than a rock,
> why is it that you do not burn out of love for this sacrament?
> Let us go therefore with confidence
> to this wonderful sacrament in order to obtain mercy.
> Come, everyone, to the great dinner because all is ready.[44]

If the text only hints at the euphoria of the nun about to receive the blessed sacrament, the music serves to heighten the elation implicit in the communicant's emotional state. The singer veers between sober declamatory reflections in common time and expressions of joy in triple (e.g., "O what a sweet and pleasant banquet" and "O, how ineffable your truth"). Notable in this regard is the passage in which the soloist criticizes her own lack of zeal. The composer repeats the text "O heart [harder than a rock]" beginning with long note values and gradually ceding to shorter ones to convey the idea of broken penitential cries. This leads directly into a triple-time passage contrasting the "hard heart" with the joyous "love" that should have a place there (Ex. 7.10).

AMONG THE MOST IMPORTANT, liturgically distinct, and musically elaborate ceremonies held in the convent were those in which a novice took the habit, professed her vows, or consecrated her virginity to God. In all three rituals, the young woman, novice, or nun was cast in the role of the bride of Christ. Two motets

Ex. 7.10.   Della Ciaia, *O dulcissime Domine* (1650), mm. 72–86

in Della Ciaia's collection seem to be designed specifically for use at nuns' rites of passage, for both are based on the conceit of a single soul seeking an intimate union with Jesus Christ.

It is appropriate that the first motet to appear in Della Ciaia's print is a setting of *Ecce venio ad te, Domine*, because its opening phrase quotes the first words a novice uttered in both the clothing and profession ceremonies at the musically active convent of S. Sebastiano in Vallepiatta.[45] The phrase is an echo from the Song of Songs; it represents a response to the repeated cries of "veni, veni" that permeate the canticle. In addition to the motif of the beloved seeking to be united with her lover, the motet alludes to pain and wounds, once again reflecting the common practice among holy women of seeking to draw nearer to Christ through involuntary or voluntary suffering:

> Behold, I come to you, O Lord my God.
> Look at me then, and have mercy on me,
> because the pains of my heart have multiplied.
> Poor me, how late I come to you, O Lord!
> Alas, how slowly I rush!
> Poor me, for I run after being wounded!
> You loved me in a unique way, O my love, before I loved you,
> and you created me in your image.
> Come, come, and do not be late!
> Take up your arms and your shield,
> and rise to my help.[46]

The confidential vein of *Ecce venio ad te, Domine* intensifies in the motet *Cognoscam te, Domine*. Here the supplicant addresses Christ as her "comforter," her "sweet consolation," and her "delight." Words taken from chapter 2, verse 5 of the Song of Songs reveal that she has passed from the state of simply loving Christ to that of pining for his love ("quia amore langueo"). In the final phrase of the motet, inspired by verse 23 of St. Paul's first letter to the Philippians, the supplicant seeks not just marriage with her celestial spouse but annihilation in him, an idea common among female mystics of the time:[47]

> I will come to know you, O Lord, you who know me;
> I will know you, O strength of my soul.
> . . . . .
> Let my great delight appear to me, my sweet consolation,
> God my Lord, my life and total glory of my soul.
> O life for whom all things live,
> who gives me life, who is my life
> by whom I live, without whom I die.
> . . . . .
> Be close to me in my soul, close in my heart,
> close in my mouth, close in my ears,
> close with your help, because I pine for love.
> I do not want to live, I want to die,
> I desire to be dissolved and to be with Christ.[48]

The intimate nature of both texts is well served by Della Ciaia's scoring for solo voice and continuo, and the composer's settings capture both the nun's suffering and her rapture. At the beginning of *Ecce venio ad te, Domine*, for example, chromaticism, dissonance, and large leaps appear in the vocal line as the nun asks for mercy on her pain. Della Ciaia does not miss the opportunity to show the redoubling of that pain by inserting a long melisma on the word "multiplicati." Likewise effective is the repetitious, rocking motive in triple time for the notion of "slowly rushing" (Ex. 7.11). *Cognoscam te, Domine* includes two long passages in triple meter, but in this motet they serve to illustrate the joyous transport of the vocalist contemplating Christ and asking him to be close to her in soul, heart, mouth, and ears. The most effective musical image is, however, conveyed in

Ex. 7.11.   Della Ciaia, *Ecce venio ad te, Domine* (1650), mm. 11–37

Ex. 7.11.   (*continued*)

common time and occurs at the end of the work. The composer renders the idea of dissolution via melodic and harmonic means: the vocal line droops downward, accompanied by a chord stated first with a raised third and then repeated with a lowered third. The motet then moves briefly into triple time as the nun reaches her desired annihilation in Christ (Ex. 7.12).

Two other motets in the collection might also have been pressed into service during rites of passage. *Quam dilecta tabernacula tua* celebrates the concept of living in God's house and praising him eternally. The first three lines of the motet quote the opening of Psalm 83, including verse 3, the one that figured so prominently in the biographies of both Catherine of Siena and Maria Francesca Piccolomini. Of greatest import are the last five lines of the motet, which quote or paraphrase (in order) Psalm 83:5; Psalm 65:4; Psalm 94:1; and Psalm 80:2 and 3. Here, the singer summons the faithful to join in musical performance:

> How lovely are your pavilions, O powerful Lord!
> My soul yearns and pines in the mansion of the Lord,
> and my heart and flesh exulted in the living God.
> Rejoice my soul, and rush toward the celestial country
> because there you will see and possess the Lord forever.
> . . . . .
> Blessed are those who live in your house, O Lord.
> Let the whole earth adore you and sing psalms in honor of your name.
> Come, people, and rejoice in God who is our salvation.
> Sing with joy to the God of Jacob,
> take up the psalms and bring drums, the merry psaltery, and the cithara.[49]

The invitation to make music is rendered, as might be expected, in lilting triple time. More suggestive is the finale of the motet, where the reference to taking up the psaltery and the cithara calls forth a mesmerizing ostinato bass (Ex. 7.13).

Ex. 7.12.   Della Ciaia, *Cognoscam te, Domine* (1650), mm. 114–25

The text of the last work in the collection, *Quemadmodum desiderat cervus*, opens with a citation of Psalm 41:2, which expresses a longing to be near God.[50] Unlike *Ecce venio ad te, Domine*, *Cognoscam te, Domine*, and *Quam dilecta tabernacula tua*, however, the text continues by depicting a blessed place, filled with music, as the final destination of a journey. The speaker then pleads with Christ (in what appears to be newly composed prose) to deliver her there:

> As a hart thirsts for the running stream,
> so my soul longs for you, O God.
> O source of my life, spring of living waters,
> when will I come to your sweet waters?
> Open the innermost part of my ears
> so that I may hear your voice.
> . . . . .
> Blessed is the soul that, liberated from an earthly prison, freely goes toward heaven.
> What songs, what instruments, what melodies are sung there continuously!
> There resound unceasingly
> the mellifluous harmonies of hymns,
> the sweetest angelic melodies.
> . . . . .

Ex. 7.13. Della Ciaia, *Quam dilecta tabernacula tua* (1650), mm. 125–56

Ex. 7.13. (continued)

O most handsome Jesus Christ,
give me a contrite heart
and a spring of tears
while I offer my prayers and orisons to you.
O Lord, listen to one who cries out from this deep sea
and take me to the harbor of eternal joy.[51]

For the verses describing musical performance, Della Ciaia relies on aria-like passages in triple meter. These frame the dramatic high point of the motet, which arrives as the singer, exploiting her full range, her virtuoso capabilities, and her declamatory intensity, prays to her "handsome" Christ for safe harbor (Ex. 7.14).

Since the journey described in these motets could well be one from the outside, troubled world to the enclosed, peaceful cloister, each is suitable for performance at rites of passage. Clearly, however, their usefulness extends beyond such ceremonies. The first phrase of *Quam dilecta tabernacula tua* is the psalm verse used in the Introit of the Mass for the dedication of a church, and therefore the work would be a seemly choice for that feast, celebrated yearly at all convents. *Quemadmodum desiderat cervus*, with its allusions to liberated souls and peaceful harbors, is a fitting composition for a funeral Mass. It takes its place as the last motet in the collection, serving as a pendant to *Ecce venio ad te, Domine*. If the first motet was indeed designed to welcome a young women into the cloister, *Quemadmodum desiderat cervus* would have been highly appropriate for ushering her out.

ALL CONVENT CHURCHES CELEBRATED with particular splendor the feast days of saints of special significance to them: founders of their order, the saint after whom the convent church was named, and saints whose relics the nuns had in their possession.[52] It is not surprising, therefore, that four of the nine motets in Della Ciaia's volume are intended unequivocally for performance on saints' days: *Ad celestem Ierusalem*; *Gaude, gaude mater Ecclesia*; *Diem faustam*; and *Gaudens gaudebo in Domino*. *Diem faustam* mentions a generic "beatum" in its opening stanza; the other three works contain at least two references each to an unnamed "N." In the musical settings, several notes, generally including one on an upbeat, fall under the "N.," allowing the nuns to insert any saint's name they desired.[53]

The "military" tone of both *Ad celestem Ierusalem* and *Diem faustam* suggests that these two motets were intended to be pressed into service on the feast days of male martyrs (e.g., S. Sebastian at Vallepiatta, S. Galgano at Santuccio, and S. Thomas at S. Petronilla).[54] This hypothesis is strengthened by the inclusion in *Ad celestem Ierusalem* of a stanza that is a variation on the second stanza of *Deus tuorum militum*, the Vespers hymn for the Common of a (male) Martyr:[55]

Ad celestem Ierusalem

Hic falsa munda gaudia	Reckoning that the false pleasures of the world
et blanda fraudum pabula	and the enticing banquets of sin
imbuta felle deputans	were soaked with bile,
forti contempsit pectore.	he despised them with a strong heart.
. . . . .	. . . . .

Ex. 7.14. (*continued*)

au - - - di, au - di cla-man-tem Do-mi-ne de hoc ma-ri

ma - gno et ad-duc me ad por - tum

fe - li - ci - ta - - - - - -

6

- - - - tis ae - ter - nae.

Hic cum dracone tartari
pugnans pro Christi nomine
dignam superno Principe
celo refert victoriam.

Fighting with the dragon of hell,
in the name of Christ
he carries to heaven
a victory worthy of the supreme commander.

Diem faustam

O quam constans, o quam fortis
Christi miles dum pugnavit!
Laeva risit arma mortis
et draconem superavit.

O how constant, o how strong
was this soldier of Christ when he fought.
He ridiculed the sinister weapons of death
and defeated the dragon.

Gaude, gaude mater Ecclesia and *Gaudens gaudebo in Domino,* on the other hand, are appropriate for any saint. The texts describe the jubilation among the faithful, both on earth and in heaven, at the crowning of a saint in the celestial court. Although the text of these motets construes the gender of "the blessed one" as male, only a few simple alterations in each work (represented by italics in the following example) are necessary to render the text suitable for a female. Thus, the works could have been performed at the much more frequent Sienese conventual celebrations in honor of female saints.

Gaude, gaude mater Ecclesia

Iste est beatus N.	This is blessed N.
qui gloriosus apparuit	who appeared full of glory
in conspectu Domini.	in the presence of the Lord.
Ista est *beata* N.	
qui *gloriosa* apparuit	
in conspectu Domini.	

In all cases, the changes do not disturb the meter of the text and thus require no musical adjustments for the performance of the work.

OF ALL THE MOTETS for saints' days, the most exuberant is *Gaudens gaudebo in Domino.* The opening phrase, borrowed from Isaiah 61:10, establishes the mood of jubilation, which is then prolonged by a series of verses inspired by or borrowed from various psalms as well as other Old Testament sources.[56] The singer first praises God, and then calls on the faithful to join in the celebration:

> I will rejoice greatly in the Lord,
> and my mouth will exult when I sing his glory,
> because he is wonderful in his saints.
> I will strongly praise and invoke the Lord
> and I will proclaim his holy name,
> because today he called Blessed N. to the heavenly kingdom.
> Play the trumpet in Zion, beat the well-tuned drums,
> call the people and announce his wonders.
> The angels exult, the archangels rejoice,
> the whole Church celebrates
> because today Blessed N., crowned in heaven,
> triumphs with the angels.[57]

References to musical performance appear in lines 2 and lines 7–8 and call forth Della Ciaia's best music in the piece. The work begins in 3/1 meter, and the soloist ascends quickly from g' to g", exploiting her high, bright range in melismatic lines that give musical expression to the concept of "singing" God's glory. The setting of lines 7 and 8 are the most musically memorable. The vocalist first performs arpeggiated motives in common time that imitate the "trumpet in Zion." As the meter shifts to 3/2, a short ostinato bass reproduces the sound of "well-tuned drums," and the singer eventually launches into a rhapsodic melisma (Ex. 7.15).

The motet *Gaude, gaude mater Ecclesia,* whose text consists of a series of six

Ex. 7.15.   Della Ciaia, *Gaudens gaudebo in Domino* (1650), mm. 69–93

irregular, often nonrhyming four- or five-line stanzas, is a reflective extension of the celebration that began in *Gaudens gaudebo in Domino*. The speaker calls on the entire community of faithful ("mother Church") to honor the joyous day on which a saint joined the celestial court. She then asks the "daughters of Jerusalem" to envision the saint crowned in heaven:

> Rejoice, rejoice, O mother Church
> with glad remembrance;
> you, who send the good tidings of a new child
> to the celestial assembly.
>
> This is the Blessed N.,
> like a morning star among the clouds,
> like a full moon in the days of plenilune,
> like a sun shining in the temple of God.
>
> . . . . .
>
> O daughters of Jerusalem, come and see
> the Blessed N. wearing the diadem
> with which the Lord crowned him
> in the day of solemnity and rejoicing.[58]

Della Ciaia's setting of the penultimate stanza (the last cited here) is notable for the repetition of the phrase "daughters of Jerusalem"; here, he is reinforcing the self-image fostered by the nuns who would perform this work. The triple-time invocation to envision the saint begins simply enough with semibreves and minims but soon plunges into a series of rapid semiminims as the crown itself and the act of crowning are mentioned. The notes lengthen briefly for the "day of solemnity" and then shorten dramatically for the word "rejoicing." The sudden shift from relatively long note values to much shorter ones might be Della Ciaia's musical depiction of the transition from a normal to an ecstatic state. It was in precisely such states that holy women such as Caterina Vannini saw visions similar to those described in this motet (Ex. 7.16).[59]

Diem faustam, like *Gaude, gaude mater Ecclesia*, is reminiscent of a hymn. The text for *Diem faustam* comprises two four-line stanzas, followed by three six-line stanzas, and a final three-line flourish. As with *Gaude, gaude mater Ecclesia*, Della Ciaia makes no attempt to mirror the formal structure of the text in his setting. The daughters of Jerusalem appear as "fellow compatriots of Jerusalem" in the penultimate stanza of *Diem faustam*, and once again they are called on to praise God in song:

> Go, O heavenly people,
> go, O fellow compatriots of Jerusalem
> and all of you sing immortal praises with me
> to the King of life,
> who extolled this strong captain of Christ
> and crowned this warrior.[60]

Several musical devices exploited to set this passage are familiar from settings already examined. Della Ciaia highlights the word "sing" (*cantate*) with a melisma over a short ostinato bass; he also sets the word "crowned" (*coronavit*) melismat-

Ex. 7.16.   (*continued*)

ically. His treatment of meter is, however, unique to this work. To create forward propulsion and a musical sense of the athleticism of the "strong captain of Christ," he moves from a swinging 3/2 to a much faster triple meter (Ex. 7.17).[61]

One can infer the presence of the daughters of Jerusalem in *Ad celestem Ieru-salem*, the lengthiest setting in the volume. The motet opens with a prose passage that sets the scene: a martyr arrives in heaven and is greeted by choirs of angels, who ask that the doors swing open for him. Ten hymnlike stanzas of four lines each follow; the eleventh and last stanza is extended with a coda.[62] The references to monastic life are obvious: the "celestial Jerusalem," angelic voices, and even a variation on verse 9 from *Domini est terra*, a psalm used in nuns' clothing cere-monies.[63] Although the motet is intended for a male martyr, the descriptions of his "heroic virtue" are tempered with references to a kind of suffering familiar to

Ex. 7.17. Della Ciaia, *Diem faustam* (1650), mm. 95–133

Ex. 7.17.   (*continued*)

nuns—the willingness to starve the body in order to taste heavenly food. The motet ends with an invitation to musical performance:

> When N. arrived at the celestial Jerusalem, the voice of the angels accompanying him was immediately heard, and they said:
>
> Princes of the celestial court, lift up your gates
> and the noble champion will enter,
> having defeated hell
> in order to be crowned in heaven.
> . . . . .
> He, feeding his mind
> with the sweet food of prayer,
> longing for celestial food,
> let down his starving body.
>
> Come to the supper of the caring Lamb
> where the angels wait;
> come, come, come,
> you will feast.
> . . . . .
> Come, come now, o beautiful
> singing crowd of heaven;
> as much as you can and as much as you dare,
> sing the praises of the immortal King,
> and celebrate with songs and citharas, with string instruments and psalteries.[64]

As in *Quam dilecta tabernacula tua*, the community of faithful are ordered to take up their instruments as they raise their voices in joyful song, and just as in that piece, Della Ciaia creates a hypnotic spell with an ostinato figure in the continuo line, over which the singer weaves ever more elaborate melismas (Ex. 7.18).

Ex. 7.18. Della Ciaia, *Ad celestem Ierusalem* (1650), mm. 156–85

Ex. 7.18. (*continued*)

IT IS PROBABLE THAT Alessandro Della Ciaia's motets found a place in the repertories of a number of different Sienese convents. The works must have appealed to the very best monastic singers, as they offered an excellent showcase for the well-trained voice. They were also eminently practical settings, for they were appropriate for use on a number of occasions of particular significance in the nunnery—rites of passage, saints' days, and funerals, for example—as well as at communion on any holiday or feast. More important, however, both the motet texts and the music with which Della Ciaia clothed them presented to the world a particular image of the cloister and its inhabitants that holy women strove assiduously to cultivate by all means possible. The emphasis in several motets on a "celestial" country far from the woes of the secular world would have been understood by an audience of the time not just as a reference to heaven but also as an allusion to the cloistered, Eden-like garden of the nunnery. Listeners would have identified their own daughters (and sisters, and cousins, and aunts) as the modern-day embodiment of the "daughters of Jerusalem" featured in more than one motet. It is also telling that in five of the nine motets, Della Ciaia employs images of musical performance in homage to monastic singers and instrumentalists, occasionally casting them in the role of angelic choirs. The composer gives these passages his loving attention, writing arialike, often rhapsodic melodies for the soloist. Most remarkable of all, however, are the two passages in *Ad celestem Ierusalem* and *Quam dilecta tabernacula tua* in which the singer urges her cohorts to take up instruments and perform. In both, the composer sets the exhortations over static, mesmerizing ostinato basses. It is in these passages that one can see Della Ciaia striving to provide a musical representation of the enchantment that gripped his contemporaries when they heard the holy concord of Siena's nuns.

Appendix 1

Documents

Doc. 1: Isidoro Ugurgieri Azzolini, *Le pompe sanesi o vero relazione delli huomini e donne illustri di Siena e suo Stato*, 2 vols. (Pistoia, 1649), 2:432–33.

Altre suonando qualsivoglia instromento musicale, o cantando leggiadrissime ariette o musiche composizioni ecclesiastiche, rapiscono gli affetti di chi le sente. Tra queste sono famosissime la Landa monaca olivetana nel monastero d'Ogni Santi, la Giarra monaca giesuata nel monastero di S. Sebastiano, detto volgarmente di Vallepiatta, la Grisona nel monastero di S. Niccolò dell'ordine serafico, ed altre quasi innumerabili tanto religiose quanto secolari non solamente gratissime nel canto ma dottissime nel contrapunto, come tra l'altre che nel suono sono maravigliose, unica è la Bargaglia in Ogni Santi, la quale oltre gli altri instrumenti che suona toccando la tiorba fa miracoli e produce stupori.

Doc. 2: *Ordinazioni e decreti per li monasteri delle monache della città e diocesi di Siena. Fabio Piccolomini Proposto della Metropolitana et Vicario generale dell'Illustrissimo e Reverendissimo Monsignore Camillo Borghesi, Arcivescovo di Siena settimo* (Siena: Luca Bonetti, 1608).

. . .

Et perché l'esperienza fin adesso ha dimostrato che a queste serve di Dio le quali vivendo con purità di cuore, posson far molte distrattioni la frequenza della persone avventitie e gli esterni concerti di musiche e canti, però espressamente comanda che per l'avvenire nessuna monaca benché fusse di offitio o superiora, faccia chiamare per occasione alcuna in qual si sia tempo né meno nella Settimana Santa (eccettuando una sol volta o due l'anno, nelle feste principali del monasterio o quando si faccia vestitura di fanciulle ed allora, volendolo, chiaminlo i parenti) concerto di musica di persone esterne, sotto pena alle monache di privatione del velo per un'anno o essendo novitie, d'altre pene a beneplacito, a i cleri di scudi due per ciascuno e ciascuna volta ed a' laici della scomunica da incorrervi subbito, e così ordina e vuole.

Doc. 3: *Decreti e costitutioni generali dell'Illustrissimo e Reverendissimo Monsignore Alessandro Petrucci Arcivescovo di Siena per il buon governo delle monache della sua città e diocesi* (Siena: Hercole Gori, 1625).

Tit. IV: Del Voto della Castità, cap. IV, Delle distrattioni (pp. 45–46): . . .

4. Ne' monasteri dove è introdotta la musica si faccia con gli offizi quello ancora della maestra del canto, la quale da per se stessa insegni all'altre, e lo facci alle debite hore et in luogo remoto acciò non s'impedischino l'ordinationi e le voci replicate non siano di troppa noia a chi le sente.

5. La musica dalle monache s'usi solamente per augumento del culto divino, e perciò non sia affettata ma grave e devota essendo specie di sacrilegio il cantare le cose sacre con musica profana.

6. Alla messa conventuale o non si canti o le musiche siano di modo prima preparate che a nissuna per il canto sia impedito l'assistere a tanto sacrificio. Né si canti né si suoni per tempo alcuno in parlatorio, né in alcun luogo o tempo si cantino cose mondane. Né in chiesa né altrove fuora degl'offizi divini si canti o suoni ad alcuna sorte di persone tanto ecclesiastiche quanto secolari, eccetto che alla venuta del Prelato.

7. Né (sotto l'istesse pene) si faccia musica nella chiesa esterna di qualsivoglia monasterio senza licenza del Prelato. Né si canti o suoni contro l'istituto della Regola e Costitutioni sotto la pena che in esse.

Tit. VI: Del Novitiato, cap. II, Regole delle novitie (pp. 62–63): . . .

11. Doppo 'l mangiare habbiano un poco di tempo per la recreatione, trattenendosi in qualche esercizio lecito per mantenere le forze corporali. Et essendogli nel tempo della probatione poco utile la musica, doveranno nel novitiato solamente imparare il canto fermo dove però s'eserciti nel coro.

Doc. 4: *Ristretto de' decreti e degl'ordini fatti per li monasteri delle monache dall'Illustrissimo e Reverendissimo Monsignore Ascanio Piccolomini d'Aragona, Arcivescovo di Siena X* (Siena, Bonetti, 1666), 11.

Le superiore non permettino si canti di canto figurato né si suoni instrumenti di sorte alcuna fuori del choro, né in choro fuorché nel celebrarsi i divini offitii. Non s'intenda però proibito il cantare e sonare fra le monache in luogo del monasterio che non sieno sentite da' secolari, né comprovare quando bisogni musiche e sinfonie in choro a chiesa serrata.

Proibiamo da' maestri secolari s'insegni alle monache o all'educande ne' tempi proibiti dell'Avvento e Quaresima.

Doc. 5: AAS, 3930, manuscript booklet of decrees dated 11 August 1666, signed by Archbishop Ascanio II Piccolomini, unn. fols.

Basterà, che quando si comprovano musiche o sinfonie la porta della chiesa sia serrata se per altro vi sia sufficiente lume; e cantanto e sonando le monache alle grati del parlatorio non siano vedute da' secolari, rimettendo il rimanente alla prudenza delle superiori.

Doc. 6: BCS, MS D.V.2, fols. 214r–v: Letter from the nuns of S. Petronilla to the Archbishop of Siena, 1668.

Illustrissimo e Reverendissimo Monsignore e Padrone Mio Colendissimo . . .

PARIMENTE REPRESENTIAMO A VOSTRA SIGNORIA Illustrissima et Reverendissima altro eguale fastidio et inquietudine già è più anni sono che la benignità sua pose rimedio a questo ma con la lunghezza del tempo si è venuto a dismettere il debito ordine qual'era delle fanciulle educhanti, che per nostra quiete di chi volessi orare e riposare le dette non venissero nelli dormitori dalle hore 24 sino a doppo la santa messa e nel'estate fatta l'oratione del hora comune, la qual si fa susseguentemente. In vero l'abitare nelli dormitori si curissi esser già incomportabile bisogniando privarci delle celle, e con l'occhasione che hora sempre ci abitano: mai si puole haver quiete, instruendole a leggere con voce alta e d'ogni tempo e con la mo[ltip]licità delle suddette educhanti è quasi un continuo, oltre il cantare [e] sonare nelli detti dormitori e stanze lì contigue, ove per tutti corr[ispon]dono apportando a ciascheduna sturbo grandissimo. . . .

Onde si supplica l'imparegiabil carità di Vostra Signoria Illustrissima e Reverendissima a rinovare suddetto ordine, e le maestri vuolliono essercitare le fanciulle a leggere altamente, cantare come anco sonare strumenti strepitosi, che prend[ino] luoghi distanti e non corrispondenti alle celle perturbando la quiete comune. . . . Del monastero di S. Petronilla il 5 agosto 1668. . . . Le Monache di Santa Petronilla.

Doc. 7: ASS, Con. sopp. 3574, unn. fols.: Selected licenze from S. Petronilla, 1686–1700.

A. Il 10 dicembre 1686. Supplico Vostra Signoria Illustrissima e Reverendissima compiacersi di conceder licenza al signor Franchini di poter venire ad insegnare la musica cinque o sei volte in quest S. Avvento in riguardo delle due feste che ci haviamo di Santa Lucia e S. Tomaso e facendoli profondamente reverenza genuflessa li domando la sua beneditione. L'Abbadessa del monastero di S. Petronilla.

[Reply:] Concedesi per tre volte quanto comporti il dovere concertare qualche composizione per l'annunciate feste e non altrimenti . . . 10 dicembre 1686. L'Arcivescovo di Siena.

B. A dì 29 dicembre 1695. Sono di nuovo a domandar licenza a Vostra Signoria Illustrissima e Reverendissima che il reverendo signor Tommasso Redi possa venire per insegniar di suono e di canto in privato e conserto per tutte che ne averanno bisognio per fino a quaresima. . . .

[Reply:] Si concede . . . 29 dicembre 1695.

C. A dì 27 aprile 1700. Domando licenza a Vostra Signoria Illustrissima e Reverendissima che il reverendo signor Tomasso Redi possi venire all monastero per insegnare di canto e di suono a monache e fanciulle et anco di conserto a tutte di cappella. . . . L'Abbadessa.

[Reply:] Si concede . . . 27 aprile 1700.

Doc. 8: ASS, Con. sopp. 3290 (S. Paolo), Libro delle licenze dal 1678 al 1693, unn. fols.

Vostra Signoria Illustrissima farà gratia concedere licentia di poter venire alle grati del nostro monistero il signor Giuseppe Fabbrini per insegnare alle solite discepole in riguardo della fessta del S. Pauolo per essere il primo anno che si facci la musica dentro. L'Abbadessa di S. Pauolo.

[Reply:] Si permette per due o tre volte in giorni utili e hore congrue con la conveniente assistenza. . . . 15 dicembre 1679. Oratio Piccolomini vicario.

Doc. 9: ASS, Con. sopp. 3289 (S. Paolo), Libro delle licenze dal 1693 al 1701, unn. fols.

Si prega Vostra Signoria Illustrissima e Reverendissima ha concedere licenza di potere venire al nostro monasterio per insegniare a cantare la musica e sonare diversi suoni il reverendo signor Giuseppe Fabbrini, il reverendo signor Andrea Pontolmi, il reverendo signor Giuseppe Cavallini e il signor Rampini maestro della tiorba . . . fino alla santa Quadragesima. L'Abbadessa

[Reply:] Si concedono li sudetti maestri fino alla Santa Quadragesima. 29 dicembre 1697. A. Sansedoni.

Doc. 10: ASS, Con. sopp. 2542, unn. fols.: Account of 27 July 1656 visit of Berenice Della Ciaia to S. Maria degli Angeli.

Quali illustrissime signore dame insieme con Sua Eccellenza al numero di sei in tutto furono ammesse in clausura e ricevute dalle nostre superiore con grande allegrezza con tutte le nostre monache e gli furono preparate vicino alla porta della clausura sei nobilissime sedie di velluto cremisino con ricche frange d'oro nelle quali postesi a sedere, dalle monache deputate sopra la musica gli fu cantato l'infrascritto madrigale a cinque voci, fatto in lode di Sua Eccellenza e composto da me, scrittore di queste memorie con concerto di varii instrumenti e vaghe sinfonie:

Madrigale a 5 voci

Mentre Donna reale
nuova stella del cielo
sorger da' monti d'Oriente appare
in questi sacri chiostri
l'ombre co 'l suo splendor fa dileguare.
Mira qual d'ostro e d'oro
e di scetri e di palme il Vaticano

lieta pompa prepara alla sua prole
il suo fido consorte
regge co 'l suo saver alto e profondo
in compagnia del sacro Atlante il mondo.

Terminato il madrigale con sinfonie fu dato principio alla visita per i luoghi più conspicui del monasterio, e di poi furono introdotte in refettorio nel quale gli fu preparata una lauta colatione con varii rinfeschi e confetture e frutti diversi con varie sorti di squisiti vini annevati e mentre satiavono il gusto e la sete, erono altresi pasciute l'orecchie con ariette musicali e concerti di varii instrumenti.

Doc. 11: BCS, MS E.V.19, "Storia del monasterio di S. Abundio e Abundanzio [1725]," fols. 117v–118r.

La sua tornata fu con tanto onore, gloria, e applauso e tanta moltitudine di religiosi, compagnie, e secolari, e musici cantando inni e cantici spirituali che era uno stupore dell'onor grande che gli fu fatto e tornò sotto il baldacchino a lui donato da detta compagnia. Quando furno usciti alla porta San Marco cominciammo a sonare le campane e l'organo e nella sua entrata cantammo in musica molte cose spirituali ad onore di Dio benedetto e del beato Giovanni Colombini. Et il padre confessore accompagnò il nostro canto coll'orazione propria del beato Giovanni Colombini. E finito il tutto gli facemmo una buona colazione a tutte le compagnie e religiosi e a tutti quelli del parentado de' Colombini et a' frati Gesuati. Quando fu finito il tutto e partisi tutti consolati, il padre confessore messe dentro la santa reliquia in clausura e noi con quella maggior reverenza che potemmo la portammo in processione cantando le litanie ad onor di Dio e del beato Giovanni [Colombini] e tutti i santi.

Doc. 12: *Relatione della general processione fatta in Siena nella domenica in Albis MDCIL dalle venerabili compagnie della medesima città il dì 11 d'aprile nella quale con solenne pompa fu portata l'insigne reliquia della sacra testa di S. Galgano Guidotti di Chiusdino nobil sanese* (Siena: Bonetti, 1649).

A. (p. 28) Al primo ingresso di essa [sacra testa] fu da esse [madri di Ognissanti] cantato in organo a due chori distinti l'hinno de' confessori con bellissime e vaghe musiche concertate con varii strumenti e doppo un bello e vago mottetto in lode del santo che pareva aperto il Paradiso.

B. (p. 36) . . . risolsero fra di loro [compagnie] andar tutte unitamente alla Porta a Santoviene, dalla parte di dentro alle mura della città nella piazza d'essa porta il qual luogo corrisponde adrittura al monasterio e clausura delle molto reverende madri di S. Maria degli Angeli, dalle quali si doveva fare la processione, e che da tal posto si poteva il tutto benissimo vedere ed osservare con devota curiosità, si accomodarono adunque in tal sito . . . concorso [anche] gran numero di gente per sodisfare alla loro curiosità. All'apparir della processione nella clausura, fu salutata la Santa Reliquia con strepitosa armonia e replicati concerti di trombe.

C. (pp. 37–38) Ma il venerabile e devoto monasterio di Santa Monaca come più vicino e confinante al suddetto e che più degli altri godeva di essa, volle anco da vantaggio con straordinarie dimostrationi maggiormente honorare la S. Testa stante che (oltre all'altre monache, che di quel monasterio si viddero in diversi luoghi stare il tutto osservando) erano circa vinti madri sopra una muraglia della clausura confinante tutte con candele accese in mano in bell'ordinanza, il che apportava insieme diletto e devotione. Ed incaminata la processione, nel passar la S. Reliquia longo detta muraglia quando fu arrivata sotto una fenestra del lor refettorio, si sentì cantare da quelle virtuose madri un bellissimo e vago mottetto nell'istrumento in honore di San Galgano. . . . seguivano dipoi cinquanta monache professe, tutte co 'l volto ricoperto di velo nero, e candele accese in mano, sempre cantando hinni in lode di S. Galgano, con reiterati giri attorno alla clausura e cortili del monasterio, ed erano accompagnati quei devoti canti delle venerande religiose da vaghi e vezzosi augelleti che anch'essi a gara in questa ridente stagione di primavera si sentivano cantare con canora e concorde armonia fra i rami verdeggianti e fiorite piante della bella clausura le divine lodi ed honori del nostro gran santo.

Doc. 13: BCS, MS C.II.24, "Piccolomini, Niccolò: Miscela. e lettere mis.," fols. 53r–v.

Fassi per tutte le monache per una parte dei parenti e dei sacerdoti che ci intervengono un pasto di spesa pur assai, come che sia ragionevole che nele nozze con Christo si spenda e si mangi fuor della misura ordenaria né si ceda in questo ale nozze secolari, anzi come queste sono di maggior merito così habbino o pari o maggiore splendidezza. La fanciulla in presentia di tutti vestita a la secolare, fa un accommodato sermone, ragionando di quanto merito sia il voto della verginità, dell'obbedienzia e della povertà voluntaria e che ella di propria elezzione abbandona il padre, la madre, i fratelli, le sorelle, e ciò che il mondo apprezza. Spoglisi le veste di drappo delle più suntuose che ha potuto trovare e si veste di vesti di panno fatte a modo loro, assai diviziose [*sic*] e benedette, dal sacerdote, dal vicario o dal vescovo proprio gli si taglia i capelli. . . . Doppo questo si fa allegrezza universale nela compagnia delle lor sorelle con hymni e suoni accommodati. In tanto la novella monaca, dedicata ala religione, si mette a sedere in mezzo di due altre vergini che tengono un baccino per una in mano, ove ciascuno degli invitati e dei circunsta[n]ti pone la eleemosina e quel che si riceve la fanciulla ripone per uso e aduopero suo particulare, tenendosi ambiziosamente conto ala minuta fra di loro di chi più o manco guadagna.

Doc. 14: BCS, MS G.XI.91 (Profession rite, S. Sebastiano in Vallepiatta), fols. 27v–28v.

Attollite portas Virgines vestras, et elevamini portae claustrales, et introibit soror vestra. / Quae est ista soror nostra quae ascendit de deserto delitiis affluens innixa super dilectum suum? / Ego sum N. sponsata Christo dilecto vestro. / Quid queris filia? recede iam inclinata est dies et dilectus pertransiit et abscondit se. / Aperi mihi mater veneranda iam guttae noctis irroraverunt caput meum. Aperi, aperi, sollicita quero dilectum meum donec inveniam, tenebam eum, nec dimictam, donec benedicat animam meam. / Filia mea non ingredieris nisi promictas te servaturam omnia quae continentur in regula ordinis Beati Johannis Columbini. / Promicto et confido dilecti Domini nostri Jesu Christi favente misericordia et gratia quia omnia possum in eo qui me confortat. Benedic me mater veneranda benedictione caritatis et amoris cum universo choro virginum harum et dignare recipere me in consortio illarum, ut sim illis socia in amore dilecti mei. / Inginocchiata la vergine, l'abbadessa da la benedittione. . . . Di poi la vergine fa riverenza profonda e ritorna col crocefisso e lume in mano avanti a Monsignor Vicario il quale dice l'oratione e finita si chiude la porta e si va in choro cantando.

Doc. 15: AAS, 3747: "Libro delle accettationi, professe, consecrationi e morti [ad Ognissanti], 1575–1738," fols. 128r–130v.

A dì 11 giugno 1684. Memoria della consacratione fatta a nostro monastero il dì sopradetto.

Comparve a hore 11 incirca Monsignore Illustrissimo Leonardo Marsilii Arcivescovo per dar principio alla funtione con tutta la sua corte, con tre dignità, e due Signori canonici da noi chiamati, et assistenza di tutto il seminario di S. Giorgio . . . entrato in chiesa, fatta oratione, fece chiamar le consecrande et interrogatele e trovatele in tutto esser sufficienti si principiò la funtione quale durò per tempo di cinque hore incirca e tutto passò con sodisfattione universale. . . .

Furono le musiche a due cori e li musici in numero vinti sette con total sodisfattione del publico. . . .

Al maestro di cappella per le compositioni delle musiche et insegnare alle consegrande £. centovinti e robba mangiativa per lire quattordici in tutto ascendente a £. cento trenta quattro, £. 134. . . .

Alli musici piastre tredici dati, e dato a ciascheduno conforme il merito e di più un fazzoletto pieno di robba mangiativa per ciascheduno ascendente il tutto a £. cento quaranta cinque, £. 145.

Al Signor Magini per prestanza dell'organo, £. quattordici, £. 17 [sic].

Doc. 16: Benvenuto Flori, *L'evangelica parabola delle vergini prudenti e delle stolte* (Siena: Ercole Gori, 1642), dedication.

Alle molt'illustri e molto reverende Madri Abbadessa e monache del monasterio di Tutti i Santi in Siena.

Mi sarei dimostrato ingrato, se la dedicatione della mia Parabola Evangelica, la quale a requisitione delle reverenze vostre composi e che fra loro fu recitata, ad altri che a loro prima cagione di essa, io havessi inviata. Per l'obligo che tengo a questo religiosissimo monastero e per non defraudare la cortesia loro, a lor medesime devotamente la consacro, e dedico. Né in alcun modo ritrarmi da questo io doveva conoscendo che le vergini prudenti a prudentissime vergini meritamente si doveano indirizzare. Non per adulare a loro, né per biasimare gli altri, ardirò dire che questa vostra congregatione sia un paradiso in terra, dove risplendono tanti soli di gloriose virtuti, ove l'otio è sbandito, paradiso sempre ricco e pieno di spirituali esercitii, un divino tempio di pace, d'obbedienza, di carità. Uscite dalle più nobili cittadinanze di Siena per farsi cittadine della celeste patria del cielo, ove fra tanto numero di anime, una sol'anima si scorge, fra tanti cuori, un sol cuore, fra tanti voleri, un sol volere, una santa concordia felice e beata in cui sì dolce e soave armonia dentro a quelle sacrate mura risuona, come che appunto gli angelici spiriti cantori del paradiso tra noi fussero scesi. Conosco che per sublimità de' loro ingegni, questa mia picciola fatica non sarà degna d'apparire al lor cospetto. Accettino il dono solo, e gradischino la servitù, e giudichino l'opera secondo il suggetto, e che il thema è santo e devoto, cavato dalla Scrittura sacra in quel meglior modo, che 'l mio debol ingegno ha saputo comporre, ed inventare, ed in premio di ciò, mi favoriranno appresso Dio, con le lor sante ed efficaci orationi con le quali mi daranno una ferma speranza, che doppo questo mortal corso, in quella immortal gloria sia per godere insieme la felicissima ed eterna beatifica visione in paradiso.

Di Siena li 15 marzo 1642.
Delle Signorie Vostre Molt'Illustri e Molto Reverende Devotissimo Servitore,
Padre Benvenuto Flori

Doc. 17: Isidoro Ugurgieri Azzolini, *Le pompe sanesi*, 2 vols. (Pistoia, 1649), 2: 404–5.

XXXIII. Una giovane sanese innominata, monica in certo monastero della patria, non contenta del buono esempio che haveva dalle compagne per battere la strada della perfezzione, cercata ogni strada di giornalmente avanzarsi, arrivò alle sue orecchie la fama della santa vita che tenevano i Padri Osservanti habitanti nel convento della Capriola vicino a Siena. Onde ella, bramosa d'avvantaggiarsi nello spirito e nella mortificazione fece la seguente generosa ma stravagante risoluzione. Si fuggì dal monastero e andò alla Capriola vestita da huomo a chiedere il santo habito di quella religione e fu esaudita. Passato l'anno fece la professione e perseverò in quel luogo con grand'esquisitezza di costumi per qualche tempo fin che finalmente conosciuta per femmina fu ridotta alla pristina clausura. Questo è raro ed incredibile esempio scritto da Fr. Luca Uvadingo ma non già nuovo a quelli che haveranno letto le vite delle sante Eugenia, Eufrasia, Marina, Eufrosina ed altre che sotto mentito habito di maschio hanno lungamente praticato ne' monasteri con santissimi monaci da' quali apprendendo la vita spirituale furono indirizzate al paradiso. Questo caso seguì circa gli anni 1400.

Doc. 18: Alessandro Della Ciaia, *Lamentationi sagre e motetti ad un voce col basso continuo, opera seconda* (Venice: Alessandro Vincenti, 1650), afterword.

Bastiano Arditi a' lettori

Ti maravigliarai per avventura, o lettore, che le presenti lamentationi e mottetti da me raccolti, tutti sotto una chiave di soprano sieno composti. Ma l'autore, al quale uscirono dalla penna non per professione o per ambitione di mandarle alla stampa, ma per gradire il suo genio e le pie richieste d'alcuni amici per monache loro parenti, ha obbedito al tuono della voce nella quale esse dovevano cantarle, e vivi felice.

Doc. 19: Isidoro Ugurgieri Azzolini, *Le pompe sanesi*, 2 vols. (Pistoia, 1649), 2: 15.

XXX. Alessandro Della Ciaia nobil sanese, fu discepolo nel contrapunto o arte della musica del dottor Desiderio Pecci sopranominato, ed essendo geloso imitatore di tanto maestro, non è maraviglia se nelle sue composizioni si riconosca da gl'intendenti quella maniera di comporre stringatissima, delle quali n'ha alcuna alle stampe che si cantano con dolcezza e si sentono con diletto, ed altre infinite n'ha appresso di se, desiderate da virtuosi, ma negate dalla sua modestia, però che per molto che vaglia, poco si stima. Oltre l'essere intelligente compositore e soave cantore, suona di monacordo, leuto e tiorba leggiadrissimamente, e non ne facendo (come vero nobile) professione per venalità, volentieri si compiace di comporre e di suonare in grazia d'amici e molto più in servigio di Dio nell'occorrenze, che se gli presentano alla giornata di solennità che si celebrano nelle chiese di Siena.

APPENDIX 2

Spiritual Autobiography of Maria Francesca Piccolomini (BCS, MS E.IV.6)

[14r] Relatione di alcune ammirabili gratie dalla Santissima Vergine conferite a Donna MARIA FRANCESCA PICCOLOMINI Olivetana nel Monasterio di Ogni Santi in Siena.[1]

[28r]   Iesus + Maria
Io Donna Maria Francesca Piccolomini olivetana havendo indegnamente e senza alcuno mio merito ricevuto dalla santissima Vergine Maria alcune segnalatissime gratie ed essendo constretta a ridirle in virtù di santa obedienza, dirolle con questo mio rozzo sì ma veracissimo racconto.

Passati appena gli sette anni cominciai sì fattamente a patire di vertigini che bene spesso ero costretta a cadere in terra tramortita. Ritrovandomi io travagliata per sì fatti avvenimenti nella nostra villa di Radi di Greta in custodia del fattore e fattoressa che tenevano cura de' beni di casa, essi disgustati oltre modo di tal caso, fecero ciò subbito intendere a mia madre che allora si ritrovava in Siena per diversi affari. La quale intendendo tal cosa, né sapendo che di me farsi, conoscendomi egualmente inhabile alle cose humane che alle divine, prese partito di porger preghiere alla Santissima Vergine Maria avvocata di noi miseri peccatori, raccommandandomi con ogni più humile e più divoto affetto alla santissima Madonna di Barontori [sic] posta in Campriano (circa un miglio a detta villa [28v] dove mi trovavo). Ciò fatto, non patii mai per l'avenire delle sopradette malatie, dalle quali ero stata per l'addietro fortemente travagliata, e per segno della ricevuta gratia e per benemerenza andai per più d'un anno vestita del santissimo habito della mia gloriosissima liberatrice.

Consacrata poscia all'Altissimo in perpetuo olocausto di castità e fatta monaca nel venerabile monasterio dell'Ogni Santi in età d'anni quattordici, m'applicai quivi al suono della tiorba per accompagnare con esso i divoti canti di queste mie religiosissime madri e carissime sorelle in Cristo. Ma ben tosto mi si guastorono in sì fatta maniera l'ogne delle dita delle mani che, quasi debil paglia divenute fragili e tenere, mi si troncavano al tocco di quelle corde e si dividevano affatto dalla carne, onde io rimasi impotente a seguire l'incominciato essercitio del mio suono restando però oltre ogni credere afflitta. Per trovare qualche rimedio al mio male, fu fatto ricorso a varii medicamenti, i quali tutti riuscirono vani et inutili, per la qual cosa ricorrendo io all'aiuto efficacissimo della nostra santissima imagine detta **[15r]** del Parto,[2] posto fra l'ogna e la carne delle dita un capello della sua santissima testa e un poca di bambage con la quale si tiene involto quel santo simulacro, mi si rassodarono in tal maniera l'ogna che a mio piacere potei e posso sonare la mia tiorba per lodare con essa la mia gloriosissima Vergine Maria operatrice verso di me vilissima creatura di miracoli così stupendi.

Mi ritrovavo nel 1650 gravemente inferma d'una incurabile malattia, la quale mi haveva già condotta a gl'ultimi periodi di mia vita. Il mio male fu da principio giudicato da' medici della città (fatti adunare a questo fine da' miei genitori) che nascesse dall'intemperie o da uno scirro, come essi dicevano, del fegato. Onde furono di comune parere ch'io dovessi pigliare l'acqua di San Casciano. Da questo medicamento non solamente non ricevei utile o giovamento alcuno, ma come se non fosse bene applicato, il mio male andò sempre crescendo e peggiorò in ogni più forte maniera, imperoché ero dalle mie gravi e lunghe malattie ridotta in un miserabile et infelice scheletro, così ero consumata **[15v]** in tutta la persona. Havevo in tal maniera perduto il gusto del magnare, che con grandissima nausea ero constretta a pigliare il poco e necessario cibo per sostentamento della mia vita. Havevo perduta ogni humana virtù et ero divenuta stitica affatto, sì che per ordinatione de' medici presi l'antimonio, il quale però non solo non mi operò cos'alcuna ma come l'havevo preso lo rigettai per la bocca. Dalli spessi vapori che dallo stomaco si sollevavano al capo pativo noiosissime infiammagioni che gravemente mi tormentavano. Haveo il corpo gonfio come se io fosse una hidropica et ero sempre perseguitata dalle continue e crudeli mie febri. Ma sopra tutto fiero et atroce fu il male che nella mano sinistra mi s'aventò, imperoché la malignità de gli humori che dentro havevo riserrati di sì fatta maniera fece capo alla mano sinistra che tutta me l'impiagò havendomi scoperto in più parti i nerbi. Oltre di questo sopra la mano mi haveva aperto una così gran piaga, che ben due dita di tasta comportava nel medicarla, gittando fuora così gran copia d'humori che tutto il braccio mi haveva consumato, non mi essendo **[16r]** altro rimasto che la nuda pelle attaccata all'osso. A così infelice e così miserabile stato ero ridotta quando venendo la mattina del 21 aprile dell'anno 1653 messer Galeazzo, conforme era solito, a medicarmi la piaga, e quella trovatala giunta al sommo d'una malignità incurabile et essere oltre ogni modo incancarita e infistolita e gittare in grandissima copia stomachevoli humori, vedendo riuscire vana ogni arte humana e prevedendo a manifesti e humanamente inevitabili segni vicina l'hora del mio morire, chiaramente me la denuntiò con dire che io mi raccommandassi con tutto il cuore alla misericordia di Dio et alla Santissima Vergine perché altronde che da celestiale virtù non potevo sperare aiuto alcuno. Per le quali parole io soprapresa da un grandissimo timore della morte vicina con le lagrime agl'occhi risposi, "Io mi sono caldamente raccommandata a quella santissima imagine della Madonna di Castelvechio che fu portata hieri per la città in processione (che fu la domenica in Albis nella quale sogliono le venerabili compagnie di Siena esporre processionalmente alla **[16v]** alla [*sic*] publica adoratione qualche reliquia o santa imagine) ma i miei peccati e le mie iniquità non meritano che le mie orationi sieno esaudite." Le quali parole interompendo misser Galeazzo con alcune delle sue replicò, "A che raccommandarsi ad altre imagini della Vergine santissima se havete nel vostro monasterio una sì miracolosa Madonna? Raccommandatevi a lei." Et a dirmi queste parole disse misser Galeazzo di sentirsi inspirato passando dal coro ove sta riposto quel santo simulacro per venire nella mia cella a medicarmi. E questo detto, havendomi già medicato la mano impiagata, si partì il cerusico. Et essendo già sul mezzo giorno io, havendo preso per desinare qualche poco di cibo che le mie debolissime forze e la gran nausea che havevo nel pigliare cos'alcuna mi permissero, con insolito avenimento e non mai più occorsomi mi adormentai. In questo sonno, felice preludio della ricuperata mia salute, mi parve di vedere in sogno la nostra santissima Vergine del Presepio che apparendomi mi dicesse di volermi guarire e liberare intieramente dalle mie infermità, e come essa Santissima Vergine **[17r]** mi haveva predetto così in effetti mi pareva di essere guarita dalla piaga infistolita della mia mano e liberata affatto dalle mie gravissime infermità. Destata con queste vive imaginationi dal sonno e dal sogno, presi una così ferma e così viva speranza nella beatissima Vergine di dovere essere guarita per mezzo del suo potentissimo aiuto, che per questa, benché languida e moribonda di corpo, ero nell'animo molto sollevata et allegra. Avvalorata da questa speranza infusa (come credo) nel mio cuore dalla santissima Vergine, chiesi con grande istanza d'havere un anello di quelli che tiene nelle dita il nostro santo simulacro. E benché il demonio fraponesse ogni sua opera accioché io non havessi il desiderato anello, dopo essere stato da me con molte preghiere addimandato e con reiterate istanze richiesto, mi fu finalmente portato da una monaca la sera dell'istesso giorno su le 22 hore. Non volli allora per decenza accostare l'anello alla mano impiagata prima che fusse medicata e ben netta e purgata dall'humore che ne scorreva. Per la qual cosa dopo ch'hebbi preso il solito pochissimo cibo, dalla madre Sor Maria Niccola mia servigiala **[17v]** mi fu con gran carità medicata la putrefatta e puzzolente mia mano. Così dunque con la maggior diligenza possibile netta e mondata la mano dal puzzolente humore che ne sgorgava (del quale haveva lordate e abondevolmente ripiene le fasce tutte e i lini co' quali era stata avvolta) con altre nuove pezze fu ben fasciata. Allora io, preso con gran confidenza nella santissima Vergine il suo anello santo, che presso havevo, e raccommandandomi con tutto il cuore a questa misericordiosissima Vergine, mi posi il detto anello nell'estremità del dito anulare dell'impiagata mia mano, peroché non poteva entrarmi più a dentro per essere il dito molto gonfio per l'humore concorsovi, e distendendo sopra i guanciali ch'a questo fine a lato havevo il braccio e la mano offesa per pigliare sonno, quella notte mi prostesi nel mio letto; et il simile fece la mia servigiala coricandosi nel suo letticciolo presso il mio letto. Allora non andò guari che per la stracchezza del male e per la debolezza delle mie forze mi addormentai continuando in questo sonno ben più di sei hore e mi destai due hore forsi innanzi giorno. Risvegliata dal sonno trovai che la mia mano piagata non era nel luogo **[18r]** dove posta la sera l'havevo a lato al fianco sopra i guanciali, ma intorno al petto piegata, cosa non mai più successami, né io la potevo muovere a fatica. Presi di questo accidente maraviglia e volendomi con la destra alzare detta mano, non sentii in far ciò dolore né gravezza alcuna; onde cominciai a credere d'haver perduto il sentimento di essa mano. Ma seguendo di tasteggiare essa mano, più non sentii né fascia né piaga né gonfiezza et humore alcuno e l'anello della santissima Vergine, che nella cima del dito posto havevo, lo sentii esser calato a basso nell'estremità di esso dito anulare. Presa allora dallo stupore e sospesa dalla maraviglia non sapevo ciò che mi credere o pensare, stando in forse se sognavo o vegliavo. Ma accertata poi dalla chiarezza della mia sensatione e dalla riflessione che buon pezzo sopra vi feci, più non stetti vacillante in credere quello che chiaramente conoscevo, d'essere miracolosamente guarita et haver riceuto dalla Santissima Vergine una gratia così stupenda e così segnalata. Ardevo allora di desiderio di far sapere alla mia servigiala la gratia et il miracolo che havevo **[18v]** riceuto dalla santissima imagine, ma non la volli destare dal sonno e dal riposo, havendo compassione alle lunghe fatiche da lei per mio servitio e per la sua carità sofferte, se bene con gran fatica mi astenni di non gridare ad alta voce e significarle il miracolo successo. Onde così taciturna e cheta mi trattenni il resto di quella notte sollevata nel letto, ringratiando nel mio cuore la misericordiosissima Vergine; né potrei fra tanto ridire i varii sentimenti dell'animo mio né spiegare i varii affetti del mio cuore. Godevo a ripensare d'haver riceuto dalla santissima Vergine una gratia così stupenda, ma temevo e tremavo perché la consideratione d'un tanto favore mi rammentava le mie obligationi, dal peso delle quali dubitavo di non rimanere oppressa e che non mi dovessero essere cagione di maggior castigo nell'altra vita col non corrispondere alle gratie della Santissima Vergine con maggior devotione, carità, e purità di cuore. Tra questi pensieri mi trattenni sino all'alba del nuovo giorno, quando a pena sentii zittire Sor Maria Niccola e la conobbi risvegliata dal sonno, che io la cominciai a chiamare dicen- **[19r]**-dole con gran festa e allegrezza ch'io ero stata quella notte guarita per miracolo della Madonna santissima del Presepio; alle quali parole ella mi rispose ch'io sarei guarita quando sarei nel cataletto. E sogiungendo e replicando come io ero guarita e che mi venisse a vedere la mano, ella sempre mi rispondeva ch'io guarirei nel punto della morte o nella sepoltura. Finalmente non fu possibile che le facessi credere la gratia riceuta, né che con replicate istanze la facessi accostare al letto a vedermi la mano, tanto era lontana dalla sua credenza una gratia così segnalata, havendomi ella la sera precedente medicata la mano e visto lo stato disperato in che mi trovavo. Vedendo allora io l'incredulità di Sor Maria Niccola, presi per espediente di medicarmi la mano con pregarla per carità che mi facesse la gratia per ciò che mi doleva. Accorse ella subbitamente al pietoso uffitio, portando varie fasce e paniere. Ma poiché vidde la mano sana e stretta colla piaga saldata, stette prima attonita per la meraviglia e per l'allegrezza baciandomi con tenerezza la mano, indi si fuggì via dalla mia camera e sparì come un baleno. **[19v]** Divulgò ella per il monasterio la gratia et il miracolo alle monache tutte, le quali accorsero ben presto alla mia cella non potendo satiarsi di mirarmi la mano, e con gran sentimento di gioia e di devotione verso la santissima Vergine baciarla, et accertatesi tutte come testimonii di vista del miracolo ne resero alla Santissima Vergine le dovute gratie cantando il Te Deum.[3] Ma perciochè le gratie divine tal hora non vengono sole, la Vergine santissima per raddoppiare a sé le glorie, a me non saprei dire se più la consolatione o la confusione, volle con un nuovo miracolo palesare le sue grandi misericordie. Imperoché una monaca fra l'altre mi persuase a pormi il sopradetto anello della Madonna santissima nel corpo perché forsi in questa maniera m'haverebbe intieramente fatta la gratia di liberarmi affatto da gl'altri miei mali. Il che fatto da me, e posto l'anello nel corpo, con raddoppiata maraviglia mi si sgonfiò, e partitesi da me le febri et ogni altro dolore mi levai dal letto, e sana e schietta, guarita e libera affatto dalle tante mie infermità passeggiai per il monasterio coll'altre monache. **[20r]** Venuto l'istesso giorno del 22 il medico per farmi secondo il solito la visita e vedendomi in questa maniera e mostrandoli io la mano guarita, stette attonito per lo stupore e dimandò se si era fatto sapere a casa de' miei parenti il miracolo. Et essendoli detto di no, replicò che non si facesse sapere il fatto fin tanto che da misser Galeazzo non fusse giudicata la carne rimessa per buona, perciochè lui non essendo della professione non se ne inten- deva. Venne il giorno doppo Misser Galeazzo e facendo motto alla porta, gli fu detto da una monaca, "La vostra ammalata è guarita." Alle quali parole egli rispose, "Oh, che è morta, eh? Orsù, requiescat!" E replicandoli pure l'istessa monaca come io ero guarita, egli soggiunse, "Oh, che mi burlate?" Ma soggiungendoli di nuovo la medesima monaca con altre da dovero come io ero guarita per miracolo della Santissima Vergine, entrato dentro misser Galeazzo nel monasterio, poiché mi vidde con gl'occhi proprii sana e guarita, "Non vel diss'io," (ridendo mi disse) "che voi vi raccommandaste alla vostra miracolosa Madonna, che havereste riceuta la gratia?" E dicendogli le altre monache che **[20v]** il medico non si assicurava se la carne rimessa nella piagata mano fusse buona o no, egli prendendomi la mano e mirando la carne rimessa nella piaga saldata, "Buona, buona!" rispose; "Fate sapere a' parenti et a tutta la città il miracolo perché veramente è grande et è maraviglioso." Allora le monache vollero di nuovo render gratie alla Vergine santissima delle sue misericordie col cantare tutto in musica il Te Deum e Letanie, et all'uno e all'altre io fui presente, e benché le mie pietose sorelle in Cristo mi havessero apprestato una sedia come a convalescente e uscita di fresco dal male acciò non stessi tanto a disagio, niente di meno io vi stetti a tutto il Te Deum et Letanie in ginochioni senza fastidio corporale sì, ma però con l'animo ondegiante fra mille cure e col cuore palpitante nel petto, hora stando in forse della mia ricuperata salute, hora ripensando d'havere senza alcuno mio merito e con infiniti peccati ricevuta dalla Santissima Vergine una gratia così stupenda e, considerando le mie grandi obligationi verso la mia gloriosissima liberatrice, meco stessa mi vergognavo, sapendo che, per la freddezza del mio spirito nel divino amore, io **[21r]** non haverei ad esse obligationi né pure in minima parte corrisposto.

Havendo io una doglia in un ginocchio, anzi havendola fin dall'infantia por- tata facendomisi più vivamente sentire con più grave dolore, non potevo di essa non lamentevolmente languire. Onde ricercata della cagione del mio lamento da Donna Caterina mia sorella, fui costretta a fare sapere la mia infermità. Per la qual cosa fui consigliata dall'istessa a far ricorso alla nostra miracolosa Madonna et al suo santo anello che altre volte era stato verso di me gratioso e accostandolo al mio languido ginocchio aspettare da esso con pura fede e con pura divotione verso la Santissima Vergine l'intera e bramata salute. Ma diversamente da' suoi santi consegli io mi regolai, imperoché in vece d'applicare l'anello al ginochio, lo posi nel petto a fine di megliorare in tal maniera la mia voce debile e languida perché gran desiderio ne tenevo acciochè meglio potessi recitare nel coro gli uffici divini. Per il che interrogandomi l'istessa come io stavo del dolore del ginochio da che vi havevo applicato il santo anello, io allora francamente risposi, "Sto peggio che mai." **[21v]** Ma facendomi poi di queste parole scrupolo consapevole a me stessa di non haver posto l'anello nel ginochio ma nel petto, come s'io volessi in sì fatta maniera col celare le gratie della Santissima Vergine torre ad essa le glorie delle sue misericordie, delle mie mal proferite parole hebbi gran pentimento. La onde emendando il fallo la sera venente posi l'anello nel ginochio infermo e da quel punto in qua sentii cessata la doglia che tante volte mi haveva per l'innanzi in fiere guise tormentata, né mai più in detto ginochio per antica habitudine infermo ho patito dolore alcuno.

Dovendosi fare nella nostra chiesa da noi novitie la nostra publica solenne consecratione, mi raccommandai con tutto il cuore alla nostra gloriosa Madonna e la pregai che terminata che fosse questa sacra funtione mi desse qualche tribulatione e qualche travaglio nella sanità per gastigo de' miei peccati. Ottenni dalla Santissima Vergine la gratia, imperoché io che in quel tempo godevo buona salute e con maggior vigore e costanza dell'altre mie compagne nella consecratione resistei a i varii disagi di essa, terminata che fù la sacra funtione, appena hebbi posto il piede nella **[22r]** porta del nostro monasterio nell'ultimo ritorno che in esso facemmo dalla chiesa dove ci consecrammo, che fui subbito assaltata da un grandissimo dolore di testa per il quale mi pareva che l'ossa mi si spezzassero, e da una noiosa infiammagione. Ricevei allora con gusto e contento dell'animo questa nuova infermità riconoscendola per dono del cielo e per gratia della Vergine Maria. Ma inasprendosi ogni hora più il mio dolore, e rendendosi travaglioso troppo a sopportare, benché lo spirito fosse pronto l'humanità inferma non haverebbe volute quelle infermità. Ond'io, per la mia debolezza quasi rimossa dalla prima volontà d'infermare e di patire, sospiravo la mia primiera salute. Non ardivo però di ricorrere all'aiuto degl'humani medicamenti per liberarmi da quei mali, sapendo che gl'havevo richiesti et impetrati dal cielo. Ma stimolata a ciò fare, anzi essendomi commandato il dovermi medicare dal nostro molto reverendo padre confessore e dalle mie superiore, bisognò lassarmi guidare dal loro consiglio e dalla loro volontà. Fra gl'altri medicamenti ch'io presi, durai per alquanti giorni **[22v]** d'ordine de' medici di pigliare il siero, dal quale medicamento, come dagl'altri, io non sentii giovamento. Per il che, essendo i miei dolori cresciuti, desideravo io di liberarmene; mi raccommandai alla nostra santissima imagine supplicandola che mi alleggerisse o togliesse [sic] affatto i dolori che per sua gratia divina havevo ottenuti. Là onde a questo fine postami in una tempia anzi in un orechio un poca della bambagie colla quale sta involto il santo simulacro della nostra miracolosa Madonna, quell'istessa Santissima Vergine che fu verso di me gratiosa in mandarmi le infermità corporali fu egualmente pietosa in ritormele, perciochè mi si partirono tutti i dolori. Le monache che guarita mi vedevano, rallegrandosi mi dicevano, "Veramente i medicamenti sono stati molto bene applicati al vostro male." Et io rispondevo loro che sì, che quel siero che havevo preso m'haveva guarita. Ma in ciò dire sentivo un vero rimordimento della conscienza che parlandomi al cuore amaramente rimproverava alla mia lingua le sue bugie. Onde io recandomi a grave peccato quanto havevo detto, fui costretta confessare alle monache, che di ciò mi fecero grand'istanza, che **[23r]** non dalle forze d'humano medicamento ma dall'efficace aiuto della Vergine santissima havevo ricevuta l'intera bramata salute.

Nell'anno passato 1658 nel mese d'ottobre un dolore che per lo spatio di sette anni portato havevo in un braccio presso la spalla destra sì fieramente mi si inasprì che mi tremava il braccio in modo tale che non potevo adoprarlo. Per la qual cosa io che havevo incominciato a sonare poco volentieri, credendo non essere il mio suono gradito alla beatissima Vergine, vedendo hora inhabile al mio suono il braccio, nella mia opinione maggiormente mi confermai. Là onde ero già a tal segno ridotta che era cosa disperata che io nella prossima solenne festività degl'Ogni Santi potessi nelle solenni musiche sonare. Alcune monache mi persuadevano che io per la liberatione di questo male ricorressi al mio potentissimo patrocinio della Vergine santissima; et una monacha fra l'altre me ne pregava e con ogni efficacia mi esortava. Ma io per alcuni giorni stetti ritrosa a ciò fare parendomi troppa presuntione d'una indegnissima serva de' servi di Dio, ripiena **[23v]** di molti difetti, quale son io, il volere in ogni sua avversità ricercare le gratie della santissima Reina degli angeli. Ma fui finalmente mossa dalle molte persuasioni della sopradetta monaca, la quale si chiama Donna Anna Maria Azzoni, a ciò fare. Disposta fra tanto di porgere alla gloriosissima Vergine Maria le suppliche delle mie oratione per la liberatione di questo male, fra me stessa dicevo, "Hora vedrò se la Vergine si compiacerà ch'io suoni o no." Onde avanti il deposito del nostro santissimo simulacro posta in ginochiuni [*sic*] et ungendo con l'olio della sua lampada il braccio infermo, legai ad esso con un filo il suo anello e, raccommandandomi col cuore ad essa santissima Vergine, di repente fui liberata dal male, né mai più sentii dolore alcuno nel detto braccio in tal maniera che nella nostra festività degl' Ogni Santi potei la mattina ne' santi sacrificii della messa et il giorno solenne nel vespero in musica continuamente e senza fastidio alcuno sonare.

Io Donna Maria Francesca Piccolomini Olivetana havendo benché immeritevolissima riceute dalla santissima Vergine le predette gratie, a gloria di sì benigna protettrice ho per **[24r]** obedienza scritto quanto sopra di propria mano.

A dì 4 Maggio 1659 Donna Maria Francesca Piccolomini mandò questa relatione al Padre Sebastiano Conti della Compagnia di Giesù, accompagnandola con una lettera in cui era il seguente paragrafo:[4]

> Le mando la relatione che per sua sola obedienza ho fatta, et humilmente la supplico che in ricompensa non si scordi mai di me con raccomandare alla Regina mia benefattrice una sua ingrata serva, acciò mi ottenga il general perdono de i miei gran falli et un vero sigillo di non mai più offendere la Divina Maestà. E questo lo spero da Sua Reverentia che me lo faccia nel santo sacrificio della messa ogni giorno, sì come ancor io per le continue obligationi non mi scordarò mai di lei.

Io Sebastiano Conti pistoiese della Compagnia **[24v]** di Giesù fo fede qualmente il dì 31 agosto 1659 essendo stato chiamato a confessare la madre Donna Maria Francesca Piccolomini nella pericolosa sua infermità della qual poi morì[5] il dì 5 settembre dell'istess'anno, ella per obedienza mi referì due altre gratie fattele dall'istessa miracolosa imagine della Madonna del Presepio, le quali per non tardar più lungamente a mandarmi la precedente relatione da me chiestale già da più mesi, haveva ella tralasciate di registrarvi di proprio pugno. La prima disse essere accaduta del 1658 per la festa del Santo Natale di Nostro Signore, mentre essendole enfiata fuor di modo la bocca, con applicarvi della bambace in cui sta involta la sacra effigie si trovò perfettamente guarita. L'altro favore attestò d'haverlo riceuto nella festa che dell'istessa miracolosa imagine si celebra nella chiesa d'Ogni Santi a 4 febraro 1659 poiché dovendo quella mattina sonar la tiorba tra le altre madri in choro, sentì sorprendersi da sì straordinario dolore ed enfiamento nella mano destra ch'era affatto impossibilitata alla predetta funtione. Ma essendo ricorsa alla sua benignissima Avvocata, appena con l'oglio della lampada di essa s'unse la **[25r]** mano offesa che speditamente libera e sana poté impiegarla nell'essercitio del suono ad honore della sua liberatrice. In fede ho scritta e soscritta la presente di propria mano.

Sebastiano Conti

Lode a Dio ed alla Santissima Madre Regina delle Vergini.

APPENDIX 3

Spiritual Biography of Maria Francesca Piccolomini by Sebastiano Conti (BCS, MS E.IV.6)

[1r] Ristretto della Vita di Donna MARIA FRANCESCA PICCOLOMINI Olivetana nel Monasterio di Ogni Santi in Siena.[1]

Composto l'anno 1659 dal P. Sebastiano Conti Pistoiese della Compagnia di Giesù.

[2r = p. 1] La christiana e religiosa pietà di Donna Maria Francesca figliuola del signore Alessandro Piccolomini Carli e della signora Laura Golia, si è data sempre a conoscere per così insigne, che si tiene per certo, non haver essa in vita sua già mai commessa colpa mortale. Né solo da' peccati gravi, ma anche da' leggieri fatti con avvertenza, procurava ella guardarsi esattissimamente, massime in materia della santa ubidienza, la qual virtù come più propia delle persone religiose, con somma accuratezza riveriva, e pregiava. A chi tal volta le diceva, che gran cosa è rompere il silentio, o far qualch'altra somigliante trasgressione, rispondeva, "Prima morire che commettere avvertentemente una inosservanza." Il suo gran timore era di peccare senza conoscerlo. Onde con non so quale occasione interrogata da un confessore, se per sorte havesse commesso qualche peccato col mirare, rispose subbito, conforme al dettame presente della coscienza, di no. Ma riflettendo poi di sì fatta interrogatione, mi scrisse con gran sentimento il successo, dicendo, che non havea mai saputo, che si potesse peccare con gli sguardi (e pur era d'indole molto vivace, e spiritosa) che per tanto ritrovavasi in singolare [2v = p. 2] afflittione, per essere probabile, che nel decorso della sua vita più volte fosse incorsa in somiglianti colpe, senza riflettervi. L'ottobre del 1658 mentre io servivo di confessore straordinario al suo religiosissimo monistero, mi disse ansiosamente, che harebbe pur voluto fuggire ogni ombra di peccato nella osservanza de' tre voti religiosi,[2] ma che in quanto a quello della castità non sapeva come si potesse meritare o demeritare. Sentì una volta dire, "Dio volesse, che tra le monache non vi fossero delle manchevoli nella integrità verginale," e per tali parole inorridita,

209

e dubbitando subbito di se stessa, si levò dal dito l'anello monastico; quasi la mera possibilità del fallo la rendesse già indegna di quell'illustre contrasegno di sposa di Giesù. Un'altra volta per un tal pensiero sopragiontole, che ad essa parve pericoloso, lassando il lavoro che haveva tra le mani, prese immantinente certe funi che servivano a stendere i panni imbiancati, e fecesi con esse lunga ed atroce disciplina. Racconta una monaca haver risaputo in confidenza da essa, che mentre sola un giorno nella sua camera stava angustiata da questi timori delle sue colpe, le apparve il demonio in forma humana; e dopo haverle detto, che erano fondati i suoi timori, la stimolò a disperarsi senza più confidare in quella **[3r = p. 3]** imagine della Vergine, la quale, soggiongeva il perfido, altro non essere che un vanissimo pezzo di legno. Ma sopravenendo un bellissimo oggetto (il quale quella, a cui essa ciò riferì non ben si ricorda se le disse essere stata la Santissima Vergine) fù il nemico costretto a fuggire, ed ella rimase mirabilmente confortata.

Era sì staccata da ciò che di riguardevole, e di amabile havea lasciato nel secolo, che per portare qualche affetto ad una signora sorella sua carnale, con cui erasi più teneramente allevata, ne domandò licenza al padre spirituale: acciò che tale affetto santificato dalla concessione della santa obbedienza procedesse più da motivo di spirito, che di carne, e di sangue. Quando era in choro a sonare non rivolgeva sguardo a quelle persone ch'erano in chiesa. Si asteneva dalle grati quanto più l'era possibile; e quando pure dalla necessità o dalla convenevolezza era costretta ad andarvi, non si udiva rispondere, né parlare con gusto se non all'hora che introducevansi ragionamenti di cose spirituali. La predetta signora sua[3] sorella attesta, che quando le voleva raccontare o travaglio o prosperità di sua casa, Donna Maria **[3v = p. 4]** Francesca non dava udienza, e stava come astratta. Ma s'ella di ciò accorgendosi mutava ragionamento in cose di spirito, allhora quella tutta attenta, e spiritosa le rispondeva. A detta signora una volta occorse, che dopo altri discorsi, a quali l'altra non mostrava di attendere, per incontrare finalmente il predetto genio cominciò a dirle, "Intendo che fa di molte gratie maravigliose cotesta vostra Madonna del Presepio." Allhora la sorella tutta lieta in quello come primo moto di spirito con ingenuità rispose, "E come se ne fa! L'ho vista io dar la benedittione alle monache mentre entravano in choro." "Voi dunque l'havete vista?" replicò ella. A queste parole riflettendo con pentimento Donna Maria Francesca soggiunse, ch'era stata vista da una monaca; e cominciò a grandemente angustiarsi del già detto. Onde per tranquillarla bisognò, che la signora [illegibile][4] le dicesse, "Già so, che non può essere, che l'habbiate vista voi, che vi conosco benissimo."

La pena maggiore di Donna Maria Francesca pareva che fosse il non poter satiarsi di pene. Importunava perciò continuamente i confessori e le superiore a concederle penitenze, particolarmente il farsi spesso la disciplina; e quando ciò otteneva, l'amor della mortificatione le faceva parer lecito di trascorrere oltre al **[4r = p. 5]** termine prescrittole con aggiongere tre colpi per ciascuno de' varii confessori che haveva hauti (poiché nella gratitudine, massime verso i padri spirituali fu eminentemente segnalata) e per molti altri raccommandati alle di lei orationi. Contro la solita inclinatione dell'humana infermità all'hora unicamente riuscivale grave la religiosa obedienza, quando venivane alleggierita da' pesi e dalle mortificationi monastiche che però quantunque ella si mostrasse prontissima in

ogni altro punto di questa virtù, all'hor che a titolo delle sue frequenti indisposi-
tioni l'era proibito il levarsi a prima, il disciplinarsi, o l'affligere in altra maniera
le proprie membra, non poteva trattenersi di proromperre con gratiosa impatienza
in tali parole, "Oh, questa obedienza." Mentre io colà servii di straordinario, le
monache, a cui era troppo cara la sanità d'una sì degna sorella ricorrevano spesso
a me dicendo, che lei in tavola beveva quasi tutt'aqua, e lasciava il meglio de'
cibi; che usava una tal'aspra disciplina fornita di punte, battendosi con istraordi-
naria violenza, e cose simili. Ridicendo poi io questi particolari a Donna Maria
Francesca con imporle la dovuta **[4v = p. 6]** moderatione, all'hora sì che si
lamentava delle sorelle, che procuravano togliierle i suoi cari patimenti. Havendo
essa una volta appresa vivamente l'atrocissima sorte di morte, che nello stagno
gelato costantemente soffrirono i quaranta santi martiri, si accese di desiderio
d'imitargli in qualche parte; onde propose di non mai accostarsi al fuoco ne' rigori
dell'inverno. E così osservò per tre anni con tal patimento della sua gracile, e
cagionevole complessione, che alle volte per l'eccessiva violenza del freddo restava
come interizzita ed inhabile ad ogni esterna operatione. E più nondimeno haverebbe perseverato in somigliante mortificatione, se da' superiori maggiori ciò
non le fosse stato espressamente vietato a titolo del grave pericolo della sanità, e
vita. Fu anche solita ne' due giorni dell'anno, che si espone in quel monistero la
miracolosa Madonna, prima d'andare a riverirla girare a piè nudi per il giardino
e per la casa in tempo che si credeva di non essere osservata dall'altre. E pure tale
espositione occorre ne' maggiori freddi, cioè a dì 25 decembre ed a' 4 di febraro.
Spesso mescolava dell'assentio con gl'altri cibi: ed essendole ciò stato proibito, essa
si raccommandava istantemente a qualcuna sua più intrinseca acciò chiedesse al
confessore licenza di tale mortificatione **[5r = p. 7]** per una monaca, senza no-
minare chi fosse. Et universalmente parlando, quello in che più industriosamente
ella impiegava l'ingegno era di trovare novi artifizii, ed efficaci ragioni per piegare
i padri spirituali a concederle penitenza. L'ultima lettera che ella mi scrisse poco
prima che s'infermasse a morte, terminava così: "Mi raccommandi al signore
confessore, e gli dica, che mi dia delle penitenze, perché le merito, e particolarmente hora."

Era fondatissima nella santa umiltà, la qual virtù ogni mattina con istantissime
preghiere soleva chiedere al Signore. Perciò abominava ogni propria lode,[5] e quella
che con le sue sorelle mostravasi sempre lieta, et affabile, non in altra occasione
dava segni di risentimento e di sdegno, che quando sentivasi nominar buona,
senza peccati, favorita della Madonna etc. Pensò con innocente errore potersi
liberare da questa persecutione di lodi, e toglier via il buon concetto, che di se
vedeva haversi con andar dicendo per il monistero, ch'era piena di peccati mortali
e così fece sinché da me e da altri confessori le fu proibito, con dimostrarle, ciò
non esser bene di dire quando anche fosse vero, **[5v = p. 8]** molto meno essendo
falso com'era in lei. Per desiderio di humiliarsi godeva di gittarsi a' piedi della
madre abbadessa in publico, e con formole straordinarie di riverente pentimento
chiederle spesso perdono di mancamenti anche non colpevoli. Non harebbe volsuto, che si publicassero le miracolose gratie fattele dalla santa Vergine, per tema
che non ne resultasse qualche gloria a se stessa. Onde nell'andare alle grati soleva
studiosamente occultare la man sinistra, ove appariva[6] il segno della piaga con sì

celebre prodigio risanata. E per sola espressa obedienza, ella vinse la somma sua ripugnanza in scrivere di proprio pugno i successi stupendi delle sanità in diverse maniere resele dalla sua gran protettrice. Fu però necessario, ch'io insieme procurassi di sodisfare alla sua umiltà con dire, che tali gratie non inferiscono necessariamente merito in chi le riceve, potendo la Vergine per sua benignità conferirle a qualsivoglia peccatore. Questa istessa sì profonda umiltà operava, ch'ella si stimasse ingratissima a tanti favori della Madonna; che perciò non ardiva accostarsi alla prodigiosa sua imagine quando si esponeva. Ed una volta doppo haver ciò negato alle replicate istanze, costretta per obedienza a levare di dito alla Vergine uno di quelli anelli, che poi sogliono mandarsi all'infermi, **[6r = p. 9]** affermò di haver ciò fatto tutta tremante; e la madre abbadessa che vi si trovò presente mi ha attestato, che la vidde impallidita, e quasi ridotta a termini di sfinimento. Mi significò una volta Donna Maria Francesca, che nell'esercitar l'ufficio di sagristana sentiva particolarissima confusione; perché dovendo adornare l'altare della Vergine non haveva fiori di virtù da offerirle, i quali la sua Signora maggiormente gradiva. Se mi occorreva raccommandarle, che pregasse il Signore per qualche infermo o altra persona bisognosa, rispondeva, "Ubbidirò, ma lei sa chi sono." Essendo essa a maraviglia insigne nel sonar di tiorba, et aborrendo ogni applauso anche in questo genere, all'hora giubilava, che per qualche male sopragiontole, massime nelle mani vedeasi impedita. Né si sarebbe mai quietata di supplicare le superiore a contentarsi che non sonasse in publico, se non che havendole miracolosamente la Vergine restituite le unghie cadutele, ed un'altra volta fattole in un subbito cessare il doloroso enfiamento della man destra[7] si accertò, che la sua Signora approvava di essere servita con quel suono nelle sacre funtioni.

Quanto intenso fosse nel cuore di Donna Maria Francesca l'amor di Dio, può primieramente raccoglersi **[6v = p. 10]** dal vivo desiderio che mostrava di sempre maggiormente accendersi in esso, onde le istanze più fervide che soleva fare agli padri spirituali erano circa l'insegnarle nuovi modi di amare il suo Signore. In una sua scrittami il 23 dicembre 1658 conchiude con queste parole, "Si ricordi in carità domandare amore, amore, amore divino per me al Santo Bambino, che vivo in miserie di peccati, di tiepidezza, anzi di ghiaccio; e lo supplichi a perdonarmi et illuminarmi il cuore sino alla fine della mia vita," etc. Dimostravano anche le tenerezze de' suoi celesti amori quelle lagrime, che dopo la santa communione lungamente genuflessa soleva spargere sino a bagnarne largamente il pavimento; le quali non poteva trattenere, ancorché per non essere notata procurasse impedirle. Più volte la settimana cioè que' giorni ne' quali non l'era espressamente proibito dal confessore, si levava la notte benché fosse di mezzo inverno senza mettersi niente in dosso, ed inginocchiata adorava amorosamente tre volte la Divinissima TRINITÀ; di poi recitava nove volte l'Ave Maria, supplicando i nove chori degl'angeli a presentare quelle salutationi alla beatissima Vergine, già che troppo indegna stimavasi di presentarsi alla gran Reina per offerirle ella stessa tal dono.[8] In una loggietta a lato alla sua camera quando credevasi esser sola, e non avvertita, ampiamente sfogava con gemiti, e con **[7r = p. 11]** sospiri i divini ardori del proprio cuore, i quali sì all'hora come ne' tempi consueti dell'oratione, conforme fu osservato da molte, le infondevano nel volto una straordinaria bellezza. Quello, che spesso mi significava di fervente desiderare era di sempre vivere nel lato aperto di Giesù, ed in quello finalmente spirar l'anima morendo. Nel che può piamente credersi, che amante sì desiderosa d'esser simile ne' patimenti al crocifisso suo sposo, sia stata esaudita. Ed appunto è piaciuto al Signore tirarla a sé in giorno di venerdì dedicato alla sua divina Passione.

Si come nelle altre anime pietose così in questa all'amor di Giesù era indivisibilmente connesso quel di MARIA. Anzi in questa tanto più segnalatamente, quanto più l'eccitavano a corrispondenza le stupende gratie concessele dalla Madre Santissima, molte delle quali, com'ella stessa le ha deposte, si soggiogneranno dopo questo breve racconto. Di niuna cosa più teneramente parlava, che di quella che soleva chiamare la sua gran liberatrice, e notavasi che in ragionare delle prerogative della Vergine diveniva ella nel viso come di fuoco, e gli occhi pareva che tramandassero vive scintille. Impiegava giornalmente ogni più accurato suo studio nel culto tanto interno quanto **[7v = p. 12]** esterno della Madre Divina, procurando al possibile, che anche altre persone s'impiegassero in honorarla, ed in particolare godendo che si dicessero messe in honore di essa. La ragione che finalmente la strinse ad ubidire e vincere l'estremo della reticenza, che provava in havere a registrare le gratie dalla Vergine ricevute, fu il non derogare alle glorie della medesima. Portava sì impressa nell'animo questa sua Signora, che ad alcune confidenti disse di havere il cuore aperto dalla parte anteriore, e che in mezzo di esso v'era la Vergine. Non si sa poi s'ella ciò asserisse in senso materialmente reale. Certo è che in premio del cordialissimo ossequio professato da Donna Maria Francesca in tutto il corso di sua vita alla sovrana protettrice, l'annuntio della vicina sua felice morte altro non fu che un'accessione di ferventissimo amore verso di essa. Poiché alcuni giorni avanti l'ultima infermità sentì sorprendersi da sì sensibili fiamme di affetto verso la Vergine che andava come smaniando per il monistero, e tenendosi la mano sul petto, quasi per reprimere gl'impeti del cuore amorosamente penante. A chi incontrandola la interrogava che si sentisse, rispondeva sospirando, "O, se sapeste." Importunata finalmente da alcune sue più confidenti disse così, "Havete voi mai provato di voler bene **[8r = p. 13]** straordinariissimamente a qualche persona? Se ciò non havete sperimentato, non potete dunque comprendere quel che prova il mio cuore nell'amor della mia Signora." Ed arrivò la cosa a tal segno, che le conveniva rattenersi dall'andare in quel choro, ove si conserva il miracoloso ritratto della Madonna, perché ivi insoffribilmente la stringevano le amorose sue pene. Onde la delicatissima coscienza di questa serva di Dio cominciò a dubbitare del troppo, e già voleva domandarne parere al suo padre spirituale, quando s'infermò a morte, ed aspettò ch'io l'andassi a confessare per assicurarla da ogni timore; conforme procurai di fare, mostrandole che anzi doveva render gratie al cielo, che come già il salmista verso Dio, così ella verso la Madre Divina potesse dire, "*Cor meum, et caro mea exultaverunt in Dominam meam.*" M'imagino che non sarebbe stimato affatto temerario il pensiero di chi affermasse, che fu forsi testimonio di questo passato incendio quel calore, che assai notabile sentirono nelle membra della defonta quelli, da' quali fu sepolta più di hore 24 dopo il suo transito. Io per me da questi sì maravigliosi sentimenti di affetto verso la Reina Celeste vengo stimolato a credere, che non senza qualche lume divino ad una delle più anziane di **[8v = p. 14]** quel monistero in gran stima appresso tutte di religiosa perfettione, paia da gran tempo in qua di continuamente vedere Donna Maria Francesca sì mentr'era viva come dopo morte, ricoverata sotto il manto della gloriosissima Vergine; e ciò è stato solito rappresentarsele, conforme essa stessa mi ha confidato, e mentre veglia, e mentre dorme, sì vivamente, che tal volta non poteva rattenersi di dire all'istessa Donna Maria Francesca, "O, felice voi che state sotto il manto." Certo è che ha dimostrato palesemente la Santissima Vergine la straordinaria protettione tenuta di questa sua serva sin dalla sua più tenera età con le frequenti gratie che le faceva; tanto che essa stessa poco avanti che s'infermasse a morte pregata che al solito si ugnesse con l'oglio della lampada la quale arde avanti la Madonna, per guarire dal dolore sopragiontole in un braccio, rispose di non voler ciò fare, perché quanto chiedeva, tanto otteneva, e harebbe volsuto men ottenere per più patire.

Agli amori celesti corrispondeva la carità verso il prossimo. Se venivale raccomandato qualche bisogno, particolarmente se spirituale, o delle sue monache, o degl'esterni, ricorreva subito affettuosamente a supplicar di aiuto il Signore e la Beatissima Vergine; ed a pericoli delle anime raccomandatele harebbe **[9r = p. 15]** volsuto col proprio sangue porgere opportuno rimedio. Pareva l'angelo di pace del suo monistero trattando sempre con tutte con sì amabile riverenza, che in 13 anni che visse religiosa non si sa che veruna mai ricevesse da essa ne pure una parola d'amarezza. Le querele, che contro Donna Maria Francesca io sentii mentre confessai quelle madri, altre non furono, se non che troppo si mortificasse con pregiudizio della sanità; e le querele di essa circa le altre monache, che ne tenessero troppa cura, che la stimassero buona, e che sovente prorompessero in lodarla. Ad essa nelle loro afflitioni, e perturbationi di animo eran solite ricorrere le velate, le servigiali, le fanciulle, ed essa con gran tenerezza accogliendole efficacemente le consolava. Sino verso il fine di sua vita con particolar gratia di Dio usò questa carità verso le sue sorelle; del che ne addurrò in testimonio parte d'una lettera scritta dopo la di lei morte da una di quelle madri, la quale agitata per longo tempo irremediabilmente da affannosissimi scrupoli, nelle risposte di consolatione, e nella intercessione appresso Dio di Donna Maria Francesca trovò finalmente il porto della tranquillità sospirata. Le parole di chi scrisse sono queste: "Ho pure riceuto quello **[9v = p. 16]** che tanto tempo ho desiderato, dico di potere tranquillare una volta la mia coscienza, non già per mio merito, ma ben sì per quelli di Donna Maria Francesca, a cui molto premeva la salute dell'anima mia. Pochi giorni avanti che lei si ammalasse le raccontai il gran travaglio che havevo; e lei subbito mi disse, 'State in pace che pregarò sempre Iddio per voi.' E il giorno innanzi che lei si communicasse per viatico, mi disse che mi sarei aggiustata in coscienza; e così è stato perché mi sono aggiustata benissimo" etc. In confermatione di sì grand'efficacia di Donna Maria Francesca nel consolar le anime soggiongerò l'attestatione d'un'altra di quelle madri, mentre scrivendo della morte di tanto riverita sorella dice così, "Veramente è stata per me una gran perdita, poiché se havevo qualche angoscia o tribolatione, benché interna, io subbito gle la dicevo, e ne restavo tanto consolata che più non mi rimaneva da desiderare, perché le sue parole, con l'accompagnatura del suo affetto non potevano non arrivare al cuore, benché agghiacciato affatto" etc. Una tanto compassionevole et affabile carità, che Donna Maria Francesca usava con tutte, la rendeva sì universalmente amabile e cara, ch'ella stessa, la quale non haveva occhi per rimirare i suoi meriti, **[10r = p. 17]** restava stupida di tanto affetto. Onde mentre io colà confessavo, venne una volta piena di maraviglia a domandarmi, donde nascesse, che le monache mostravano sì gran cura della sanità di essa. In prova di che raccontommi, ch'essendosi poco avanti messa sopra una loggia inavvertentemente al sole, quante da varie parti del monistero la viddero, tutte corsero a far che se ne levasse.

Ma per quanto quelle madri custodissero con ogni sollecitudine un sì caro tesoro, è piaciuto alla Divina Maestà arrichirne presto il cielo, concedendo a Donna Maria Francesca nell'anno ventesimo settimo dell'età sua la morte sospirata da essa, e come può anche congetturarsi preveduta, poiché spesso con asseveranza diceva, che presto morirebbe. Una volta tra le altre ad una fanciulla, che rallegravasi con essa di vederla in buona salute, rispose prontamente, "È vero che hora sto bene, ma sapete, tra poco ho da morire." E replicandole quella, che non si facesse tali augurii, soggionse essa, "Voi lo vedrete per certo." A Donna Caterina sua sorella maggiore, monaca nell'istesso monistero spesso sorridendo diceva, "Non occorre badare all'haver più età di me, perché io pur tanto ho da andare avanti." Più specificatamente però ad **[10v]** un'altra fanciulla disse di se stessa quest'anno 1659, che l'anno seguente non sarebbe viva. Non molto avanti che morisse, chiamando un giorno alcune sue più familiari fanciulle in un angolo del giardino, si distese in terra nella positura propria de' morti nel cataletto, dicendo di volersi provare come star dovea dopo la sua vicina morte; e si fece da dette fanciulle ricoprire di fiori, come appunto si fa a' cadaveri delle sacre vergini defonte. Finalmente nella malattia di cui morì, quando le si proponevano i medicamenti soleva rispondere, "Datemi pure quel che volete, ma non gioverà." E tanto più facilmente possiamo indurci a credere ch'ella havesse qualche particolar lume dal cielo circa la propria morte, quanto che per indutione non mai fallita è stato osservato, che quando Donna Maria Francesca diceva d'essersi sognata, che nella tal cella del monistero era entrata la communione (il che più e più volte essa fu solita dire con ingenua semplicità) sempre si ammalava di lì a poco qualcuna in quella cella con infermità, che riducevala sino al prendere il santissimo viatico. Parve alla prudenza di quelle madri, che al merito non ordinario di questa inferma si convenisse l'honore straordinario di recarle in camera il ritratto della sua riveritissima Vergine, come seguì il giorno ch'ella si **[11r]** communicò per viatico. E poté essa con estremo giubilo del suo spirito non sol baciare più volte quella mano miracolosa, ma in quel gratiosissimo volto pascere a suo agio gli occhi un giorno, et una notte. Anzi stimasi che in tale occasione qualche bellezza sopra naturale ella fosse fatta degna di rimirare nel volto di quel sacro ritratto; poiché all'improviso chiamando l'abbadessa, le replicò tutta lieta più volte, "Madre, madre mirate hora la Vergine, miratela miratela." In tutto il tempo dell'infermità diede segni di perfetta rassegnatione nel divino volere con imperturbabile patienza; e se pure tal volta lo sdegno dello stomaco la moveva a dire di non voler qualche cosa che stimavasi opportuno di darle, bastava ricordarle la santa obedienza, che subito vincendosi rispondeva, "Orsù, sforziamoci." Morì questa innocentissima vergine a cinque di settembre del 1659, quanto più amata in vita tanto più pianta in morte inconsolabilmente dalle sue sacre sorelle; sì che non vi è memoria che in quel monistero la perdita di verun'altra sia a tutte sì vivamente dolsuta. Fu notato che appunto alli 5 di settembre un'anno prima, mentre Donna Maria Francesca stava chiusa in camera, tre volte le fu picchiata forte la porta, e sentì dirsi con una voce che ad essa parve di Donna Orsola Benvoglienti poco avanti [11v] defonta, "Donna Maria Francesca voglio venir da voi." Certo è ch'ella dopo la terza volta accorrendo alla porta non vi trovò alcuna; ed havendo poi con spavento ciò raccontato all'abbadessa et ad altre monache, per quanto queste facessero esatta diligenza, non si trovò che veruna delle viventi fosse in tal hora stata a chiamarla. Per ultimo circa il passaggio di essa non mi pare indegno di risapersi un particolare ch'io riconosco per favore ricevuto dal cielo contro ogni mio merito. Verso il fine di agosto havendo Donna Maria Francesca[9] risaputo l'ordine venutomi da miei superiori di dover partir di Siena, mi scrisse una lettera che fu l'ultima, di cui il principio era tale: "Intendendo sì acerba nuova della sua partenza mi sono accertata che nulla vagliono le mie preci, poiché sallo Dio, quanto di cuore lo havevo supplicato; et hora ben conosco, che i miei peccati ne sono cagione, e mi par rimanere abbandonata d'ogni consolatione" et c. Ma in realtà in quell'istesso in cui stimava di non essere stata esaudita fu esaudita, poiché non rimase abbandonata come doleasi, ma dopo scritta questa lettera quasi subbito infermatasi fu da me benché indegnissimo servita degl'aiuti spirituali sino all'ultimo istante della sua vita; e potei chiuderle quegli occhi, de' quali con ordinaria sua formola ella diceva, che sino che gl'havesse tenuti aperti non harebbe mai [12r] cessato di fare oratione per me.

Dopo la morte di Donna Maria Francesca è parso ad alcune persone religiose di provare gl'influssi benefichi della sua protettione dal cielo. Una tra l'altre in un monistero di Siena trovavasi tormentata da estremissima ripugnanza in havere ad esseguire l'ordine datole dalla sua superiora di applicare la mattina seguente un tal medicamento ad una inferma, per dubbio che somigliante essercitio dovesse turbarle fortemente la quiete della sua anima. Tra sì fatte angoscie sentì ispirarsi di ricorrere all'intercessione di Donna Maria Francesca poco avanti defonta. Appena genuflessa si raccomandò a questa serva di Dio, che le sparirono dalla mente tutti i pensieri affannosi che l'ingombravano, e sentì placidissimamente animarsi a quella caritativa funtione, in cui poi la mattina s'impiegò senza provare pure una minima perturbatione.[10] È vero che le ombre de' sogni non possono esser fondamento sostantiale della nostra credenza; con tutto ciò anche tra esse può ravvisarsi qualche luce divina, quando ne risultano straordinarii sentimenti di christiana pietà. Però non reputo disdicevole il riferire qualmente due settimane dopo la morte di Donna Maria Francesca parve ad una monaca d'Ogni Santi di veder ch'ella risuscitata era accolta con giubilo universale nel [12v] monastero. All'hora essa, che con singolare affetto l'amava, tiratala destramente in disparte, cominciò a pregarla che le dicesse dov'era stata sin all'hora, e n'hebbe per risposta che subbito morta se n'era andata dirittamente in paradiso, ove godeva d'un grado di gloria molto sublime. "E che potrei far io," replicò l'altra, "per acquistar sì gran gloria?" "Due sono le virtù, con cui potrai acquistarla," replic[ò] Donna Maria Francesca, "umiltà, et obedienza," e ciò replicolle più volte. Seguì poi a discorrere della importanza di queste virtù, e della eccellenza de' gaudii eterni con sì dolce ed espressiva affettuosa [sic], che l'altra, la quale con inesplicabile suo contento la udiva, svegliata che fu (quasi quella fosse stata non imaginatione di sogno, ma ammonimento di celeste visione) propose fermamente di approfittarsi con sin-golarissimo studio in queste due virtù per arrivare alla gloria di cui l'havevano fatta sopra modo invaghire le parole della sua cara sorella; né potrei a bastanza esprimere, con che pietosi sentimenti ella mi ragionò di questo suo sognato col-loquio e del singolar frutto che da esso haveva raccolto. Fu anche cosa notabile, che appunto l'istessa notte in cui il predetto sogno successe, un'altra monaca dell'istesso monistero pur dormendo fu mirabilmente ricreata dalla vista di questa felice defonta nel modo ch'ella stessa ha **[13r]** deposto con le seguenti parole: "Per l'affetto professato da me a Donna Maria Francesca sempre l'ho tenuta, e la tengo scolpita nella mia mente, bramosa di potere imitare le sue virtù. Or stando io una sera in tal pensiero mi addormentai, e parvemi di vederla. Ricordandomi che più non viveva, le domandai come havesse temuto nel punto del suo passaggio,[11] ed essa con lieto volto mi disse che haveva in quel punto ricevuta gratia d'una straordinaria cognitione divina, che la ricreò sopra modo; essendole parso di vedere una luce che l'infondeva nel petto un'ardente amore verso Dio, di gran lunga maggior di quello, ch'era solita sentire nel communicarsi, tanto che con parole non me lo poteva esplicare. Soggionse all'hora di haver visto il choro de gl'ardenti serafini, che maggiormente l'accendevano d'amore; e dopo questi esserle apparsi gli apostoli, i quali prenderono l'anima sua, e così trionfante passò di questa misera vita. Mentre che io ancor piùattendevo lieta il suo ragionamento, mi parve che lei fosse chiamata da Donna Caterina sua sorella[12] e come obedientissima sparì da gl'occhi miei, rimanendomi scolpito nel cuore questo mio gustevol sogno, il quale per obedienza ho narrato, ancorché in esso Donna Maria Francesca mi havesse fatta grand'istanza, che non ne parlassi a veruno."[13]

[13v] Piacemi in fine per saggio de' santi sentimenti, che circa il pregio della vocatione religiosa, e circa altre delle virtù sopranarrate haveva questa gran serva di Dio, soggiognere una intiera lettera scrittami da essa nel novembre del 1658 alcuni giorni avanti all'anniversario della sua monastica professione.

Iesus Maria

Si avvicina quel dì solenne da me così spensieritamente speso, dico il santo giorno, nel quale il Celeste Sposo per sua pietà mi volle aggregare nel numero delle sue religiose, vestendomi l'habito del glorioso S. Benedetto. Ma io stolta, et indegna di così gran privilegio, non gustai in sì solenne festa le gratie che mi concedeva il liberale Signore; e ben è noto a Sua Riverenza il dolore che al presente provo d'haver fatta scioccamente una sì importante atione. E però la supplico umilmente a domandar perdono il dì 16 novembre al misericordiosissimo Iddio, acciò non mi discacci come vergine stolta, che tanto merito. Trovandomi in così grandi affanni, ricorro alle orationi di tutti cotesti padri, che m'impetrino perdono, et ottengano che io adempisca sempre il divin beneplacito, e possa ancorché indegna corrispondere a tanto amore. Io non lascio di ricordarmi di Vostra Riverenza; ma sa benissimo, che le mie preci **[29r]** sono da misera peccatrice; e benché per l'obligo ch'io le tengo vorrei essere esaudita, tutta via se non sono aiutata da' suoi santi sagrificii, niente vagliono le mie fredde preghiere. Ma confido nel pretioso sangue di Giesù, medianti le sue orationi affettuose, d'essere posta nel sacrato lato aperto in croce per noi peccatori. Vorrei che mi concedesse licenza di farmi la disciplina sette volte in questi dodici giorni per penitenza de' miei peccati; però son contenta di fare l'obedienza, che ben so che meriterei altro che sette discipline. Le fo sapere che la Madre Donna N. l'altro giorno mi disse, "Eh, voi siete buona; non havete peccati." Le gridi, altrimente sarò tentata di dire ch'ho peccati mortali. Poi vorrei pure che m'insegnasse ad amar questo Dio, e mi dicesse, che cosa potrei fare per amarlo; perché ne sono molto lontana, essendo sempre la medesima; e questo è segno che non ci è l'amor di Dio; però lei sente in che termine si trova l'anima mia. Supplichi dunque la Divina Maestà che si muova a pietà di quest'anima. Finalmente devo dirle che la vita del padre Vincenzo Caraffa, che Vostra Riverenza mi ha prestata, non gliela vorrei rimandare ancora, perché ci ho gusto grande; ma non per questo ne cavo frutto alcuno, massime nel patir **[29v]** qualche cosa, perché io non fo veruna penitenza. Quando ci venne Sua Riverenza mi scordai di chiederle licenza di fare delle mortificationi interne, perché il tutto vò fare con l'obedienza. Con che humilissimamente la riverisco. Mi benedica. Dal nostro sacro monasterio di Ogni Santi 14 novembre 1658.

Obligatissima figliuola in Cristo
Donna Maria Francesca Olivetana

GLOSSARY

basso continuo:	the continuous bass line, often figured, that appears in most compositions from the seventeenth to the mid-eighteenth centuries. The basso continuo provided a convenient shorthand guide for the accompanist, who played the chords implied by the musical line and its figures on an instrument such as a harpsichord, organ, or theorbo.
beato:	"blessed." A title conferred as an acknowledgment that someone has obtained the blessedness of heaven and is worthy of limited religious honor; the first step toward sainthood.
cappella:	musical ensemble dedicated to performing polyphony.
cittern:	a plucked string instrument resembling a lute, but strung with wire and played with a plectrum.
clausura:	enclosure. The post-Tridentine convent was expected to be completely walled off from the outside world; nuns who resided in a such a convent thus lived in clausura.
clothing:	the ceremony in which a young girl "took the habit" and began her year as a novice in a convent.
concerted music:	music arranged for and performed by an ensemble of voices and instruments.
consecration:	the ceremony in which a nun dedicated her virginity to God. The rite was performed only at certain institutions in Siena: the Benedictine house of S. Abbondio, the Cistercian convent of Le Trafisse, and the Olivetan institution of Ognissanti.
conversa (pl. *converse*):	servant nun. These women paid smaller dowries than the coriste, and they were released from singing the Divine Office so that they could do the heavy chores around the convent, including cooking, cleaning, laundry, and so on.

corista (pl. *coriste*):

choir nun. Choir nuns were expected to be able to read and write so that they could participate in the Divine Office and take roles in convent administration. They were not expected to do any menial chores; such tasks were left to the converse.

Divine Office:

the eight canonical devotional services (Matins, Lauds, Prime, Terce, Sext, None, Vespers, and Compline) that all members of Roman Catholic monastic orders are required to recite daily.

educanda (pl. *educande*):

girl boarder in a convent. Parents often sent their young daughters to convents for "education," either to keep them in a safe environment until they could be married or to prepare them for the monastic life. *Educande* were supposed to be no younger than seven and no older than twenty-five when they entered the convent.

grates:

the grilles placed over openings in the convent walls, through which nuns could communicate with the outside world. Grates separated the nuns' internal church from their external church and were also present in the parlors. See figure 1.

interdiction:

an ecclesiastical censure in which a prelate withdraws all sacraments and the right to Christian burial from a specified group, such as a convent of nuns.

lauda (pl. *laude*):

a non-liturgical religious song in Italian.

licenza:

license. The official, written permission that nuns had to obtain from the archbishop or his deputy in order to allow lay persons to approach or enter a convent.

madrigal:

a musical composition based on an Italian text, often set in polyphony, and intended for entertainment purposes.

maestra di coro (*maestra di canto fermo*):

the female director who led the choir of nuns in singing plainchant.

maestra di musica (*maestra di cappella*):

the female director of the monastic ensemble that performed polyphony in the convent.

maestro di musica, maestro di cappella:

the male music director called in from the lay community to teach the nuns music, or to direct a musical ensemble of secular musicians and/or nuns, or to provide compositions for the nuns' use.

melisma:

a passage from a vocal work in which the singer is required to sing many notes on one syllable of text.

motet:

a musical composition based on a Latin text, often set in polyphony, and intended for performance at a liturgical or devotional service. Seventeenth-century motets range from works scored for solo voice (and the ever-present accompanying basso continuo) to those for multiple choirs and continuo.

parlor:

grated room in the convent that was set aside for communication between the nuns and those outside the cloister. Parlors served as the site of music lessons; they often adjoined the convent church. See figure 1.

polyphony:

music featuring several independent melodic lines of greater or lesser complexity that are intended to be performed simultaneously.

profession:

the ceremony in which a novice professes the solemn vows of chastity, poverty, and obedience. In early modern Sienese convents, profession generally occurred almost exactly a year after a girl had taken the habit.

regular:

a man belonging to an established monastic order.

rule:

a set of regulations established by the founder of a religious order for observance by its members.

Sacred Congregation of Bishops and Regulars:

the standing committee for the control of religious orders set up in Rome after the Council of Trent. The committee had the authority to grant exemptions from established rules or procedures and also served as a court of final appeal in matters of dispute in convents and monasteries the world over.

theorbo:

a large member of the lute family, featuring one set of fretted strings as well as an extended neck and extra set of long, unstopped bass strings. The theorbo was used primarily as an accompanying instrument.

vita (pl. *vite*):

a biography ("life") of a holy woman, usually written by a confessor or other holy man with close ties to her.

NOTES

Introduction

1. See Robert L. Kendrick, *Celestial Sirens: Nuns and their Music in Early Modern Milan* (Oxford: Clarendon Press, 1996), Craig A. Monson, *Disembodied Voices: Music and Culture in an Early Italian Convent* (Berkeley: University of California Press, 1995), and Kimberlyn Montford, "Music in the Convents of Counter-Reformation Rome," (Ph.D. diss., Rutgers University, 1999). Nuns in many other Italian cities cultivated music during the seventeenth century; their activities remain to be studied in the same detail found in the three monographs just cited. For an overview of what went on in other urban centers, see Gian Ludovico Masetti Zannini, *Motivi storici della educazione femminile, 1500–1650*, 2 vols. (Bari: Editorialebari, 1980; Naples: M. D'Auria Editore, 1982), 1:139–56, and "Documenti sulla musica sacra a Viterbo (1583–1692)," *Lunario romano* 15 (1986): 309–24; Jonathan Glixon, "Images of Paradise or Worldly Theaters? Toward a Taxonomy of Musical Performances at Venetian Nunneries," in *Essays on Music and Culture in Honor of Herbert Kellman*, ed. Barbara Haggh (Paris: Éditions Klincksieck, 2001), 429–57; Gabriella Zarri, "Monasteri femminili e città (secoli XV–XVIII)," in *Storia d'Italia, annali 9: La chiesa e il potere politico dal Medioevo all'età contemporanea*, ed. Giorgio Chittolini and Giovanni Miccoli (Turin: Giulio Einaudi, 1986), 394–95; Carolyn Gianturco, "Caterina Assandra, suora compositrice," in *La musica sacra in Lombardia nella prima metà del Seicento. Atti del convegno internazionale di studi, Como 31 maggio–2 giugno 1985*, ed. Alberto Colzani, Andrea Luppi, and Maurizio Padoan (Como: Antiquae Musicae Italicae Studiosi, 1987), 117–27.

2. The full text of Bossi's report is preserved in the Archivio Arcivescovile, Siena; the portions related to convents are admirably summarized by Giuliano Catoni, "Interni di conventi senesi del Cinquecento," *Ricerche storiche* 10 (1980): 171–203.

3. The statistics on Siena's noble families and the information about their economic status is taken from George R. F. Baker, "Nobiltà in declino: Il caso di Siena sotto i Medici e gli Asburgo-Lorena," *Rivista storica italiana* 84 (1972): 592–96. The list of the thirty-seven families of the ruling elite may be found as table 4 on p. 596. For an even more detailed examination of Sienese aristocracy, see Danilo Marrara, *Riseduti e nobiltà: Profilo storico-istituzionale di un'oligarchia toscana nei secoli XVI–XVIII* (Pisa: Pacini Editore, 1976).

4. Many thanks to Nello Barbieri, who produced figure 1 from the sketch in BCS, MS A.X.19, fol. 154v.

Chapter 1

1. See *Archivio di Stato di Siena: Guida-Inventario*, 2 vols., Pubblicazioni degli Archivi di Stato, 5–6 (Rome: Ministero dell'Interno, 1951), 2:174–75; Girolamo Gigli, *Diario sanese*, 2nd ed., 3 vols. (Lucca, 1723; Siena: Tip. dell'Ancora di G. Landi e N. Alessandri, 1854; reprint ed., Bologna: Arnaldo Forni Editore, 1974), 2:237–41; Giuliano Catoni, "Interni di conventi senesi del Cinquecento," *Ricerche storiche* 10 (1980): 186 n. 57; Feo Belcari, *Vita del Beato Giovanni Colombini da Siena*, ed. Rodolfo Chiarini (Lanciano: R. Carabba Editore, 1914), 30–32; BCS, MS E.V.19: "Storia del monasterio di S. Abundio e Abundanzio," fol. 104v; Karen Scott, "Urban Spaces, Women's Networks, and the Lay Apostolate of Catherine Benincasa," in *Creative Women in Medieval and Early Modern Italy: A Religious and Artistic Renaissance*, ed. E. Ann Matter and John Coakley (Philadelphia: University of Pennsylvania Press, 1994), 114.

2. *ASS: Guida-Inventario*, 1:39–40; Gigli, *Diario sanese*, 2:12–14; Alfredo Liberati, "Chiese, monasteri, oratori e spedali senesi: Ricordi e notizie," *BSSP* 47 (1940): 251–54; Catoni, "Conventi senesi," 186 n. 57.

3. ASV, SCVR, Pos. 1604, Lett. P–T, letter of 6 May 1604: "questo convento è al parer mio il più facultoso che lei habbia in questa sua diocesi non solo in riguardo delle entrate, e delle rendite sue, che non sono inferiori ad alcun altro per avvicinarsi a 1700 scudi senza computarvi il guadagno de' lavori delle suore particolari, ma principalmente per essere in questo monasterio prefisso minor numero di bocche che negli altri onde possono più commodamente e con più larghezza vivere." Bossi thought the convent could support five more women than were actually living there in 1575; see Catoni, "Conventi senesi," 186 n. 57.

4. *ASS: Guida-Inventario*, 1:8–9, 29, 34; 2:178, 181–82; 186–87, 188; Gigli, *Diario sanese*, 1:265; 2:97–98; 181; Alfredo Liberati, "Chiese, monasteri," *BSSP* 51–54 (1944–47): 130–36; 57 (1950): 131–36; and "Monastero di Santa Margherita in Castelvecchio," *BSSP* 41 (1934): 120–26; Catoni, "Conventi senesi," 177, 186 n. 57; Bruno Chiantini et al., *Santa Petronilla: Eventi storici e vicende* (Roccastrada: Editrice "Il mio amico," 1995), 27–43.

5. The social status of the nuns at S. Margherita is clear in a letter that the Bishop of Novara wrote to the Sacred Congregation concerning Siena's open convents: "S. Margherita di Castelvecchio has a noble and ancient structure and is full of sixty nuns from [Siena's] principal families, but the women are so lax about their living arrangements that it is a great, open scandal." See ASV, SCVR, Pos. 1585, Lett. R–V, letter of 20 November 1585: "uno che si chiama Santa Margherita di Castelvecchio è di struttura nobile et antico et anche pieno di 60 monache principali della città, ma tanto larghe nel suo vivere ch'è un scandalo troppo grande e aperto."

6. The noble status of the girls who professed at open institutions is often noted in documents sent to the Sacred Congregation of Bishops and Regulars in Rome during the 1580s and 1590s; see especially ASV, SCVR, Pos. 1588, Lett. P–T, letter of 28 August 1588, and Pos. 1591, Lett. S–V, letter of 25 November 1591. For the letter from the poor aristocrat Silvestro de' Vecchi, dated 15 October 1585, see Pos. 1585, Lett. R–V.

7. The picture of the "Madonna della palla" used to hang outside S. Petronilla and derived its nickname from a story about boys playing ball. Upon losing a game, a boy threw the ball at the picture and hit the Virgin's left cheek. The painted cheek supposedly turned livid with blood, and this miraculous event prompted the nuns to move the painting

to their internal church. See *Notizie istoriche riguardanti la miracolosa immagine di Maria Santissima detta della palla che conservavasi nella chiesa del soppresso monastero delle RR MM di ‵S. Petronilla* (Siena: Bindi [1824]), 7.

8. That is, S. Chiara, S. Niccolò, and S. Lorenzo did not hold the same prominent place as S. Petronilla on Gigli's calendar of feasts (see chapter 2).

9. Philippa Jackson is currently completing a dissertation on the patronage of Pandolfo Petrucci, in which the convent of S. Maria Maddalena figures prominently.

10. *ASS, Guida-Inventario*, 1:30–32; 2:178–79; Gigli, *Diario sanese*, 2:33–35, 55, 580–82; Liberati, "Chiese, monasteri," *BSSP* 47 (1940): 162–65; 48 (1941): 73–80; 55 (1948): 122–28; Catoni, "Conventi senesi," 186 n. 57.

11. *ASS: Guida-Inventario*, 1:33–34; 2:185–86; Gigli, *Diario sanese*, 1:174; Liberati, "Chiese, monasteri," *BSSP* 47 (1940): 244–48; 56 (1949): 149–51; Catoni, "Conventi senesi," 186 n. 57; Gian Ludovico Masetti Zannini, *Motivi storici della educazione femminile (1500–1650)*, 2 vols. (Bari: Editorialebari, 1980; Naples: M. D'Auria Editore, 1982), 2: 361; ASV, SCVR, Pos. 1621, Lett. P–T, letter of 25 May 1621.

12. See ASV, SCVR, Pos. 1579, busta unica, undated letters from the "impoverished gentlemen" Bartolomeo Buoninsegni and Fulvio Marretti asking permission to place their daughters at Vita Eterna. Feliciani's daughter took the habit at Paradiso sometime early in the seventeenth century; see ASV, SCVR, Pos. 1604, Lett. P–T, letter from Giovanbattista Piccolomini dated 7 March 1604. Frank D'Accone identifies the daughter as Urania, who was born in 1580 and died in 1649 after serving the convent as prioress; see *The Civic Muse: Music and Musicians in Siena during the Middle Ages and the Renaissance* (Chicago: University of Chicago Press, 1997), 360.

13. *ASS: Guida-Inventario*, 1:41; 2:178, 180; Gigli, *Diario sanese*, 1:176–78; 2: 116–17; ASS, Con. sopp. 1150, fol. 113r; ASV, SCVR, Pos. 1586, Lett. S–V, letter of 27 April 1586.

14. *ASS: Guida-Inventario*, 2:187; Liberati, "Chiese, monasteri," *BSSP* 57 (1950): 146–51; 62–63 (1955–56): 241–49; Catoni, "Conventi senesi," 186 n. 57; Giorgio Picasso, "Congregazione benedettina olivetana," *DIP*, 9 vols. (Rome: Edizioni Paoline, 1974–), 2: 1493–96. For more on the miraculous statue of the Virgin and Child, see chapter 5.

15. Liberati, "Le Gesuate di Vallepiatta," *BSSP* 40 (1933): 411–18; Romana Guarnieri, "Gesuate" and "Gesuati," *DIP*, 4:1114–16; 1116–30. The family names of nuns who professed at the institution in the seventeenth century are taken from ACRFS, S. Sebastiano 1 (old 1248), fol. 60r.

16. A house for reformed prostitutes, extant in mid-fifteenth-century Siena, was defunct by the mid-sixteenth century; see Sherrill Cohen, "The Convertite and the Malmaritate: Women's Institutions, Prostitution and the Family in Counter-Reformation Florence" (Ph.D. diss. Princeton University, 1985), 275, 318 n. 2. See also Catoni, "Conventi senesi," 178–79.

17. *ASS: Guida-Inventario*, 2:179; Gigli, *Diario sanese*, 1:307–8; ASV, SCVR, Pos. 1624, Lett. R–V, letter of 7 February 1622/23. For more on Vannini and the Convertite, see chapter 5.

18. Such protective institutes arose all over Italy during the sixteenth century; see Sherrill Cohen, *The Evolution of Women's Asylums since 1500* (New York: Oxford University Press, 1992), 19–21.

19. See *Ragguaglio della vita della serva di Dio Suor Chiara Birelli della Congregazione dell'Abbandonate di Siena disteso dal P. Giuseppe Scapecchi della Compagnia di Gesù* (Florence: Michele Nestenus and Antonmaria Borghigiani, 1712), 22–25, for a brief history of the Abbandonate.

20. *ASS: Guida-Inventario*, 1:35; 2:181; Gigli, *Diario sanese*, 1:44, 2:294–95; Liberati,

"Chiese, monasteri," *BSSP* 56 (1949): 152–53; ASS, Con. sopp. 3860; Stefano Moscadelli, "I Conservatorî riuniti femminili di Siena e il loro archivio," *BSSP* 95 (1988): 97.

21. *ASS: Guida-Inventario*, 2:177; Eugenio Lazzareschi, "Una mistica senese: Passitea Crogi, 1564–1615," *BSSP* 23 (1916): 20–23. For more on Crogi, see chapter 5. The Capuchin women were so serious about their austere lifestyle that in 1617, they wrote to the Sacred Congregation to ask permission to give away the 4,000–5,000 scudi they had received in alms, as it was contrary to their vow of poverty; see ASV, SCVR, Pos. 1617, Lett. S–T, letter of 22 December 1617.

22. Not included among the twenty-one convents (or in figure 2) is S. Francesco delle Mantellate, which apparently had been suppressed by 1605, and S. Orsola delle Derelitte, which remained a true conservatory in nature.

23. The value of a musical education as an ornament to the nobility was well-ingrained in the Sienese by the sixteenth century; see D'Accone, *The Civic Muse*, 634–41. The pride the nobility took in musical performances by their offspring is reflected in a letter the Sienese noblewoman Olimpia Chigi Gori Pannilini wrote to her half-brother Cardinal Sigismondo Chigi (see chapter 2).

24. Picasso, "Congregazione benedettina olivetana," *DIP*, 2:1495.

25. See Belcari, *Vita del Beato Giovanni Colombini*, 36, 38, 50, 53, 60, 61, 87, 89.

26. S. Apollonia is the patron saint of dentists. Artists often depicted her holding one of her teeth in pincers, and stories surrounding her martyrdom either mention that her teeth were smashed or that she was tortured by having her teeth extracted; see David Hugh Farmer, *The Oxford Dictionary of Saints* (Oxford: Oxford University Press, 1992), 28. In an era before dentists, barbers were responsible for pulling teeth. A marble plaque dated 1492 that originally adorned a "cappella de' barbieri" shows the barber's tools of trade: razor, scissors, and pincers; it still hangs in the entrance to Siena's Biblioteca Comunale.

27. ASS, Con. sopp. 3589, fol. 21v: "Item. Che le dette reverende madri sieno obligate a fare celebrare, arrivati che saranno li detti huomini et Università collegialmente in detta chiesa et altare destinato dell'immagine di detta Santa Appollonia, una messa secondo il costume antico, cioè con mottetti."

28. See Robert L. Kendrick, *Celestial Sirens: Nuns and their Music in Early Modern Milan* (Oxford: Clarendon Press, 1996), 44.

29. The summary of Sienese history that follows is distilled largely from Judith Hook, *Siena: Una città e la sua storia* (Siena: Nuova immagine editrice, 1988), 143–61, with additional information gleaned from Eric Cochrane, *Florence in the Forgotten Centuries, 1527–1800* (Chicago: University of Chicago Press, 1973), 88–89, and J. R. Hale, *Florence and the Medici: The Pattern of Control* (New York: Thames and Hudson, 1977), 131–32.

30. Hook, *Siena*, 155 (my translation).

31. See Gigli, *Diario sanese*, 2:102–3; BCS, MS E.V.19, fols. 79r–99r. The women at S. Abbondio managed to retain their ancient seat even after the Council of Trent legislated the suppression of extraurban houses because they were too exposed to the perils of war and were often loosely regulated; see Gabriella Zarri, "Monasteri femminili e città (secoli XV–XVIII)," in *Storia d'Italia, annali 9: La chiesa e il potere politico dal Medioevo all'età contemporanea*, ed. Giorgio Chittolini and Giovanni Morandi (Turin: Giulio Einaudi, 1986), 401–2.

32. Giuseppe Pardi, "La popolazione di Siena e del territorio senese attraverso i secoli," *BSSP* 30 (1923): 113–17. I would like to thank Stefano Moscadelli for bringing this article to my attention.

33. ASS, Con. sopp. 2542, unn. fol.: "Le monache di Santa Bonda, e quelle di Ogni Santi e Santa Chiara entrorono tutte in Siena la mattina seguente . . . che era un fango a ginocchio."

34. BCS, MS E.V.19, fols. 88r, 92v–93r.

35. For the following summary of Bossi's character, the political situation in Siena c. 1575, and the details of the apostolic visit, I am most indebted to Catoni, "Conventi senesi," 171–203.

36. The definitive account of Carlo Borromeo's attempts to regulate music in Milanese convents may be found in Kendrick, *Celestial Sirens*, 58–72.

37. Catoni, "Conventi senesi," 174.

38. Ibid., 177.

39. Kendrick, *Celestial Sirens*, 38–39; Craig A. Monson, *Disembodied Voices: Music and Culture in an Early Modern Italian Convent* (Berkeley: University of California Press, 1995), 6. Kimberlyn Montford notes that in Rome, the convent population increased during times of social and economic instability. Even so, Roman families consigned far fewer of their daughters to the convent than did families in Siena, Bologna, or Milan; see "Music in the Convents of Counter-Reformation Rome" (Ph.D. diss., Rutgers University, 1999), 37.

40. See table 1.1. Figures for the general population in mid-Seicento Siena may be found in George R. F. Baker, "Nobiltà in declino: Il caso di Siena sotto i Medici e gli Asburgo-Lorena," *Rivista storica italiana* 84 (1972): 586. In order to estimate the number of nuns in convents at midcentury, I compiled information from letters, as well as convent contracts and deliberations. When such sources were not available, I relied on the figures preserved in a document from ASV, SCVR, Pos. 1600, Lett. P–T, letter of 16 October 1600 (transcribed by Masetti Zannini, *Motivi storici della educazione femminile*, 2:360–61). This document reproduces the population limits Bossi prescribed for the twelve cloistered convents he visited in 1575 (the *bocche*, or "mouths," that he deemed those houses could support), as well as the bocche for the four convents that had accepted cloistering by 1600. (The only institution for which I could find no information was the Cappuccine; for this house, I proposed a number roughly equal to the population of the smallest convents in Siena.) Although the author of the 1600 letter wanted to reduce the bocche at many convents, there is no evidence that this ever occurred; in fact, most convents were granted permission to accept women "over the number." Thus, my estimates are often very conservative. Even with the conservative figures, the percentage of the Sienese female population in religious institutions by the mid-Seicento lags only slightly behind that for contemporary Milan and Bologna; see Monson, *Disembodied Voices*, 6, and Kendrick, *Celestial Sirens*, 38–39.

41. Baker points out the preference of the Sienese for seeking marriages exclusively within their own city. Between 1560 and 1779, for example, about 95 percent of the sons from the Borghesi, Pecci, Petrucci, and Piccolomini clans married noblewomen from Siena. By the mid–seventeenth-century, Siena's ruling elite needed approximately 3,474 scudi to contract a secular marriage. In contrast, my research shows that a normal convent dowry was approximately 400–450 scudi. See Baker, "Nobiltà in declino," 609–11, especially n. 78 and n. 92. Siena's situation was not unique; Venetian families also found that ever-increasing dowries and a shrinking class of suitable bridegrooms made it difficult to arrange marriages for their daughters. Jutta Gisela Sperling has postulated that the decreasing number of marriages in Venice during the late sixteenth and early seventeenth centuries and the exploding convent population did not result from a simple desire to contain costs but were the result of a self-destructive form of competitive gift-giving, a conspicuous destruction of wealth, in which the "ritual waste of patrician women's reproductive capacities" was the result of the requirement that "gifts" (in this case, women) had to be returned "with interest"; see her *Convents and the Body Politic in Late Renaissance Venice* (Chicago: University of Chicago Press, 1999), 58–59.

42. Catoni, "Conventi senesi," 201 (decree 22): "Quelle che si han da vestire o da

velare con gran diligenza siano essaminate dall'ordinario in luogo dove esse liberamente possino scoprire l'intentione et animo loro."

43. For the rules issued by Bossi, see Catoni, "Conventi senesi," 199–203. These can be compared to the decrees issued by various ecclesiastical authorities for nuns in Piacenza; see Franco Molinari, "Visite pastorali dei monasteri femminili di Piacenza nel secolo XVI," in *Il Concilio di Trento e la riforma tridentina: Atti del convegno storico internazionale, Trento 2– 6 settembre 1963*, 2 vols. (Rome: Herder, 1965), 2:679–731. I take up Bossi's admonitions concerning the clothing ceremony and convent theater in subsequent chapters.

44. BCS, MS E.V.19, fol. 100r: "Comandò [Bossi] di più che le converse facessero professione e chi di loro non la volesse fare, gli fosse cavato l'abito della Religione e cacciata via e che non uscissero mai più di clausura. Ma in questa parte per questa prima volta non fu ubbidito per impotenza." Ten years after Bossi's visit, Siena's cloistered nuns and members of the Balìa wrote a collective letter to the Sacred Congregation in Rome explaining why it was impossible for servant nuns to refrain from exiting the convent; see ASV, SCVR, Pos. 1585, Lett. R–V, letter of 20 July 1585. It is not clear when Siena's female monastics finally bowed to the inevitable.

45. All cloistered houses were under the archbishop's control by the late 1500s. Many had been under the jurisdiction of male members of their order (regulars), but the political and social troubles of the sixteenth century probably gave Siena's archbishops an excellent excuse for transferring that authority to themselves; see Gigli, *Diario sanese*, 2:14.

46. For an overview of Piccolomini's life and career, see Narciso Mengozzi, "Ascanio Piccolomini quinto Arcivescovo di Siena," *BSSP* 19 (1912): 249–353.

47. ASV, SCVR, Pos. 1583, Lett. S–V, letter of 10 May 1583: "sarà opra di charità far gratia a dette monache che possin vestire le prefate dodici zitelle allevate nel lor mona- sterio per il buono effetto detto da che anco ne seguirà che forse si disporranno a servar perfetta clausura il che non hanno potuto fare fin adesso non havendo da vivere." The response of the Sacred Congregation was "Nihil" ("No").

48. See Monson, *Disembodied Voices*, 41–42.

49. The various controversies and their resolution are documented in a series of letters and decrees sent to the Sacred Congregation; see ASV, SCVR, Pos. 1587, Lett. P–T, letter of 8 August 1587; Pos. 1588, Lett. P–T, letters of 21 August, 28 August, and 11 September 1588; Pos. 1590, Lett. R–V, letter of 21 January 1590; Pos. 1591, Lett. S–V, letters of 21 May and 25 November 1591; Pos. 1592, Lett. R–T, edict of 9 September 1592, and letters of 27 September, 9 October, and 4 November 1592. ASV, SCVR, Pos. 1593, Lett. R–S, preserves the printed edict of 17 July 1593 allowing the nuns to exit the city walls during the harvest season. See AAS, 3922, for the interdiction of 26 August 1591, the decree of 6 December 1591 lifting that interdiction and absolving the girls who had taken the habit, and the printed broadsheet of rules permitting open convents to accept educande (dated 19 June 1593). See also ASS, Con. sopp. 1160, fol. 78r.

50. ASV, SCVR Pos. 1594, Lett. S, letter of 28 November 1594: "Primo, egli ha oppinione di se medesimo troppo grande e sicura . . . 7⁰, Non si scorge in lui zelo della salute delle anime, né della riforma de' costumi, non havendo più cura che tanto di estirpare i vitii della cità et piantarci buoni costumi, di promovere le opere spirituali et il servicio di Dio, solamente si mostra severissimo e poco discreto verso li poveri monasterii delle monache della cità. . . ." The letter also attacked Piccolomini for having taken his "im- moderate delight in the Tuscan language" so far as to have his own amorous love poetry published.

51. ASV, SCVR, Pos. 1595, Lett. R–T, letter of 18 September 1595.

52. Tarugi hailed from Montepulciano. His life and career are briefly summarized in

Alessandro Castellini, "Il Cardinale Francesco Maria Tarugi arcivescovo di Siena," *BSSP* 50 (1943): 88–109.

53. See ASV, SCVR, Pos. 1599, Lett. S–V, letters of 10 February, 15 February, and 18 May 1599. The nuns of Vita Eterna and of Paradiso, who maintained close ties to the Dominican friars, vigorously protested the transfer of authority. Their letters of 22 and 26 June 1599, as well as the archbishop's response on 9 August 1599, are preserved in the same source.

54. The conditions negotiated by the nuns were based on those obtained by Vita Eterna in 1595. ASV, SCVR, Pos. 1604, Lett. P–T, preserves an undated letter from the archbishop describing the deal worked out with S. Sebastiano. See also Liberati, "Santa Margherita in Castelvecchio," 139–40, for a transcription of the document describing the 1602 ceremony during which the nuns at that house took their solemn vows.

55. The letters suggesting that the Mantellate be forced to join with the Franciscans of S. Margherita are preserved in the ASV, SCVR, Pos. 1585, Lett. R–V, letters of 12 and 20 November 1585; Pos. 1587, Lett. P–T, letter of 16 November 1587, and Pos. 1591, Lett. S–V, letter of 4 April 1591. The nuns describe their own pitiful situation in an undated letter preserved in SCVR, Pos. 1604, Lett. P–T. I could find no references to the convent after this date. Nevertheless, female Franciscan tertiaries did not disappear from the Sienese urban landscape. One of them, Francesca Toccafondi, came under investigation by the Sienese inquisition after her death in 1685; see Adelisa Malena, "Inquisizione, 'finte sante,' 'nuovi mistici.' Ricerche sul Seicento," in *Atti dei Convegni Lincei 162. L'inquisizione e gli storici: un cantiere aperto, Roma, 24–25 giugno 1999* (Rome: Accademia Nazionale dei Lincei, 2000), 292–97.

56. See *ASS: Guida-Inventario*, 1:29; ASV, SCVR, Pos. 1612, Lett. O–S, letter of 2 May 1612; Pos. 1615, Lett. R–S, letter of 5 July 1615; Pos. 1624, Lett. R–V, letter of 7 February 1622/23 with attachments, letter of 24 May 1624.

57. I would like to express my gratitude to Craig Monson, who examined all the documents regarding music sent to the Sacred Congregation from 1625 to 1670 and graciously allowed me complete access to his research.

58. AAS, 3922, unn. fol.: "Che si rimuovano et tolgano via i leuti e le cetere del convento e non vi se ne riceva mai più che sono inditio e principio di male affetto." The decrees for the Convertite were also sent to the Sacred Congregation in Rome; see ASV, SCVR, Pos. 1597, Lett. R–S, unn. fol.

59. The phrase "purity of heart" (*purità di cuore*) occurs at least twice in the early-seventeenth-century decrees issued by Antonio Seneca for the convents of Rome. Unlike Borghesi, Seneca wanted to restrict the nuns to singing plainchant. See Gian Lodovico Masetti Zannini, " 'Suavità di canto' e 'purità di cuore': Aspetti della musica nei monasteri femminili romani," in *La cappella musicale nell'Italia della Controriforma. Atti del Convegno internazionale di studi nel IV Centenario di fondazione della Cappella musicale di S. Biagio di Cento, Cento 13–15 ottobre 1989*, ed. Oscar Mischiati and Paolo Russo (Florence: Leo S. Olschki Editore, 1993), 137–39.

60. Gaetano Greco, "Dopo il Concilio di Trento," in *Storia di Siena*, 3 vols. (Siena: ALSABA, 1996), 2:28.

61. AAS, 3930, fol. 42v: "È parso bene a Monsignore Illustrissimo e Reverendissimo Arcivescovo ridurre a memoria i buoni ordini che sono a monasterii di non permettere che o monache o fanciulle piglino lettione di musica o di suono senza la presenza d'altra monaca d'età per tutto il tempo della lettione. 6 aprile 1668. Carlo Piochi."

62. Monson, *Disembodied Voices*, 38–39; Kendrick, *Celestial Sirens*, 67, 81; Montford, "Convents of Counter-Reformation Rome," 56–57, 81, 91, 97.

63. Kendrick, *Celestial Sirens*, 67–68; see also Monson, *Disembodied Voices*, 37; and Montford, "Convents of Counter-Reformation Rome," 81.

64. Kendrick, *Celestial Sirens*, 70, 81, 101.

65. Ibid., 103; Monson, *Disembodied Voices*, 39–48.

66. Piccini's service at S. Maria in Provenzano, Siena's second most important non-monastic church, is reported by Silvia Calocchi, "Musica e feste in Siena durante il governatorato del Principe Mattias de' Medici, 1629–1667" (Tesi di laurea, Università degli Studi di Siena, 1988–89), 198. The letter from the Archbishop of Siena concerning Piccini is preserved in the ASF, Mediceo del Principato 5479, fol. 364r: "Al Piccini musico di Vostra Altezza ho fatto fin'hora godere tutte le habilità che da me potevano dipendere, havendolo liberalmente introdotto ad insegnare alle monache de' monasteri. Ma per un eccesso succeduto questo Carnevale passato per il quale fu formato processo tanto nel tribunale laico quanto nel mio, egli è venuto così malamente diffamato di qualche gioventù che io per decoro de' monisteri no ho potuto far di meno di non allontanarmelo. . . . 15 aprile 1664, Arcivescovo di Siena." I would like to thank Beth Glixon for supplying me with a transcription of this document. I was unable to find records of the court case against Piccini in Sienese archives.

67. See Franco Daniele Nardi, "Aspetti della vita religiosa a Siena nell'età della Controriforma," part 2, *BSSP* 94 (1987): 151–75. The documents describing the case of the secret grate are preserved in ASV, SCVR, Pos. 1616, Lett. P–S, letter of 29 July 1616; Lett. S–T, letter of 20 December 1616.

68. ASV, SCVR, Pos. 1604, Lett. P–T, letter from Giovanbattista Piccolomini, dated 28 March 1604: "ho trovato e scoperto una di loro gravida vicinissima a' giorni del parto che lei medesima me l'ha confessato, affermandomi che l'ha ingravidata un frate del convento loro di San Domenico se ben da' altri mi vien detto che la si sia impacciata con frati d'altre religioni ancora e che questo non sia il primo errore da lei commesso . . . et il mantello monacale fa pur qualche buon effetto poiché serve a coprire il corpo pieno mentre caminano per le strade."

69. *Celestial Sirens*, 91–106.

70. Both Accarigi and Forteguerri led the musical ensemble at S. Sebastiano; see ACRFS, S. Sebastiano 1 (old 1248), fols. 41r, 61r.

71. See ASV, SCVR, Reg. monialium 7 (1655), pp. 170–71, letter of 25 June 1655; the full text of the document is quoted in chapter 2.

72. BCS, MS E.V.19, fols. 109v–110r. The patrician organists hailed from nine different families: Colombini, Gionti, Luti, Mandoli, Placidi, Sani, Santi, Savini and Turamini. Their nonaristocratic companion was Orsola Silvestri (see chapter 2). The situation at S. Abbondio may be compared to the bitter rivalry over the organist's position at the Bolognese house of S. Cristina; see Monson, *Disembodied Voices*, 111–17.

73. BCS, MS E.V.19, fols. 108v–109r. Ascanio I received musical training as a young man; see Mengozzi, "Ascanio Piccolomini," 331.

74. See Frederick J. McGinnis, *Right Thinking and Sacred Oratory in Counter-Reformation Rome* (Princeton: Princeton University Press, 1995), 108–9.

75. Stillman Drake, *Galileo* (Oxford: Oxford University Press, 1980), 78.

76. My translation is based on the document given in Laura Corso, "Relazioni fra Lorenzo Magalotti e Ascanio II Piccolomini Arcivescovo di Siena," *BSSP* 44 (1937), 339; it may be compared with that published in Karl von Gerber, *Galileo Galilei and the Roman Curia*, trans. Mrs. George Sturge (London: Kegan Paul, 1879), 274.

77. Alexander VII approved of nuns performing polyphony inside the cloister but banned men from teaching at Roman convents; see Montford, "Convents of Counter-Reformation Rome," 91–98.

78. Hook, *Siena*, 105.

79. See Doc. 16, appendix 1.

Chapter 2

1. ASS, Con. sopp. 2329, fol. 214v: "venne l'acqua la prima volta del ponte el dì 17 di maggio che fu el primo giorno della pasqua della Pentechoste, quale con molta festa et allegrezza andando a processione per tutto el giardino cantando el Te Deum con molte lacrime spandendo per l'allegrezza che ebbero tutte le madri."

2. At S. Sebastiano and Le Trafisse, the leader of the plainchant choir was designated *maestra del coro* or *maestra del canto fermo*, and her name was recorded in the Deliberazioni alongside those of other nuns who, at regular intervals, were tapped to fill important convent offices. See ACRFS, S. Sebastiano in Vallepiatta 1 (old 1248), fols. 2r–117v; and ASS, Con. sopp. 3630 (Le Trafisse), fols. 138v, 153r–v, 157r–v, 162r, 182r–v.

3. See ASS, Con. sopp. 909 (S. Abbondio), unn. fol.: "Aprile 1677 [A dì 4] e £. 23.13.4 per un libro di canto fermo e lire due e soldi 5 per farci fare le cuperte, in tutto £. 25.18.4"; Con. sopp. 2649 (S. Marta): "Uscita di spese diverse (1619–20), Per un antifonario per il canto fermo, £. 44."

4. ASV, SCVR, Sezione monache, 1644, luglio–dicembre, letter of 14 October 1644: "Suor Francesca Tarari gentildonna della città di Cagliari et monacha professa nel monasterio di Santa Catherina di Siena di detta città espone humilmente all'Eminenze Vostre come nell'ingresso che fece in detto monasterio diede l'elemosina dotale solita darsi dalle monache coriste et per non saper leggere né cantare non ha potuto godere li privilegii che godono dette coriste. E perché al presente è d'età grave e non puol imparare di leggere né cantare supplica humilmente l'Eminenze Vostre che si voglino degnare concederli indulto che non ostante non sappie leggere possa nondimeno godere tutti li privilegii et indulti che godono tutte le altre monache coriste et ancora quanto alla voce attiva e passiva." The only "privilege" mentioned in this letter is the right to speak and to be spoken to in the cloister (active and passive voice); Tarari was probably also denied the right to vote in chapter meetings. I would like to thank Craig Monson for providing me with his transcription of this document.

5. AOMS, MS 39–I, M24 (old G.V.16). At least two hands are evident in the 163 numbered parchment folios comprising the choirbook. The second hand begins on fol. 99v; it is in this portion of the manuscript, on fol. 133r, that one finds the signature of the scribe and the date of 1543. I would like to express my gratitude to Frank D'Accone, who brought this source to my attention.

6. Ibid., fol. 95r: "Duos sorores ex parte hebdomadarii cantant in medio chori."

7. BCS, MS F.VI.20, containing 42 folios. Before its recent restoration and rebinding, it suffered the indignities often inflicted on decorated manuscripts: an illuminated initial and several folios were cut away.

8. Ibid., fol. 11r: "Quando repetitur versus 'Quid facimus' procedant moniales iuxta refectorium, quo verso finito, incipiat cantatrix 'Ave rex.' Inclinet ad crucem conventus se in terra genibus et manibus positis exceptis ministris. Et omnes stent erepti conversi deinceps ad crucem quousque incipiatur 'Gloria laus' et cetera."

9. ASS, Con. sopp. 2841, consisting of 82 parchment folios. This is the only document from S. Monaca that survives in ASS.

10. BCS, MS I.VIII.29, containing 156 folios. I would like to thank Philippa Jackson, who brought this manuscript to my attention. See Scipione Borghesi and Luciano Banchi, *Nuovi documenti per la storia dell'arte senese* (Siena: Enrico Torrini, 1898; reprint ed., Soest:

Davaco, 1970), 210, for references to the nuns' work as scribes and illuminators in the late fifteenth century.

11. MS I.VIII.29, fols. 152r–56r. The treatise is not found in the manuscript from S. Monaca.

12. ACRFS, S. Maria Maddalena 131 (old 1331), [fol. 1r], "Per le molto Reverende Madri del venerabile Monastero di S. Maria Maddalena ad istanza della molto reverenda Suor Caterina Angela Carli, Priora del coro. FF. Dionysius Amadorius senensis scripsit anno 1675." The manuscript contains 21 paper folios.

13. See Herbert Thurston and Donald Attwater, *Butler's Lives of the Saints*, 4 vols. (New York: P. J. Kennedy, 1956), 3:544; and F. Roth, "St. Thomas of Villanova," *The New Catholic Encyclopedia*, 15 vols. (New York: McGraw-Hill, 1967), 14:123–24.

14. In 1675, the nuns of S. Petronilla paid Girolamo Lenzi to copy antiphons and plainchant for the feasts of the Most Holy Name of Mary and for S. Peter of Alcantara, a Franciscan reformer canonized in 1669; see ASS, Con. sopp. 3394, fol. 138r: "1675. Ottobre il [dì] 16, a messer Girolamo Lenzi £. 7 e soldi 5 per aver copiato l'antifone del Santissimo Nome della Vergine Maria e di S. Pietro d'Alcantara ed il canto fermo, £. 7.5." The Clarissan nuns, like their Augustinian sisters, evidently wanted to be able to celebrate recently added feast days by singing the appropriate chants.

15. See ASS, Con. sopp. 3630, fols. 112r–v, 125r–v, 148r–v, 168r–v, 207v.

16. ASS, Con. sopp. 2327, unn. fols., entries for 21 September 1663 and for 23 August 1676.

17. ASS, Con. sopp. 904, fol. 103v: "A dì 17 settembre 1651, per libbre dieci carne grossa per polpette per le cantore . . . £. 2.6.8"; Con. sopp. 909, fol. 26r: "A dì 18 marzo (1674/75), in pesce anguilla e limoni per le cantore, £. 2"; Con. sopp. 906, fol. 94r: "(15) settembre 1670, e più giuli quattro e mezzo per li piccioni per darli alle cantore al solito, £. 3."

18. BCS, MS A.IX.10, "Mescolanze di cose diverse appartenenti a Siena," fol. 238r: "1576. Suor Orsola Silvestri ne' Santi Abbondo e Abbondanzio. Così gratiosa nel sonare gli organi ch'era veramente miracolo di natura." The other woman to whom Montebuoni Buondelmonti accords a separate entry in the manuscript is Maddalena Casulana (see fol. 238v).

19. BCS, MS E.V.19, fol. 101r: "Nel suo triennio [Elisabetta Buoninsegni, elected abbess on 30 April 1576] prese 6 fanciulle per monacarsi . . . fra le quali fanciulle l'ultima si domandava Aurora Silvestri, e alla religione Suor Orsola. Lei fu la prima che ci portasse la perfezzione del sonare l'organo e per lei molte dell'altre impararono"; fols. 109v–110r: "(Novembre 1593). I nomi delle organiste sono questi, cioè Suor Pia Santi, Suor Orsola Silvestri, Suor Tecla Mandoli, Suor Francesca Turamini, Suor Innocenza Turamini, Suor Lisabetta Placidi, Suor Petra Sani, Suor Eufemia Savini, Suor Barbara Luti, Suor Battista Colombini, Suor Giulia Gionti." The date of Suor Orsola's consecration is given in the same source on fol. 104r.

20. See ASS, Con. sopp. 3630. The names of organists appear haphazardly from 1620 until about 1665 (see fols. 112v–183v); after that, the job seems to have been subsumed under the duties of the maestra di cappella.

21. Plucked string instruments were widely cultivated in Siena by both amateur and professional musicians; see Isidoro Ugurgieri Azzolini, *Le pompe sanesi*, 2 vols. (Pistoia, 1649), 2:3–16; BCS, MS A.IX.10, fols. 238r–240v; and Dinko Fabris, "Tre composizioni per liuto di Claudio Saracini e la tradizione del liuto a Siena tra Cinque e Seicento," *Il flauto dolce* 16 (April 1987): 14–25.

22. See chapter 5 for a discussion of the theorbists at Ognissanti; the presence of a lute teacher at S. Marta is discussed hereafter.

23. See ASS, Con. sopp. 2332 (Santuccio), fol. 100r: "A dì 8 detto (dicembre 1651) . . . lire dodici a maestro Matteo leutaio per haver accomodato il violone, £. 12"; Con. sopp. 3289, 3290 (S. Paolo), unn. fols.

24. For the inventory from S. Marta, see ASS, Con. sopp. 2671, fol. 7r; a lute is named in the outlay of expenses for 1618–19 in Con. sopp. 2649, unn. fol. Repair records for the spinetta, theorbo, and violone at S. Petronilla are in Con. sopp. 3394, fols. 140r and 144v; violins are cited specifically in the same convent's book of licenze, Con. sopp. 3574, unn. fols. A string ensemble consisting of violins, violones, theorbos, and spinet was apparently common in contemporary Roman churches; Alexander Silbiger has noted that the spinet was often preferred to a harpsichord in such ensembles as it took less space; see "The Roman Frescobaldi Tradition, c. 1640–1670," *JAMS* 33 (1980): 59–60.

25. ASV, SCVR, Reg. Monialium 7 (1655), pp. 170–71, Letter of 25 June 1655: "[Le] monache del Santuccio rappresentano alla Sacra Congregatione che il servitio della lor chiesa patisce quanto alla musica per non esservi chi supplisca alla parte di soprano, hanno supplicato di poter ricevere gratis per qualche tempo con titolo d'educanda Caterina Alessandri povera zitella esperta nel canto e suono." I would like to thank Craig Monson for providing me with a transcription of this letter.

26. BAV, Archivio Chigi 3871, fol. 46r, letter of 21 January 1671: "Domenica fu festa alle monache dell Refugio dove ci fu tutta Siena che per non essere niente in Piazza si ste a tutto il vespero, e la mia Lala suonò l'organo alla messa grande e a tutto il vespero."

27. The title bestowed on the woman who led the polyphonic ensemble (*maestra di musica* or *maestra di canto figurato*; that is, "music director" or "director of polyphonic music") clearly distinguishes her from the woman who led the plainchant choir; see note 2 of this chapter.

28. See ASS, Con. sopp. 3630 (Le Trafisse), fols. 125v, 133r, 138v, 148v; ACRFS, S. Sebastiano in Vallepiatta 1 (old 1248), fols. 91v, 99r, 103v, 107r, 112v. Suor Marzocchi is actually listed as the assistant to the maestra di musica in 1629, but since no maestra is named among the officers that year, I have assumed that Marzocchi shouldered the responsibility.

29. See ASS, Con. sopp. 3517 (S. Petronilla), unn. fol.; ACRFS, S. Maria Maddalena 13 (old 681), fol. 62r.

30. For references to the maestre (sometimes unnamed), see Con. sopp. 2337, fols. 61r, 72v, 74v, 81v, 105r, 109v; Con. sopp. 2339, p. 203; Con. sopp. 2340, fols. 68r, 73v; Con. sopp. 2341, unn. fols.; Con. sopp. 2342, unn. fols.; Con. sopp. 2343, unn. fols.; Con. sopp. 2344, 53v and unn. fols.; Con. sopp. 2345, p. 63. Suor Nicola Caterina Chigi is credited with "maestranza di cappella" in Con. sopp. 2340, fols. 68r, 73v. For Suor Geltruda Chigi, see Con. sopp. 2341, unn. fol.: "Il dì 10 luglio 1686. Alla maestra della musica e per essa a Suor Maria Geltruda Chigi, piastre una, £. 7"; Con. sopp. 2342, unn. fols.: "Il 14 ottobre 1691. Alla maestra di cappella e per essa a Suor Maria Geltruda Chigi, piastra una, solita annua, £. 7"; Con. sopp. 2343, unn. fols.: "Il dì detto (2 ottobre 1695). Alla maestra di musica e per essa a Suor Maria Geltruda Chigi, piastra una, £. 7"; "Il 7 agosto 1696. Alla maestra della musica Suor Maria Geltruda Chigi, piastra una, £. 7." The exact relationship between Suor Nicola Caterina and Suor Maria Geltruda is not clear; they might have been sisters, cousins, or aunt and niece. Craig Monson traces the development of a similar "modest musical dynasty" at S. Cristina; see *Disembodied Voices*, 48–50.

31. See chapter 7.

32. BAV, Archivio Chigi 3852, fol. 26r: "Si conpiacca gradire questo piccolo segnio delle mie obligationi e mantenermi la promessa della carità de' mottetti. Che sieno smarrite le parole, non importa a me. Basta che Vostra Eminenza me ne favorischa purché sieno di

soprano e contralto. . . . Siena, di Santa Margherita 12 maggio 1670. . . . serva e zia, Suor Lutugarda Chigi."

33. Robert Kendrick summarizes the various possibilities for arranging music not specifically composed for women's voices in *Celestial Sirens: Nuns and their Music in Early Modern Milan* (Oxford: Clarendon Press, 1996), 203.

34. Records showing the purchase of music are rare and always vague; see for example, Con. sopp. 3382 (S. Petronilla), fol. 174v: "Ferraio [1613]. Per alcuni libri di musica, lire cinque, £. 5.12.4"; and Con. sopp. 2656 (S. Marta), unn. fol.: "6 detto (settembre 1677) £. dodici al maestro del canto e per libri di musica, £. 12."

35. The *Diario sanese* was first published in Lucca in 1723; a Sienese firm published a second, expanded edition in 1854.

36. The table includes only those feast days that fell under the particular province of a specific convent and thus (in a certain sense) "belonged" to that convent on the civic-religious calendar (titular feast days, for example). For this reason, neither the feast of S. Augustine nor the feast of S. Francis of Assisi appear on this list. The Franciscan and Augustinian convents in the city certainly observed these feast days, but the main celebrations involving the public were held at the two male monastic churches in Siena bearing the names of those saints, S. Agostino and S. Francesco. For a similar and obvious reason, the feast of the Nativity, on which nuns of S. Margherita in Castelvecchio unveiled their miraculous painting of the Virgin, does not appear on the list. Only two feast days are shown as "split" between two convents, and in each case, evidence is strong that equally splendid rites were held at both institutions.

37. At both S. Girolamo and S. Lorenzo, musicians were called in to sing on the titular feasts. See, for example, ASS, Con. sopp. 1950 (S. Girolamo), fols. 41r, 53v, 67r; and Con. sopp. 2215 (S. Lorenzo), fols. 90v, 93v, 98v, 102v, 104r, 107v, 108v, 109v, 111v, 121v. Frank D'Accone furnishes a document showing that the musicians at the Palazzo Pubblico were hired to perform for the feast of the Immaculate Conception at SS. Concezione in 1577 and were expected to continue the practice every year thereafter; see *The Civic Muse: Music and Musicians in Siena during the Middle Ages and the Renaissance* (Chicago: University of Chicago Press, 1997), 588–89; 662 (Doc. 13.5).

38. Payments to outside musicians are preserved in ASS, Con. sopp. 885–895, and are easy to locate, as they usually appear within a few days of the date of the feast. See, for example, Con. sopp. 891, fols. 73r, 75r, 83r, 90r, 92v, 98v, 103v, 104v, 109r.

39. Payments for the years 1597–1610 are in ASS, Con. sopp. 2646–2648. For the names of the Cathedral maestri, see Con. sopp. 2648, fols. 3v, 7r, 9v, 34v.

40. See ASS, Con. sopp. 891, fol. 92v; Con. sopp. 892, fols. 51v, 52r. For more on Gulini's career, see Colleen Reardon, *Agostino Agazzari and Music at Siena Catheral, 1597–1641* (Oxford: Clarendon Press, 1993), 49–52.

41. ASS, Con. sopp. 3385, unn. fol. D'Accone has uncovered a document showing that Cathedral musicians came to sing figural polyphony at S. Petronilla for Good Friday services in 1559; see *The Civic Muse*, 631.

42. Music at the consecration rites is explored in chapter 3. For the translation of the relics of SS. Abbondio and Abbondanzio, see *Vita de' gloriosi santi martiri Abbondio e Abbondantio con l'interventione e translatione de' corpi loro* (Siena: Salvestro Marchetti, 1616), 33–34: "e li due signori vicari e'l padre confessore portarono dentro in clausura le sante reliquie e le monache ricevettoro con canti e hinni cantati in musica ad honore di questi santi."

43. See ASS, Con. sopp. 3385, unn. fols. The use of the boys from the cappella at S. Maria della Scala is unique among the records of outside musicians at convents. For an overview of musical activities at this charitable institution, see D'Accone, *The Civic Muse*, 625–29; and Reardon, "*Insegniar la zolfa ai gittatelli*: Music and Teaching at Santa Maria

della Scala, Siena, during the Late Sixteenth and Early Seventeenth Centuries," in *Musica Franca: Essays in Honor of Frank A. D'Accone*, ed. Irene Alm, Alyson McLamore, and Colleen Reardon (Stuyvesant, NY: Pendragon Press, 1996), 119–38.

44. BCS, MS A.IX.10, fol. 238r: "1505. Ser Pietro, maestro di cappella nel Duomo nel 1505. . . . Questo perfettionò nella professione di canto musicale Suor Gismonda d'Agostino ceraiolo che di conversa fu fatta monaca nel medesimo convento [di S. Abbondio] per la sua delicatissima voce e per la grazia inpareggiabile che haveva nel cantare. Et allora fu introdotta in quel convento la musica, e vi si mantiene ora." Montebuoni Buondelmonti's "Ser Pietro" was probably Ser Piero di Domenico d'Asciano, who sang with the choir at the Duomo from 1493 to 1495 and then took a post at a parish church before being officially appointed to lead the chapel in 1512. Montebuoni Buondelmonti clearly mixed up his dates, but aside from this, there seems little reason to doubt his story. Certainly, his accuracy cannot be questioned in the case of Suor Orsola Silvestri. See D'Accone, *The Civic Muse*, 286–87.

45. Only four volumes of licenze are extant from the seventeenth century: ASS, Con. sopp. 3574 (S. Petronilla, 1685–1700), Con. sopp. 2272 (S. Lorenzo, 1653–93), and Con. sopp. 3289, 3290 (S. Paolo, 1678–1701). None of the four sources is foliated.

46. At S. Lorenzo, the vicar turned down a 1665 petition for Dorotea Piccolomini to take lessons in singing and playing because he needed the advice of the archbishop, Ascanio II Piccolomini, who took a personal interest in the girl. At S. Petronilla, a 1698 request for a novice to study with a "maestro del conserto" was also turned down, probably because of the unusual wording of the document. Usually, the nuns asked for permission to allow the maestri to come to the convent; this is the only entreaty I have found asking that the novice be allowed to go to the maestro. The vicar probably thought that the clever nuns might have interpreted a positive response to such a request as a license to allow the girl to exit the cloister for her studies. See ASS, Con. sopp. 2272, 3574.

47. The fact that in 1668, Ascanio II Piccolomini felt it necessary to issue a decree declaring that no cloistered girl or woman be left alone in the presence of a music teacher suggests that some convents may have been lax about assigning older nuns to supervise music lessons. See chapter 1, note 61.

48. ASS, Con. sopp. 3599, unn. loose sheet: "Io Cosimo Fantastichi fo fede come ho insegnato a cantare alla Signora Supplitia Verucci nelle monache di Santa Petronilla più mesi cominciando nel 1652 fino al 1654 spezzatamente e dalla molto Reverenda Suor Maria Giovanna Abbadessa di quel tempo ho riceuto per mia recognitione in tutto il tempo lire ottanta otto per la sopradetta Signora Supplitia e per fede ho scritto mano propria. Il medesimo Cosimo Fantastichi." For more on Fantastichi's career, see Reardon, *Agostino Agazzari and Music at Siena Cathedral*, 51, 57, and "Music and Musicians at Santa Maria di Provenzano, Siena, 1595–1640," *The Journal of Musicology* 11 (1993): 113, 115, 121.

49. This distinguishes Siena from Rome, where it appears that the "smaller, less aristocratic" convents were more apt to request licenses for music teachers; see Kimberlyn Montford, "Music in the Convents of Counter-Reformation Rome" (Ph.D. diss., Rutgers University, 1999), 16.

50. ASS, Con. sopp. 3290, unn. fols., requests of 7 April 1690 and 11 May 1690. See also a request to which the vicar responded on 3 September 1691, insisting that the nuns "content themselves with one maestro as all the others do."

51. Monson, *Disembodied Voices*, 2; Kendrick, *Celestial Sirens*, 36, 72, 183–84; Montford, "Convents of Counter-Reformation Rome," 16.

52. Books of licenze do not record the amount of money the maestri received, but debit-credit registers sometimes do. Then, as now, music teachers were not paid very much; they might hope to earn about £. 14–21 (2–3 scudi) for helping to prepare a convent

ensemble for a feast-day celebration (see notes 53–56). A normal convent dowry, on the other hand, ran between 400 and 450 scudi; renouncing even a portion of this sum to attract a poor but talented woman to serve as a teacher-performer made little economic sense.

53. See ASS, Con. sopp. 2649, unn. fol.: "Uscita di spese diverse (1618–19). Al cappellano (Girolamo Gulini) per havere insegnato la regola del leuto per sonar nel'organo, £. 14; Al medesimo per il canto fermo, £. 28"; Con. sopp. 2651, unn. fol.: "Uscita settembre 1640–agosto 1641. Al maestro di musica e assettimi di strumenti, £. 11"; Con. sopp. 2652, unn. fol.: "Uscita settembre 1649–agosto 1650. Al maestro di musica per più mottetti hauti da lui, £. 21." The use of lay music teachers at S. Marta was such a normal activity that a seventeenth-century copy of the convent's constitution instructs the abbess to delegate a nun to supervise all lessons "when teachers come to the grates to teach music or singing." See BCS, MS E.II.8, p. 59: "E quando saranno alle grati maestri per insegnare musica o canto . . . la superiora deputi una o più che vi assistino sempre."

54. Payments to Piochi are in ASS, Con. sopp. 2656, unn. fols; a typical example: "A dì detto (24 luglio 1672) £. dieci . . . date al Reverendo signor Christofano Piochi per conposisioni e haver rivisto le cantore in occasione della festa, £. 10."

55. ASS, Con. sopp. 2325, fol. 95v: "1638. A dì detto (18 dicembre) lire sette date al signor Montini per aver consertato la musica colle nostre monac[h]e, £. 7"; Con. sopp. 2332, fol. 112v: "A dì 3 settembre (1656). Uscita detta (di nostro monasterio), lire quattordici al molto reverendo signor Girolamo Gagliardi maestro di musica per havere insegnato al conserto alle nostre cantatrici, £. 14"; Con. sopp. 2327, unn. fol.: "1664. A dì detto (8 settembre) lire vintuna al reverendo signor Alesandro Bartalucci maestro di musica per avere insegniato el conserto di musica . . . £. 21"; unn. fol. "Settembre 1675 (a dì 8). Lire quattordici date al signor Brazzi per il conserto, £. 14." Montini and Brazzi were members of the Cathedral cappella, and Bartalucci served both the Cathedral and S. Maria in Provenzano.

56. ASS, Con. sopp. 2331, fol. 97r: "A dì 7 detto (settembre 1636). A spese di nostro convento £. quarantasei tanti si sono pagati al signor Andrea Calderoni maestro della musicha per havere insegniata due mesi alle nostre monache et questo per non haver volsuto pigliare la musicha il giorno della nostra festa, e in detta somma vi è incluso £. quatordici pagati al medesimo che ci ha assetto l'organo, £. 46." Con. sopp. 2339, p. 95: "A dì 3 dicembre 1678. Lire diciotto al maestro della musica (Giuseppe Fabbrini) per conserto e molte musiche date, £. 18"; Con. sopp. 2342, unn. fol.: "Il dì detto (6 settembre 1693). Al signor Giuseppe Fabrini maestro della musica per l'aver consertato a quelle che cantano per la prossima festa, piastre 4, £. 28."

57. Monson, "Disembodied Voices: Music in the Nunneries of Bologna in the Midst of the Counter-Reformation," in *The Crannied Wall: Women, Religion and the Arts in Early Modern Europe*, ed. Monson (Ann Arbor: University of Michigan Press, 1992), 202–4.

58. BCS, MS E.V.19, fol. 143v: "(9 novembre 1689) Uscendo [Leonardo Marsili] pertanto di chiesa, essendo venuti tutti questi signori, rientrò in Pontificale, cantando noi *Ecce sacerdos magnus* in musica et i suoi preti cantorno l'antifona *Gaudent in celis* per il titolo della chiesa cioè nostri santi Abundio et Abundantio martiri . . . doppo finito si parò per celebrare la santa messa. Si cantorno 2 mottetti in musica, uno a 2 voci, et uno a voce sola." This document offers a good example of the mixture of large-scale and small-scale repertory that must have been typical at houses that cultivated polyphonic music.

59. BCS, MS E.V.19, fol. 112v: "25 gennaro 1598/99 . . . [Tarugi arrives and begins his examination of the nuns] e alla prima [monaca] che gl'andò innanzi gli comandò che tirasse giù il velo negro per infino negl'occhi, il qual comandamento gl'impose a questa prima acciò lo dovesse far noto a tutte l'altre che gl'avevano andare innanzi. . . . E finita la

detta visita et esamina ci lassò molti commandamenti ma pochi ne potemmo osservare et adempire per l'incomodità."

60. Kendrick, *Celestial Sirens*, 103.

61. Suor Anna Bichi became abbess at Santuccio in the late 1690s; see ASS, Con. sopp. 2529, fols. 184r–85r.

62. Both visits are recorded in ASS, Con. sopp. 2542, unn. fols., prefaced with the year 1676/77: "[Bichi] celebrò la santa messa essendo la nostra chiesa ripiena di popolo mentre dalle nostre monache deputate sopra la musica furono cantati devoti mottetti e sonate vaghe sinfonie con variati strumenti." The entry on the Polish countess notes that she came to Siena "raccomandata dal Serenissimo Gran Duca" and that she heard a Mass "durante la quale dalle nostre monache deputate sopra la musica fu cantato un vago mottetto a piene voci."

63. The 23 May 1656 decree allowing Della Ciaia into the cloisters of all Sienese convents is preserved in AAS, 3930, fols. 15r–v. Montford notes that women of the Roman aristocracy held it an ancient right to enter female monastic establishments in their city; see "Convents of Counter-Reformation Rome," 47. For more on the Chigi family, see chapter 6.

64. It is unclear if the scribe composed only the text or both the text and the music. No musical setting for this text has yet surfaced in Sienese archives or libraries.

65. See *Celestial Sirens*, 160. For Bynum's thesis and her examination of the role food played in the life of S. Catherine of Siena, see *Holy Feast and Holy Fast: The Religious Significance of Food to Medieval Women* (Berkeley: University of California Press, 1987), 1–29; 165–80.

66. See AAS, 3941 bis, fols. 13v–14r (decree of 27 maggio 1656), and ASS, Con. sopp. 1150, *Ristretto de' decreti e degl'ordini fatti per li monasteri delle monache dall'Illustrissimo e Reverendissimo Monsignore Ascanio Piccolomini d'Aragona Arcivescovo di Siena X* (Siena: Bonetti, 1666), 18–19.

67. The food metaphor helps to explain the custom of giving monastic performers special treats at the dining table; see note 17.

68. See ASS, Con. sopp. 2542 (Santuccio), unn. fol. The chronicle relates that in 1649, when the lay confraternities wanted to borrow the head of S. Galgano, the nuns drew up a legal document specifying a fine of 20,000 scudi "in caso di mancanza."

69. BCS, MS E.V.19, fol. 117v: "con torce accese, con molta reverenza e canti musici messero detta reliquia sotto un baldacchino."

70. BCS, MS E.V.19, fols. 138v–140r contain a full description of the events of procession week. The passages cited in the text come from fol. 138v: "Venne la Santa Pasqua alli 2 d'Aprile nel 1684 et il secondo giorno di Pasqua venne qua al monastero la compagnia di S. Michel Arcangelo in processione e reverirono la santa reliquia e li cantorno un inno composto da loro, bello, nel tono dell'*Iste Confessor* e si cantò un bel mottetto in musica e poi si partirono"; fol. 139v: "La domenica in Albis il commune di Munistero fece insegnare ad alcune fanciulle parole adattate al detto santo [Colombini] come che noi l'avevamo perso e cose simili. Vestite dette citte ad angeli andorno alla città cercando il beato cantando tutte insieme. N'ebbero molto gusto i sanesi e muovevano proprio a divozione"; fol. 140r: "si cantò da noi [monache] la messa in musica e con mottetti facendoli quelli onori che la nostra povertà li poteva fare."

71. Prince Mattias served three terms as governor of Siena: 1629–31, 1641–43, and 1644–67. He played an important role in promoting operatic performance in the city (see chapter 6). Kendrick speculates that Mattias was in contact with the Milanese nun composer Chiara Margarita Cozzolani, for she dedicated her *Concerti sacri* of 1642 to the Medici prince; see *Celestial Sirens*, 269–70.

72. The summary of events found here and hereafter is taken from *Relatione della general processione fatta in Siena nella domenica in Albis MDCIL dalle venerabili compagnie della medesima città il dì 11 d'aprile nella quale con solenne pompa fu portata l'insigne reliquia della sacra testa di S. Galgano Guidotti di Chiusdino nobil sanese* (Siena: Bonetti, 1649), 21–36.

73. See chapter 4 for more on convent theater.

74. See note 26.

75. See chapter 3.

76. See Monson, *Disembodied Voices*, 41.

77. Gabriella Zarri, "Dalla profezia alla disciplina (1450–1650)," in *Donna e fede: Santità e vita religiosa in Italia*, ed. Lucetta Scaraffia and Gabriella Zarri (Bari: Editori Laterza, 1994): 208.

78. ASS, Con. sopp. 2542, unn. fol.: "Se questo è il monasterio di Santa Maria degli Angeli, deve essere habitato da tanti Angeli del Paradiso."

79. Kendrick, *Celestial Sirens*, 161–62; Monson, *Disembodied Voices*, 40.

80. BCS, MS E.V.19, fol. 66r: "In quel tempo [mid–fourteenth century] erano governate dalli Reverendi Padri monaci di S. Eugenio, e non mangiavano carne e andavano fuori e il popolo entrava nella loro chiesa di dentro a udir la messa e'l divino uffizio . . . e per testimonio di ciò essendo venuto il popolo la notte della Natività del Nostro Signore Gesù Cristo al matutino, un fanciullo piccolo nella braccia della madre disse a gran voce, 'Gl'Angeli mettano la corona alla monaca che canta,' la qual monaca cantava la lezzione del matutino." Although in modern Italian "mettano" would be an imperative, Sienese dialect admits its use as simple present tense.

Chapter 3

1. See Giuliano Catoni, "Interni di conventi senesi del Cinquecento," *Ricerche storiche* 10 (1980): 202–3: "35. Quella fanciulla che si vorrà vestire dell'habito monacale per fuggire ogni tumulto, sia accompagnata la mattina al monasterio dalle più prossime parenti senz'alcuna pompa et invito d'altre persone, et solo sia introdotta nella chiesa interiore del monastero ove, udita la messa et ricevuta la santissima eucharestia et fatte l'altre solenne cerimonie, sia vestita dall'ordinario o da chi sarà deputato da lui alla presenza delle altre monache. . . . Il che anco s'osservi quando si fa la professione. 36. Nel giorno che la fanciulla si vestirà, come di sopra, o che farà la professione non si faccino conviti sontuosi alle monache, ma si proceda tanto moderatamente che non si spenda nel convito in tutto fra ogni cosa più di dieci scudi per ciascuna suora che si vesti o che si veli."

2. See Gian Lodovico Masetti Zannini, " 'Suavità di canto' e 'purità di cuore': Aspetti della musica nei monasteri femminili romani," in *La cappella musicale nell'Italia della Controriforma, Atti del Convegno internazionale di studi nel IV Centenario di fondazione della Cappella Musicale di S. Biagio di Cento, Cento, 13–15 ottobre 1989*, ed. Oscar Mischiati and Paolo Russo (Florence: Leo S. Olschki Editore, 1993), 130; Craig A. Monson, *Disembodied Voices: Music and Culture in an Early Modern Italian Convent* (Berkeley: University of California Press, 1995), 185–86; Jutta Gisela Sperling, *Convents and the Body Politic in Late Renaissance Venice* (Chicago: University of Chicago Press, 1999), 138; Robert L. Kendrick, *Celestial Sirens: Nuns and their Music in Early Modern Milan* (Oxford: Clarendon Press, 1996), 135 n. 48.

3. The printed broadsheet preserving the grand duke's decrees is bound together with similar papers in a register from S. Caterina del Paradiso; see ASS, Con. sopp. 1150, fol. 67r: "Proibisce espressamente in occasione d'ingressi, vestimenti, professioni, e sacramenti l'uso di condurre in giro le spose monache in gala, come pure gli strascichi, rinfreschi,

musiche, apparati, inviti, regali, mancie, ed ogni altra festa, pubblicità, e spettacolo tanto in chiesa che ai parlatori e nella clausura."

4. *Decreti e costitutioni generali dell'Illustrissimo e Reverendissimo Monsignore Alessandro Pe-trucci Arcivescovo di Siena per il buon governo delle monache della sua città e diocesi* (Siena: Hercole Gori, 1625), 22. The minimum age requirement in Siena seems to have been an exception to the rule. Monson notes that Tridentine decrees specified that girls should be over the age of fifteen in order to begin the novitiate; see *Disembodied Voices*, 183.

5. *Decreti e costitutioni generali*, 21–23.

6. ASV, SCVR, Pos. 1585, Lett. R–V, letter of 2 July 1585: "Nella città di Siena è un monasterio chiamato Santa Maria Madalena con monache dell'ordine di Santo Agostino, nel quale per antichissima consuetudine è stato solito sempre che quelle che si monacano pigliano l'habito nella loro chiesa fuori del monasterio, stando presenti le monache velate nella chiesa di dentro et quella fa un sermone et dice molte orationi ordinate dall Santi Padri fundatori di esso ordine, et ciò con intervento de tutti li parenti di quella giovane alla quale finite tali ceremonie, et mentre si canta il *Te Deum* si da una elemosina de circa 30 scudi più o meno secondo la possibilità di essi parenti."

7. Monson, *Disembodied Voices*, 185, 187.

8. ASV, SCVR, Pos. 1616, Lett. P–S, letter of 18 September 1616: "non può altri-menti vestirsi nella Chiesa esterna con quelle cerimonie e satisfationi che si sogliono."

9. Masetti Zannini, "Aspetti della musica nei monasteri femminili romani," 130.

10. For more on the theatrical traditions of Sienese nuns, see chapter 4. Bolognese convents also staged plays and operas to celebrate investitures; see Monson, *Disembodied Voices*, 190.

11. The score is preserved in BAV, Fondo Chigi, MS Q.VI.84. For more on the opera, the Chigi family, and Campansi, see chapter 6.

12. ASS, Con. sopp. 3863, 62. One of the audience members at the performance was Princess Violante of Bavaria, governor of Siena.

13. ASS, Con. sopp. 1151, unn. fol.: "Illustrissimo e Reverendissimo Monsignore Vicario. Avendo Vostra Signoria Illustrissima impostomi che deva mandare il libro per dover compiacersi far la licenza per la figlia del signor Girolamo Piccolomini a ciò possa andare ad imparare alcune ariette per la commedia che deve farsi in occasione del vistiario della signora sposa Rocchii dal signor Domenico Mazzoli. . . . La Priora. [Reply:] Concedesi per l'effetto accennato. . . . 2 settembre 1719. Ambrogio Sansedoni."

14. See Monson, *Disembodied Voices*, 183; and Kendrick, *Celestial Sirens*, 132–33.

15. ASS, Con. sopp. 2152, fols. 302r, 332v.

16. ASS, Con. sopp. 1947, fol. 62v: "E più lire cinquanta due soldi 13:4 date al signor Magini che tanto à dato a' musici che ànno cantato avanti nostra porta nel ingresso della detta signora Donna Angiola, $£$. 52.13.4."

17. ASS, Con. sopp. 1948, fols. 72v, 77r. Magini was apparently in charge of hiring and directing the secular musicians who performed on Campansi's titular feast day in the years 1687–90; see Con. sopp. 1950, fols. 41r, 53v, 67r; Con. sopp. 1951, fol. 41v. He also served as Leonardo Marsili's maestro di casa (majordomo) from at least 1673; see BAV, Archivio Chigi 3847, fol. 116r.

18. ASS, Con. sopp. 2670, unn. fol.: "E la musica fuore o drento come si puole, e si compiace la fanciulla."

19. I have based my calculations on the amounts paid to musicians for performing at the elaborate consecration ceremonies at S. Abbondio in 1632 and 1680; the ensemble singers received $£$. 3.10 each and the organist, theorbist, violone player, and director, between 6 and 8 lire apiece. See the discussion of consecration ceremonies hereafter.

20. ASS, Con. sopp. 2670, 44 right: "la musica per essersi cantata dentro non si è fatta pagare." For the Borghesi clothing, see 34 left in the same source.

21. ACRFS, S. Sebastiano in Vallepiatta 1 (old 1248), lists the number of choir nuns in selected years between 1632 and 1639; it ranges from thirty-four to thirty-eight (see fols. 12r, 13v, 18v, 20r, 27r). A letter of 11 January 1686 reports thirty-five "monache di coro" at the institution; see ASV, SCVR, Sezione monache, 1686 gennaio–marzo.

22. See Doc. 1, appendix 1. I have not been able to find a nun with this surname among the convent's records.

23. See the discussion in chapter 2.

24. BCS, MS G.XI.91, a parchment manuscript of small dimensions with gold-embossed decorations on the leather cover. Although the convent of S. Sebastiano is never named in the manuscript, the *ordo* was designed for followers of Giovanni Colombini, as the rubric on fol. 23r makes clear ("Antiphonae decantandae quando puellae habitum recipiunt in Monasterio Sancti Ioannis Columbini, vel Professionem faciunt"). A prayer mentioning Mary's visitation of Elizabeth confirms that the manuscript was intended for the Gesuate (who called themselves the "Poor Sisters of the Visitation of Mary") rather than for the Benedictines of S. Abbondio, who possessed the body of Colombini. The investiture ceremony is on fols. 2r–13r.

25. The first two psalms and antiphons were used for tonsure up to Vatican II; see the *Liber usualis* (Paris: Desclée, 1964), 1845–47. Psalm 132, *Ecce quam bonum*, was used on a variety of occasions.

26. I am indebted to Robert Kendrick for his observations on the symbolic content of the rite of profession; see *Celestial Sirens*, 134–35.

27. Gabriella Zarri, "Ursula and Catherine: The Marriage of Virgins in the Sixteenth Century," in *Creative Women in Medieval and Early Modern Italy: A Religious and Artistic Renaissance*, ed. E. Ann Matter and John Coakley (Philadelphia: University of Pennsylvania Press, 1994), 238.

28. BCS, MS G.XI.91, fols. 24r–25v.

29. Ibid., fol. 6r: "Hic puella sermonem aggreditur, quo habito, dum vestimenta deponit, cantetur mottectum."

30. See AAS, 3713: "Ordo vestiendi puellam quando intrat Monasterium Divi Laurentii ad serviendum Altissimo Deo [late seventeenth century]"; and 3739, "Ordo vestiendi puellas in Monasterio S. Nicolai prope muros civitatis Senarum (1636)." The core of the Clarissan rites—the tonsure psalms and use of the *Te Deum*—is identical to that for the Gesuate. Neither Clarissan ceremony, however, includes the *Ecce venio ad te*. Instead the girl sings the great responsory *Regnum mundi* (reserved for profession among the Gesuate). The psalm *Miserere mei* is also included in both Clarissan rites before tonsure.

31. See *Ordinazioni e decreti per li monasteri delle monache della città e diocesi di Siena. Fabio Piccolomini Proposto della Metropolitana e Vicario generale dell'Illustrissimo et Reverendissimo Monsignore Camillo Borghesi, Arcivescovo di Siena settimo* (Siena: Bonetti, 1608). The single broadsheet is preserved among papers from the convent of S. Petronilla (ASS, Con. sopp. 3598). The wording of Archbishop Petrucci's decree on investiture practices is very similar to that issued in 1575 by Bossi; see Petrucci, *Decreti e costitutioni generali*, 23.

32. For Celio Piccolomini's decrees, see AAS, 3641 bis, fols. 28v, 29r. A handwritten copy of Leonardo Marsili's 1685 injunction is found in ASS, Con. sopp. 1150, fol. 107r.

33. See Borghesi, *Ordinazioni e decreti per li monasteri delle monache della città e diocesi di Siena*, and Petrucci, *Decreti e costitutioni generali*, 25.

34. BCS, MS G.XI.91, fols. 13v–22v.

35. "I held in contempt the [secular] world and all its trappings for love of our Lord Jesus Christ, whom I loved, in whom I believed, whom I held dear, whom I chose."

36. BCS, MS G.XI.91, fols. 27v–28v.

37. For the images of the beloved seeking her lover, knocking on a door (her head wet with dew), and rising from the desert, leaning upon her lover, see the Song of Songs 3:1–4, 5:2, and 8:5. Kendrick discusses the text and its importance to both monastic women and men in " 'Sonet vox tua in auribus meis': Song of Songs Exegesis and the Seventeenth-Century Motet," *Schütz Jahrbuch* 16 (1994): 99–118.

38. See BCS, MS G.XI.91, fol. 25v, for the chant transcriptions; the rubrics are on fols. 15v, 19v, 20r, and 21r.

39. See Masetti Zannini, "Aspetti della musica nei monasteri femminili romani," 130; Kendrick, *Celestial Sirens*, 135–37; and Monson, *Disembodied Voices*, 190–91.

40. *La consécration des vierges dans l'église romaine: Étude d'histoire de la liturgie*, Bibliothèque de l'institut de droit canonique de l'Université de Strasbourg 4 (Paris: Presses universitaires de France, 1954).

41. Given that eight to twenty years could elapse between consecrations, and that no nun could hold office or vote in chapter meetings until completing the ceremony, nuns at houses requiring the consecration rite often asked for and received exceptions so that women younger than twenty-five could participate. See ASV, SCVR, Sezione monache, 1680, gennaio–marzo, letter of 26 January 1680 from nuns of SS. Abbondio e Abbondanzio.

42. See Monson, *Disembodied Voices*, 195–97, for an outline of the rite. The full ordo of the Roman pontifical is given in Metz, *La consécration des vierges*, 411–55. See also Anne Bagnall Yardley, "The Marriage of Heaven and Earth: A Late Medieval Source of the *Consecratio virginum*," *Current Musicology* 45–47 (1990): 305–24.

43. Metz, *La consécration des vierges*, 341.

44. *Disembodied Voices*, 198–238.

45. The only document about the rite at Le Trafisse is a letter from the Cistercian nuns to the Sacred Congregation requesting permission to include six women under the age of twenty-five in their upcoming consecration rite (see ASV, SCVR, Sezione monache, 1685, novembre–dicembre, letter of 26 November 1685). I was unable to find further references to the ceremony in the documents from the institution.

46. AAS, 3747. The consecrations took place in 1585 (fol. 114v), 1593 (fol. 115r), 1598 (fol. 115v), 1613 (fol. 116r), 1619 (fol. 117r), 1633 (fol. 118r), 1644 (fol. 120r), 1656 (fol. 123r), 1669 (fol. 124v), and 1684 (fols. 128r–132v).

47. The 1669 consecration featured music for two rather than three choirs. See AAS, 3747, fol. 124v.

48. AAS 3747, fol. 120r: "La funtione fu bellissima con musica a 3 chori; teatro superbissimo e grandissimo concorso, e passò il tutto con sodisfattione universale."

49. BAV, Archivio Chigi 33, fol. 295r: "Domenica passata si fece all'Ognisanti da Monsignor Arcivescovo la consacrasione di 13 monache. La funzione e l'apparato fu fatto da quelle madri con ogni maggiore suntuosità e vi concorse quasi mezza la città, almeno di nobili."

50. See BCS, MS E.V.19, fols. 59r–165v. Notes on fols. 103r and 174r confirm that the chronicle and the "spoglio delle antiche scritture" that follows the chronicle were copied in 1725. The lacunae in the manuscript are noted on fols. 128r and 130v–131r.

51. Monson notes the same trend in Bologna, perhaps because the daily fare of the nuns was anything but appetizing; see *Disembodied Voices*, 189–90.

52. See ASV, SCVR, Sezione monache, 1680, maggio–agosto, letter of 31 May 1680: "Le monache del monasterio di S. Abundio di Siena umilmente espongono all'Eminenze Vostre che in riguardo della poca capacità della chiesa esteriore sono state solite fare la funzione della consecrazione nella chiesa interiore più capace con l'intervento di qualche

numero di musici e d'altre persone conveniente alla solennità e decoro della detta funzione." The nuns used the same argument in a subsequent request to the Sacred Congregation; see ASV, SCVR, Sezione monache, 1702, luglio–agosto, letter of 28 July 1702.

53. The writer of the chronicle could remember only a portion of the Latin incipit the nuns sang and left a space. It was clearly the first item entrusted to the consacrees during the consecration ceremony; see Monson, *Disembodied Voices*, 196.

54. BCS, MS E.V.19, fols. 147r–v: "perché non si poté ottenere dalla Sacra Congregatione licenza di fare la funzione dentro in clausura conforme al solito, fu necessario mandare giù la grata e presso a quella si fece una bellissima cappelletta con belli parati che sembrava un paradiso, dove sterno le madri consacrande le quali uscite che furono la prima volta si diportorno cantando l'[*Et nunc*] *sequimur*. Dove era mandata giù la grata e muro solo mezzo braccio vi era restato vicino a terra dove era assiso nel faldistorio Monsignore con tutti gli altri signori sacerdoti."

55. Ibid., fol. 76v: "Queste sopradette professe furono le prime che cantassero tutto quello che si canta in cerimonia della consacrazione e cantorno di canto fermo secondo che è notato nel Pontificale. E quelle che erano precedute avanti avevano detto il tutto leggendo."

56. Ibid., fol. 92r: "cantorno in musica a 2 voci tutto quello che è solito di cantare e per gratia di Dio ebbero non piccolo onore. E Monsignore ne fece gran lode all'abbadessa e disse non aver avuta mai maggior consolazione di quel giorno, laude a Dio donatore di ogni gratia. Ci venne a vederla tanta la gran moltitudine delle persone che s'ebbe a mettere la guardia alla porta della chiesa; nondimeno ci entrò più di 500 secolari." This particular consecration was held in Siena at the male monastery of S. Girolamo (not to be confused with the female house of S. Girolamo in Campansi), where the Benedictine nuns had lived since being forced to leave their own convent nearly ten years earlier, during the siege of Siena.

57. Ibid., fol. 104r: "Furono le prime che cantassero a 3 voci in musica."

58. Ibid., fol. 119r: "E le citole tutto quello ebbero a cantare, lo cantorno in musica e col organo."

59. Ibid., fol. 92r, notes that "ci fu la musica del Duomo e l'organo" at the consecration that year.

60. ASS, Con. sopp. 890, fol. 181v: "El maestro di cappella ebbe due piastre, la coppia di fazzoletti e la camicia. / E tutti gli altri musichi ebbero una mezza piastra per uno."

61. ASS, Con. sopp. 893, fol. 136r: "Sei musici si dè giuli cinque et una coppia di fazoletti per uno, fra quali el maestro del tronbone ebbe £. 9 per esserci venuto due volte avanti per prova del canto. / Et più al maestro che gli aveva insegnato la musica et venuto più volte a conprovarle e sonato ancora l'organo donorno piastre 18 in una borsa che costò 2 piastre et 2 coppie di fazoletti."

62. ASS, Con. sopp. 899, unn. folios at end of register: "Alli musici che furno 12, co' sonatori e prima: / Al maestro di cappella, £. otto e due coppie di fazzoletti. / A quello che sonò la tiorba, una piastra e fazzoletti. / A quello del violone, £. 6 e la coppia de' fazzoletti. / E più 9 musici, cinque giuli e una coppia di fazzoletti per ciascheduno. . . . / E più al maestro che gl'haveva insegnato la musica e venuto più volte a conprovarle e sonato l'organo, li donorno una cotta che ci spesero piastre 16 e piastre 4 in detti due coppie di fazzoletti e altri regali mangiati[vi]."

63. ASS, Con. sopp. 913, fol. 95v: "per un paio di camicie per donare alle velande acciò se ne servissero per il signor maestro della musica Giuseppe Fabbrini, £. 13. / Al signor organista £. sette con un paro di fazzoletti, £. 7. / A' quattordici musici computati li sonatori si diede a ciascuno una paniera con un paro di fazzoletti, ciambellini e stiacciatelle e lire tre soldi 10 per ciascun, £. 49"; fol. 96v: "Al signor Giuseppe Fabbrini maestro

della musica per haverli insegnato, piastre vinti quattro, due panducali, stiaccciatelle, ricciarelli, un baccino d'altre paste e confettioni e il monastero aggiunse una coppia di camicie."

64. See "*Veni sponsa Christi*: Investiture, Profession and Consecration Ceremonies in Sienese Convents," *Musica Disciplina* 50 (1996): 290–91.

65. See Kendrick, *Celestial Sirens*, 136, and Dinko Fabris, "Dal Medioevo al decennio francese e oltre: Continuità e metamorfosi nella tradizione napoletana," presentation at the conference "Produzione, circolazione e consumo: Per una mappa della musica sacra dal tardo Medioevo al primo Seicento," Venice, Italy, Fondazione Ugo e Olga Levi, 28–30 October 1999.

66. Carolyn Gianturco, "Caterina Assandra, suora compositrice," in *La musica sacra in Lombardia nella prima metà del Seicento. Atti del convegno internazionale di studi, Como, 31 maggio–2 giugno 1985*, ed. Alberto Colzani, Andrea Luppi, and Maurizio Padoan (Como: Antiquae Musicae Italicae Studiosi, 1987), 125.

67. Agostino Agazzari was related to Alfonso Agazzari, who served as rector of the German College in Rome in the 1590s. In 1594, Alfonso wrote the Sacred Congregation, asking permission to visit his sisters, aunts, and cousins in the Sienese houses of S. Marta, S. Girolamo in Campansi, S. Sebastiano in Vallepiatta, and S. Petronilla (see ASV, SCVR, Pos. 1594, Lett. S, letter of 2 August 1594). The composer thus must have known some of the same women, several of whom inhabited convents famous for their music.

68. A transcription of the transposed motet is appended to my "*Veni sponsa Christi*," 292–97.

69. Once the catalogue of the musical collection at the Biblioteca Comunale, Siena, is complete, some manuscript compositions for nuns may emerge. My colleagues Chiara Palazzuoli and Silvia Paghi have seen no such works thus far, however, and have informed me that most of the music appears to be from the eighteenth century. The publications of seventeenth-century Sienese composers—Annibale Gregori, Giovanbattista Baccinetti, Orindio Bartolini, Cristofano Piochi, Giuseppe Fabbrini, Giuseppe Cini, and Giovanni Andrea Florimi—reveal no compositions with obvious links to female monasteries.

70. See his "Song of Songs Exegesis and the Seventeenth-Century Motet," 105–6.

71. Della Ciaia used the same figure for the same text in his solo setting of *Ecce venio ad te*, published in 1650. For more on this work, see chapter 7.

72. Pope Alexander VII Chigi was Flavio Chigi's uncle. Della Ciaia was also uncle to Flavio, who was the son of his sister, Berenice Della Ciaia. Berenice was married to Mario Chigi, brother to Pope Alexander VII. See the abbreviated genealogical chart of the Chigi family in chapter 6.

73. *Celestial Sirens*, 135.

74. Neither Della Ciaia's investiture motet nor his works from 1650 can be linked to a specific occasion or a specific nun. They were clearly intended for general use by aristocratic Sienese women at a number of different convents.

Chapter 4

1. I have benefited greatly from Elissa B. Weaver's essays on Florentine convent theater. In addition to the essays cited hereafter, see her edition of Beatrice Del Sera, *Amor di virtù: Commedia in cinque atti, 1548* (Ravenna: Longo Editore, 1990); "Convent Comedy and the World: The Farces of Suor Annalena Odaldi (1572–1638)," *Annali d'italianistica* 7 (1989): 182–92; and "Suor Maria Clemente Ruoti, Playwright and Academician," in *Creative Women in Medieval and Early Modern Italy*, ed. E. Ann Matter and John Coakley (Philadelphia: University of Pennsylvania Press, 1994), 281–96. I am also indebted to Pro-

fessor Weaver for reading an earlier draft of this chapter and offering suggestions for its improvement.

2. See Alessandro D'Ancona, *Origini del teatro italiano*, 2 vols. (Turin, 1891; reprint ed., Rome: Bardi Editore, 1966), 1:282. Curzio Mazzi reports that a sacred comedy was performed in Siena when Francesco Todeschini-Piccolomini became Pope Pius III in 1503; see *La Congrega dei Rozzi di Siena nel secolo XVI*, 2 vols. (Florence: Le Monnier, 1882), 1:26.

3. See *Il Malatesta: Comedia spirituale del miracolo della sacra vergine Santa Caterina da Siena, nuovamente ridotta in ottava rima e publicamente rappresentata nella contrada dove ella nacque di Fonteblanda* [sic] *la prima domenica di maggio giorno della sua solennissima festa 1569* (Florence, 1575) and Annibale Lomeri, *Conversione di Iacomo Tolomei per mezzo di S. Caterina da Siena, rappresentata in Siena l'anno 1601 per la festività della medesima santa* (Siena: Salvestro Marchetti, 1606), both preserved in the Biblioteca Comunale, Siena.

4. *Rappresentatione eremitica spirituale distinta in atti e scene dal molto Reverendo Padre Ercolano Ercolani de la Congregatione del Chiodo di Siena* (Siena: Matteo Florimi, 1608). The play was sent to press by Ottavio Cinuzzi, who dedicated the work to Suor Camilla Della Stufa, a nun at S. Agata in Florence; Cinuzzi recalls Ercolani's efforts in the dedication to the volume. Ercolani was a well-respected religious figure in late sixteenth-century Siena. He was one of two priests chosen to give communion and confession to the faithful who flocked to worship the statue of the Madonna in Provenzano, and he was twice elected to lead the Congregazione dei Sacri Chiodi; see Franco Daniele Nardi, "Matteo Guerra e la Congregazione dei Sacri Chiodi (secc. XVI–XVII): Aspetti della religiosità senese nell'età della Controriforma," *BSSP* 91 (1984): 54–59.

5. Angelo Solerti, *Musica, ballo e drammatica alla Corte Medicea dal 1600 al 1637* (Florence, 1905; reprint ed., New York: Benjamin Blom, 1968), 66, 161.

6. *Cicilia sacra in drammatica poesia, del dottore Annibale Lomeri sanese, nell'Accademia de' Filomati detto il Satirico. Alle molto illustri e molto reverende madri abbadessa e monache del monasterio di Santa Cicilia in Roma. Recitata in Siena all'Altezze Serenissime di Toscana il 18 giugno 1621* (Arezzo: Ercole Gori, 1636), 28, 50.

7. See D'Ancona, ed., *Sacre rappresentazioni dei secoli XIV, XV, e XVI*, 3 vols. (Florence: Le Monnier, 1872), 1:129, 130n., 167, 191, 211, 255; 2:71, 93, 123, 269, 323, 409; 3: 235, 317, 361.

8. At least one copy of each of the plays on the lives of these saints, printed by the Sienese firm "alla Loggia del Papa," is still preserved in the Biblioteca Comunale, Siena. For the texts of the works featuring S. Mary Magdalen and S. Margaret, see D'Ancona, *Sacre rappresentazioni*, 1:255–302; 2:123–39. A document confirms that the women of S. Petronilla staged a play about S. Apollonia in February 1621; see ASS, Con. sopp. 3383, fol. 259r.

9. For the text of the play on S. Eufrasia, see D'Ancona, *Sacre rappresentazioni*, 2:269– 322. The *Rappresentatione di Santa Uliva* also includes scenes set in the convent; see D'Ancona, *Sacre rappresentazioni*, 3:235–315. Prints of both plays can be found in the Biblioteca Comunale, Siena.

10. See Weaver, "The Convent Wall in Tuscan Convent Drama," in *The Crannied Wall: Women, Religion, and the Arts in Early Modern Europe*, ed. Craig A. Monson (Ann Arbor: University of Michigan Press, 1992), 74–75.

11. See Giuliano Catoni, "Interni di conventi senesi del Cinquecento," *Ricerche storiche* 10 (1980): 184, 201: "17. Non si rappresentino dentro commedie o altre rappresentazioni d'alcuna sorte, né si tenghino per tal effetto nel monastero barbe posticcie o zazzere finte o vesti rappresentative o altre simil cose per così fatto uso."

12. Decrees on theater by Sienese prelates may be compared with the considerably more restrictive controls that vicars in Milan and Bologna attempted to impose; see Robert

Kendrick, *Celestial Sirens: Nuns and their Music in Early Modern Milan* (Oxford: Clarendon Press, 1996), 81, and Craig Monson, *Disembodied Voices: Music and Culture in an Early Modern Italian Convent* (Berkeley: University of California Press, 1995), 190–91. For a survey of theater in Venetian convents, see Jonathan Glixon, "Images of Paradise or Worldly Theaters? Toward a Taxonomy of Musical Performances at Venetian Nunneries," in *Essays on Music and Culture in Honor of Herbert Kellman*, ed. Barbara Haggh (Paris: Éditions Klincksieck, 2001), 429–57.

13. See *Decreti e costitutioni generali dell'Illustrissimo e Reverendissimo Monsignore Alessandro Petrucci Arcivescovo di Siena per il buon governo delle monache della sua città e diocesi* (Siena: Hercole Gori, 1625), 45: "E per questo non si rappresentino mai dentro al monasterio commedie mondane né altro spettacolo che habbia del profano. E se dal prelato otterranno licenza di fare qualche festa spirituale o di recitare qualche devota rappresentatione, si faccia in luogo del tutto remoto e lontano da ogni prospetto di persone esterne. E non ardischino di deporre il proprio habito, ma sopra di esso a giuditio della superiora e delle maggiori potranno vestire habiti che habbino del grave."

14. *Ristretto de' decreti e degl'ordini fatti per li monasteri delle monache dall'Illustrissimo e Reverendissimo Monsignore Ascanio Piccolomini d'Aragona, Arcivescovo di Siena X* (Siena: Bonetti, 1666), 17: "Non vi sia permesso far commedie o rappresentationi se prima queste non havrete fatto vedere al nostro vicario ed esso ve n'habbia data licenza e resti proibito tanto alle professe e novitie quanto all'educande il farsi vedere travestite e senza il solito habito da qualsivoglia secolare."

15. ASV, SCVR, Pos. 1597, Lett. R–S, letter of 2 March 1597. The archbishop of Siena wrote to the Sacred Congregation complaining of general disobedience in the open monasteries; he attached an undated letter referring specifically to the performance of comedies at S. Sebastiano and S. Margherita: "In questi giorni di Carnovale le monache del monastero aperto di Ca[s]telvecchio e le monache del monastero aperto di Vallepiatta di Siena senza stimare punto l'ordine dato dall'Illustrissimo e Reverendissimo signor Cardinale Alissandrino hanno recitato rappresentazioni dentro li loro monasteri e senza haver riguardo alcuno alla clausura assegnatali conforme alla bolla di Papa Gregorio XIIII Sanctae Memoriae vi hanno introdotto donne laiche d'ogni qualità e ritenutovi per la notte delle zittelle, e perché la religiosa facendo tanto poco conto del voto dell'obbedienza e delle censure ecclesiastiche passa con scandalo gravissimo del secolo, si supplicano le Signorie Vostre Illustrissime e Reverendissime a comomandarne [*sic*] castigo per le delinquenti e moderatione per l'avenire all'universale."

16. ASV, SCVR, Pos. 1597, Lett. R–S, letter of 24 March 1597: "Le monache del monasterio aperto di Vallepiatta fanno sapere alle Signorie Vostre Illustrissime come questo Carnevale hanno recitata nel loro monasterio una rappresentatione et ivi anno [illegible] intromesse nella clausura altre donne che per ciò da Monsignor Vescovo sono state dechiarate scomunicate. Onde si supplica per parte loro et di quelle ch'erano introdutte per l'assolutione, che si riceverà a gratia."

17. ASV, SCVR, Pos. 1597, Lett. R–S, undated letter: "Le monache di Santa Margarita dette le povere di Castelvecchio di Siena havendo fatto una rappresentatione nella quale sono intervenute alcune zitelle secolari in una lor stanza dove si dice potere andar ogn'uno per esser dette monache aperte, et che escono fuora, sono state dechiarate sospese dal Vicario di Monsignor Vescovo benché per il passato si sia compatito sempre a questo et benché potrebbe dubitarsi di detta sospensione. Ricorreno a questa sacra congregatione humilmente supplicando comettersi a detto Signor Vicario che chiarito bene del tutto assolva non tanto le monache quanto li secolari che fossero incorsi acciò in questi santi giorni quadragesimali non restino prive di messe, communioni, prediche et altri cibi spirituali."

18. Alessandro Forteguerri, for example, sent no fewer than four letters (dated 27 August 1585, 15 October 1585, 14 January 1586, and 18 March 1586) to the Sacred Congregation asking that his daughter Dionora be allowed to become a nun at the open monastery of S. Girolamo in Campansi, Siena. See ASV, SCVR, Pos. 1585, Lett. R–V; Pos. 1586, Lett. S–V.

19. See for example, ASV, SCVR, Pos. 1585, Lett. R–V, letter of 12 March 1585/86. The anonymous writer complains about the "licentious" nuns of Paradiso who allow "many gentlewomen" into their cloister to see the comedies they stage.

20. BCS, MS G.XI.58, fol. 1r: "Io se ben ero per prima molto desideroso (o così obligato per li molti meriti vostri) di compiacervi, non dimeno restai con tanti altri honorati uditori così appagato e sotisfatto della nobile recitatione qual faceste della vaga representatione di San Galgano, che haverei reputato commetter mancamento non piccolo se, quantunque l'impresa fusse dalla mia professione assai lontana, non vi havesse prontamente sotisfatte ricercandomene con tanto affetto di compositione di alcun altra per recitarla l'anno presente a vostro gusto e di chi altri per gratia havessi commodo di sentirla, tra li quali bramo essere anch'io."

21. For evidence of men attending convent performances, see Weaver, "Spiritual Fun: A Study of Sixteenth-Century Tuscan Convent Theater," in *Women in the Middle Ages and the Renaissance: Literary and Historical Perspectives*, ed. Mary Beth Rose (Syracuse, NY: Syracuse University Press, 1986), 179.

22. ASF, Mediceo del Principato 1942, fol. 7r: "et vo alli rapresentazioni spiritulai [*sic*] che fano qua le monac[h]e molto bene." Both Christine of Lorraine and her daughter-in-law Maria Maddalena of Austria attended musical and theatrical productions at the Florentine convent of La Crocetta, where the Medici princess Maria Maddalena had withdrawn to live. For more on Medici patronage at this house, see Kelley Harness, "*Regine dell'Arno:* Court Life in a Seventeenth-Century Florentine Convent," presentation at the annual meeting of the American Musicological Society, Phoenix, AZ, 30 October–2 November 1997.

23. Weaver, "Spiritual Fun," 175.

24. See Weaver, "Spiritual Fun," 178. Kendrick notes that Milanese nuns' parlors often served as sites for secular music-making and theatrical performances; see *Celestial Sirens*, 81, 117. I have been able to document the construction of a theater room in the eighteenth century at the convent of Il Refugio; see ASS, Con. sopp. 3863, 62–63.

25. BCS, MS K.X.53, fol. 27v: "Ora la mettino a cavallo se si può, e vadino alla lor via con la lor gente." See also Weaver, "Spiritual Fun," 178–79.

26. Weaver notes that the performers of many Florentine convent comedies seem to have been drawn primarily from the novices and schoolgirls; see "Spiritual Fun," 177–78.

27. BCS, MS G.XI.59, fol. 1v: "La concludo così come christiana battezzata e come monaca professa."

28. BAV, Archivio Chigi 3847, fol. 80v (letter of 7 January 1671): "Per avere il carnovale corto ànno messo su due commedie; io però ò preso la parte solo a una perché al mio coliro sono um poco incatanata che questa mia distibatione di testa mi da sempre noia e poi ora bisogna che lasci il luogo a le giovane che il mio tempo è passato."

29. My information on the maggio comes from Paolo Toschi, "Maggio," *Enciclopedia dello spettacolo*, vol. 6 (Rome: Le Maschere, 1959), 1848–50; and D'Ancona, *Origini del teatro italiano*, 2:241–345. I would like to thank Elissa Weaver for her help on this subject.

30. See ASS, Con. sopp. (S. Petronilla) 3383, 3387, 3389, 3391, 3394, 3401, 3403, 3404, 3510, 3511, 3516, 3517; Con. sopp. (Santuccio) 2325, 2326, 2327, 2338, 2341, 2342, 2343, 2344. Not all registers are foliated, but the payments are easy to find, as they are always disbursed in early May. Traces of the maggio tradition can also be

found at S. Abbondio (ASS, Con. sopp. 904, fol. 58v, records a 1650 payment for "sausages for the girls who sang the May song") and at SS. Concezione (see Con. sopp. 1374, fol. 87v).

31. I was able to find only one maggio in the Biblioteca Comunale, Siena, and it does not appear to be linked to a convent performance: *Maggio cantato l'anno 1796 in onore dell'Annunziazione di Maria Vergine* (Siena: Francesco Rossi e figlio, n.d.).

32. See, for example, ASS, Con. sopp. 2326 (Santuccio), fol. 63v: "A dì 3 maggio 1650. A dì detto lire quattro e soldi sette 4 date alle nostre secolare, cioè £. due in denari per aver cantato maggio et il restante per libbre 6 prosciutto e libbre tre formaggio compro dalle sopradette, £. 4.7.4."

33. See Mazzi, *Congrega dei Rozzi*, 1:318; 2:307–30.

34. BCS, MS G.XI.56, unn. fol.: "il giorno che ebbi la nuova certa che Camilla haveva da entrar fra di voi che fu il 17 di luglio che poi entrò il 21 corriva la festa di Santa Marina." I would like to thank Elissa Weaver for the information that Camilla might have been Tregiani's niece.

35. See Reardon, *Agostino Agazzari and Music at Siena Cathedral, 1597–1641* (Oxford: Clarendon Press, 1993), 48–51. Flori signed the dedication to his play on 15 March 1642 and was buried on 18 March 1642.

36. See Doc. 16, appendix 1. The copy of Flori's play preserved in the Biblioteca Comunale, Siena, has a parchment cover on which is written "Suor Maria Elena, Ogni Santi." On the flyleaf, two names are written in ink: "Suor Giulia" and "Suor Maria Elena." A 1642 contract from Ognissanti lists the names of all the nuns in the convent. Among them were two women from the Benvoglienti clan: Suor Giulia and Suor Maria Eletta (misspellings of names by scribes were not uncommon in this period); see ASS, Con. sopp. 3024, fols. 96v–97r. This copy of the play can thus be linked directly to the convent for which it was written.

37. BCS, MS K.X.53, fol. 2r: "E col favor di quel divo Austino / el qual ci guida in questo monasterio / or noi cominciaremo a suo onore / se state attenti e non fate rumore."

38. Catoni reports that the Biblioteca Comunale holds another play on S. Galgano that probably can be associated with Santuccio, but I was unable to locate it. See his "Conventi senesi," 184 n. 49.

39. James Wyatt Cook, for example, speculates that the printing history of Antonia Pulci's works may be evidence for "a continued popular interest in reading the plays, if not in their production"; see his translation of Pulci, *Florentine Drama for Convent and Festival: Seven Sacred Plays* (Chicago: University of Chicago Press, 1996), 35.

40. BCS, MS G.XI.53, fol. 102v: "Hora li vescovi e gli abbati chantando qualcosa seppelliscano il santo e l'angelo licentia la festa."

41. Ibid., fol. 1r: "Un giovanetto con la cetara esce fuore e dice al popolo."

42. See John Anson, "The Female Transvestite in Early Monasticism: The Origin and Development of a Motif," *Viator* 5 (1974): 15–17, for a discussion of the legend, which was well known in the Tuscan vernacular through a translation by Domenico Cavalca. According to Raymond of Capua, S. Catherine was inspired by this legend; see *The Life of Catherine of Siena by Raymond of Capua*, trans. and ed. Conleth Kearns (Wilmington, DE: Michael Glazier, 1980), 27, 37–38. S. Marina's story deeply affected Passitea Crogi, the founder of the Sienese convent of the Cappuccine (see chapter 5). The popularity of these stories as subjects for convent theater might have been the fact that they gave monastic actresses an ironclad excuse to dress up in men's clothing.

43. See BCS, MS G.XI.59, fols. 48v–49r, 51r.

44. See Enrico Cattaneo, "Le monacazioni forzate fra Cinque e Seicento," in *Vita e*

processo di Suor Virginia Maria de Leyva monaca di Monza (Milan: Garzanti Editore, 1985), 147–95, and Catoni, "Conventi senesi," 178–80.

45. BCS, MS G.XI.59, fol. 1v: "La donna maritata di figluoli aggravata et spesso per gl'affanni disperata, sempre si duol non esser monacata."

46. Ibid., fols. 12v–13r.

47. BCS, MS G.XI.58, fol. 3r; MS G.XI.59, fol. 16r.

48. When, early in the play, Eufrosina is told to bow to her aunt's wishes, she responds, "I want to obey God." See BCS, MS G.XI.59, fol. 5r.

49. BCS, MS G.XI.58, fol. 7r.

50. BCS, MS K.X.53, fol. 25r: "Caro mio padre a me deve piacere / d'esser ora al mio sposo obbediente / ch'essendo ormai sotto la sua signoria / devo far cosa ch'in piacer gli sia."

51. Ibid., fol. 10r.

52. BCS, MS G.XI.58, fol. 20v: "Donque s'a Dio servir vi compiacete / spinta dalla sua santa inspiratione / nel stato virginal nel qual hor sete / dir ne potete la vostra intentione."

53. Ibid., fol. 13v.

54. BCS, MS G.XI.59, fol. 25r–v.

55. Ibid., fol. 25v: "mi par ben duro figla, che tu non vogli né veste, né gioie, et ornamenti da nostri pari, e come al tempo nostro si costuma. . . . compiace tu a me figliuola di vestirti et ornarti secondo lo stato nostro, e come fanno l'altre fanciulle par tue, che così sarebbe il dovere."

56. See Monson, *Disembodied Voices*, 186–87.

57. BCS, G.XI.59, fol. 48r: "Non si fa cosa per la città che le monache non la sappino subito, e se bene lor non cerchan di sapere non dimeno ogni cosa è rapportata loro di chi le va a visitare."

58. Ibid., fol. 48r: "Sapete pur hor mai come son fatte le monache. . . . Quella domanda d'una cosa, quel'altra d'un altra; bisogna pur rispondere a tutte . . . bisognò dirli dall'A insino al ronne, ogni cosa per ordine."

59. BCS, MS G.XI.58, fol. 15v: "Quelle suore m'han tanto intertenuta / a mio dispetto con molto ciarlare / ch'a gran fatica me ne son venuta."

60. Ibid., fols. 29v–30r: "frettolosa al convento me n'invio / a pregar quelle venerabil suore / ch'affettuose lor preghiere a Dio / porger voglino acciò che tanto horrore / cessi, ch'altro remedio non vegg'io / a questo mal."

61. BCS, MS G.XI.59, fol. 6r: "Eufrosina è fanciulla savia, parla poco, non si lassa intendere; sta ritirata, non escie si può dir mai di camera, o dell'oratorio; non si vede in lei altro che spirito, una devotione straordinaria. Ella disprezza il mondo, lei mortifica la carne; a lei non si vede in mano altro che libri spirituali, corone, pater nostri, e simil cose. Chi vuol sua amicitia ragioni di Iddio, e della Vergine Maria sua advocata, e delli santi."

62. Ibid., fol. 34v: "Beate le monache che son fuor di tanti affannacci di questo mondaccio."

63. BCS, MS G.XI.58, fol. 41r: "Anzi a me par con gl'Angeli habitare / e fuor di lor son in tutto smarrita."

64. The play opens with ottave "recited" by a young man accompanied by an instrument; see BCS, MS K.X.53, fol. 2r: "E prima un giovinetto in sul suono dice al populo queste stanze."

65. Ibid., fol. 39r: "Il giovane adesso canti nel suono in bel modo le seguenti stanze: Per onorar così degno convito / io mi so' mosso a comparirvi avanti / per la pubblica fama havendo udito / di queste nozze l'alta lode e vanti. / E che per ogni strada e ogni

lito / degne son che ciascun ne parli e canti / et io che bramo d'onorarle ancora / dironne alquanto in breve spatio d'ora." The remaining stanzas continue on fols. 39r–40v.

66. Ibid., fol. 41v: "Or che rendute son le gratie a Dio / quando saremo al quanto riposati / che qui si facci festa è il voler mio / con canti e suoni onesti e costumati."

67. Ibid.: "Ora levata via la mensa, si ponghino a sedere ordinatamente la sposa sia allato alo sposo e presso a lei stieno le donne da una banda e dall'altra gl'huomini e qui si balli, canti, suoni cose allegre et oneste."

68. BCS, MS G.XI.58, fol. 2r: "Mosso dal casto zelo / dei novelletti sposi / si rasserena il cielo / i più sublimi eroii / manda quaggiù tra noi / e il paradiso tutto / gioisce lieto del futuro frutto." The performing forces for this madrigal are not specified; the libretto says only that it is to be sung.

69. Ibid., fol. 31v: "Chi brama al ciel salire / e mai sempre ivi la gloria fruire / convien che sprezzi le cose terrene / e 'n Dio ponghi sua spene. / Così poi 'n paradiso / fie di tormenti e morte herede il riso." Again, the libretto simply instructs that this *settina* is to be sung.

70. BCS, MS G.XI.59, fol. 9v: "O sacre verginelle / se Dio del suo amore / acceso ha 'l vostro core / spente son le facelle / rotte le freccie, e l'arco di Cupido. / Non puonno nuocer quelle / a chi del core a Dio ha fatto nido."

71. Ibid., fol. 26v: "La via ch'al ciel conduce / per fede e per sua luce / scoperta hor mai havete / ma quella, dati al senso, non tenete. . . . Erta è la via del cielo / facil la rende il zelo. / Sprezza quello ogni cosa / che ama Iddio e 'n Dio sol si riposa."

72. Ibid., fol. 5v.

73. See Emil Vogel, Alfred Einstein, François Lesure, Claudio Sartori, *Bibliografia della musica italiana vocale pubblicata dal 1500 al 1700*, 3 vols. (Pomezia: Staderini-Minkoff, 1977), 2:1608 (no. 2593). The text of the madrigal in *Eufrosina* is nearly identical to the work published by Scotto, except for the last two lines, which retain the metrical cast of the original but alter both words and meaning. I would like to thank Robert Kendrick, who examined the Scotto print for me.

74. BCS, MS G.XI.59, fol. 54r: "Dolci, amorose, e leggiadrette Ninfe / che col dolce cantar, e dolci accenti / fate ecco risonar, placar i venti / venite a cantar nosco. / Nozze per noi bramate / felici più d'ogn'altro hoggi ci fate."

75. Ibid., fol. 30r: "Spiriti infernali, a che fate consiglio / contro la casta sposa? / A lei nuocer non puote il vostro artiglio. / Sicura si riposa / nel seno di Giesù di Maria figlio. / Gite giù maladetti hor all'Inferno / lì state in fuoco e 'n ghiaccio in sempiterno."

76. BCS, MS G.XI.58, fols. 7r–v.

77. Ibid., fol. 22v: "Superati l'inganni / dell'antico serpente, non temete / ché per vessillo, anzi per scudo havete / dell'eserciti il Dio / ch'a porto condurrà vostro desio."

78. Music serves the same functions in Florentine convent theater of the period; see Elissa B. Weaver, "Canti, suoni e balli nel teatro delle suore toscane," presentation at the conference of the International Association of Italian Literary Studies, University of Odense, Denmark, 1–5 July 1991. I thank Professor Weaver for sending me a copy of this presentaion.

79. AAS, 3747, fols. 19r–v.

80. ASS, Con. sopp. 2649, "Salarii e provisioni (1618–19)," and "Uscita di spese diverse (1618–19)," unn. fols.

81. The liturgical drama from S. Martial de Limoges is preserved in Paris, Bibliothèque Nationale, MS 1139, transcribed in E. de Coussemaker, *Drames liturgiques du moyen age* (Rennes, 1860; reprint ed., New York: Broude, 1964), and discussed in Fernando Liuzzi, "Drammi musicali dei secoli XI–XIV," *Studi medievali*, n. s. 3 (1930): 82–109. The

reference to a German production of a play on the parable comes from [E. Alvise], *Commedia di dieci vergine* (Florence: Libreria Dante, 1882), 82.

82. [Alvise], *Commedia di dieci vergine*, is a modern edition of the Florentine convent play. I am indebted to Elissa Weaver for bringing this work to my attention. Professor Weaver's book, *Convent Theatre in Early Modern Italy: Spiritual Fun and Learning for Women* (Cambridge: Cambridge University Press, 2001), includes a survey and discussion of a number of Florentine convent plays on the parable of the wise and foolish virgins.

83. Rob C. Wegman includes a brief transcription of a portion from the Flemish play in "From Maker to Composer: Improvisation and Musical Authorship in the Low Countries, 1450–1500," *JAMS* 49 (1996): 419.

84. [Alvise], *Commedia di dieci vergine*, 12: "I' vo imparare a sonar el liuto e danzar di ballecti."

85. The wise virgins sing a verse of *Exurgat Dominus* to frighten away a demon; they greet the bridegroom with *Desidero te millies*; they sing *Gaudete et exultate* as they enter the wedding feast, and they perform *Laudate Dominum omnes gentes* and *Sanctus, Sanctus* from behind the locked doors to the feast; see [Alvise], *Commedia di dieci vergine*, 35, 48, 56, 57, 65.

86. For more on the consecration rite, especially as practiced in Siena, see chapter 3. The parable of the wise and foolish virgins made a lasting impression on at least one inhabitant of Ognissanti. The theorbist Maria Francesca Piccolomini referred to herself as a "vergine stolta" ("foolish virgin") in a letter to her confessor; see appendix 3, fol. 13v. Piccolomini's life is discussed in chapter 5.

87. See the *Liber Usualis* (Paris: Desclée, 1964), 262⁹, 1215: "Prudentes Virgines, aptate lampades vestras: ecce sponsus venit, exite obviam ei." This text is also used as the antiphon for the Magnificat at the Common of a Virgin and Martyr and at the Common of Several Virgins.

88. All the passages cited in the text are taken from the 1642 Siena edition of Flori's *L'evangelica parabola* (BCS, VI₂ O 15); notes hereafter provide act, scene, and page numbers.

89. Prologue, 17–18: "Partito il prologo si sentirà una voce dentro a la scena, che canterà in stile recitativo i sotto versi, invitando le vergini a comparire co' vasi d'olio, e con le lampade accese per andare ad incontrar la sposa con lo sposo: Vergini saggie e belle / da le luci sgombrate il pigro sonno, / alle nozze novelle / chiamate siete di due sommi heroi. / Gitene alla gran corte / ove regna la gioia alta immortale. / Già perdon lo splendor l'aurate stelle / all'apparir del sol nell'Oriente, / già de' canori augelli / il musico concento, al poggio, al piano / con dolcezza si sente, / che loda il suo fattor almo e sovrano. / Rompete le tardanze: / a così grande invito / pronta la voglia sia, il piè spedito. / Su, su del verde olivo / il pretioso humor preste prendete, / e provide accendete / le vostre faci, e frettolose andate / dove invita, ed aspetta l'amoroso / con la sposa del ciel celeste sposo."

90. See Weaver, "Spiritual Fun," 181.

91. Act I, sc. 5, 39–40: "*Aurilla*: Sento un di qua che grida / la carità chiedendo ad alta voce. *Povero*: Deh, per l'amore di Dio, donne da bene / aiutate qui 'l povero meschino / perché 'l nostro Signore / un per cento daravvi in paradiso. *Aquilina*: Guardate il bel spettacol che gl'è questo / . . . menalo in loco / che da nessun possa esser veduto. *Povero*: Deh, habbiate pietà d'un povarello. *Aurilla*: Omai tu ci hai stordite, / a l'udir qui costui è un monello / che messo si sarà nella carretta, / acciò che cavar possa da la gente / con quest'arte, ed inganno / de denar. . . . *Odorosa*: Sentite che fetore! / O puzzolente odore! / Gitene via furfanti. . . . *Povero*: Guardatelo, e toccatelo, e vedrete / se dico falsità, dico bugia. . . . / *Tangifila*: Sciagurato! Ch'il tocchi? Vanne via. . . . / *Gustante*: Leviamoci di qui perché quel cibo / che poco fa gustai, col suo fetore / costui nel sen mi turba. *Aurilla*: Lascianlo, e gridi poi quant'egli vole."

92. Act I, sc. 6, 42–44: "*L'infermo*: Deh, se pietate alberga / in voi (care sorelle) / porgete alcun soccorso / a me pover meschino. . . . *Deifila*: Che dite dolci e care mie sorelle / voi che di carità ripiene sete? / Vorrei poter portar questo meschino / ne la pupilla di quest'occhi miei; / sento i miei sensi muoversi a pietate. *Beatrice*: Chi ascolta le miserie di costui / havrebbe il cor di diaccio e di macigno / se trafitto non fusse da pietade. . . . *Diletta*: Questo sarà l'odore / con cui li piedi s'unge al Redentore. . . . *Felice*: Chi de' miseri al fin have pietade, / la dolcezza di quel divino amore / soavemente poi gusta, e sapora. . . . *Innocenza*: Ma chi puote haver mai maggior diletto / di quello che s'adopra e che fatica / sol per piacer al suo Signor sovrano / e l'opra sia de la sua, propria mano?"

93. For the pilgrims' song and the scene with foolish virgins, see Act II, sc. 4, 72–75.

94. Act II, sc. 5, 75–78.

95. Act III, sc. 4, 91–92.

96. Act III, sc. 5, 93: "Ed ancor ho sentito / che da voi stesse hora vi procurate / sotto habiti mentiti, e mascherati / mesti infelici augurii."

97. Act IV, sc. 8, 141: "Han gl'abiti mutati, / co' cappelli impiumati / mostrando appunto sieno i lor cervelli / simili a gl'augelli / che svolazzando van per tutti i lati."

98. For more on the subject, see Weaver, "The Convent Wall in Tuscan Convent Drama," 73–86.

99. Sc. 3, 124.

100. Sc. 9, 190: "U' sono i meriti vostri / ch'intrar possiate ne' sacrati chiostri?"

101. BCS, MS G.X.24, "Confessionario utilissimo pertinente solo ad aprire e mostrare le conscientie di ciascuna religiosa moniale di qualunque ordine, stato, grado e età le sieno che per loro medesime voglino imparare ad confessare e dire li lor proprii peccati senza essere interrogate dal confessoro [*sic*]," fol. 39v: "Mia colpa se mi fussi delectata o havesse hauto desiderio e piacere d'udir canti e suoni secolareschi e provocativi ad vanità e dilecto del mondo."

102. *Disembodied Voices*, 85.

103. Act I, sc. 9, 21.

104. Act I, sc. 3, 27: "Sirene ingannatrici, che col canto / visco tenace, e forte / danno con la dolcezza amara morte."

105. Sc. 3, 86: "Che tutte queste giovane vedreste / nel cantar, nel sonare, e poi col ballo / qual damme svelte, risolute, e preste."

106. Sc. 2, 123: "Venga Orfeo, Anfion con la sua lira, / che gli augelli, e le belve, / con il soave suon, col dolce canto / ad ascoltarlo uscian fuor delle selve, / per honorar co' i lor canori accenti / il Diletto, il Piacer, cuor delle genti."

107. See Act II, sc. 2, 51–58.

108. Act II, sc. 3, 67–68.

109. The complete scene is on pp. 81–91. The peasants use words such as "citto" for a young boy, as well as locutions such as "chesta" and "chello" for "questa" and "quello" (e.g., pp. 83–4) and "a du" for "dove" (p. 86), a manner of speaking associated with the countryside of Siena. The stupidity of the peasants is revealed by the fact that they do not really understand how to construct the word games so typical of the "giuochi senesi"; see James Haar, "On Musical Games in the Sixteenth Century," *JAMS* 15 (1962): 22–34.

110. Act III, sc. 3, 89–91: "*Senso*: Hor cantate, ed hor danzate / con diletto, gusto, e gioia / scacciate ogni tedio e noia / e 'l gentil Piacer lodate. . . . *Aurilla*: Chiare voci, percotete / nell'orecchie i dolci accenti / che maggior gioie e contenti / a noi porger non potrete. . . . *Tutti insieme*: Cantiamo hor con dolci accenti / del Piacer la somma gioia. / Fuggi ogn'un il tedio e noia; / viva Amor, e suoi contenti."

111. Act IV, sc. 5, 133–34: "Il Piacere viene in scena sonando, e quasi danzando con le sopra nominate [vergini stolte] cantando i sotto madrigali: Chi vuol levare dal core / tedio fastidio e noia / e scacciare il dolore, / e riempirlo d'allegrezza e gioia / venga chi brama havere / felice in questo mondo almo Piacere. / Sentirà dal diletto / disgombrarsi dal petto / ogni pena, ogni duolo / dileguarsi dal cor, levarsi a volo."

112. Act IV, sc. 5, 135: "Poscia che le sue dolci cantilene / avanzan di gran lunga le canore / de' boschi cittadine alme sirene."

113. Sc. 3, 130: "Hor qui finiam questi lunghi sermoni / che ci havete stordite."

114. See pp. 140–46.

115. Act V, sc. 4, 173–74: "Dall'ancilla [*sic*, for "Da' all'ancilla"] tua, dolce Signore, / ch'altro l'orecchie sue / non sappin ascoltar né d'altro udire, / se non le lodi tue de' dolci carmi, / e quelle melodie / de le canore voci / delli alternanti chori / di quei pennuti augei del paradiso, / chi [*sic*] stanno avanti al tuo divin cospetto, / e con quei cantar possa / quel dolce, e nuovo canto / amoroso, dicendo oh santo, oh santo."

116. Act V, sc. 7, 180: "E voi Spirti divini / ardenti serafini, / fate ch'udiam da voi angeli santi / vaghe canzoni con soavi canti, / e sentinsi concenti / d'armonici strumenti, / dolci laudi cantando all'amorosa / per noi al Re del cielo, alla sua sposa."

117. Act V, sc. [8], 188–89: "Gloria, gloria! Al Signore / rendiam laude, ed honore, / che ci diede quel chiaro e santo lume / e di poggiar al ciel spedite piume, / d'operar al bel desio / del dolce amore Dio, / amante sposo, che corona l'alme / di verdi olive e trionfanti palme." Patrick Macey has informed me that this text does not appear in his database of sixteenth-century Florentine lauda repertory. It also does not correspond to a work with a similar title published in Filippo Vitali's *Arie a tre voci* (Rome: Vincenzo Bianchi, 1639); see Vogel-Sartori, *Bibliografia della musica italiana vocale*, 2:1834 (no. 2940).

118. Act V, sc. 9, 195.

119. See sc. 11, 160. Nino Pirrotta defines the moresca as "a representational dance whose performers impersonate exotic, bizarre or comic characters"; see *Music and Theatre from Poliziano to Monteverdi* (Cambridge, UK: Cambridge University Press, 1982), 54–55. In Flori's play, four of the five peasants, upset at having been duped by the foolish virgins, perform "two strains of a moresca with sticks" ("Qui fanno co' bastoni due mutanze di moresca"). Apparently, the moresca was a mimed dance, frequently associated with pastoral scenes, and "mock skirmishes were common"; see Guglielmo Ebreo of Pesaro, *De Pratica Seu Arte Tripudii* (*On the Practice or Art of Dancing*), trans. and ed. Barbara Sparti (Oxford: Clarendon Press, 1993), 53–4.

120. Act V, [sc. 8], 181–88.

121. Peter Burke, *Popular Culture in Early Modern Europe* (London: Temple Smith, 1978), 188. As Burke notes on p. 201, Carnival served as a "safety-valve," allowing those suffering most from the inequalities of early modern society to vent their frustrations. At the same time, the "lifting of normal taboos and restraints" reaffirmed their place in the normal scheme of things.

122. Weaver, "Spiritual Fun," 183.

123. See Doc. 16, appendix 1.

Chapter 5

1. The literature on women's spiritual biographies and autobiographies is substantial and growing. For an introduction to seventeenth-century works in the genre from Europe and New Spain, see Electa Arenal and Stacey Schlau, *Untold Sisters: Hispanic Nuns in Their Own Words* (Albuquerque: University of New Mexico Press, 1989); Sara Cabibbo and

Marilena Modica, *La santa dei Tomasi: Storia di suor Maria Crocifissa, 1645–1699* (Turin: Giulio Einaudi, 1989); E. Ann Matter, "The Personal and the Paradigm: The Book of Maria Domitilla Galluzzi," in *The Crannied Wall: Women, Religion, and the Arts in Early Modern Europe,* ed. Craig A. Monson (Ann Arbor: University of Michigan Press, 1992), 87–103; Isobel Grundy, "Women's History? Writings by English Nuns," in *Women, Writing, History, 1640–1740,* ed. Isobel Grundy and Susan Wiseman (Athens: University of Georgia Press, 1992), 126–38; Jacques Le Brun, "L'institution et le corps, lieux de la mémoire: D'après le biographies spirituelles féminines du XVIIe siècle," *Corps ecrit* 11 (1984): 111–21; Kathleen Myers, *Word from New Spain: The Spiritual Autobiography of Madre Maria de San José, 1656–1719,* Hispanic Studies: Textual Research and Criticism (Liverpool: Liverpool University Press, 1993); and Ronald E. Surtz, *Writing Women in Late Medieval and Early Modern Spain: The Mothers of Saint Teresa of Avila* (Philadelphia: University of Pennsylvania Press, 1995). Two further studies are indispensable for understanding the intersections between sanctity and culture: Caroline Walker Bynum, *Holy Feast and Holy Fast: The Religious Significance of Food to Medieval Women* (Berkeley: University of California Press, 1987), and Gabriella Zarri, "Living Saints: A Typology of Female Sanctity in the Early Sixteenth Century," in *Women and Religion in Medieval and Renaissance Italy,* ed. Daniel Bornstein and Roberto Rusconi (Chicago: University of Chicago Press, 1996), 219–303.

2. See Catherine M. Mooney, "The Authorial Role of Brother A. in the Composition of Angela of Foligno's Revelations," in *Creative Women in Medieval and Early Modern Italy: A Religious and Artistic Renaissance,* ed. E. Ann Matter and John Coakley (Philadelphia: University of Pennsylvania Press, 1994), 34.

3. See, for example, Alison Weber, *Teresa of Avila and the Rhetoric of Femininity* (Princeton: Princeton University Press, 1990), 42–76.

4. For a short description of seven of the manuscripts in question, see Lorenzo Ilari, *La Biblioteca pubblica di Siena disposta secondo le materie: Catalogo,* 7 vols. (Siena: Tipografia dell'Insegna dell'Ancora, 1844–48), 6:531–32. Two other manuscripts were added to the collection after Ilari's catalogue was published (MS E.IV.10 and MS K.VII.50). For this discussion, I used K.VII.50: "La vita della venerabilissima Madre Passitea Crogi da Siena scritta dal molto Reverendo Padre Don Ventura Venturi da Siena Abbate Olivetano," a seventeenth-century copy that is both complete and easy to read. Venturi based his account on information provided by Padre D. Marchi, who had served as Crogi's confessor; see G. Formichetti, "Crogi, Passitea," in *DBI,* 51 vols. (Rome: Istituto della Enciclopedia italiana, 1960-), 31:227–29. The *terminus ante quem* of Venturi's original biography is clear from the title page of BCS, MS K.VII.35: "Passitea Crogi: Opera del molto reverendo Padre Don Ventura Venturi Abbate Olivetano . . . Copiata dal suo originale dal D.A.A. l'anno 1628. Di nuovo riveduta e ricopiata dal medesimo l'anno 1647." Eugenio Lazzareschi includes passages from Ventura's biography in his three-part article, "Una mistica senese: Passitea Crogi, 1565–1615," *BSSP* 22 (1915): 419–33; 23 (1916): 3–46; 25 (1918): 123–64.

5. *Vita della venerabile Madre Passitea Crogi senese fondatrice del monasterio delle religiose cappuccine nella città di Siena* (Rome: Filippo Maria Mancini, 1669). Marracci, a native of Lucca, dedicated the volume to two prominent Sienese citizens: "Signor Cardinale Chigi" and "Principessa Donna Berenice Della Ciaia Chigi." The "Cardinal Chigi" in question is probably Flavio, the son of Berenice.

6. See Zarri, "Living Saints," 234, for a description of sixteenth-century holy women who also received their education in a supernatural manner.

7. The life and actions of S. Marina were included in Jacobus de Voragine's *Golden Legend,* and the saint must have been popular in Siena at this time; in 1589 Domenico Tregiani wrote a play on this subject for the Convertite (see chapter 4).

8. See Lazzareschi, "Passitea Crogi," *BSSP* 23 (1916): 15, 20–23; and Alessandro Castellini, "Il Cardinale Francesco Maria Tarugi Arcivescovo di Siena," *BSSP* 50 (1943): 101.

9. The strictness of religious observance at this institution may be inferred from a letter written in 1623 to Federigo Borromeo, archbishop of Milan, by a certain Suor Fulvia, a nun at the convent of the Convertite in Siena. Suor Fulvia asked the prelate to grant her wish to go the convent of the Capuchin sisters in Siena or another institution in Milan where there is "obedience and observance of the rule . . . because since Nina died, there is no longer any vestige of religion here" (che io possa andare a stare dalle madri cappuccine qua in Siena o vero mi metta costà in qualche luogo dove si viva con obbedienza et osservanza di regola . . . che da che morta Nina, qua non v'è più vestigio di religione). The "Nina" in question is Caterina Vannini, the Sienese mystic who so fascinated Borromeo that he wrote her biography (see the discussion hereafter). Borromeo maintained a correspondence with several holy women, including Vannini; perhaps this explains why Suor Fulvia would think of writing to him for help with her unusual request. For a plate showing the pertinent portion of Suor Fulvia's letter, see Agostino Saba, *Federico Borromeo ed i mistici del suo tempo con la vita e la corrispondenza inedita di Caterina Vannini di Siena* (Florence: Leo S. Olschki Editore, 1933), 160–61.

10. This charming story is related in MS K.VII.50 on fols. 132r–v.

11. Lazzareschi speculates that Crogi's involvement in court intrigues, especially her possible complicity in the death of the marshal of Ancre and his wife, may explain the Catholic Church's reluctance to canonize her; see his "Passitea Crogi," *BSSP* 23 (1916): 41–46.

12. One of Crogi's few connections to Sienese musical life was her prophecy to the musician Alberto Gregori that his son Annibale would recover from an illness; see BCS, MS K.VII.50, fol. 182v.

13. See Zarri, "Living Saints," 251–54.

14. *Ragguaglio della vita della serva di Dio Suor Chiara Birelli della Congregazione dell'Abbandonate di Siena disteso dal Padre Giuseppe Scapecchi della Compagnia di Giesù* (Florence: Michele Nestenus e Antonmaria Borghigiani, 1712).

15. BCS, MS K.XI.35: "Vita di Suor Colomba monaca in Campanzi."

16. See chapter 6.

17. Zarri, "Living Saints," 232.

18. See Bynum, *Holy Feast*, 141–42.

19. BCS, MS K.XI.35, fol. 38v: "pregò [Suor Colomba] però in quel tempo al suo Signore che la privasse della favella per non mai più haver ad offenderlo in modo alcuno con la lingua."

20. Le Brun's observations on the important role doctors played in the lives of seventeenth-century holy women are discussed hereafter.

21. According to the author of the manuscript, Fabio Chigi's sister and niece were too modest to rejoice in Suor Colomba's prediction; see BCS, MS K.XI.35, fols. 107r–v.

22. I would like to thank Honey Meconi for her observation that it is perhaps more correct to say that the womens' *vite* follow patterns laid down by earlier *vite*. It is difficult, if not impossible, to determine if what the biographers say happened actually did happen. In this case, what is "true" is less important than what is reported to be true and what meanings that "truth" held for the readers; see Bynum, *Holy Feast*, 7.

23. Ibid., pp. 1–8, 140–49.

24. Such symbolism is useful for understanding the "nourishing" quality attributed to nun's music; see chapter 2.

25. For a discussion of the importance of illness and various forms of discipline in the spiritual lives of medieval holy women, see Bynum, "Women Mystics and Eucharistic Devotion in the Thirteenth Century," in *Fragmentation and Redemption: Essays on Gender and the Human Body in Medieval Religion* (New York: Zone Books, 1991), 131–32, and "The Female Body and Religious Practice in the Later Middle Ages," in the same volume, 184–89. Zarri examines some of the same traits, commonly found in biographies of early sixteenth-century holy women; see her "Living Saints," 227–29; 234–40.

26. Bynum discusses the role food and food symbolism played in S. Catherine's life in *Holy Feast*, 165–80. Most of her information comes from the biography of the saint written by Raymond of Capua; for an English translation, see Conleth Kearns, *The Life of Catherine of Siena by Raymond of Capua* (Wilmington, DE: Michael Glazier, 1980).

27. See BCS, MS K.VII.50, fol. 8r; MS K.XI.35, fol. 3v; and Lazzareschi, "Passitea Crogi," *BSSP* 23 (1916): 5–6. Zarri notes that Catherine served as a model for many holy women in cities other than Siena; see her "Living Saints," 225, 235.

28. Ambrogio Caterino Spannocchi, ed., *Vita della serva di Dio Suor Rosa Maria Generali monaca conversa del Terz'Ordine di S. Domenico nel monastero di Santa Caterina da Siena, detto il Paradiso, nella città di Siena, raccolta da una religiosa del medesimo monastero d'ordine de' suoi superiori* (Venice: Andrea Poleti, 1722), 40: "Sì, sta a vedere che sarà venuto il tempo di Suor Colomba da Campansi. Devi esser qualche santa tu, che ti abbino ad accettare per l'amore di Dio e senza dote?"

29. The familiar motifs are all present in Generali's short life (1648–80): harsh penitence, fasting, ecstasies, frequent illnesses, devotion to Christ's Passion, and the ability to see into the future.

30. Zarri, "Living Saints," 251–53, notes the Church's "sharpening mistrust" of holy women with "mystical or visionary tendencies."

31. Among those Birelli healed, for example, was Periteo Malvezzi of Bologna, who served as governor of Siena from 1614–22; see Scapecchi, *Vita di Suor Chiara Birelli*, 58. See also the discussion of Maria Francesca Piccolomini hereafter.

32. BAV, Archivio Chigi 33, fol. 291r: "Perdemmo in Castelvechio quella monicha buona tenuta in concetto di gran serva di Dio chiamata Suor Maria Caterina Stefanoni. Il giorno che stiede esposta in chiesa vi concorse un'infinità di populo e raccontono un miracolo quale se sia vero non lo so: la Signora Alessandra Gori fece toccare con un suo anello il volto della defonta, ed essendo poi andata da non so quale infermo gravemente amalato glel'applicò e dicono habbia riportato da questo notabile sollevamento." The letter is dated "7 agosto 1669" on fol. 291v.

33. The description of Crogi's mystic marriage to Christ (BCS, MS K.VII.50, fol. 81r) includes the following passage: "Indi a poco comparve l'istesso Giesù con aspetto e forma di estrema bellezza circondato da un'altra moltitudine d'angioli li quali vestiti d'habiti sontuosi e vaghissimi sonando e cantando facevano un'armonia et un concerto." Zarri notes that a holy woman's "heavenly visions were always accompanied by angelic music"; see "Living Saints," 238.

34. For the references to vite of Bolognese nuns, I am grateful to Craig Monson, who supplied the passages cited in the text.

35. Bologna, Biblioteca Universitaria, MS 1318, "Breve compendio della vita e virtù della venerabile Madre Suor Angiola Gozzadini monaca nel monastero di Santa Maria delli Angioli di Bologna, MDCLX," fol. 33v.

36. A fuller passage from the vita and all pertinent bibliographical information may be found in Monson's introduction to *The Crannied Wall*, 10–11.

37. Bologna, Biblioteca Universitaria, MS 123: "Vita succinta di Suor Laura Catterina Maria al secolo Giulia figlia del Co. Filippo Albergati e Laura Bolognetti," fols. 2r–v.

38. See Monson, *Disembodied Voices: Music and Culture in an Early Modern Italian Convent* (Berkeley: University of California Press, 1995).

39. *Celestial Sirens: Nuns and their Music in Early Modern Milan* (Oxford: Clarendon Press, 1996), 155–56.

40. Kendrick, *Celestial Sirens*, 76–81; 161–63.

41. Borromeo's biography of Vannini may be found in Saba, *Federico Borromeo ed i mistici del suo tempo*, 125–91.

42. Borromeo's letters to Vannini remain to be discovered; Vannini's missives are transcribed in Saba, *Federico Borromeo ed i mistici del suo tempo*, pp. 193–259; they are also reproduced in Piero Misciattelli, *Caterina Vannini: Una cortigiana convertita senese e il cardinale Federigo Borromeo alla luce di un epostolario inedito* (Milan: Edizioni Fratelli Treves, 1932).

43. The synopsis of Vannini's life is based on books one and two of Borromeo's biography; see Saba, *Federico Borromeo ed i mistici del suo tempo*, 125–75.

44. If practices in Siena were similar to those in Florence, officials may have required all prostitutes to attend the sermon, which was perceived as an "opportunity for conversion"; see Sherill Cohen, *The Evolution of Women's Asylums since 1500* (New York: Oxford University Press, 1992), 46.

45. Saba, *Federico Borromeo ed i mistici del suo tempo*, 187–88.

46. For examples other than those cited hereafter see Saba, *Federico Borromeo ed i mistici del suo tempo*, 145, 168, 197, 219, 221–22.

47. Ibid., 140: "quando ella si trovava in chiesa alla messa, le pareva veder la chiesa tutta risplendente, e sentire un'angelica melodia, la quale si raddoppiava nel pronuntiarsi dal sacerdote quelle parole, Sanctus, Sanctus, Sanctus, Dominus Deus Sabaoth, venendo le medesime replicate dagli angeli con un canto così soave, che l'anima stava quasi per separarsele dal corpo."

48. Ibid., 144: "sentì formarsi sopra un soavissimo concerto di musicali strumenti, accompagnato da una dolcissima armonia di angeliche voci, che per più hore cantarono delle laudi di San Giorgio, e di San Francesco di Paola, la cui festa appunto in quel giorno dalla chiesa si celebrava."

49. Ibid., 111.

50. Kendrick, *Celestial Sirens*, 158.

51. I have translated this passage from the transcription given in Kendrick, *Celestial Sirens*, 450–51.

52. Cited in Kendrick, *Celestial Sirens*, 156.

53. I have translated this passage from the transcription given by Robert L. Kendrick, "Genres, Generations and Gender: Nuns' Music in Early Modern Milan, c. 1550–1706," (Ph.D. diss., New York University, 1993), 836. Kendrick uses this passage to examine Borromeo's ideas concerning the association of female mysticism and music; see *Celestial Sirens*, 156–57.

54. Karen-edis Barzman, "Cultural Production, Religious Devotion, and Subjectivity in Early Modern Italy: The Case Study of Maria Maddalena de' Pazzi," *Annali d'italianistica: Women Mystic Writers* 13 (1995): 284, 295 (reproduction of oil painting showing de' Pazzi painting blindfolded).

55. Kendrick, *Celestial Sirens*, 158.

56. Monson, *Disembodied Voices*, 87. Monson's discussion of how the nun composer Vizzana justified her authorization to "speak" by casting herself as a "passive instrument of the divine" is most useful for understanding the manner in which Vannini exploited her performing skills.

57. Barzman, "The Case Study of Maria Maddalena de' Pazzi," 285.

58. See chapter 1.

59. The association of lutes with prostitutes was common; see Georgina Masson, *Courtesans of the Italian Renaissance* (New York: St. Martin's Press, 1975), 31, 37, 38–39, 64, 91; and Monson, *Disembodied Voices*, 85.

60. Piccolomini's two-part vita survives in manuscript—BCS, MS E.IV.6—copied sometime in the late seventeenth century from an earlier source. The first part consists of a spiritual biography by her confessor Sebastiano Conti (transcribed as appendix 3), and the second part is given over to Piccolomini's autobiographical account (transcribed as appendix 2). The manuscript copy was badly bound and foliated after being copied: the biographical portion by Conti runs from fols. 1r–13v (folios 1–10 have also been numbered by a later hand) and then skips to fols. 29r–v. The title page for Piccolomini's autobiographical account (clearly labeled "copia" in this manuscript) is given on fol. 14r; her account begins on fol. 28r–v and then continues on fols. 15r–24r. A letter from Piccolomini to Conti is appended on fols. 24r–25r. Folio 1r of the manuscript documents its purchase on 19 July 1818 by a certain Francesco Burzagli. He may have been responsible for several marginal annotations, as well as additions and deletions that run throughout the manuscript. In several cases, he tried to modernize spellings; in other cases, he edited lines or phrases to make the prose smoother, often reproducing the prose that appeared when Piccolomini's story was reproduced in a printed book (published 1668) telling the story of the miraculous statue (see note 73). The print, however, reproduces neither the biography nor the autobiography in full. My own transcriptions are therefore based on MS E.IV.6 and follow the seventeenth-century text as closely as possible, except when it is unreadable. In such cases, I use the text added by the volume's owner. I have also added modern punctuation for readability. Important marginal additions are given in the notes. In the discussion that follows, passages from the biography or autobiography are followed by citations of folio numbers in parentheses in the text; interested readers may then turn to appendices 2 and 3, locate the appropriate folios, and read the passages in Italian.

61. Very little of the "normal" kinds of documentary material survive for Ognissanti (e.g., debit-credit registers, deliberations) in ASS; what is extant there is mostly from the eighteenth century. On the other hand, we have the short passages in the volume printed to record the events of the 1649 Domenica in Albis procession (see chapter 2), a single volume at AAS that describes several consecration ceremonies (see chapter 3), the 1642 play by Flori (see chapter 4), and Piccolomini's vita.

62. ASS, MS A51: Tommaso Mocenni, "Raccolta di nomi di persone nobili battez-zate in Siena nate da fameglie che sono esistenti nel presente anno 1713," fol. 261r. See also ASS, Pieve di S. Giovanni Battista 113, unn. fol.

63. ASS, MS A51, fol. 259v; AAS, 3747, fols. 19v, 184v.

64. ASS, MS A51, fols. 260v–261r. See the discussion hereafter for references to one of Piccolomini's sisters.

65. Ibid., fols. 260r–v. According to the convent necrology, Piccolomini's brothers took care of all the funeral arrangements; see AAS, 3747, fol. 173r.

66. AAS, 3747, fol. 22r.

67. ASS, Con. sopp. 3024, fols. 96v–97r. Suor Caterina Piccolomini was not among the six who signed the contract of 1642, despite the fact that she had entered the convent in 1636. Nuns at Ognissanti, S. Abbondio, and Le Trafisse had to take part in the conse-cration rite before being able to hold office, vote in chapter meetings, and sign contracts, and they could not participate in that ceremony until reaching the age of twenty-five (although exceptions to this rule were common). Caterina took part in the consecration ceremony of 1644; see AAS, 3747, fol. 120r.

68. Radi di Creta is approximately 13 kilometers south of Siena.

69. Cabibbo and Modica note that hagiographic literature of the post-Tridentine pe-

riod often emphasizes the important role of the mother in the formation of a child's spiritual vocation; see *Storia di suor Maria Crocifissa*, 83. Campriano, where Piccolomini's mother went to pray, was only a mile or so from the family villa at Radi di Creta.

70. AAS, 3747, fol. 123r: "la funtione fu bellissima con musica a tre cori, teatro superbissimo e grandissimo concorso." The names of all fifteen nuns who participated in the rite, including the Piccolomini women, are also preserved on this folio.

71. Spannocchi, *Vita di Suor Rosa Maria Generali*, 175–76.

72. Scapecchi, *Vita di Suor Chiara Birelli*, 84–87.

73. *Relazione della miracolosa Madonna del Presepio che si conserva dalle monache benedettine aggreggate alla congregazione olivetana nel venerabile monistero di Ogni Santi in Siena composta dal Padre Sebastiano Conti pistoiese della Compagnia di Giesù* (Siena: Stamperia del Publico [1668]). This is the printed volume to which I have referred in note 60. The volume was reprinted in 1743.

74. *The Hours of the Divine Office in English and Latin*, 3 vols. (Collegeville, MN: Liturgical Press, 1963), 3:1500. Electa Arenal and Stacey Schlau have noted that "the visual elaboration of Marian themes" by Spanish nuns often depicted Mary as a "figure of wisdom": reading, writing, or playing music; " 'Leyendo yo y escribiendo ella': The Convent as Intellectual Community," *Journal of Hispanic Philology* 13 (1989): 220.

75. *Celestial Sirens*, 89.

76. AAS, 3747, fol. 19r. I was unable to find any record of Suor Maria Benedetta's death.

77. AAS, 3747, fol. 18r. The girls were daughters of Pietro Bargagli and Onesta Borghesi. Artemisia was baptized on 18 December 1610 and Petra on 11 March 1612 (ASS, MS A48: Mocenni, "Raccolta di nomi di persone nobili battezzate in Siena," fol. 118v). Artemisia died of a fever on 19 September 1660 when she was only forty-nine. Petra died on 25 May 1681 at the age of seventy-nine; she was blind for the last eleven years of her life (AAS, 3747, fols. 174v, 182v). Girolamo and Scipione Bargagli, the brothers who made the "veglie di Siena" famous by their late-sixteenth-century publications, are perhaps the most famous representatives of the family; see Dinko Fabris, "Giochi musicali e veglie 'alla senese' nelle città non toscane dell'Italia rinascimentale," in *Musica Franca: Essays in Honor of Frank D'Accone*, ed. Irene Alm, Alyson McLamore, and Colleen Reardon (Stuyvesant, NY: Pendragon Press, 1996), 213–29; and James Haar, "On Musical Games in the Sixteenth Century," *JAMS* 15 (1962): 22–34.

78. Kenneth Grahame, *The Wind in the Willows* (New York: Holt, Rinehart and Winston, 1980), 188.

79. My sincere thanks to Ms. Liddell for her letter of 10 October 1995 and her most informative comments in a conversation on 20 April 1996.

80. Absinthe (the herb wormwood) contains a volatile oil that is a narcotic poison. I would like to thank H. Colin Slim and Gary Towne for bringing this fact to my attention.

81. Kearns, *The Life of Catherine of Siena by Raymond of Capua*, 42.

82. See Cabibbo and Modica, *Storia di Suor Maria Crocifissa*, 85.

83. Emilia, daughter of Orazio Piccolomini, was vested as a nun on 26 November 1625 and took the name Maria Vittoria; she died on 29 January 1663. See AAS, 3747, fols. 18r, 176r.

84. *Relazione della miracolosa Madonna del Presepio*, 11–17.

85. Ibid., 18.

86. Ibid., 46–47.

87. Ibid., 19–27.

88. Ibid., 46–52.

89. Jacques Le Brun, "Mutations de la notion de martyre au XVIIe siècle d'après les

biographies spirituelles féminines," in *Sainteté et martyre dans les religions du livre*, ed. Jacques Marx, Problèmes d'Histoire du Christianisme 19 (Brussels: Éditions de l'Université de Bruxelles, 1989), 84.

90. Ibid., 77–78; 83–84.

91. See appendix 2, note 3.

92. "The Female Body and Religious Practice," 187. Bynum notes that incorruptibility was claimed for all six female saints added to the universal Roman calendar between 1400 and 1900.

93. Alfredo Liberati, "Chiese, monasteri, oratori, e spedali senesi," *BSSP* 57 (1950): 146–51.

94. See Gregorio Lombardelli, *Vita del gloriosissimo San Galgano senese da Chiusdino* (Siena: Bonetti, 1577), 111–13.

95. The story is related on a document dated 10 April 1649 that was attached to the convent chronicle; it is fully transcribed in Narciso Mengozzi, "Il convento detto del Santuccio," *BSSP* 29 (1922), 14n. The chronicle and attached document were possibly in private hands when Mengozzi examined them, for he provides no bibliographic citations. I have been unable to locate the chronicle among the surviving records from the convent.

96. "Interni di conventi senesi del Cinquecento," *Ricerche storiche* 10 (1980): 184–85.

97. *Relazione della miracolosa Madonna del Presepio*, 1–7.

98. In May 1660, the abbess of Ognissanti called a chapter meeting to discuss what to do with the 200 scudi that had been donated to the miraculous statue of the Madonna of the Manger; see AAS, 3747, fol. 26v.

99. The 1743 edition of the *Relazione della miracolosa Madonna del Presepio* adds a ninth chapter recounting the events of the 1693 procession.

100. Ibid., (1668 ed.), 78–80 names witnesses from Carpentras and Rome who had been healed by oil from the Virgin's lamp.

101. Ibid. (1743 ed.), 84–90. Many of those miraculously cured were nuns at the convent of San Donato in Polverosa, whose Sienese confessor, Giovanbattista Barili, carried some oil from the lamp of the Madonna of the Manger with him. Barili used the oil to cure Florentine priests and lay men as well.

102. Kearns, *The Life of Catherine of Siena by Raymond of Capua*, 175–76.

103. Some of the occasions on which the Sienese appealed to the Virgin for protection are represented in the Biccherna paintings from the fifteenth and sixteenth centuries; see *Le Biccherne: Tavole dipinte delle magistrature senesi (secoli XIII-XVIII)*, ed. L. Borgia et alii (Rome: Ministero per i Beni Culturali e Ambientali, 1984), 156–57, 170–71, 182–83, 184–85, 190–91, 194–95, 226–27. See also Frank A. D'Accone, *The Civic Muse: Music and Musicians in Siena during the Middle Ages and the Renaissance* (Chicago: University of Chicago Press, 1997), 185n.

104. Piccolomini's funeral is described in AAS, 3747, fol. 173r. Conti recounts the stories of the two nuns who saw her appear to them after her death in BCS, MS E.IV.6, fols. 12r–13r.

Chapter 6

1. Cesare Brandi, ed., *Palazzo Pubblico di Siena: Vicende costruttive e decorazione* (Milan: Silvana Editoriale, 1983), 121–22; 326–27.

2. Lorenzo Bianconi and Thomas Walker, "Dalla *Finta pazza* alla *Veremonda*: Storie di Febiarmonici," *Rivista italiana di musicologia* 10 (1975): 435–36; Michael Tilmouth, "Music on the Travels of an English Merchant: Robert Bargrave (1628–61)," *Music and Letters* 53 (1972): 145–46.

3. See Richard Krautheimer, *The Rome of Alexander VII, 1655–67* (Princeton: Princeton University Press, 1985), 12; Monika Butzek, ed., *Il Duomo di Siena al tempo di Alessandro VII: Carteggio e disegni (1658–1667), Die Kirchen von Siena*, Supplement 2 (Munich: Bruckmann, 1996), 59–60; E. Stumpo, "Chigi, Agostino," *DBI*, 24:744.

4. For an overview of Alexander VII's accomplishments in Rome, see Krautheimer, *The Rome of Alexander VII*, and Francis Haskell, *Patrons and Painters: A Study of the Relations between Italian Art and Society in the Age of the Baroque*, 2nd ed., rev. and enl. (New Haven: Yale University Press, 1980), 151–52; for Siena, see Butzek, *Il Duomo di Siena al tempo di Alessandro VII*. A forthcoming catalogue of the exhibition "Alessandro VII Chigi tra Siena e Roma" (Siena, 20 April 2000–10 January 2001) should provide a wealth of information on Chigi patronage at a number of Sienese institutions.

5. Haskell, *Patrons and Painters*, 154, goes so far as to maintain that neither Flavio nor Agostino "showed any great intelligence or culture." Recent scholarship offers a more favorable opinion of Flavio Chigi's tastes in architecture; see Patricia Waddy, *Seventeenth-Century Roman Palaces: Use and the Art of the Plan* (Cambridge: MIT Press, 1990), 300–320.

6. See, for example, Vincenzo Golzio, *Documenti artistici sul Seicento nell'Archivio Chigi* (Rome: Fratelli Palombi, 1939), 205–7, 226–27, 240–43, 373–76; Jean Lionnet, "Les activités musicales de Flavio Chigi, cardinal neveu d'Alexandre VII," *Studi musicali* 9 (1980): 287–302; Frank A. D'Accone, *The History of a Baroque Opera: Alessandro Scarlatti's "Gli equivoci nel sembiante"* (New York: Pendragon Press, 1985), 20–22, 29, 104–5, 117–18; Renato Lefevre, "Gli 'Sfaccendati,'" *Studi romani* 8 (1960): 154–65, 288–301; Lorenzo Bianconi and Thomas Walker, "Production, Consumption, and Political Function of Seventeenth-Century Italian Opera," *Early Music History* 4 (1984): 251–53; Robert Lamar Weaver, "Materiali per le biografie dei fratelli Melani," *Rivista italiana di musicologia* 12 (1977): 273–80; Margaret Murata, "Il Carnevale a Roma sotto Clemente IX Rospigliosi," *Rivista italiana di musicologia* 12 (1977): 94–95; Alexander Silbiger, "The Roman Frescobaldi Tradition, c. 1640–1670," *JAMS* 33 (1980): 73–75; Wolfgang Witzenmann, "Autographe Marco Marazzolis in der Biblioteca Vaticana," *Analecta musicologica* 7 (1969): 54–55, 62–63, and *Cantatas by Marco Marazzoli, c. 1605–1662* (New York: Garland, 1986).

7. BAV, Archivio Chigi 277, fol. 22r–v: "Havendo il dramma dell'Antigone eletto da questi signori deputati per rappresentarsi nel nuovo theatro perduta la qualità più singolare che pregiavano di non essere stato rappresentato altrove già che si ha riscontro sia stato recitato a Venetia, Bologna ed anco si dice in altre città della Lombardia, si trovano per ciò assai sconsolati, non sapendo a qual opera appigliarsi, onde quando Vostra Eminenza, hora che il signor Contestabile si trova in Roma, credesse poterli favorire di quella nuova comedia messa in musica che là discorreva l'estate passata e mai recitata, o di altra che Vostra Eminenza giudicasse a proposito, consolarebbe tutti singolarmente, e sarebbe favore della sua consueta beneficenza in tempo molto opportuno et in bisogno presente. . . . Siena 10 dicembre 1668 . . . Leonardo Marsilii."

8. BAV, Archivio Chigi 3847, fol. 21r: "Sento che sia per passare qua una tale Signora Giulia famosa cantatrice. Mi vien detto che spesso viene costì a cantare. Se Lei gli imponesse il venir un poco qui e farsi sentire da me si assicuri che mi farebbe un favore grandissimo. . . . Siena, li 12 dicembre 1667 [*sic, recte* 1668]." The date is obviously wrong, for Suor Maria Pulcheria wrote another letter six days later, lamenting the fact that the cardinal was not able to communicate her desire to hear Masotti perform to the singer herself. That letter is clearly a follow-up to the one given here and is correctly dated "18 dicembre 1668": see BAV, Archivio Chigi 3847, fol. 35r.

9. See Beth L. Glixon, "Private Lives of Public Women: Prima Donnas in Mid-Seventeenth-Century Venice," *Music and Letters* 76 (1995): 524–26.

10. I have not been able to determine precisely what branch of the Della Ciaia hosted Masotti. It is possible that she stayed at the home of the composer Alessandro Della Ciaia, who was related to the Chigi through his sister Berenice's marriage to Mario Chigi. See figure 3.

11. BAV, Archivio Chigi 3871, fols. 16r–v: "Ieri arrivò la Signora Giulia in casa Ciai e iarsera ci andammo a veglia e veramente canta molto bene e con una gran maniera e disinvoltura ma levato questo è una gran brutta figliola vestita a quella maniera mezza da huomo. Così da donna mi presuppongo che sia molto peggio. Ci fu di molte dame a sentirla e di cavalieri moltissimi. . . . Siena, il 19 dicembre 1668, serva e sorella, Olimpia Chigi Gori."

12. BAV, Archivio Chigi 33, fol. 263r–v: "Questi signori deputati doppo molti discorsi fatti dell'opera da eleggersi nuovamente instigati da me e persuasi dalla Signora Giulia, la quale nel suo passaggio di qui cantò l'altra sera con sommo contento di molte dame et infiniti cavalieri li quali vi furno presenti, hanno risoluto rappresentare l'Argia per l'esibitioni fatteli qua dal signor Apolloni di scorciarla e col supposto di poterne conseguire ad intercessione di Vostra Eminenza una copia da chi l'ha acciò che si possano poi cavare le parti e distribuirle a chi la doverà recitare. . . . Siena, 19 dicembre 1668 . . . Leonardo Marsilii."

13. See William C. Holmes, "Cesti's *L'Argia*: An Entertainment for a Royal Convert," *Chigiana* 26–27, n.s. 6–7 (1971): 35–52.

14. BAV, Archivio Chigi 33, fol. 266r: "Questi signori deputati dal theatro vanno disponendosi per la recitatione dell'opera, già che la fabrica trovasi ridotta in assai buono stato, e sperano dalla generosità di queste dame una copiosa contributione per il soffitto alle quali presentano le loro supliche in due sonetti che stampano a questo effetto. Si studia tutti li modi per fare denaro acciò si compisca questa fabrica singolare in se stessa e più in una città picciola e ciò mercé delle generosi donationi della casa Chigi. . . . Siena, 16 gennaro 1669 . . . Leonardo Marsilii." The Medici were also involved in the effort to repair the theater; see Bianconi and Walker, "Dalla *Finta pazza* alla *Veremonda*," 435 n. 230.

15. See BAV, Archivio Chigi 277, fol. 24r (letter of Leonardo Marsili to Sigismondo Chigi, dated 5 June 1669): "Qui siamo stati tutti impacciati nella recitatione dell'opera, la quale è riuscita ricca di abiti, di scene, musica esquisita coll'assistenza continua del signor Cesti." Marsili also mentions the repeat performances.

16. The undated letter on Campaluci's behalf, preserved among the documents received by the deliberative body of the Concistoro during the months of November and December 1669 (ASS, Concistoro 2269), is transcribed in full by Silvia Calocchi, "Musica e feste in Siena durante il governatorato del Principe Mattias de' Medici (1629–1667)" (Tesi di laurea, Università degli Studi di Siena, 1988–89), 167–68. Campaluci began his career as a "clerk and singer" at Siena Cathedral in 1655; see AOMS 1087 (old 797), fol. 292r. He remained with the cappella up until 15 November 1669, when the payment records note the license granted for the trip to Venice. In April 1670, he was given permission to go to Florence. He returned to the Cathedral cappella in mid-May 1670 but is noted as absent from the singers during Carnival season of 1671. In November 1672, he went to Rome, never to return to the Cathedral. See AOMS 1088 (old 798), fol. 294r and 1089 (old 799), fols. 22r, 41v.

17. Lefevre, "Gli 'Sfaccendati,'" 298 n. 29.

18. A sonnet dedicated to Botteghi "while she sang to universal applause in the drama *Argia*" was printed in Siena in 1669; see Warren Kirkendale, *The Court Musicians in Florence during the Principate of the Medici* (Florence: Leo S. Olschki, 1993), 416. I would like to thank Beth Glixon for bringing this to my attention.

19. See Ellen Rosand, *Opera in Seventeenth-Century Venice* (Berkeley: University of California Press, 1991), 239–40; and Glixon, "Private Lives of Public Women," 526.

20. Masotti's presence in Siena in the spring of 1669 is documented in two letters. Verginia Chigi Piccolomini included the following in a letter addressed to Cardinal Sigismondo Chigi, dated 26 April 1669: "Noi siamo state quattro sere a sentire cantare la Donna Giulia che in vero canta molto bene che non si pole desiderare di più" (BAV, Archivio Chigi 3888, fol. 33r). Giulia Masotti also wrote to Cardinal Sigismondo from Siena on 24 April 1669, telling him of her travel plans (BAV, Archivio Chigi 33, fol. 577r).

21. BAV, Archivio Chigi 3888, fol. 35r: "Lunedì si fece la comedia essendo indugiato quel giorno primediante Jacomo che è infreddato et il venerdì e sabato hebbe la febbre e nonostante si è portato bene et a questi Cavalieri fiorentini che ci erano li è piaciuto assai. Et li musici delli cattivi non ce ne era: boni e qualcheduno mediocre et la commedia è bella. . . . Siena, 29 maggio 1669 . . . serva e sorella, Verginia Chigi Piccolomini."

22. BAV, Archivio Chigi 3871, fols. 92r–v: "veramente credrei che ci avesse avuto gusto alla comedia che non si fece domenica a cacione che il Campi Luci era infredato e sabato ebbe la febre e però la fecero ier che entrò a 22 ore e mezo e finì vicino alle quator e veramente è riuscita bellissima ben rescitata e guidata benissimo e di suoni dicano che a Venetia non stavano tanto bene quanto sono qua. Posso dire a Vostra Eminenza che ci era de' fiorentini et altri forestieri che tutti la lodarono di molto et un francese che passava di qui si trattene per vederla disse che a Parigi avrebero fatto pagare una doppia. Et io si assicuri che mi sono molto invaghita della musica perché non credo veramente che si possa sentire né più delicata né più galante di questa. . . . Io però fo pensiero d'andarci tutte le volte et ieri cavai tutte le citte delle monache e ce le condussi . . . serva e amatissima sorella, Olimpia Chigi Gori." I have rendered the hours mentioned by Olimpia in modern terms by consulting Nello Barbieri, "Note di cronologia: Le ore a Siena dal XIV al XVIII secolo," *BSSP* 90 (1983): 148–51.

23. Both Chigi sisters lamented the cancellation of the opera performance; see BAV, Archivio Chigi 3871, fols. 35r–36v; 3888, fols. 47r–v.

24. See Robert Lamar Weaver, "Biografie dei fratelli Melani," 277–80, 283–84. The Chigi may have also been involved with the Sienese production of the Jacopo Melani/Filippo Acciaiuoli *Il Girello* in 1672; see Robert Lamar Weaver, "*Il Girello*: A seventeenth-Century Burlesque Opera," *Quadrivium* 12 (1971): 141, 152.

25. See *History of a Baroque Opera*, 117–18, 164.

26. Golzio, *Documenti artistici sul Seicento nell'Archivio Chigi*, 374.

27. The trip is recorded in BAV, Archivio Chigi 1809, fols. 16r–21r.

28. Lefevre discusses the activities of the academy in "Gli 'Sfaccendati,' " 154–65 and 288–301. For more on the 1672 opera, see Gino Roncaglia, " 'Il Tirinto' di B. Pasquini e i suoi 'Intermezzi,' " *Rassegna musicale* 4 (1931): 331–39; and Carolyn Gianturco, "Il melodramma a Roma nel secolo XVII," in *Storia dell'opera*, ed. Alberto Basso (Turin: UTET, 1978), 213–14. See also Lowell Lindgren, "Acciaiuoli, Filippo," and Thomas Walker, "Apolloni, Giovanni Filippo," *The New Grove Dictionary of Opera*, 4 vols. (London: Macmillan, 1992), 1:8, 152–53.

29. Golzio, *Documenti artistici sul Seicento nell'Archivio Chigi*, 207 n. 8, 226.

30. See the discussion in chapter 1.

31. See Stumpo, "Chigi, Agostino," 744; Golzio, *Documenti artistici sul Seicento nell'Archivio Chigi*, 3–4, 149–55; and Waddy, *Seventeenth-Century Roman Palaces*, 301.

32. The children's names and dates of birth (and sometimes death) appear in BAV, Fondo Chigi, MS Rve (III), fols. 33r–37v. Steven Plank provides a complete list of the children in "Music for a Chigi Princess: A Study of an Anonymous 'Operina Sacra' of 1686" (Ph.D. diss., Washington University, St. Louis, 1980), 5, although some of the dates cited are incomplete or incorrect.

33. BAV, Archivio Chigi 3871, fol. 58r (Letter to Sigismondo Chigi dated 16 No-

vember 1672): "Ora avrebbe a essere fenito il numero delle femmine della Signora Principessa perché sono arrivate al numero de' cori del'angioli che potrebbero veramente bastare."

34. Laura (b. 1659) took the habit as Suor Flavia in 1676, and her investiture featured music by Alessandro Melani (see the preceding discussion). Sulpizia (1664–1725) became Suor Maria Lutugarda at the institution, and Anna (1674–1738) entered the convent as Suor Maria Berenice. SS. Domenico e Sisto was one of the convents that featured lavish music during the Jubilee Year of 1675; see Kimberlyn Montford, "Music in the Convents of Counter-Reformation Rome" (Ph.D. diss., Rutgers University, 1999), 60–62.

35. The presence of four or five sisters in one religious institution was not unheard of in early modern Italy; see Silvana Seidel Menchi, "Characteristics of Italian Anticlericalism," in *Anticlericalism in Late Medieval and Early Modern Europe*, ed. Peter A. Dykema and Heiko A. Oberman (Leiden: E. J. Brill, 1993), 275. Montford reports that Fabrizio Massimo sent three daughters from a first marriage and three from a second marriage to the Roman convent of Tor de' Specchii; see "Convents of Counter-Reformation Rome," 41 n. 13. The Chigi family's placement of seven daughters at one convent was, however, probably some kind of record for the time.

36. See ASS, Con. sopp. 1949, fols. 4v–5r.

37. See George R. F. Baker, "Nobiltà in declino: Il caso di Siena sotto i Medici e gli Asburgo-Lorena," *Rivista storica italiana* 84 (1972): 609 n. 78.

38. See ASS, Con. sopp. 1947, fol. 62v, "E più lire cinquanta due soldi 13:4 date al signor Magini che tanto à dato a' musici che ànno cantato avanti la nostra porta nel ingresso dell detta signora Donna Angiola, £. 52.13.4." ASS, Con. sopp. 1948, fol. 72v, records a payment of £. 42 to Magini in connection with music for the investiture of Berenice.

39. ASS, Con. sopp. 1949, fol. 37r: "[Expenses for the clothing of Eleonora] E più lire quaranta quattro date per 8 piedistalli aggiustati Monsu Arrigo legnaiolo per li palchi delli musici quando si farà la musica fuore, £. 44."

40. See, for example, BAV, Archivio Chigi 1000, 121. An entry made on 31 August 1686 records the expenses (including music) for the clothing of Olimpia Chigi in June of that year.

41. BAV, Fondo Chigi, MS Q.VI.84, title page: "Operina sacra in musica . . . rappresentata in occasione che prende l'abito francescano nel venerabile monastero di San Girolamo detto Campanzi di Siena l'eccellentissima signora principessa Donna Olimpia Chigi . . . l'anno 1686." The score contains eighty-nine numbered folios; the foliation begins with Act I. Preceding Act I are three unnumbered folios, including the title page and the opening sinfonia. The score is neatly copied and well preserved. Its connection to the Chigi family is not only proclaimed on the title page but trumpeted at the opening of each act. The first initial of the text with which each act begins is rendered as a large, decorative letter around which are intertwined the Chigi emblems (the star, the leafy oak, the six *monti*). The winged dragon and the crowned eagle of the Borghese family make an appearance at the beginning of Act III.

42. See the extant designs in BAV, Fondo Chigi, MS P.VII.11, fols. 95v–96r.

43. Ugo Frittelli, *Albero genealogico della nobil famiglia Chigi patrizia senese* (Siena: Arti Grafiche Lazzeri, 1922), 139; *Alessandro VII Chigi tra Siena e Roma: Itinerari Chigiani* (Siena: Comune di Siena, 2000), 22.

44. The subject of this theatrical piece links it to the tradition of the oratorio, which was very similar in style to opera during the mid-to-late seventeenth century; see Howard E. Smither, *A History of the Oratorio*, vol. 1, *The Oratorio in the Baroque Era* (Chapel Hill: University of North Carolina Press, 1977), 292–308. I have simply chosen to refer to the work using the term the scribe provided; that is, "little sacred opera."

45. Mario Praz, *Studies in Seventeenth-Century Imagery*, 2nd ed. (Rome: Edizioni di Storia e Letteratura, 1964), 169. For the background on emblem books and their contents, I am indebted to Praz, pp. 83–168 (chapter 3, "Profane and Sacred Love"). Descriptions (and sometimes pictures) of the specific emblems mentioned in this paragraph may be found on pp. 105, 111, 112, 114, 121, 136, 138, 148.

46. Ibid., 54.

47. The initials "L.M." appear on the title page and at the beginning of each act, intertwined with the large decorative initial and repeated in the upper right corner of the same folio (see fols. [1r], 33r, 67r). Plank says that they are proably those of the illuminator rather than the composer, although he does suggest that they might point to Leonardo Marsili, friend of the Chigi and archbishop of Siena in 1686; see "An Anonymous 'Operina Sacra' of 1686," 13. Although Marsili was musically knowledgeable, no documentary evidence uncovered thus far suggests that he had the ability or the time (during the first years of his reign as archbishop) to compose the operina.

48. See Carolyn Gianturco, "Evidence for a Late Roman School of Opera," *Music and Letters* 56 (1975): 5–14.

49. The number of keys used is small: G major, F major, and A minor predominate. The work opens and closes in G major, the key exploited the greatest number of times for arias and duets.

50. A detailed scene-by-scene formal analysis of the score is available in Plank, "An Anonymous 'Operina Sacra' of 1686."

51. For the dates the girls entered Campansi, see BAV, Archivio Chigi 1809, fols. 22r–26v; and ASS, Con. sopp. 1949, fol. 3r. Musical training for little girls was not uncommon during this period, and their expertise at a young age was often astonishing. Settimia Caccini was performing at the Florentine court by age eleven, and Francesca Caccini and Caterina Martinelli were considered virtuoso singers at age thirteen. See Suzanne G. Cusick, "Caccini, Francesca," and Susan Parisi, "Caccini, Settimia," *New Grove Dictionary of Opera*, 1:669–70, and Edmond Strainchamps, "The Life and Death of Caterina Martinelli: New Light on Monteverdi's 'Arianna,' " *Early Music History* 5 (1985): 157–64. Colleen Baade reports that an eleven-year-old girl who entered Toledo's convent of S. Clara in the seventeenth century could already play the organ, compose in five parts, realize accompaniments from a figured bass, and sight-sing vocal polyphony; see "Spanish Nun Musicians: Early Modern Career Girls?" presentation at the eighth Annual Meeting of the Society for Seventeenth-Century Music, Vermillion, South Dakota, 28 April 2000.

52. BAV, Fondo Chigi, MS Q.VI.84, fols. 17r–18v: "Divino Amore / se i gigli miei / riserbo a te / io non vorrei / tanto rigore / contro di me."

53. Ibid., fols. 19v–22v: "Al candor di puro giglio / provo il foco in mezzo al cor. / All'ardor d'intatto giglio / vinto cede il sacro Amor."

54. Ibid., fols. 2v–7v: "Sembra il mar sereno un dì / et alletta al navigar; / soffia il vento in un momento / e si cangia il regno infido / e dal lido chi ridendo si partì / vi ritorna a sospirar." ("The sea appears calm / and invites one to sail. / In a moment, the wind blows / and the untrustworthy kingdom changes / and whoever left the shore smiling / returns there sighing.")

55. Ibid., fols. 82v–84r: "La voce del cielo è incanto dell'alma, / combatte et abbatte un cor che repugna, / ma nella pugna virtù n'ha sempre il vanto, / Iddio la palma."

56. Ibid., fols. 47r–48r: "Se morto mi vuoi / contento sarò."

57. See Robert L. Garretson, *Conducting Choral Music*, 8th ed. (Upper Saddle River, NJ: Prentice Hall, 1998), 142.

58. Arias for soprano voices in Alessandro Scarlatti's *Gli equivoci nel sembiante* (1679) and *La Statira* (1690) frequently ascend to f" and g" and sometimes touch a" to show off

the brilliance of the high register. See *Gli equivoci nel sembiante*, ed. Frank A. D'Accone, *Operas of Alessandro Scarlatti*, vol. 7 (Cambridge: Harvard University Press, 1982), and *La Statira*, ed. William C. Holmes, *Operas of Alessandro Scarlatti*, vol. 9 (Cambridge: Harvard University Press, 1985).

59. "An Anonymous 'Operina Sacra' of 1686," 104.

60. "A Seventeenth-Century Franciscan Opera: Music for a Chigi Princess," *Franciscan Studies* 42 (1982): 186–87.

61. Identical DNA would explain why both twins were talented musicians.

62. BAV, Fondo Chigi, MS Q.VI.84, fols. 13v–16r: "Il bello diviso / in tanti sembianti / natura formò. / Un solo chi n'ama / chi un solo ne brama / goderlo non può."

63. ASS, Con. sopp. 1992, 2 right.

64. See chapter 5 for a more detailed account of Suor Colomba Tofanini's life.

65. BAV, Fondo Chigi, MS Q.VI.84, fols. 24r–v: "*Innocenza*: No, che soffrire non voglio più, troppo è noiosa la servitù. *Amor Divino*: Sì, che soffrire devi ancor più, troppo è noiosa la servitù."

66. See chapter 5.

67. *Right Thinking and Sacred Oratory in Counter-Reformation Rome* (Princeton: Princeton University Press, 1995), 119, 136, 189–90. I am grateful to Robert Holzer for bringing this work to my attention.

68. Murray Bradshaw, "Right Thinking, Spirituality, and the 'Representation of Soul and Body'," presentation at the Eighth Biennial Conference on Baroque Music, Exeter, England, 11 July 1998.

69. BAV, Fondo Chigi, MS Q.VI.84, fols. 88v–89r: "*Diletto*: Il Diletto è sol perfetto, *Innocenza*: L'Innocenza sol è vaga, *Amor Divino, Diletto, Innocenza*: quando l'Amor Divino i cori impiaga."

70. Ibid., fol. 54r.

71. Ibid., fol. 8r: "*Innocenza*: Diletto, amico mio! *Diletto*: Innocenza gradita! *Innocenza*: Tra queste mura e qual desio ti chiama?"

72. See BAV, Archivio Chigi 1809.

73. Ibid., fols. 51r–52v.

74. BAV, Fondo Chigi, MS Q.VI.84, fols. 75v–76r: "Il servire, l'obbedire al Amor quand'è divino, è gran dono del ciel, non del destino."

75. Innocence's first statement is a variation on the beginning of Psalm 41, a verse that the composer Della Ciaia used in a motet that may have been intended for monastic rites of passage. For more on this motet, see chapter 7. The librettist might also have had emblematic literature in mind, for both the image of a stag pierced by an arrow and that of a stag slaking its thirst at a spring appear in a well-known emblem book of the time; see Praz, *Seventeenth-Century Imagery*, 95–96.

76. BAV, Fondo Chigi, MS Q.VI.84, fols. 81v–82v; 84r–v: "*Innocenza*: Errai folle, il confesso, e qual cerva ferita io givo in traccia d'un fonte d'acqua viva et in selva romita, in foresta selvaggia qual delle sacre carte la sposa innamorata dell'amato ben andavo in traccia. . . . *Amor Divino*: Dunque, intendesti pure ch'esser devi bersaglio al dardo mio? *Innocenza*: Voglio così, così comanda Iddio. . . . *Amor Divino*: Dimmi dunque, mi giuri fedeltà, eterno amore? *Innocenza*: Sarà tuo questo core fin quanto duri a' cieli il moto, il raggio al re dell'ore."

77. Ibid., fols. 61r–v: "Credi a me che t'inganni. Alla città ritorna, ivi l'amor soggiorna ch'a te brama ferir il sen pudico."

78. Ibid., fols. 68r–v: "Ma donzella gentil, nel cui bel volto per man di brio vezzoso versa natura i rari suoi tesori, ami pur la città, fugga gli orrori."

79. Ibid., fol. 71v: "Alla città ritorna, di sue fughe pentita."

80. "An Anonymous 'Operina Sacra' of 1686," 98.

81. BAV, Fondo Chigi, MS Q.VI.84, fols. 67r–68r: "Mal accorta Innocenza, dunque fuggir volesti pellegrina da me torcere i passi? E l'Amore Divino ch'il moto arresta ai fiumi, al cielo, agl'astri, non può fermare il piede ai tuoi disastri? Erri fra le foreste, de le belve t'esponi al dente ingordo e fra nemici artigli non intendi o non vedi i tuoi perigli."

82. Ibid., fols. 55r–58r: "Bei giacinti, viole gradite, / rose care, amaranti vezzosi, / puri gigli, narcisi odorosi, / voi nel sen dolce piaga m'aprite."

83. See Bianconi and Walker, "Production, Consumption and Political Function," 252; Golzio, *Documenti artistici sul Seicento nell'Archivio Chigi*, 241–42.

84. "Production, Consumption, and Political Function," 252.

85. See figure 3. Fabio Chigi, Pope Alexander VII, had no children. Mario Chigi's only son was Cardinal Flavio Chigi, who was also childless. Gismondo, the only other brother to the Chigi pope, never married and left no heirs; see P. Sforza Pallavicino, *Della vita di Alessandro VII* (Prato, 1839), 26.

86. Golzio, *Documenti artistici sul Seicento nell'Archivio Chigi*, 203–7, 229.

Chapter 7

1. *Lamentationi sagre e motetti ad una voce col basso continuo del signor Alessandro Della Ciaia, nobil sanese e Accademico Filomato, opera seconda, raccolta e data in luce da Filippo Succhielli* (Venice: Alessandro Vincenti, 1650). The role Filippo Succhielli played in "bringing the works to light" is unclear.

2. Robert L. Kendrick, *Celestial Sirens: Nuns and their Music in Early Modern Milan* (Oxford: Clarendon Press, 1996), 137. I extend my warmest thanks to Professor Kendrick for bringing the Della Ciaia print to my attention.

3. ASS, MS A49, Tommaso Mocenni, "Raccolta di nomi di persone nobili battezzate in Siena nate da fameglie che sono esistenti nel presente anno 1713," vol. 2, fol. 104r, records 26 May 1600 as the date of Della Ciaia's baptism; baptism dates for his children are listed on fols. 106r–v. ASS, Gabella dei contratti 459, fol. 56v, preserves the date of Della Ciaia's marriage contract with Santi, who brought a higher-than-average dowry of 4,000 scudi to her union with a member of the ruling elite. ASS, Con. sopp. 3000, 40 right, shows the transfer of a financial contract from Alessandro to his son and heir Filippo in 1678.

4. *Lamentationi sagre e motetti*, dedication: "L'autore ha composto il presente libro non per professione, ma per sola vaghezza, quando glielo permettano (il che è di rado) gli affari gravissimi della sua casa."

5. See Carolyn Gianturco, "Della Ciaia, Azzolino Bernardino," *The New Grove Dictionary of Music and Musicians*, 2nd ed., 29 vols. (London: Macmillan, 2001), 7:170.

6. *Saints and Sinners: The Latin Musical Dialogue in the Seventeenth Century* (Oxford: Clarendon Press, 1992), 75. Noske provides a complete transcription of the piece on pp. 283–314 and discusses another work from the collection (again, with admiration) on pp. 86–87. See chapter 3 for a discussion and complete transcription of *Veni, veni soror nostra*, also from the *Sacri modulatus*.

7. See Isidoro Ugurgieri Azzolini, *Le pompe sanesi*, 2 vols. (Pistoia, 1649), 2:10–11; and Laura Buch, "Pecci, Desiderio," *New Grove Dictionary*, 2nd ed., 19:226.

8. *Madrigali a cinque voci, con basso continuo, opera prima* (Venice: Bartolomeo Magni, 1636). The dedication to Pecci begins: "Queste mie note che imparai a formare dalla dotta lingua di Vostra Signoria Eccellentissima tornano hora, quasi ecchi fortunati a risonare nelle di lei orecchie con devotissimi accenti." See note 3 for the source preserving the record of Della Ciaia's marriage.

9. I was not able to determine if Della Ciaia himself had sisters or aunts in convents. Of the six children born to Della Ciaia and his wife Sulpizia Santi, only one was female. If she survived to adulthood, the chances are good that her rich parents contracted a secular marriage for her. Della Ciaia's music thus cannot be linked to his own offspring.

10. ASS, Con. sopp. 3000, 40 left. The annuity was derived from an investment of 200 scudi. For more on Piccolomini, see chapter 5.

11. *Fragmentation and Redemption: Essays on Gender and the Human Body in Medieval Religion* (New York: Zone Books, 1991), 131.

12. See Conleth Kearns, trans. and ed., *The Life of Catherine of Siena by Raymond of Capua* (Wilmington, DE: Michael Glazier, 1980), 97, 186, 197, 201; Agostino Saba, *Federico Borromeo ed i mistici del suo tempo* (Florence: Leo S. Olschki, 1933), 184; Giuseppe Scapecchi, *Ragguaglio della vita della serva di Dio Suor Chiara Birelli* (Florence: Michele Nestenus and Antonmaria Borghigiani, 1712), 36, 51; BCS, MS K.XI.35, "Vita di Suor Colomba monaca in Campanzi," fol. 28v; and Ambrogio Caterino Spannocchi, *Vita della serva di Dio Suor Rosa Maria Generali* (Venice: Andrea Poleti, 1722), 116–23. For more on these women's lives, see chapter 5.

13. See BCS, MS G.XI.3: "Vita di Christo con una breve contemplatione del Crocifisso fatta per poter contemplare brevemente tutta la vita di Christo per potersi preparare con humiltà et devotione alla consagra et sponsalitio dello sposo Giesù Christo per le monache di Santa Chaterina;" and BCS, MS G.IX.8, "Intelligenze di misterii della Passione di Giesù." On the cover of the latter manuscript, whose text is attributed to Suor Domitilla, a Capuchin sister of Pavia, is a rubric showing that it once belonged to the nuns at Santuccio.

14. See ASS, Con. sopp. 2841 (S. Monaca), fols. 38r–v; and Con. sopp. 1038 (S. Abbondio), unn. fols. The account of Christ washing his disciples' feet is related in John 13:2–11.

15. ASS, Con. sopp. 3589, fol. 8r: "La domenica del ulivo dare le palme al populo et fare dire il passio et la settimana santa le solite cerimonie di mattutini, passi, et altro che si sogliono fare in simili giorni."

16. *Ristretto de' decreti e degl'ordini fatti per li monasteri delle monache dall' Illustrissimo e Reverendissimo Monsignor Ascanio Piccolomini d'Aragona, Arcivescovo di Siena X* (Siena: Bonetti, 1666), 11: "Ne' giorni di Mercoledì, Giovedì, e Venerdì santo all'Ave Maria della sera le monache habbiano terminato l'Offitio e la chiesa rimanga serrata."

17. See Hans Joachim Marx, "Monodische Lamentationen des Seicento," *Archiv für Musikwissenschaft* 28 (1971): 5–6.

18. For references to Archilei, see Murray C. Bradshaw, ed., *Emilio de' Cavalieri: The Lamentations and Responsories of 1599 and 1600*, Publications of the American Institute of Musicology, Miscellanea 5, vol. 3 (Neuhausen-Stuttgart: Hänssler-Verlag, 1990), XXXVI. The activities of Archilei and the Caccini sisters are recorded in documents transcribed by Angelo Solerti, *Musica, ballo e drammatica alla Corte Medicea dal 1600 al 1637* (Florence, 1905; reprint ed., New York: Benjamin Blom, 1968), 58, 64, 85, 129, 144, 154, 158, 184–85.

19. Lesson 1 of Maundy Thursday, Lesson 3 of Good Friday, and Lesson 1 of Holy Saturday are all scored for soprano and basso continuo. Nuns with low voices might also have been able to perform the *altus* setting of Lesson 2 for Maundy Thursday.

20. *Celestial Sirens,* 137 n. 56. See also Gabriella Zarri, "Monasteri femminili e città (secoli XV–XVIII)," in *Storia d'Italia, annali 9: La Chiesa e il potere politico dal Medioevo all'età contemporanea,* ed. Giorgio Chittolini and Giovanni Miccoli (Turin: Giulio Einaudi, 1986), 394. A number of late seventeenth- and early-eighteenth-century Lamentation settings for nuns are found in Neapolitan archives; see Dinko Fabris, "Dal Medioevo al decennio francese e oltre. Continuità e metamorfosi nella tradizione napoletana," presen-

tation at the conference "Produzione, circolazione e consumo: Per una mappa della musica sacra dal tardo Medioevo al primo Seicento," Venice, Italy, Fondazione Ugo e Olga Levi, 28–30 October 1999.

21. "Dalla profezia alla disciplina (1450–1650)," in *Donna e fede: Santità e vita religiosa in Italia*, ed. Lucetta Scaraffia and Gabriella Zarri (Bari: Editori Laterza, 1994), 208: "trasformare i monasteri di monache in luoghi protetti, isolati dal mondo esterno con chiavistelli e grate, resi sempre più gradevoli all'interno per gli ampiamenti degli edifici e l'estensione di cortili e giardini che, a compensazione di una guardinga clausura, fossero in grado di fornire all'immaginario monastico e cittadino la riproduzione in terra del giardino dell'Eden e della Gerusalemme celeste."

22. See *Celestial Sirens*, 162, and Craig A. Monson, *Disembodied Voices: Music and Culture in an Early Modern Italian Convent* (Berkeley: University of California Press, 1995), 89.

23. From Lesson 1 on Maundy Thursday. The translation is from *The Hours of the Divine Office in English and Latin*, 3 vols. (Collegeville, MN: Liturgical Press, 1963), 2: 1106–7. All of the translations of Lamentations cited in the text are based on this source (see 2:1106–9; 1133–35; and 1156–59). In some cases, however, I have altered the translations slightly to reflect more literally the meaning of the text.

24. From Lesson 3, Good Friday; see *The Hours of the Divine Office*, 2:1135.

25. A helpful introduction to the subject may be found in Gail Holst-Warhaft, *Dangerous Voices: Women's Laments and Greek Literature* (London: Routledge, 1992), 1–39. See also Paul C. Rosenblatt, R. Patricia Walsh, and Douglas A. Jackson, *Grief and Mourning in Cross-cultural Perspective* ([New Haven]: HRAF Press, 1976), 1–2, 17, 22–23; Elizabeth Tolbert, "Magico-Religious Power and Gender in the Karelian Lament," in *Music, Gender and Culture*, ed. Marcia Herndon and Susanne Ziegler (Wilhelmshaven: Florian Noetzel Verlag, 1990), 41–56; and Susan Auerbach, "From Singing to Lamenting: Women's Musical Role in a Greek Village," in *Women and Music in Cross-cultural Perspective*, ed. Ellen Koskoff (New York: Greenwood Press, 1987), 25–43.

26. Robert Davidsohn, *Storia di Firenze*, 5 vols. (Berlin, 1896–1927; transl. by Giovanni Battista Klein, Florence: Sansoni, 1972), 1:1129–30; 4, pt. 3, 708; John Henderson, "Religious Confraternities and Death in Early Renaissance Florence," in *Florence and Italy: Renaissance Studies in Honour of Nicolai Rubenstein*, ed. Peter Denley and Caroline Elam (London: Westfield College, University of London, 1988), 386; Sharon Strocchia, "Death Rites and the Ritual Family in Renaissance Florence," in *Life and Death in Fifteenth-Century Florence*, ed. Marcel Tetel, Ronald G. Witt, and Rona Goffen (Durham, NC: Duke University Press, 1989), 126. So powerful was the association of death and lamenting women in Northern Italian urban centers that the custom was incorporated into popular, public processions commemorating the burial of Christ on Good Friday. Although women's laments had an impact on the texts incorporated into the processions, the women's roles were, ironically enough, appropriated by the male clergy. See Donald G. La Salle, Jr., "Liturgical and Popular Lament: A Study of the Role of Lament in Liturgical and Popular Religious Practices of Good Friday in Northern Italy from the Twelfth to the Sixteenth Centuries," (Ph.D. diss., Catholic University of America, 1997), 172–93. For a stunning visual representation of women's emotional expressions "as they acted out the ritual grief of the community" over the death of Christ, see Randi Klebanoff, "Passion, Compassion, and the Sorrows of Women: Niccolò dell'Arca's *Lamentation over the Dead Christ* for the Bolognese Confraternity of Santa Maria della Vita," in *Confraternities and the Visual Arts in Renaissance Italy, Ritual, Spectacle, Image*, ed. Barbara Wisch and Diane Cole Ahl (Cambridge, UK: Cambridge University Press, 2000), 146–68.

27. Strocchia, "Death Rites," 126–27.

28. Angelomichele De Spirito, "La comunicazione tra i vivi e i morti: Preliminari e fonti di una ricerca antropologica," *Ricerche di storia sociale e religiosa*, n.s. 11 (1982): 295.

29. *Histories of a Plague Year: The Social and the Imaginary in Baroque Florence*, trans. Dario Bocca and Bryant T. Ragan, Jr. (Berkeley: University of California Press, 1989), 104–8. Giovanni Boccaccio describes a similar abandonment of traditional funeral customs for victims of the Black Death: "Few indeed were those to whom the lamentations and bitter tears of their relatives were accorded"; *The Decameron*, trans. G. H. McWilliam (London: Penguin Books, 1972), 55. See also Strocchia, *Death and Ritual in Renaissance Florence* (Baltimore: The Johns Hopkins University Press, 1992), 57–59.

30. Ernesto De Martino, *Morte e pianto rituale nel mondo antico: Dal lamento pagano al pianto di Maria* (Turin: Edizioni Scientifiche Einaudi, 1958), 322–30; Holst-Warhaft, *Dangerous Voices*, 3–4.

31. For example, when Ognissanti's famous theorbo-playing nun, Maria Francesca Piccolomini, was on the point of death, both her biographer, Padre Sebastiano Conti, and the convent's regular confessor, Ermonide Bardi, were with her; see AAS, 3747, fol. 173r. Books of *licenze* from convents are filled with frequent requests for confessors to assist dying nuns.

32. See Claus Westermann, *Lamentations: Issues and Interpretation*, trans. Charles Muenchow (Minneapolis: Augsburg Fortress, 1994), 1–11.

33. For reasons of consistency, I am limiting my comparison of Della Ciaia's works to Gregori's three cantus settings only.

34. Günther Massenkeil, "Lamentations," *New Grove Dictionary*, 2nd ed., 14:188, cites Osee 14:1; the Vulgate assigns the phrase to the second verse. See *Biblia sacra iuxta vulgatam versionem*, 3rd emended ed. (Stuttgart: Deutsche Bibelgesellschaft, 1983), 1384.

35. Falsobordone passages may be found in Lamentations settings beginning in the 1580s. Gregori was doubtless influenced by Cavalieri's incorporation of the practice in his settings of 1600; see John Bettley, "*La compositione lacrimosa*: Musical Style and Text Selection in North-Italian Lamentations Settings in the Second Half of the Sixteenth Century," *Journal of the Royal Musical Association* 118 (1993): 181–83.

36. Massenkeil, "Lamentations," 188.

37. "Quomodo obscuratum est aurum, mutatus est color optimus."

38. "In tenebrosis collocavit me, quasi mortuos sempiternos."

39. It is possible that the composer was influenced by his older countryman and fellow aristocrat-composer Claudio Saracini; see Éva Pintér, *Claudio Saracini: Leben und Werk*, 2 vols. (Frankfurt: Peter Lang, 1992), 1:223–30.

40. "Parvuli petierunt panem, et non erat qui frangeret eis."

41. Massenkeil, "Lamentations," 189.

42. Bynum, *Fragmentation and Redemption*, 119–31, and *Holy Feast and Holy Fast: The Religious Significance of Food to Medieval Women* (Berkeley: University of California Press, 1987), 172–74.

43. See Alison Weber, *Teresa of Avila and the Rhetoric of Femininity* (Princeton: Princeton University Press, 1990), 42–76.

44. "O dulcissime Domine Iesu, quanta est dulcedo devotis [*sic*] animae tecum epulantis in convivio tuo ubi ei non alius cibus manducandus proponitur nisi tu, unicus dilectus eius super omnia desideria cordis eius desiderabilis. O quam suave et iucundum convivium cum te ipsum in cibum donasti! O quam admirabilis operatio tua, Domine! O quam potens virtus tua! O quam ineffabilis veritas tua! O cor plusquam lapideum quomodo amore non ardes de hoc sacramento? Adeamus ergo cum fiducia ad admirabile sacramentum ut misericordiam consequamur. Venite omnes ad cenam magnam quia parata sunt omnia."

45. See chapter 3. *Ecce venio ad te, Domine* was used in profession ceremonies for a

number of different orders. See AAS, 3739; and Jutta Gisela Sperling, *Convents and the Body Politic in Late Renaissance Venice* (Chicago: University of Chicago Press, 1999), 139.

46. "Ecce venio ad te, Domine Deus meus. Respice ergo et miserere mei, quia dolores cordis mei multiplicati sunt. Heu mihi, quam sero venio ad te, Domine! Heu, quam tarde festino! Heu me, quia curro post vulnera! Dilexisti me unice, amor meus, ante quam diligerem te, et ad imaginem tuam creasti me. Veni, veni, et noli tardare. Apprehende arma et scutum et exurge in adiutorium mihi."

47. See Kendrick, *Celestial Sirens*, 380 n. 15.

48. "Cognoscam te, Domine, cognitor meus; cognoscam te, virtus animae meae. . . . Appareat mihi delectatio mea magna, solatium meum dulce, Domine Deus meus, vita mea, et gloria tota animae meae. O vita cui omnia vivunt, quae das mihi vitam, quae es mea vita, per quam vivo, sine qua morior . . . Prope esto in animo, prope in corde, prope in ore, prope in auribus, prope in auxilio, quia amore langueo. Nolo vivere, volo mori, dissolvi cupio et esse cum Christo."

49. "Quam dilecta tabernacula tua, Domine virtutum! Concupiscit et deficit anima mea in atria Domini; cor meum et caro mea exultaverunt in Deum vivum. Iubila, anima mea, et ad celestem patriam festinanter propera quia in illa Deum videbis et habebis in aeternum. . . . Beati qui habitant in domo tua, Domine. Omnis terra adoret te et psalmum dicat nomini tuo. Venite gentes et exultate Deo salutari nostro. Iubilate Deo Jacob, sumite psalmum et date tympana, psalterium iucundum cum cithara."

50. In Venice, the entire text of Psalm 41 was recited during clothing ceremonies; see Sperling, *Convents and the Body Politic*, 137–38.

51. "Quemadmodum desiderat cervus ad fontes aquarum, ita desiderat anima mea ad te, Deus. O fons vitae, vena aquarum viventium, quando veniam ad aquas dulcedinis tuae? Aperi penetralia aurium mearum ut audiam vocem tuam. . . . Felix anima quae terreno resoluta carcere libera celum petit. Quae cantica, quae organa, quae melodiae ibi sine fine decantantur! Sonant ibi semper melliflua hymnorum organa, suavissima angelorum melodia. . . . Pulcherrime Iesu Christe, da mihi cordis contritionem et lacrymarum fontem dum praeces et orationes tibi offero. Audi clamantem, Domine, de hoc mari magno et adduc me ad portum felicitatis aeternae."

52. See chapter 2.

53. See Ex. 7.16, mm. 75–76.

54. See Kendrick, *Celestial Sirens*, 391.

55. The second stanza of *Deus tuorum militum* reads as follows: "Hic nempe mundi gaudia, / et blanda fraudum pabula, / imbuta felle deputans, / pervenit ad caelestia." See the *Liber usualis* (Paris: Desclée, 1964), 1126.

56. In the translation, line 2 is from Psalm 70:23; line 3 from Psalm 67:36; line 5 from Psalm 53:8; line 7 from Joel 2:1 and Psalm 80:3; line 8 from Psalm 104:2.

57. "Gaudens gaudedo in Domino et exultabunt labia mea cum cantavero gloriam eius qui est mirabilis in sanctis suis. Laudans laudabo et invocabo Dominum et confitebor nomini sancto eius qui hodie Beatum N. ad celestia regna convocavit. Canite tuba in Sion, pulsate tympana bene sonantia, vocate gentes et annuntiate mirabilia eius. Exultant angeli, gaudent archangeli et universa gratulatur Ecclesia quia hodie Beatus N. coronatus in celis cum angelis triumphat."

58. "Gaude, gaude mater Ecclesia, laeta agens memoriam quae novae prolis gaudia, mittis ad celi curiam. Iste est beatus N., quasi stella matutina in medio nebulae, et quasi luna plena in diebus suis, et quasi sol refulgens in templo Dei. . . . Filiae Ierusalem, venite et videte, beatum N. cum coronis, quibus coronavit eum Dominus, in die solemnitatis et laetitiae."

59. Craig Monson draws a parallel between melismas and ecstatic rapture in music

by the nun composer Vizzana; see *Disembodied Voices*, 98, 103. For more on Vannini, see chapter 5.

60. "Ite celestes, ite, Jerusalem sodales, et laudes immortales cantate mecum omnes Regi vitae, qui fortem Christi ducem exaltavit, et athletam coronavit."

61. I am grateful to Professor Jeffrey Kurtzman, who helped me sort out the possibilities for interpreting the relationship between duple and triple passages in Della Ciaia's compositions. The triple passage beginning at m. 109 and notated in 3/4 in my transcription appears in the original print under a time signature of 3, in black notation (that is, with three black minims grouped into a single measure, over a black, dotted semibreve). The meaning of the text at this point in the motet leads me to believe that Della Ciaia chose the notation in order to prompt the singer to launch into the quickest triple meter possible, as advocated by Frescobaldi in the preface to his *Capricci* of 1624; see Étienne Darbellay, "Tempo Relationships in Frescobaldi's *Primo libro di capricci*," in *Frescobaldi Studies*, ed. Alexander Silbiger (Durham, NC: Duke University Press, 1987), 301–2, 320–21.

62. As already mentioned, the first hymnlike stanza is a variation on stanza 2 of the hymn for the feast of a martyr, *Deus tuorum militum*. The motet also includes lines from the hymn used at Vespers on the feast of the Resurrection (*Ad cenam Agni providi*).

63. See chapter 3.

64. "Ad celestem Ierusalem cum venisset N., facta subito vox est comitantium angelorum, et dixerunt: Celestis aulae principes, portas vestras attollite, et triumphator nobilis intrabit, victis inferis, coronandus in aethera. . . . Hic dulce mentem pabulo, orationis nutriens, cibis supernis inhians, ieiuna membra detulit. Ad cenam Agni providi, in qua ministrant angeli, veni, veni, veni, veni, epulaberis. . . . Age, age nunc canora, turba celitum decora, quantum potes, quantum audes, immortali Regi laudes, modulare et letare, in canticis et cytharis, et chordis et psalterio."

Appendix 2

1. See chapter 5, note 60, for a description of the manuscript and its peculiarities of foliation.

2. The statue was more commonly referred to as the "Madonna del Presepio."

3. At this point in the text, a note appears in the left margin: "Nota che per maggior testimonianza di tal miracoloso risanamento, molti mesi dopo la morte di Donna Maria Francesca si è trovato nel sepolcro il di lei cadavero tutto corrotto fuor che la mano col suo braccio sinistro."

4. At this point in the text, a note appears in the right margin: "Portolla il signor canonico Bardi confessore di quel monistero."

5. At this point in the text, a note appears in the left margin: "tra le hore 21 e 22 in venerdì."

Appendix 3

1. See chapter 5, note 60, for a description of the manuscript and its peculiarities of foliation.

2. The word "regolari" is inserted above "religiosi."

3. The words "La predetta signora sua" written in the margin to replace a line of words now scratched out and illegible.

4. The illegible word was obviously the name of the cited "signora"; it is now scratched out and illegible.

5. In the right margin, the following passage—"la quale sapeva ella essere sì propria

della Vergine sua Signora, che di essa unicamente si pregia nel famoso suo cantico. Perciò oltre il chiedere al Signore questa virtù istantissimamente ogni mattina, aborriva anzi abominava ogni propria"—was added to replace the portion of text beginning at "la qual virtù" and ending at "abominava."

6. In the left margin appears this addition: "nella mera diversità del colore."

7. In the right margin, the following phrase is added: "ed in altra occasione toltole lo spasimo et il tremore del braccio destro, finalmente si accertò, etc."

8. In the left margin the words "quel riverente suo ossequio" are meant to replace "tal dono."

9. These words are added in the left margin: "allhora sana e vigorosa."

10. At this point, a long passage appears in the right margin: "Un'altra persona regolare agitata per gran tempo da grave tentatione con indicibile amarezza del suo spirito, mi ha scritto tre mesi in circa dopo la morte di Donna Maria Francesca, che in raccomandarsi a lei non solamente svanisce detta tentatione, ma di più è solita sentirsi subbito agevolare qualunque difficoltà e ripugnanza, che le s'incontri nella vita Religiosa. È vero etc."

11. Note added in right margin: "Notisi che Donna Maria Francesca mentre visse mostrò spesso uno straordinario timore del giudizio da farsi della sua anima nel punto della morte."

12. The words "Donna Caterina sua sorella" badly scratched out in the manuscript for reasons unknown.

13. A long marginal note appears beginning at the bottom of 13r and continues on the bottom of 12v: "Molte del medesimo monistero affermano di haver udito da Donna Maria Elena Benvoglienti (la quale non molto sopravisse alla nostra felice defonta e fu sempre in gran concetto di perfetione) che mentre una mattina orava in choro, vidde all'altar maggiore Donna Maria Francesca di volto e di habito vaghissimo e risplendente. Certo è che Suor Maria Nicola con ogni assicuranza a me stesso ha attestato che mentre una mattina a giorno già chiaro essa salì alla loggietta contigua alle stanze ch'erano di Donna Maria Francesca, chiaramente la vidde vicina a certi vasi di gelsomini ridente in viso e vestita a quella guisa che sogliono tal volta vestirsi da angelo le fanciulle, ma in voler correre ad essa, le disparve dagli occhi." In the marginal note, the name of Suor Maria Nicola is scratched out and replaced by "un'antica compagna dell'amantissima Donna Maria Francesca." The second time the name of Donna Maria Francesca appears, it is replaced by "già di questa felice defonta."

SELECTED BIBLIOGRAPHY

I. Early Printed Sources

Decreti e costitutioni generali dell'Illustrissimo e Reverendissimo Monsignore Alessandro Petrucci Arcivescovo di Siena per il buon governo delle monache della sua città e diocesi. Siena: Hercole Gori, 1625.

Della Ciaia, Alessandro. *Lamentationi sagre e motetti ad una voce col basso continuo, opera seconda, raccolta e data in luce da Filippo Succhielli.* Venice: Alessandro Vincenti, 1650.

Gregori, Annibale. *Cantiones ac sacrae lamentationes singulis vocibus concinendae cum basso continuo, opus V.* Siena, 1620.

Ordinazioni e decreti per li monasteri delle monache della città e diocesi di Siena. Fabio Piccolomini Proposto della Metropolitana e Vicario generale dell'Illustrissimo et Reverendissimo Monsignore Camillo Borghesi, Arcivescovo di Siena settimo. Siena: Luca Bonetti, 1608.

Ragguaglio della vita della serva di Dio Suor Chiara Birelli della Congregazione dell'Abbandonate di Siena disteso dal P. Giuseppe Scapecchi della Compagnia di Giesù. Florence: Michele Nestenus and Antonmaria Borghigiani, 1712.

Relatione della general processione fatta in Siena nella domenica in Albis MDCIL dalle venerabili compagnie della medesima città il dì 11 d'aprile nella quale con solenne pompa fu portata l'insigne reliquia della sacra testa di S. Galgano Guidotti di Chiusdino nobil sanese. Siena: Bonetti, 1649.

Relazione della miracolosa Madonna del Presepio che si conserva dalle monache benedettine aggreggate alla congregazione olivetana nel venerabile monistero di Ogni Santi in Siena composta dal Padre Sebastiano Conti pistoiese della Compagnia di Giesù. Siena. Stamperia del Publico [1668].

Ristretto de' decreti e degl'ordini fatti per li monasteri delle monache dall'Illustrissimo e Reverendissimo Monsignore Ascanio Piccolomini d'Aragona Arcivescovo di Siena X. Siena: Bonetti, 1666.

Spannocchi, Ambrogio Caterino, ed. *Vita della serva di Dio Suor Rosa Maria Generali monaca conversa del Terz'Ordine di S. Domenico nel monastero di Santa Caterina da Siena, detto il Paradiso, nella città di Siena, raccolta da una religiosa del medesimo monastero d'ordine de' suoi superiori.* Venice: Andrea Poleti, 1722.

Ugurgieri Azzolini, Isidoro. *Le pompe sanesi o vero relazione delli huomini e donne illustri di Siena e suo Stato.* 2 vols. Pistoia, 1649.

273

Vita de' gloriosi santi martiri Abbondio e Abbondantio con l'inventione e translatione de' corpi loro. Siena: Salvestro Marchetti, 1616.

Vita della venerabile Madre Passitea Crogi senese fondatrice del monasterio delle religiose cappuccine nella città di Siena. Rome: Filippo Maria Mancini, 1669.

II. Literature

[Alvise, E.]. *Commedia di dieci vergine.* Florence: Libreria Dante, 1882.

Anson, John. "The Female Transvestite in Early Monasticism: The Origin and Development of a Motif." *Viator* 5 (1974): 1–32.

Archivio di Stato di Siena: Guida-Inventario. 2 vols. Pubblicazioni degli Archivi di Stato, 5– 6. Rome: Ministero dell'Interno, 1951.

Arenal, Electa, and Stacey Schlau. " 'Leyendo yo y escribiendo ella': The Convent as Intellectual Community." *Journal of Hispanic Philology* 13 (1989): 214–29.

———. *Untold Sisters: Hispanic Nuns in Their Own Words.* Albuquerque: University of New Mexico Press, 1989.

Baade, Colleen. "Spanish Nun Musicians: Early Modern Career Girls?" Presentation at the Eighth Annual Meeting of the Society for Seventeenth-Century Music, Vermillion, South Dakota, 28 April 2000.

Baker, George R. F. "Nobiltà in declino: Il caso di Siena sotto i Medici e gli Asburgo-Lorena." *Rivista storica italiana* 84 (1972): 584–616.

Barbieri, Nello. "Note di cronologia: Le ore a Siena dal XIV al XVIII secolo." *BSSP* 90 (1983): 148–51.

Barzman, Karen-edis. "Cultural Production, Religious Devotion and Subjectivity in Early Modern Italy: The Case Study of Maria Maddalena de' Pazzi." *Annali d'italianistica: Women Mystic Writers* 13 (1995): 283–305.

Belcari, Feo. *Vita del Beato Giovanni Colombini da Siena.* Edited by Rodolfo Chiarini. Lanciano: R. Carabba Editore, 1914.

Bettley, John. "*La compositione lacrimosa*: Musical Style and Text Selection in North-Italian Lamentations Settings in the Second Half of the Sixteenth Century." *Journal of the Royal Musical Association* 118 (1993): 167–202.

Bianconi, Lorenzo. *Music in the Seventeenth Century.* Translated by David Bryant. Cambridge, UK: Cambridge University Press, 1987.

Bianconi, Lorenzo, and Thomas Walker. "Dalla *Finta pazza* alla *Veremonda*: Storie di Febiarmonici." *Rivisita italiana di musicologia* 10 (1975): 379–454.

———. "Production, Consumption and Political Function of Seventeenth-Century Italian Opera." *Early Music History* 4 (1984): 209–96.

Borghesi, Scipione and Luciano Banchi. *Nuovi documenti per la storia dell'arte senese.* Siena: Enrico Torrini, 1898; reprint ed., Soest: Davaco, 1970.

Bradshaw, Murray C., ed. *Emilio de' Cavalieri: The Lamentations and Responsories of 1599 and 1600.* Publications of the American Institute of Musicology, Miscellanea 5. Vol. 3. Neuhausen-Stuttgart: Hänssler-Verlag, 1990.

———. "Right Thinking, Spirituality, and the 'Representation of Soul and Body.' " Presentation at the Eighth Biennial Conference on Baroque Music, Exeter, England, 11 July 1998.

Brandi, Cesare ed. *Palazzo Pubblico di Siena: Vicende costruttive e decorazione.* Milan: Silvana Editoriale, 1983.

Burke, Peter. *Popular Culture in Early Modern Europe.* London: Temple Smith, 1978.

Butzek, Monika, ed. *Il Duomo di Siena al tempo di Alessandro VII: Carteggio e disegni (1658– 1667).* Die Kirchen von Siena. Supplement 2. Munich: Bruckmann, 1996.

Bynum, Caroline Walker. *Fragmentation and Redemption: Essays on Gender and the Human Body in Medieval Religion.* New York: Zone Books, 1991.

————. *Holy Feast and Holy Fast: The Religious Significance of Food to Medieval Women.* Berkeley: University of California Press, 1987.

Cabibbo, Sara, and Marilena Modica. *La santa dei Tomasi: Storia di Suor Maria Crocifissa (1645–1699).* Microstorie 17. Turin: Giulio Einaudi, 1989.

Calocchi, Silvia. "Musica e feste in Siena durante il governatorato del Principe Mattias de' Medici (1629–1667)." Tesi di laurea, Università degli Studi di Siena, 1988–89.

Calvi, Giulia. *Histories of a Plague Year: The Social and the Imaginary in Baroque Florence.* Translated by Dario Bocca and Bryant T. Ragan, Jr. Berkeley: University of California Press, 1989.

Castellini, Alessandro. "Il Cardinale Francesco Maria Tarugi Arcivescovo di Siena." *BSSP* 50 (1943): 88–109.

Cattaneo, Enrico. "Le monacazioni forzate fra Cinque e Seicento." In *Vita e processo di Suor Virginia Maria de Leyva, monaca di Monza,* 147–95. Milan: Garzanti Editore, 1985.

Catoni, Giuliano. "Interni di conventi senesi del Cinquecento." *Ricerche storiche* 10 (1980): 171–203.

Chiantini, Bruno et al. *Santa Petronilla: Eventi storici e vicende.* Roccastrada: Editrice "Il mio amico," 1995.

Coakley, John. "Friars as Confidants of Holy Women in Medieval Dominican Hagiography." In *Images of Sainthood in Medieval Europe,* edited by Renate Blumenfeld-Kosinski and Timea Szell, 222–46. Ithaca, NY: Cornell University Press, 1991.

Cochrane, Eric. *Florence in the Forgotten Centuries, 1527–1800.* Chicago: University of Chicago Press, 1973.

Cohen, Sherrill. *The Evolution of Women's Asylums since 1500: From Refuges for Ex-Prostitutes to Shelters for Battered Women.* New York: Oxford University Press, 1992.

Corso, Laura. "Relazioni fra Lorenzo Magalotti e Ascanio Piccolomini, arcivescovo di Siena (da un carteggio inedito)." *BSSP* 44 (1937): 335–64.

Creytons, Raymond. "La riforma dei monasteri femminili dopo i decreti tridentini." In *Il Concilio di Trento e la riforma tridentina: Atti del convegno storico internazionale, Trento 2–6 settembre 1963.* 2 vols. 1:45–84. Rome: Herder, 1965.

D'Accone, Frank A. *The Civic Muse: Music and Musicians in Siena during the Middle Ages and the Renaissance.* Chicago: University of Chicago Press, 1997.

————. *The History of a Baroque Opera: Alessandro Scarlatti's "Gli equivoci nel sembiante."* New York: Pendragon Press, 1985.

D'Ancona, Alessandro. *Origini del teatro italiano.* 2 vols. Turin, 1891; reprint ed., Rome: Bardi Editore, 1966.

————, ed. *Sacre rappresentazioni dei secoli XIV, XV, e XVI.* 3 vols. Florence: Le Monnier, 1872.

Darbellay, Étienne. "Tempo Relationships in Frescobaldi's *Primo Libro di Capricci.*" In *Frescobaldi Studies,* edited by Alexander Silbiger, 301–26. Durham, NC: Duke University Press, 1987.

Davidsohn, Robert. *Storia di Firenze.* 5 vols. Berlin, 1896–1927. Translated by Giovanni Battista Klein. Florence: Sansoni, 1972.

Del Cavalliere, Emilio. *Rappresentatione di anima, e di corpo.* Rome, 1600; facsimile ed., Franborough, UK: Gregg International, 1967.

Del Sera, Beatrice. *Amor di virtù: Commedia in cinque atti, 1548.* Edited by Elissa Weaver. Classici italiani minori 17. Ravenna: Longo Editore, 1990.

De Martino, Ernesto. *Morte e pianto rituale nel mondo antico: Dal lamento pagano al pianto di Maria.* Turin: Edizioni Scientifiche Einaudi, 1958.

De Spirito, Angelomichele. "La comunicazione tra i vivi e i morti. Preliminari e fonti di una ricerca antropologica." *Ricerche di storia sociale e religiosa*, n. s. 11 (1982): 293–318.

Dizionario biografico degli Italiani. 51 vols. Rome: Istituto dell'Enciclopedia Italiana, 1960–.

Dizionario degli Istituti di Perfezione. 9 vols. Rome, Edizioni Paoline, 1974–.

Donahue, Darcy. "Writing Lives: Nuns and Confessors as Auto/Biographers in Early Modern Spain." *Journal of Hispanic Philology* 13 (1989): 230–39.

Drake, Stillman. *Galileo*. Oxford: Oxford University Press, 1980.

Fabris, Dinko. "Dal Medioevo al decennio francese e oltre: Continuità e metamorfosi nella tradizione napoletana." Presentation at the conference "Produzione, circolazione e consumo: Per una mappa della musica sacra dal tardo Medioevo al primo Seicento," Venice, Italy, Fondazione Ugo e Olga Levi, 28–30 October 1999.

Fabris, Dinko. "Tre composizioni per liuto di Claudio Saracini e la tradizione del liuto a Siena tra Cinque e Seicento." *Il flauto dolce* 16 (April, 1987): 14–25.

Frittelli, Ugo. *Albero genealogico della nobil famiglia Chigi, patrizia senese*. Siena: Arti Grafiche Lazzeri, 1922.

Gianturco, Carolyn. "Caterina Assandra, suora compositrice." In *La musica sacra in Lombardia nella prima metà del Seicento, Atti del convegno internazionale di studi, Como, 31 maggio–2 giugno 1985*, edited by Alberto Colzani, Andrea Luppi, and Maurizio Padoan, 117–27. Como: Antiquae Musicae Italicae Studiosi, 1987.

———. "Evidence for a Late Roman School of Opera." *Music and Letters* 56 (1975): 4–17.

Gigli, Girolamo. *Diario sanese*. 3 vols. Lucca, 1723; 2nd ed., Siena: Tip. dell'Ancora di G. Landi e N. Alessandri, 1854; reprint ed., Bologna: Arnaldo Forni Editore, 1974.

Glixon, Beth L. "Private Lives of Public Women: Prima Donnas in Mid-Seventeenth-Century Venice." *Music and Letters* 76 (1995): 509–31.

Glixon, Jonathan. "Images of Paradise or Worldly Theaters? Toward a Taxonomy of Musical Performances at Venetian Nunneries." In *Essays on Music and Culture in Honor of Herbert Kellman*, edited by Barbara Haggh, 429–57. Paris: Éditions Klincksieck, 2001.

Golzio, Vincenzo. *Documenti artistici sul Seicento nell'Archivio Chigi*. Rome: Fratelli Palombi, 1939.

Greco, Gaetano. "Dopo il Concilio di Trento." In *Storia di Siena*, 3 vols., 2:25–40. Siena: ALSABA, 1996.

Grundy, Isobel. "Women's History? Writings by English Nuns." In *Women, Writing, History, 1640–1740*, ed. Isobel Grundy and Susan Wiseman, 126–38. Athens: University of Georgia Press, 1992.

Guglielmo Ebreo of Pesaro. *De Pratica Seu Arte Tripudii (On the Practice or Art of Dancing)*. Edited and translated by Barbara Sparti. Oxford: Clarendon Press, 1993.

Haar, James. "On Musical Games in the Sixteenth Century." *JAMS* 15 (1962): 22–34.

Hale, J. R. *Florence and the Medici: The Pattern of Control*. New York: Thames and Hudson, 1977.

Harness, Kelley. "*Regine dell'Arno*: Court Life in a Seventeenth-Century Florentine Convent." Presentation at the annual meeting of the American Musicological Society, Phoenix, AZ, 2 November 1997.

Haskell, Francis. *Patrons and Painters: A Study of the Relations between Italian Art and Society in the Age of the Baroque*. 2nd rev. ed. New Haven: Yale University Press, 1980.

Henderson, John. "Religious Confraternities and Death in Early Renaissance Florence." In *Florence and Italy: Renaissance Studies in Honour of Nicolai Rubenstein*, edited by Peter Denley and Caroline Elam, 383–94. London: Westfield College, University of London, 1988.

Holmes, William C. "Cesti's *L'Argia*: An Entertainment for a Royal Convert." *Chigiana* 26–27, n.s. 6–7 (1971): 35–52.

Holst-Warhaft, Gail. *Dangerous Voices: Women's Laments and Greek Literature*. London: Routledge, 1992.

Hook, Judith. *Siena: Una città e la sua storia*. Siena: Nuova immagine editrice, 1988.

The Hours of the Divine Office in English and Latin. 3 vols. Collegeville, MN: Liturgical Press, 1963.

Ilari, Lorenzo. *La Biblioteca pubblica di Siena disposta secondo le materie: Catalogo*. 7 vols. Siena: Tipografia dell'Insegna dell'Ancora, 1844–48.

Kearns, Conleth, ed. and trans. *The Life of Catherine of Siena by Raymond of Capua*. Wilmington, DE: Michael Glazier, 1980.

Kendrick, Robert L. *Celestial Sirens: Nuns and Their Music in Early Modern Milan*. Oxford: Clarendon Press, 1996.

———. "Genres, Generations, and Gender: Nuns' Music in Early Modern Milan, c. 1550–1706." Ph.D. diss., New York University, 1993.

———. " 'Sonet vox in auribus meis': Song of Songs Exegesis and the Seventeenth-Century Motet." *Schütz-Jahrbuch* 16 (1994): 99–118.

Kirkendale, Warren. *The Court Musicians in Florence during the Principate of the Medici*. Florence: Leo S. Olschki, 1993.

Klebanoff, Randi. "Passion, Compassion, and the Sorrows of Women: Niccolò dell'Arca's *Lamentation over the Dead Christ* for the Bolognese Confraternity of Santa Maria della Vita." In *Confraternities and the Visual Arts in Renaissance Italy: Ritual, Spectacle, Image*, edited by Barbara Wisch and Diane Cole Ahl, 146–72. Cambridge, UK: Cambridge University Press, 2000.

Krautheimer, Richard. *The Rome of Alexander VII, 1655–67*. Princeton: Princeton University Press, 1985.

La Salle, Donald G. "Liturgical and Popular Lament: A Study of the Role of Lament in Liturgical and Popular Religious Practices of Good Friday in Northern Italy from the Twelfth to the Sixteenth Centuries." Ph.D. diss., Catholic University of America, 1997.

Lazzareschi, Eugenio. "Una mistica senese: Passitea Crogi, 1564–1615." *BSSP* 22 (1915): 419–33; 23 (1916): 3–46; 25 (1918): 123–64.

Le Brun, Jacques. "L'institution et le corps, lieux de la mémoire: D'après le biographies spirituelles féminines du XVIIe siècle." *Corps écrit* 11 (1984): 111–21.

———. "Mutations de la notion de martyre au XVIIe siècle d'après les biographies spirituelles féminines." In *Sainteté et martyre dans les religions du livre*, edited by Jacques Marx, 77–90. Problèmes d'Histoire du Christianisme 19. Brussels: Éditions de l'Université de Bruxelles, 1989.

Lefevre, Renato. "Gli 'Sfaccendati.' " *Studi romani* 8 (1960): 154–65; 288–301.

Liberati, Alfredo. "Chiese, monasteri, oratori e spedali senesi: ricordi e notizie." *BSSP* 47 (1940): 162–65; 244–48; 251–54; 48 (1941): 73–80; 51–54 (1944–47): 130–36; 55 (1948): 122–28; 56 (1949): 149–53; 57 (1950): 131–36; 146–51; 62–63 (1955–56): 241–49.

———. "Le Gesuate di Vallepiatta." *BSSP* 40 (1933): 411–18.

———. "Monastero di Santa Margherita in Castelvecchio (Memorie storiche ed artistiche)." *BSSP* 41 (1934): 120–40.

Lionnet, Jean. "Les activités musicales de Flavio Chigi cardinal neveu d'Alexandre VII." *Studi musicali* 9 (1980): 287–302.

Liuzzi, Fernando. "Drammi musicali dei secoli XI–XIV. Part 1. Le vergini savie e le vergini folli." *Studi medievali*, n. s. 3 (1930): 82–109.

Malena, Adelisa. "Inquisizione, 'finte sante,' 'nuovi mistici.' Ricerche sul Seicento." In *Atti dei convegni Lincei 162. L'inquisizione e gli storici: un cantiere aperto, Roma 24–25 giugno 1999*, 289–306. Rome: Accademia Nazionale dei Lincei, 2000.

Marrara, Danilo. *Riseduti e nobiltà: Profilo storico-istituzionale di un'oligarchia toscana nei secoli XVI–XVIII*. Pisa: Pacini Editore, 1976.

Marx, Hans Joachim. "Monodische Lamentationen des Seicento." *Archiv für Musikwissenschaft* 28 (1971): 1–23.

Masetti Zannini, Gian Ludovico. "Documenti sulla musica sacra a Viterbo (1583–1692)." *Lunario Romano* 15 (1986): 309–24.

―――. *Motivi storici dell'educazione femminile (1500–1650). Vol. 1. Morale, religione, lettere, arte, musica*. Bari: Editorialebari, 1980.

―――. *Motivi storici dell'educazione femminile. Vol. 2. Scienza, lavoro, giuochi*. Naples: M. D'Auria Editore, 1982.

―――. " 'Suavità di canto' e 'purità di cuore': Aspetti della musica nei monasteri femminili romani." In *La Cappella musicale nell'Italia della Controriforma: Atti del Convegno internazionale di studi nel IV Centenario di fondazione della Cappella Musicale di S. Biagio di Cento, 13–15 ottobre 1989*, edited by Oscar Mischiati and Paolo Russo, 123–41. Florence: Leo S. Olschki, 1993.

Matter, E. Ann. "The Personal and the Paradigm: The Book of Maria Domitilla Galluzzi." In *The Crannied Wall: Women, Religion, and the Arts in Early Modern Europe*, edited by Craig A. Monson, 87–103. Ann Arbor: University of Michigan Press, 1992.

Mazzi, Curzio. *La Congrega dei Rozzi di Siena nel secolo XVI*. 2 vols. Florence: Le Monnier, 1882.

McGinnis, Frederick J. *Right Thinking and Sacred Oratory in Counter-Reformation Rome*. Princeton: Princeton University Press, 1995.

Menchi, Silvana Seidel. "Characteristics of Italian Anticlericalism." In *Anticlericalism in Late Medieval and Early Modern Europe*, edited by Peter A. Dykema and Heiko A. Oberman, 271–81. Leiden: E. J. Brill, 1993.

Mengozzi, Narciso. "Ascanio Piccolomini quinto Arcivescovo di Siena." *BSSP* 19 (1912): 249–353.

―――. "Il convento detto del Santuccio." *BSSP* 29 (1922): 3–53.

Metz, René. *La consécration des vierges dans l'église romaine: Étude d'histoire de la liturgie*. Bibliothèque de l'institut de droit canonique de l'Université de Strasbourg 4. Paris: Presses universitaires de France, 1954.

Misciattelli, Piero. *Caterina Vannini: Una cortigiana convertita senese e il cardinale Federigo Borromeo alla luce di un epistolario inedito*. Milan: Edizioni Fratelli Treves, 1932.

Molinari, Franco. "Visite pastorali dei monasteri femminili di Piacenza nel sec. XVI." In *Il Concilio di Trento e la riforma tridentina: Atti del convegno storico internazionale, Trento 2–6 settembre 1963*. 2 vols. 2:679–731. Rome: Herder, 1965.

Monson, Craig A. *Disembodied Voices: Music and Culture in an Early Modern Italian Convent*. Berkeley: University of California Press, 1995.

―――. "Disembodied Voices: Music in the Nunneries of Bologna in the Midst of the Counter-Reformation." In *The Crannied Wall: Women, Religion, and the Arts in Early Modern Europe*, edited by Craig Monson, 191–209. Ann Arbor: University of Michigan Press, 1992.

Montford, Kimberlyn. "Music in the Convents of Counter-Reformation Rome." Ph.D. diss., Rutgers University, 1999.

Mooney, Catherine M. "The Authorial Role of Brother A. in the Composition of Angela of Foligno's Revelations." In *Creative Women in Medieval and Early Modern Italy: A*

Religious and Artistic Renaissance, edited by E. Ann Matter and John Coakley, 34–63. Philadelphia: University of Pennsylvania Press, 1994.

Moscadelli, Stefano. "I Conservatorî riuniti femminili di Siena e il loro archivio." *BSSP* 95 (1988): 9–129.

Murata, Margaret. "Il Carnevale a Roma sotto Clemente IX Rospigliosi." *Rivista italiana di musicologia* 12 (1977): 83–99.

Myers, Kathleen. *Word from New Spain: The Spiritual Autobiography of Madre Maria de San José (1656–1719).* Hispanic Studies: Textual Research and Criticism 4. Liverpool: Liverpool University Press, 1993.

Nardi, Franco Daniele. "Aspetti della religiosità senese nell'età della Controriforma." Part 2. *BSSP* 94 (1987): 52–175.

———. "Matteo Guerra e la Congregazione dei Sacri Chiodi (secc. XVI–XVII): Aspetti della religiosità senese nell'età della Controriforma." *BSSP* 91 (1984): 12–148.

Noske, Frits. *Saints and Sinners: The Latin Musical Dialogue in the Seventeenth Century.* Oxford: Clarendon Press, 1992.

Pardi, Giuseppe. "La popolazione di Siena e del territorio senese attraverso i secoli." *BSSP* 30 (1923): 85–132.

Paschini, Pio. "I monasteri femminili in Italia nel '500." In *Problemi di vita religiosa in Italia nel Cinquecento. Atti del Convegno di storia della chiesa in Italia nel Cinquecento, Bologna, 2–6 settembre 1958,* 31–60. Padua: Editrice Antenore, 1960.

Pecci, Giovanni Antonio. *Storia del vescovado della città di Siena.* Lucca: Salvatore e Gian-Domenico Marescandoli, 1748.

Petrocchi, Massimo. *Roma nel Seicento.* Storia di Roma, 14. Bologna: Licinio Cappelli, 1970.

Pintér, Éva. *Claudio Saracini: Leben und Werk.* 2 vols. Frankfurt: Peter Lang, 1992.

Pirrotta, Nino. *Music and Theatre from Poliziano to Monteverdi.* Cambridge: Cambridge University Press, 1982.

Plank, Steven Eric. "Music for a Chigi Princess: A Study of an Anonymous 'Operina Sacra' of 1686." Ph.D. diss., Washington University, St. Louis, 1980.

———. "A Seventeenth-Century Franciscan Opera: Music for a Chigi Princess." *Franciscan Studies* 42 (1982): 180–89.

Praz, Mario. *Studies in Seventeenth-Century Imagery.* 2nd ed. Sussidi eruditi 16. Rome: Edizioni di Storia e Letteratura, 1964.

Pulci, Antonia. *Florentine Drama for Convent and Festival: Seven Sacred Plays.* Translated by James Wyatt Cook. Edited by James Wyatt Cook and Barbara Collier Cook. Chicago: University of Chicago Press, 1996.

Reardon, Colleen. *Agostino Agazzari and Music at Siena Cathedral, 1597–1641.* Oxford: Clarendon Press, 1993.

———. "*Insegniar la zolfa ai gittatelli:* Music and Teaching at Santa Maria della Scala, Siena, during the Late Sixteenth and Early Seventeenth Centuries." In *Musica Franca: Essays in Honor of Frank A. D'Accone,* edited by Irene Alm, Alyson McLamore, and Colleen Reardon, 119–38. Stuyvesant, NY: Pendragon Press, 1996.

———. "*Veni sponsa Christi:* Investiture, Profession and Consecration Ceremonies in Sienese Convents." *Musica Disciplina* 50 (1996): 271–97.

Roncaglia, Gino. " 'Il Tirinto' di B. Pasquini e i suoi 'intermezzi.' " *Rassegna musicale* 4 (1931): 331–39.

Rosand, Ellen. *Opera in Seventeenth-Century Venice: The Creation of a Genre.* Berkeley: University of California Press, 1991.

Saba, Agostino. *Federico Borromeo ed i mistici del suo tempo con la vita e la corrispondenza inedita di Caterina Vannini.* Florence: Leo S. Olschki Editore, 1933.

Scott, Karen. "Urban Spaces, Women's Networks and the Lay Apostolate in Siena of Catherine Benincasa." In *Creative Women in Medieval and Early Modern Italy: A Religious and Artistic Renaissance*, edited by E. Ann Matter and John Coakley, 105–19. Philadelphia: University of Pennsylvania Press, 1994.

Settecento monastico italiano: Atti del I Convegno di studi storici sull'Italia benedettina, Cesena, 9–12 settembre 1986. Edited by Giustino Farnedi and Giovanni Spinelli. Cesena: Badia S. Maria del Monte, 1990.

Silbiger, Alexander. "The Roman Frescobaldi Tradition, c. 1640–1670." *JAMS* 33 (1980): 42–87.

Smither, Howard E. *A History of the Oratorio*. Vol. 1. *The Oratorio in the Baroque Era*. Chapel Hill: University of North Carolina Press, 1977.

Solerti, Angelo. *Musica, ballo e drammatica alla Corte Medicea dal 1600 al 1637*. Florence, 1905; reprint ed., New York: Benjamin Blom, 1968.

Sperling, Jutta Gisela. *Convents and the Body Politic in Late Renaissance Venice*. Chicago: University of Chicago Press, 1999.

Strocchia, Sharon T. "Death Rites and the Ritual Family in Renaissance Florence." In *Life and Death in Fifteenth-Century Florence*, edited by Marcel Tetel, Ronald G. Witt, and Rona Goffen, 120–45. Durham, NC: Duke University Press, 1989.

Surtz, Ronald E. *Writing Women in Late Medieval and Early Modern Spain: The Mothers of Saint Teresa of Avila*. Philadelphia: University of Pennsylvania Press, 1995.

Tilmouth, Michael. "Music on the Travels of an English Merchant: Robert Bargrave (1628–61)." *Music and Letters* 53 (1972): 143–59.

Waddy, Patricia. *Seventeenth-Century Roman Palaces: Use and Art of the Plan*. Cambridge: MIT Press, 1990.

Weaver, Elissa B. "Canti, suoni e balli nel teatro delle suore toscane." Presentation at International Association of Italian Literary Studies, University of Odense, Denmark, 1–5 July 1991.

———. "Convent Comedy and the World: The Farces of Suor Annalena Odaldi (1572–1638)." *Annali d'italianistica* 7 (1989): 182–92.

———. "The Convent Wall in Tuscan Convent Drama." In *The Crannied Wall: Women, Religion, and the Arts in Early Modern Europe*, edited by Craig A. Monson, 73–86. Ann Arbor: University of Michigan Press, 1992.

———. "Spasso spirituale, ovvero il gioco delle monache." In *Passare il tempo: La letteratura del gioco e dell'intrattenimento dal XII al XVI secolo: Atti del Convegno di Pienza 10–14 settembre 1991*. 2 vols. 1:351–71. Rome: Salerno Editrice, 1993.

———. "Spiritual Fun: A Study of Sixteenth-Century Tuscan Convent Theater." In *Women in the Middle Ages and the Renaissance: Literary and Historical Perspectives*, edited by Mary Beth Rose, 173–205. Syracuse, NY: Syracuse University Press, 1986.

———. "Suor Maria Clemente Ruoti, Playwright and Academician." In *Creative Women in Medieval and Early Modern Italy: A Religious and Artistic Renaissance*, edited by E. Ann Matter and John Coakley, 281–96. Philadelphia: University of Pennsylvania Press, 1994.

Weaver, Robert Lamar. "*Il Girello*, a Seventeenth-Century Burlesque Opera." *Quadrivium* 12 (1971): 141–63.

———. "Materiali per le biografie dei fratelli Melani." *Rivista italiana di musicologia* 12 (1977): 252–95.

Weber, Alison. *Teresa of Avila and the Rhetoric of Femininity*. Princeton: Princeton University Press, 1990.

Wegman, Rob C. "From Maker to Composer: Improvisation and Musical Authorship in the Low Countries, 1450–1600." *JAMS* 49 (1996): 409–79.

Westermann, Claus. *Lamentations: Issues and Interpretation*. Translated by Charles Muenchow. Minneapolis: Augsburg Fortress, 1994.

Yardley, Anne Bagnall. "The Marriage of Heaven and Earth: A Late Medieval Source of the *Consecratio virginum*." *Current Musicology* 45–47 (1990): 305–24.

Zarri, Gabriella. "Dalla profezia alla disciplina (1450–1650)." In *Donna e fede: Santità e vita religiosa in Italia*, edited by Lucetta Scaraffia and Gabriella Zarri, 177–225. Bari: Editori Laterza, 1994.

———. "Le istituzioni dell'educazione femminile." In *Le sedi della cultura nell'Emilia-Romagna. I secoli moderni: Le istituzioni e il pensiero*, 85–109. Milan: Silvana Editoriale, 1987.

———. "Living Saints: A Typology of Female Sanctity in the Early Sixteenth Century." In *Women and Religion in Medieval and Renaissance Italy*, edited by Daniel Bornstein and Roberto Rusconi, 219–303. Chicago: University of Chicago Press, 1996.

———. "Monasteri femminili e città (secoli XV–XVIII)." In *Storia d'Italia, annali 9: La Chiesa e il potere politico dal Medioevo all'età contemporanea*, edited by Giorgio Chittolini and Giovanni Miccoli, 359–429. Turin: Giulio Einaudi, 1986.

———. *Le sante vive: Cultura e religiosità femminile nella prima età moderna*. Turin: Rosenberg and Sellier, 1990.

———. "Ursula and Catherine: The Marriage of Virgins in the Sixteenth Century." In *Creative Women in Medieval and Early Modern Italy: A Religious and Artistic Renaissance*, edited by E. Ann Matter and John Coakley, 237–78. Philadelphia: University of Pennsylvania Press, 1994.

INDEX